Uneasy Dreams

Uneasy Dreams

The Golden Age of British Horror Films, 1956–1976

BY
GARY A. SMITH

FOREWORD BY *James Bernard*

McFarland & Company, Inc., Publishers
Jefferson, North Carolina, and London

The present work is a reprint of the illustrated case bound edition of Uneasy Dreams: The Golden Age of British Horror Films, 1956–1976, *first published in 2000 by McFarland.*

Frontispiece: Frankenstein's monster (Kiwi Kingston) carries Katy Wild in *The Evil of Frankenstein* (1964).

LIBRARY OF CONGRESS CATALOGUING-IN-PUBLICATION DATA

Smith, Gary A., 1950–
Uneasy dreams : the golden age of British horror films, 1956–1976 / by Gary A. Smith ; foreword by James Bernard.
p. cm.
Includes bibliographical references and index.

ISBN 0-7864-2661-6 (softcover : 50# alkaline paper) ∞

1. Horror films — Great Britain — History and criticism.   I. Title.
PN1995.9.H6.S618   2006
791.43'6164'0941—dc21   99-55753

British Library Cataloguing-in-Publication data are available

©2000 Gary A. Smith. All rights reserved

No part of this book may be reproduced or transmitted in any form or by any means, electronic or mechanical, including photocopying or recording, or by any information storage and retrieval system, without permission in writing from the publisher.

On the cover: Zombie Ben Aris carries off Jacqueline Pierce in *The Plague of the Zombies* (1965)

Manufactured in the United States of America

McFarland & Company, Inc., Publishers
Box 611, Jefferson, North Carolina 28640
www.mcfarlandpub.com

For Michael —
"Fish Gotta Swim…"

ACKNOWLEDGMENTS

My gratitude to the following people who assisted me in writing this book: Glenn Lindemer and Richard Korting, longtime friends who sat through many of these movies with me during the original releases. Mike Meriano, who supplied me with endless amounts of information and provided copies of many obscure films. Jim Spears, who collaborated with me on an unrealized project, parts of which found their way into this manuscript.

Other helpful material came from Carol Schmidt, Bill Richardson and Dick Klemensen.

Most important of all, I want to thank Michael Hirschbein, who is a constant source of love, inspiration and encouragement in all things I do.

Table of Contents

Acknowledgments vii
Foreword (by James Bernard) 1
Preface 3
Introduction 5

Recollections: Four Interviews
 Max J. Rosenberg 15
 Louis M. Heyward 17
 Aida Young 21
 Gordon Hessler 23

THE FILMS 29

Bibliography 245
Index 247

FOREWORD

Vampires — the Undead — Count Dracula! Bram Stoker would surely be delighted to know of the apparently limitless consequences of his creation.

To take a small example: I was born in 1925 in the foot-hills of the Himalayas (in the days of the now-vanished British Empire), and Gary Smith was born in 1950 in San Diego, California, 25 years and thousands of miles apart.

Yet in 1991, Count Dracula brought us unerringly together; Gary wrote to me about my recently recorded concert suite from *Taste the Blood of Dracula*, and not long afterwards I met him and his companion Michael for a happy lunch in London.

Since then, we have become firm friends, and I have come to realize with awe the vast extent of Gary's knowledge, not only of horror films, but of almost all categories of film (witness his comprehensive and fascinating book *Epic Films*). He possess not only knowledge, but witty and trenchant critical perception, allied to a great capacity for enjoyment (of both the good and the bad).

He is also an ardent Anglophile — misguided perhaps, but I'm not complaining.

This is only a foreword, so I will now shut up, and leave you confidently in the hands of the expert.

— James Bernard

PREFACE

In 1958, when I was a child, I badgered my mother into taking me to see the new color Dracula film ("The chill of the tomb won't leave your blood for hours!"). It didn't take much wheedling as my mother was a movie fan who had been raised on a steady diet of Universal horrors. However, *Horror of Dracula* was a surprise to us both. As we came out of the theater, my somewhat shaken mother turned to me and said, "This isn't the way they made them in my day." I don't remember her going to see many horror films after that. For me, it was only the beginning.

During the next few years I saw *The Revenge of Frankenstein, Curse of the Demon, Blood of the Vampire, Horrors of the Black Museum* and *The Mummy*. By the time *The Brides of Dracula* rolled around in 1960, I was a confirmed Anglophile, fascinated by anything British, especially their horror movies. This obsession happily endures to this day.

In recent times there has been a tremendous amount of interest in the output of Hammer Films. More than two decades after their last theatrical feature was released, Hammer seems to have finally gained the respectability and attention it deserves.

There were, however, a great number of noteworthy horror films made in Britain at the same time by other companies. Many of these have received little or no attention.

My goal in writing this book is to create what I hope will be a comprehensive listing of all the horror, science fiction and fantasy films to come out of Britain during what I consider to be their roughly twenty-year "Golden Age."

Sprinkled throughout are a handful of films which were made either before or after this time period. I have also included a number of suspense thrillers which contain genre elements. The entries are listed alphabetically under the original British title. The American release information follows. At the end of each entry, I have listed whether the film is available on commercial video in the United Kingdom and the United States.

Some of the names which recur in the credits for these films are pseudonyms. The most frequent of these are screenwriters Peter Welbeck (who is actually Harry Alan Towers), Henry Younger (Michael Carreras), Jay Fairbank (Jennifer Jayne and Art Fairbank) and John Elder (Anthony Hinds).

INTRODUCTION

The "Golden Age" of the British horror film began with the international success of *The Quatermass Xperiment* in 1956 and ended with the failure of *To the Devil...a Daughter* in 1976. That this era of film production should have started and finished with two films from Hammer is fitting and not at all surprising. Hammer "led the way" and was the most prolific producer of horror during the twenty years that the genre flourished in the British film industry.

Despite a literary heritage that is especially rich in horror subjects, British film studios were slow to tap this resource. The horror film has played such an integral part in British film history that it is hard to believe it didn't evolve into a major genre there until the mid–50s. Prior to this time, horror movies had not been a staple of the British cinema. This was in reaction to the strict censorship which automatically labeled these films "Horrific" and thereby limited the potential audience to adults.

The first American "horror cycle" began in 1931 with the success of Universal Pictures' *Dracula*, starring Bela Lugosi in the title role. This was quickly followed by *Frankenstein*, featuring a relatively unknown British actor named Boris Karloff as the Monster. The following year Karloff starred in *The Mummy* and *The Old Dark House* for Universal and *The Mask of Fu Manchu* for MGM. These films established him as the top horror star in America. In 1933, Karloff returned home to England for a visit and to star in *The Ghoul* for Gaumont–British. *The Ghoul* was a horror film very much in the Universal mode, unlike any motion picture previously produced in Britain. However, it did not start a trend. A few years later, Bela Lugosi journeyed to England to appear in one of Hammer's earliest productions, *The Mystery of the Marie Celeste* (1936). This sea going melodrama gave no hint of what would eventually issue forth from that tiny British company 20 years later.

The second "horror cycle" in Hollywood began in 1939 with the release of *Son of Frankenstein*. Universal soon resurrected all of their classic monsters and added some new ones. That same year Bela Lugosi returned to England to star in *The Dark Eyes of London*, which has the distinction of being the first British horror movie to be given an "H" certificate ("Horrific," persons over 16 only). As the decade progressed, RKO gave Universal competition with a series of inexpensive, but highly effective, shockers produced by Val Lewton. In England, the horror output at this time consisted mainly of a cycle of melodramatic thrillers starring Tod Slaughter. Then in 1945, as Universal's second horror series was coming to a close, Britain's Ealing Studios produced an omnibus film called *Dead of Night*. The film featured five horror stories with a framing

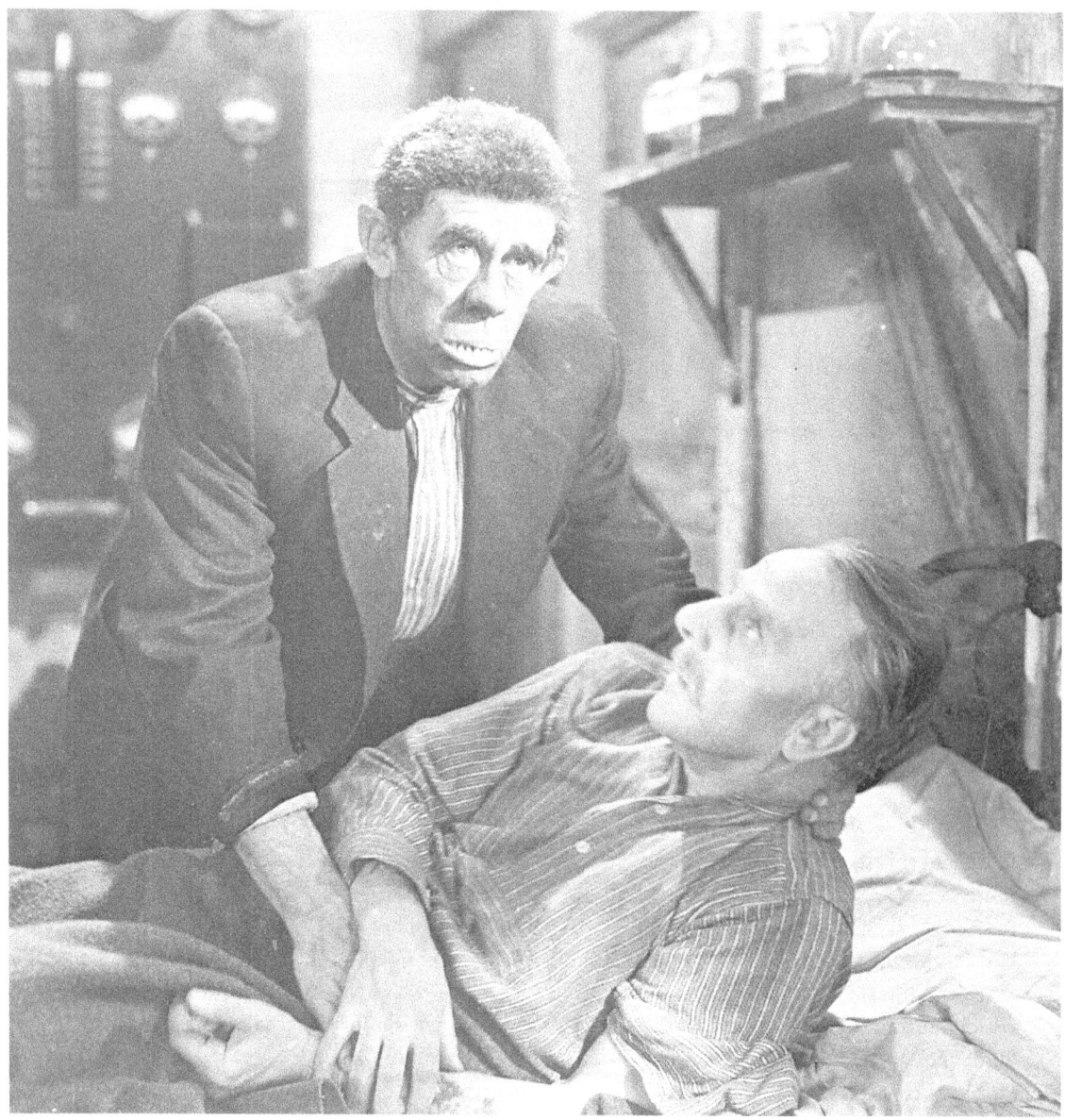

Dark Eyes of London (aka *The Human Monster*) was the first film to be given the "H for Horrific" rating.

device linking them together. This idea would evolve into a subgenre of its own with the Amicus films of the 60s, but in *Dead of Night* it presented a fairly unique concept. The film began the tradition of the British horror film as we have come to know it. It was well-written and expertly acted by an ensemble cast but, once again, it did not start a trend in the British film industry.

In 1948, America's "Golden Age" of classic horror films came to an inglorious end when comedians Bud Abbott and Lou Costello met Dracula, the Wolf Man and Frankenstein's Monster in *Abbott and Costello Meet Frankenstein*. On a return to England, Bela Lugosi parodied the genre in

Mother Riley Meets the Vampire (1952). The advent of the atomic age had rendered the familiar monsters passé. During the early 50s, the ever-growing threat of atomic warfare and its radioactive aftermath, combined with the menace of Communist infiltration, spawned a new breed of movie monsters. Science fiction films flourished, with gigantic beasts and alien invaders replacing the Gothic creatures of yore.

In the summer of 1953, the BBC television network in England presented a six-part serial, written by Nigel Kneale, called *The Quatermass Xperiment*. This science fiction story about a monstrous life form from outer space captured the British television audience and held them enthralled. Executives at Hammer Films realized the powerful potential of the material and purchased the motion picture rights. Hammer knew that they already had a built-in domestic audience. Brian Donlevy was imported from the United States to star as Prof. Quatermass, helping insure distribution in American. Where once the British film companies had avoided having the "H" certificate attached to their product, Hammer now adapted the title of their film to incorporate the new "X" (Adults Only) certificate by calling it *The Quatermass Xperiment*.

Upon its 1955 release in Britain, the film became, not too surprisingly, a big success. When the film was shown a year later in the United States under the title *The Creeping Unknown*, it garnered some favorable reviews as well as some respectable box office receipts.

DIRECTOR FREDDIE FRANCIS EXAMINES THE SCRIPT FOR *EVIL OF FRANKENSTEIN* AS KATY WILD LOOKS ON.

In America, television had captured most of the adult audience while teenagers flocked to cinemas and drive-in theaters where films were now geared to the lucrative juvenile market. American-International Pictures produced a series of bargain basement thrillers, short on cash but long on imagination, which pandered to this youthful audience. In England, while Hammer was searching for another science-fiction

OAKLEY COURT, LOCATION FOR COUNTLESS BRITISH HORROR FILMS.

subject, American producers Max J. Rosenberg and Milton Subotsky were attempting to find backing for a script that Subotsky had written based on *Frankenstein*. It was brought to the attention of Hammer executives who liked the idea but thought the script was little more than a rehash of the original Universal film. In addition to this, Rosenberg and Subotsky wanted a substantial amount of money for a property based on a novel that was in public domain. Hammer agreed to pay the two producers considerably less than they were asking plus a percentage of the profits on any film that might result from this proposed Frankenstein project. The Subotsky script was discarded and Hammer began to develop their own Frankenstein story. Universal's lawyers warned that if the new film resembled the 1931 version in any way, other than what was in the original novel, they would bring an injunction against Hammer to prevent them from showing it.

The new screenplay, entitled *Frankenstein and the Monster*, was written by former Hammer production manager Jimmy Sangster. To meet with Universal's demands, Sangster emphasized the character of the doctor rather than focus on his ghastly creation. At first, Hammer considered using

Boris Karloff as Baron Frankenstein to ensure U.S. box office appeal. This idea was soon abandoned in favor of casting the popular British television star Peter Cushing in the lead role. Christopher Lee was signed to play the part of the Monster, but the concept of its appearance was still under consideration. Should it in anyway resemble the Universal monster, Hammer was liable to be hit with a lawsuit. Makeup artist Phil Leakey solved the problem by creating a totally original design that Lee has often likened to a "road accident" victim. To avoid further problems with Universal, the Monster would now be known as "The Creature" and the title was changed to *The Curse of Frankenstein*.

Originally *The Curse of Frankenstein* was to have been little more than another of Hammer's inexpensive assembly line productions, shot in black-and-white with a 21 day shooting schedule. Associate producer Anthony Nelson-Keys saw more potential in the project and felt that the picture must be filmed in color. This would also set the film apart from its predecessors and give it a unique quality unlike anything yet seen in the horror genre. The color and Gothic trappings would also help to disguise the relatively small budget. Filming commenced in November 1956 and shortly thereafter some of the completed sequences were taken to the United States with the hope of finding an American distributor. After viewing these "rushes," the executives at Warner Bros. were enthusiastic enough to strike a deal with Hammer for the distribution rights. *The Curse of Frankenstein* was released in the United Kingdom in May 1957 and many critics were shocked by the more grisly aspects of Baron Frankenstein's experiments. The public loved it and the film broke box office records in England. The critical reaction following the July 1957 U.S. release was significantly more favorable and, once again, house records for attendance were broken. Hammer was so pleased with this initial response that they began to prepare a sequel, tentatively titled *The Blood of Frankenstein*, before the official box office counts were in. Not only had Baron Frankenstein revived the dead, he had given both the horror genre and the British film industry a much-needed shot in the arm.

Sensing the box office potential of horror and science fiction subjects, independent producer Richard Gordon formed Producers Associates and soon had four inexpensive black-and-white chillers ready for release. He was the first producer to utilize the talents of Christopher Lee following his appearance in *The Curse of Frankenstein*. After inexpensively securing the services of Lee, the role of "Resurrection Joe" was then written into the script of the Boris Karloff thriller *Corridors of Blood*. Gordon would continue to produce horror films in Britain throughout the following two decades with varying degrees of artistic success.

Hammer's next remake of a classic horror subject was *Dracula* (1958), made this time with the full blessing of Universal, who had secured the distribution rights. Utilizing the same creative team that helmed *The Curse of Frankenstein*, it proved to be an even bigger success than the previous film. Once again, most of the British critics were appalled, but in the United States the reviews were enthusiastic. Critic Vincent Canby said: "This is certainly one of the best of its type... It's hard to see how *Horror of Dracula* will not clean up at the box office." And "clean up" it certainly did — on both sides of the Atlantic. Prior to this, there had never been a version of Dracula which made the sexual aspects of vampirism so explicit. Henceforth, sex would become an important ingredient in the majority of Hammer's output.

The producing team of Robert S. Baker

BARBARA SHELLEY AND VICTOR MADDERN IN A PUBLICITY PHOTOGRAPH FOR *BLOOD OF THE VAMPIRE*.

and Monty Berman were among the first to capitalize on the success of Hammer's early Gothic horror movies. In 1958 they produced *Blood of the Vampire*, an opulent-looking color film which greatly resembled a Hammer production. To strengthen this connection, publicity material proclaimed: "Story and Screenplay by Jimmy (*Frankenstein*) Sangster." Baker and Berman quickly followed with *The Trollenberg Terror* and *Jack the Ripper*. Both of these were also scripted by Sangster and carried on the terrifying tradition of British horror recently established by Hammer. The following year, the Baker-Berman collaboration reached its apex with the outstanding *The Flesh and the Fiends*, a definitive depiction of the Burke and Hare story. Baker and Berman would eventually achieve their biggest success producing television series, including *The Saint* starring Roger Moore.

By 1959, the British film companies were being recognized in the United States as the preeminent creators of quality horror films. Herman Cohen, one of American-International's most successful producers, moved to England and joined forces with Britain's Anglo-Amalgamated to produce inexpensive films for AIP. The first of these coproductions was *Horrors of the Black Museum*. This was immediately followed by *The Headless Ghost*, thereby fulfilling AIP's request for a double bill for the United States Cohen soon ended his affiliation with AIP, but continued to produce horror films in the United Kingdom until 1974.

Most of Hollywood's major companies were now vying for the rights to distribute the Hammer product. When Hammer's remake of *The Mummy* was released, *Time* magazine published an article entitled "Gold from Ghouls." It stated: "In three years, Hammer's remakes of *Curse of Frankenstein*, *Dracula* and other items from Hollywood's library of horror classics have earned more dollars from world sales than the products of any other British moviemaker in the last decade." An American run magazine reviewing yet another import said: "Those English are trying to scare us silly! Like their new versions of the 'Dracula' and 'Mummy' stories, this one is dead-serious and mighty gruesome." British horror had become a high-profile commodity.

In the 60s, the British studios continued to turn out "class" product, much of it distributed in the United States by Universal–International or Columbia. American-International, obviously feeling the heat of the competition, engaged Roger Corman to direct a series of color Gothic horror movies based on the works of Edgar Allan Poe. These proved immensely popular with audiences and continued to be made throughout the decade in both America and Britain. Hammer remained the most prolific producers of horror films and had no true rival until 1964. The production team of Rosenberg and Subotsky, who had once taken their script of *Frankenstein* to Hammer, formed Amicus Productions in 1962. *Dr. Terror's House of Horrors* (1964) was the first horror production from Amicus and it used Hammer personnel both in front of and behind the camera. However, the format of the film was unlike anything Hammer had ever attempted. Taking its lead from *Dead of Night*, this was a multi-story, modern-day excursion into the supernatural. This format became an Amicus specialty and they continued to use it for six more films. Unlike Hammer, Amicus' productions seldom showed great quantities of "Kensington Gore" theatrical blood and relied on name guest stars, rather than sex appeal, to attract their audience.

Also in 1964, Compton Films, a company formed by distributors Tony Tenser and Michael Klinger, departed from their usual softcore sexploitation fare to produce *The Black Torment*, a moderately successful color horror film in the Hammer style. Their next genre offering was Roman Polanski's *Repulsion* (1965). The popularity of this film convinced Tenser that there was money to be had from horror. In 1967, Tenser ended his partnership with Klinger and established another company called Tigon-British, and the first production was Michael Reeves' *The Sorcerers*. Tenser went on to become Britain's third most prolific producer of horror and science fiction films. (Tensor resigned from Tigon in 1972. In 1974, he co-financed Peter Walker's *Frightmare*, his final film production.)

In 1964, Hammer entered into a financial agreement with Seven Arts which enabled them to increase production. They made a further deal with 20th Century-Fox to produce 17 pictures over the next three years. Fox would distribute their films outside of the United Kingdom. During those three years, Hammer brought £3,000,000 in revenue into the United Kingdom. Because of this unprecedented success, Hammer became the first film company to win the Queen's Award to Industry for export. This encouraged other independent companies to produce more horror films and by 1970 the market was completely inundated with British product. Horror films had become the perfect antidote for the ailing British film industry. They could be produced inexpensively and generally turned a tidy profit. One person who took advantage of this climate was Peter Walker, a former director of softcore porn films. He entered the horror market in 1971 with *Die Screaming, Marianne*. Over the next several years, Walker specialized in directing slasher films which usually featured much female nudity and even more blood.

Sir James Carreras decided to retire from his position as head of Hammer in 1972. Tony Tenser had suggested a merger with Tigon or even the possibility of a buyout, but Sir James preferred to keep Hammer

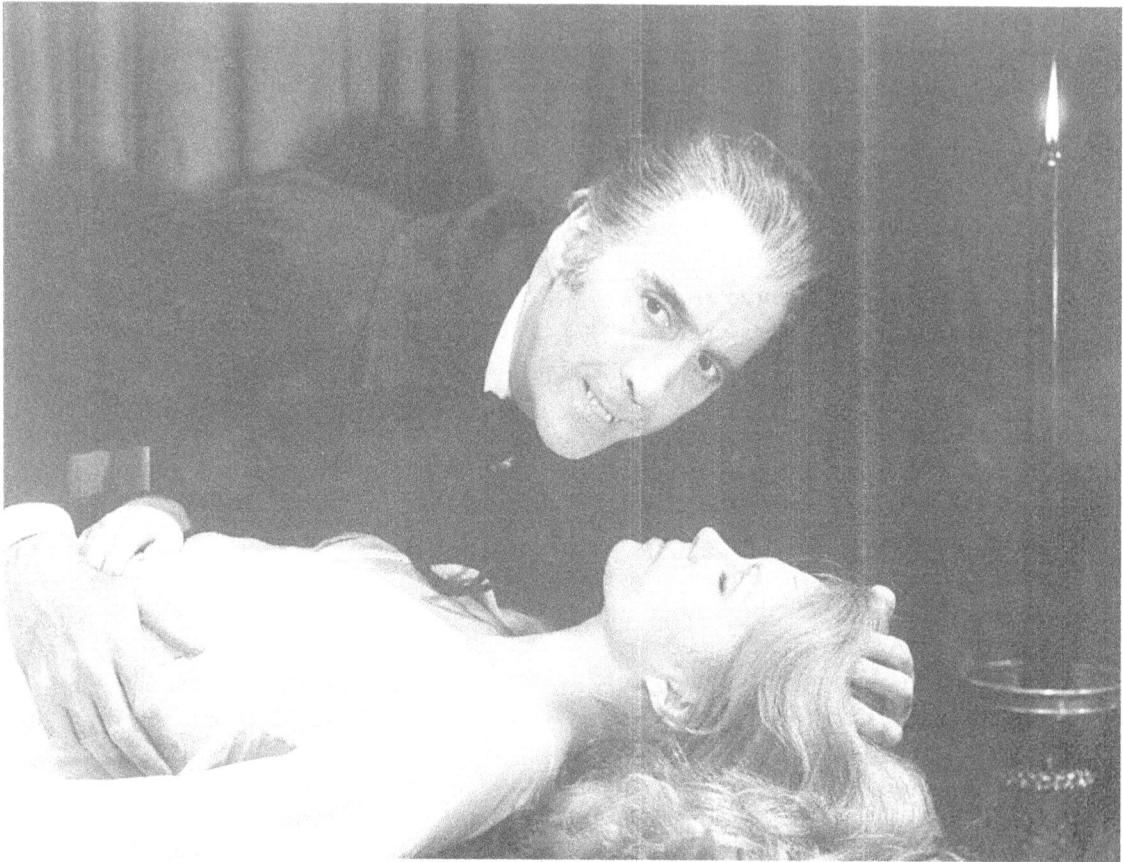

CHRISTOPHER LEE IN HIS FINAL APPEARANCE AS THE VAMPIRE COUNT THREATENS JOANNA LUMLEY IN *THE SATANIC RITES OF DRACULA*.

in the family. Michael Carreras assumed his father's position as the managing director of Hammer and it soon became apparent that he did not plan on allowing the company to rely solely on their past reputation. He intended to diversify their output and take advantage of merchandising tie-ins that would help promote Hammer's image. It has been conjectured that this diversification would eventually prove to be Hammer's undoing.

In 1973, *The Exorcist* took horror out of the past and firmly rooted it in the present day. Its staggering box office totals inspired the major American studios to try their hands at big-budget thrillers. The inexpensive Gothic horrors from Britain, which had once seemed so daring, suddenly began to look like arcane fairy tales. That same year, producer Kevin Francis, son of director-cinematographer Freddie Francis, announced that his newly acquired company, Tyburn Films, would devote itself to producing the type of films Hammer had made in their early days as horror specialists. He felt that both Hammer and Amicus had lost their touch through repetition. Curiously, Tyburn's first completed production, *Persecution* (1974), was quite unlike anything Hammer or Amicus had done, but Francis had been able to secure Lana Turner for the lead and this did help the film to obtain an American distributor. Getting a distribution deal in America had already become increasingly difficult for the British companies and, in the wake of *The Exorcist*, it became nearly impossible. Tyburn's next two films, *The Ghoul* and *Legend of the Werewolf* (both 1975), were never shown theatrically in the United States. Despite an extensive roster of proposed projects, including titles such as *Dracula's Feast of Blood* and *The Satanists*, Tyburn was unable to mount another theatrical feature. Warner Bros. shelved the two Hammer films they had ready for release (*The Satanic Rites of Dracula* and *Legend of the 7 Golden Vampires*) and these remained unseen in the United States until Max Rosenberg's new company, Dynamite Entertainment, finally distributed them in the late 70s.

Amicus had abandoned horror in 1974 to produce the Edgar Rice Burroughs adventure fantasy *The Land That Time Forgot*. After one more picture, Milton Subotsky left Amicus to form his own company. Rosenberg solo-produced *The People That Time Forgot* and then moved his operation back to the United States. In 1976, Hammer endeavored to contemporize their product with an updated version of Dennis Wheatley's story of Satanic possession and black magic, *To the Devil...a Daughter*. Unwisely, most of the elements that had made the novel so memorable were eliminated in the screen treatment. Despite a good performance by Christopher Lee and the youthful beauty of Nastassja Kinski, the film failed badly at the box office.

Michael Carreras attempted a film based on the *Vampirella* comics as a coproduction with American-International. With John Hough directing a script by Jimmy Sangster and Christopher Wicking, and featuring Peter Cushing in an important role, the project held promise. Unfortunately, Sam Arkoff became dissatisfied and withdrew AIP's financial support. The film was never made. To date, the last theatrical feature to bear the Hammer name was an ill-advised remake of Alfred Hitchcock's *The Lady Vanishes*. Released in 1979, it received few playdates outside of the United Kingdom; later that same year, Hammer passed into the hands of Brian Lawrence and Roy Skeggs. During the early 80s, Skeggs and Lawrence were able to keep the Hammer name alive with two series made for television, "The Hammer House of Horror" and "The Hammer House of Mystery and Suspense." Tyburn also delved into television production with the films *Sherlock Holmes and the Masks of Death* (1984) and *Murder Elite* (1986), but eventually this company also vanished from the scene. Over the years the Hammer name has been often mentioned in the press. A highly publicized deal between Roy Skeggs, Richard Donner and Warner Bros. produced no results. In June 1997, *U.S. News and World Report* stated that "a group of British investors that includes wealthy ad impresario Charles Saatchi recently purchased 50 percent of [Hammer] for $9 million." Their intent seems to be on merchandising Hammer's assets and selling off the remake rights to American companies, rather than mounting their own film productions. Action directors Jan DeBont, Renny Harlin and Alex Proyas were mentioned in conjunction with various Hammer remakes projects but, despite Roy Skeggs statement that his company had become "the flavor of the month," these too fell by the wayside. In 1999, Skeggs lost his control of Hammer when the company went into receivership. Now, more than ever, a major horror movie revival in the England seems unlikely.

While discussing the virtual demise of Hammer Films on the 1987 BBC television documentary "Hammer—The Studio That Dripped Blood," producer Aida Young summed up the end of Britain's "Golden Age" of horror in simple terms: "I think the moment came to an end... You know, there was a time and then there wasn't a time."

Recollections: Four Interviews

Max J. Rosenberg

Max J. Rosenberg was born in New York and studied there to become an attorney. In 1943, he produced his first motion picture, a compilation film entitled *The Good Old Days*. The success of this venture inspired him to purchase the rights to the 1932 German film *Unheimliche Geschichten* (*Extraordinary Tales*).

He recut it, incorporated additional footage and added a dubbed English soundtrack. The resulting film, retitled *Dr. Terror's House of Horrors*, was released in 1944. This was Rosenberg's introduction into the horror genre. In 1962, he and partner Milton Subotsky formed Amicus Productions. Amicus became one of the major forces during the Golden Age of British Horror.

Interview conducted on April 10, 1996:

Q: How did you and Milton Subotsky become partners?

A: At the time, I had a distribution company and Milton came to me with a film he had coproduced with a group of students from Harvard. I passed on the film, but I was impressed enough with Milton to go into partnership with him to produce the TV series *Junior Science* in 1954. We became the best of friends almost immediately. You know, during all those years we never had any agreement on paper.

Q: What's the story on the Frankenstein script you sold to Hammer?

A: Milton had written a script based on *Frankenstein*. It wasn't a very good script because, frankly, Milton wasn't a very good writer. The hook was that we wanted it to be the first film of its kind to be shot in color. I took the script to Eliot Hyman and David Stillman at Associated Artists Productions. Hyman knew James Carreras, so he took the script to him. We were paid for the screenplay, which they didn't use, and eventually received a percentage of the profits on the finished film, *The Curse of Frankenstein*.

Q: Why did you decide to produce films in England?

A: Milton and I had produced two rock 'n' roll pictures in New York, *Rock, Rock, Rock!* and *Jamboree*, which had been very successful for us. I had heard about the Eady Plan which had been passed in England to stimulate film production there. The gist of it was that the government paid film producers a subsidy based on a percentage of the box office take. It sounded like a good idea to us. Milton came to England in 1959 to work on *City of the Dead*, and I was also involved in the production end of that deal, but we didn't actually form Amicus Productions Ltd. until 1962. Our first production as Amicus was another rock 'n' roll picture called *It's Trad, Dad*. By this time, horror was already big business in England. Milton and I didn't care for the Hammer films at all. Jim Carreras was a great businessman but he didn't know much about making pictures. So we decided to make our own horror film. We got the idea for an anthology from the British classic *Dead of Night* and I borrowed the title from a picture I had produced back in the 40s. *Dr. Terror's House of Horrors* was the final outcome.

DOUG MCCLURE (LEFT; SHOWN WITH PETER CUSHING IN *AT THE EARTH'S CORE*) STARRED IN AMICUS' THREE EDGAR RICE BURROUGHS ADAPTATIONS.

Q: Who chose the material for your films?
A: It was a joint decision between Milton and myself. I usually thought up the titles. Sometimes we were able to sell the film on the strength of the title alone.

Q: How about some thoughts on your films.
A: My favorite of the anthology films is *Asylum*. I thought Robert Bloch was a terrific writer and the script for that one was especially good. *Tales from the Crypt* was a big moneymaker for us. I had met Bill Gaines in New York when he was doing *Mad* magazine and we became friends. His EC Comics had been banned for years. He was delighted that we were interested in making a film based on them. *And Now the Screaming Starts* was a lovely Gothic tale. This was one of the few films where my wife visited the set. She saw the dismembered hand crawling around and was horrified! The one film I didn't like was *Scream and Scream Again*. It was uninvolving and also was one of our only productions that ran over budget.

Q: Was From Beyond the Grave *well received by the critics?*

A: Warner Bros. had asked us to do an anthology film called *Tales from Beyond the Grave*. When we finished it, everybody thought it was one of our best efforts, but the executives at Warner Bros. hated it and declined to release it. I eventually got the rights back, shortened the title to *From Beyond the Grave* and made my own distribution deal. I also designed the poster art.

Q: Any particular performer standout in your mind?

A: Peter Cushing. A very sweet man and a true gentleman. He was the best. Vincent Price was suave and urbane. A real professional. On the other hand, Christopher Lee was an idiot.

Q: Would you comment on the Edgar Rice Burroughs films?

A: *The Land That Time Forgot* was our biggest moneymaker ever. I think it still has a charming naivete. The property was turned down by every studio we approached, so Milton and I financed it ourselves. Sam Arkoff eventually picked it up for distribution in the United States. Doug McClure was a nice guy and he was just the type of leading man we were looking for. He was married to my secretary. Milton finally left Amicus during the production of *The People That Time Forgot*. He and producer John Dark hated each other. It had also become difficult for us to maintain our close friendship and remain business partners as well. After Milton left, I overheard John Dark say about me, "What do we need the old man for?" so I decided I had enough too and returned to the United States. By then, the horror film was dead in England anyway.

Q: Your distribution company, Dynamite Entertainment, released two Hammer films that Warner Bros. had shelved. Any comments?

A: They were terrible pictures but I was able to get the rights inexpensively. I re-titled both of them and reedited one of them rather extensively. *Legend of the 7 Golden Vampires* was a bad picture when we got it and an even worse one when we finished with it.

Q: What is your favorite of all the films you have been involved with?

A: *Thank You All Very Much*, based on the novel *The Millstone*. It starred Sandy Dennis and Ian McKellen. I have always thought it was an important picture.

Louis M. Heyward

Louis "Deke" Heyward began writing as a child and by the age of 13 he had published a story in *Esquire* magazine. He wrote his first radio show at 15. As a young adult he studied to become a doctor, but abandoned this ambition and instead became a lawyer. Writing, however, remained his first love. In 1948, with some 5000 radio shows behind him, he moved on to television to work on *The Faye Emerson Show*. He wrote for *The Garry Moore Show*, and the wildly innovative *Ernie Kovacs Show* and later produced Dick Clark's television programs. In 1961, he joined 20th Century–Fox as vice president of television development. He later became vice president in charge of production for the European branch of American-International Pictures. In 1972, he resigned his position at AIP and went into independent production.

Interview conducted on July 10, 1996.

HILARY DWYER IN A PUBLICITY PHOTO FOR *THE OBLONG BOX*.

Q: How did you become involved with American-International Pictures?

A: A colleague of mine suggested that I write a script about my son. I took it to Jim Nicholson and Sam Arkoff at AIP and the end result was *Pajama Party* (1964) starring Tommy Kirk and Annette Funicello.

Q: How did you end up working on the British end of AIP's output?

A: Sam Arkoff originally used me as a "trouble shooter." I had already been to Italy to straighten out some problems that had arisen on one of Mario Bava's AIP films. When there was trouble in England on *War-Gods of the Deep*, Sam sent me there with the important parting words, "seize the power." This turned out to be the best piece of advice he ever gave me. At the request of Roger Corman, Sam had given art director Daniel Haller the opportunity to coproduce the film with veteran British producer George Willoughby. Haller and his wife came on like gangbusters and Willoughby was thoroughly intimidated. I went in and threatened to shut down the production unless a compromise could be reached.

A couple of years later I went back to England to discuss a deal with Harry Alan Towers, a charming rogue and scoundrel who should be known as the "Father of Coproductions." We had planned on shooting *House of 1,000 Dolls* in Ireland but that fell through and we ended up filming in Spain instead.

Q: When did you decide to move to England?

A: In 1967, I opened a European branch office for AIP in a townhouse opposite the American Embassy on Grosvenor Square in London. Sam told me that if I would stay there as vice president in charge of production, he would allow me to realize a particular pet project of mine. But more about that later.

Q: Please comment on some of the films you made while there.

A: The first American–International Ltd. film was a coproduction with Tigon called *Witchfinder General*. I thought that the script was excellent, but it lacked the romantic angle that would make it more appealing to American audiences. I reworked some of the script and added the love interest. I thought that Hilary Dwyer was a real find. We signed her to a five-picture contract. She later married, had children and quit making films altogether.

The director, Michael Reeves, was a brilliant and sensitive young man, but he was emotionally tormented. He was supposed to direct our next picture, *The Oblong Box*, but, tragically, he died. I brought in Gordon Hessler to replace him. I had known Gordon from his Universal days when he was a story editor for Alfred Hitchcock. He felt trapped in directing for television in America, so he jumped at the chance to direct *The Oblong Box*. I enjoyed working with Gordon immensely. We shared similar visions and Gordon was able to realize them. What we did not want to do was try and copy Corman's style on the Poe films. Sam Arkoff felt very differently and he was constantly tampering with Gordon's work. I was always having to fight for Gordon with Sam.

Q: Were you disappointed with any of the films you made?

A: *De Sade* was one of the unhappiest experiences I was involved with. It was a British-German coproduction for AIP. The original screenplay by Richard Matheson was splendid ... a very fine piece of writing. We brought in Cy Endfield as director because of the terrific work he had done on *Zulu*. I tend to favor shooting in sequence as much as possible to maintain character continuity for the actors. Endfield ignored this and avoided shooting any of the scenes involving sexual content. The production had fallen way behind schedule. Cy Endfield couldn't cope and was eventually hospitalized. Roger Corman was brought in to shoot the last quarter of the picture. When it came time to release *De Sade*, AIP edited the film severely to try and please the Motion Picture Ratings Board and the Catholic Legion of Decency. It was condemned and got an "X" rating anyway.

Q: Any thoughts on The Vampire Lovers, *AIP's only coproduction with Hammer?*

A: At the time we made *The Vampire Lovers*, James Carreras was getting ready to step down as head of Hammer. There was almost a feeling of "absentee ownership" about the company. His son Michael eventually took over and he turned out to be a very competent filmmaker. AIP was just discovering sex and pressured Hammer to include more and more nudity. It got to be a bit much after a while, so my main job here became trying to convince them to show less bare bosoms. Ingrid Pitt was a fun lady and good to work with.

Q: Scream and Scream Again *was a coproduction with Amicus. How did this come about?*

A: Max Rosenberg and Milton Subotsky brought us a book called *The Disoriented Man*. It had some interesting ideas, so we agreed to make the film with them. It was not a particularly good experience. Max and Milton were nice people but their over-enthusiasm was often crazy-making. Subotsky was sometimes aggressive, pushy and even offensive. He tried to interfere with every aspect of the production. I finally had him barred from the set.

Q: About this time, you produced one of Boris Karloff's last films.

A: Yes, it was called *The Crimson Cult*. I had worked with Karloff years before on a radio play called "The Babysitter." Sam Arkoff didn't want me to hire him because he was uninsurable. I hired him anyway. He was a study in everything right about acting, a thorough professional. I never saw him refer to a script once, but he came in everyday and knew his lines letter perfect. This was another coproduction with Tigon, which was an odd company. Sort of the "Dead End Kids" of the British movie industry. They enjoyed the movie biz but were a bit half-assed about everything.

Q: How about The Abominable Dr. Phibes?

A: Robert Fuest was a former scenic designer and that, combined with his experience directing episodes of *The Avengers* television series, made him the perfect choice to direct this film. He brought in Brian Eatwell as the production designer and he was able to work wonders with very little money. I rewrote bits of the script as if Ernie Kovacs were playing the Price role, and Vincent loved it. At first, Sam Arkoff hated the film and wanted his name taken off of it, but when he realized what a potential success he had, Sam decided to put his name back on.

Q: Now can we discuss your pet project?

A: As I mentioned earlier, Sam Arkoff told me that if I moved to England, he would allow me to film a property that was very important to me. It was my dream to remake *Wuthering Heights*.

As the years passed, Sam kept putting me off. Finally I had to sell the project to him as a horror film, which was something he could understand. We had a first-rate cast and I was very pleased with the outcome. It's a film of which I'm truly proud.

Q: Was Who Slew Auntie Roo? *one of the last films you worked on for AIP?*

A: Someone came to us with a story called "The Gingerbread House" which we felt had potential. Jim Nicholson had seen *What's the Matter With Helen?* and enjoyed it, so he decided to get the director, Curtis Harrington, and the star, Shelley Winters, for *Who Slew Auntie Roo?* Curtis Harrington was great to work with but Shelley was difficult. There were problems between her and co-star Michael Gothard. She also kept insisting that I get a "Sir" for a supporting role. I got Ralph Richardson but she had meant Laurence Olivier. I insisted on casting Hugh Griffith in a minor role. Although he had a reputation as an alcoholic, he never drank during filming and was a supreme delight to work with.

Q: Would you care to say anything about Vincent Price, who was such a major part of most of AIP's British productions?

A: One story, that I have often told, sums up Vincent perfectly. During the production of *Witchfinder General*, we were all staying at a country hotel near Bury St. Edmunds. The food was abominable and the cast and crew were beginning to show signs of mutiny. Vincent gave me a grocery list and sent me off to purchase the needed items. That evening he took over the hotel kitchen and, complete with chef's hat, prepared a gourmet banquet for everyone.

Vincent didn't get along with Sam Arkoff and much of the time I found myself acting as a mediator between them. By the time we started American-International Ltd. in England, he was fairly fed up with AIP. Vincent came to enjoy working in England because he knew that I believed in quality, not quantity. Sam Arkoff seemed to hate the British productions for the very same reason.

Aida Young

Aida Young was born in London and joined a documentary film unit when she left college. She stayed with them in the capacity of a researcher-writer and eventually became involved in directing, producing and editing as well. She moved on to feature films at Highbury Studios as an assistant director. She freelanced as a production manager-production assistant at numerous studios.

In 1962 she was associate producer on the MGM film *Light in the Piazza*. Young has also been involved in a number of television series including *Danger Man (Secret Agent)*, starring Patrick McGoohan, and, more recently, *Covington Cross*.

Interview conducted on September 10, 1996:

Q: Did you always aspire to a career in motion pictures?

A: I wanted to be an actress and performed, as an amateur, at a famous London club theater. There I met people in films and, as it seemed to me then that I wasn't going to play Hedda Gabler for some time, I decided that maybe films were the answer. I started in documentary films before trying for features. I didn't then realize that there were no women doing certain jobs in the film industry. I was offered all kinds of jobs ... secretary, wardrobe, continuity, etc., but I persevered and became the first woman assistant director. After that I became the first woman associate producer.

OLINKA BEROVA WAS THE GLAMOROUS STAR DISCOVERY OF *THE VENGEANCE OF SHE*.

Q: Your first credits for Hammer are as associate producer on Michael Carreras' first two spectaculars, She *and* One Million Years B.C. *How did you come to work for Hammer?*

A: In 1963, I was associate producer on a musical called *What a Crazy World* that Michael Carreras directed away from Hammer. That began my association with him and led to my working for Hammer.

Q: Although Hammer had always been known for their beautiful leading ladies, after She *and* One Million Years B.C. *glamour became an even more important element in their films. Did you have any input in casting Ursula Andress and Raquel Welch?*

A: I had no hand in casting Raquel Welch or Ursula Andress. They were cast by the head office. On later films I had more input.

Q: Your first film as a full producer was The Vengeance of She. *Although this film has been much maligned, I think it is very good and Olinka Berova gives a very sympathetic performance, in addition to being incredibly beautiful. Were you pleased with this film and its star?*

A: I didn't realize that *The Vengeance of She* was maligned. It wasn't very good, although Olinka was both beautiful and intelligent. The director and I found her in a Czech film.

Q: Prior to this, Hammer announced a She *sequel to be called* Ayesha, the Daughter of She, *to star Susan Denberg. Were you involved in the development of this project?*

A: I had nothing to do with the *Ayesha* project.

Q: Your next film was Dracula Has Risen from the Grave, *which (along with* She *and* One Million Years B.C.*) were three of Hammer's all-time biggest moneymakers. You certainly must have been doing something right! Was it difficult being a woman producer in what was essentially a man's domain at that time?*

A: After each film for Hammer, I left and did other things like *Danger Man*, which I finally produced. It was extremely difficult being a woman producer. There was only one other here, Betty Box, sister of writer-producer-director Sidney Box. I hadn't expected to make horror films, but I really enjoyed doing them. Maybe *Dracula Has Risen* was good because I was fresh to it.

Q: James Bernard told me that originally Peter Sasdy didn't want him to compose the score for Taste the Blood of Dracula. *You intervened on his behalf, provided he would compose a less dissonant score that the one he had done for* Dracula Has Risen from the Grave. *Mr. Bernard said that at first he was a bit resentful that you should tell him what type of music to compose, but later he realized that you were perfectly right.* Taste the Blood of Dracula *and* Scars of Dracula *are two of his loveliest scores, no small thanks to you.*

A: I'm still a producer and I still have input into music. I work closely with the composers—whom I choose. I worked very closely with Phil Martell, who did a wonderful job as music supervisor for Hammer.

Q: Following three Dracula films, you produced the very large-scale When Dinosaurs Ruled the Earth. *I have read that this film ran into production problems because of the complexity of the special effects.*

A: I worked with Victoria Vetri on *When Dinosaurs Ruled the Earth*. It was full of problems, not the least of which was the fact that it was the first film of this type without Ray Harryhausen, who was unavailable to do the special effects.

Q: Were there any Hammer projects that you helped to develop that never saw the light of day?

A: As I said, after each film I left Hammer to do other things, so I wasn't in on any developments.

Q: In 1978 you produced a remake of The Thief of Baghdad, *which is a very handsome looking production. Would you comment on this film?*

A: *The Thief of Baghdad* was special, but it was difficult to follow the original, which was extraordinary. The director (Clive Donner) hadn't worked on a special effects film before, but he did a very good job. We had a good cast and we tried out a lot of new ways to do special effects. For instance, we used "front projection" for the first time. We were due to shoot the location photography in Israel and, two weeks prior to our departure, Israel marched into Lebanon. Our plans were in disarray but I went to Israel myself to shoot plates for the flying carpet shots. While I was there, Roddy McDowall and Marina Vlady fell off the carpet onto the studio floor when one of the steel stilts inexplicably snapped. Fortunately, although they were badly bruised, it wasn't worse than that, but I had to fly back anyway. I finally got the plates and they're used in the film. It's been a long time since I've seen it, so I can't really discuss it, but I guess if we'd had more money we could have done more miraculous special effects.

Q: What are your current projects?

A: I am about to produce a feature film on Handel. What a difference from Hammer!

Q: Looking back on your association with Hammer, was this a happy time in your career? Do you think they allowed you to realize your full potential as a producer?

A: I learned more at Hammer about real filmmaking than before or since. We were a very hardworking, happy family and very loyal. It was unthinkable to go over schedule or budget. More than that, we all enjoyed what we were doing. We all helped one another and there was no pecking order or histrionics.

I guess we were always short of money, but we made sure that the quality was first-class and all the money was on the screen. It's a philosophy that has remained with me.

Gordon Hessler

Gordon Hessler was born in Berlin, Germany, and moved with his family to England when he was three years old. As a young adult he served in the British army and studied to be an aeronautical engineer. The school he attended also had a theater program that he became involved in. Eventually his interests turned toward motion pictures. He found it difficult to get into the British film industry, so at the age of 22 he moved to New York. Interview conducted on September 17, 1997:

Q: How did you break into the movie industry?

A: When I moved to New York, I got a job as a delivery boy for Warner Pathe News. This enabled me to meet people in the film industry and I eventually got a job for a company which made documentary films. I became an editor and later a director of documentaries. I moved over to Fordel Films, which also made documentaries, and later became vice president of that company. I directed a film called *St. John's Story* (1958), which received a considerable amount of acclaim, and a television program called *March of Medicine*, for which I received the Dr. Albert Lasker Award.

Q: How did you begin your association with Alfred Hitchcock?

GORDON HESSLER AND ESSY PERSSON FILMING *CRY OF THE BANSHEE*.

A: I moved to California in 1960 and got a job with Universal. They assigned me to Hitchcock's production unit. I think it may have been because of my British accent ... I can't think of any other reason. I became a "reader" for Hitchcock, which meant I read stories to find suitable material for his television series *Alfred Hitchcock Presents*. I directed some of the episodes, but Hitchcock was always reluctant to let me direct because then he had to hire someone else to do my job. I eventually became an associate producer on the series, moving up to producer for the final season.

Q: *When did you move into directing feature films?*

A: I had found a story for Hitchcock that I thought was quite good, but he rejected it. I took it to Robert Lippert, who had been producing some inexpensive horror films for 20th Century-Fox in England. Lippert was able to set up a three-week production schedule at Shepperton Studios. I was given a temporary leave from Universal and flew over to direct it. The film was called *Catacombs* but it was released as *The Woman Who Wouldn't Die* in America. Bob Lippert originally intended *Catacombs* for Fox, but he showed it to someone at Warner Brothers first. Warners liked the film and offered much more money than Fox would have, so Lippert sold it to them outright. Warners also offered me a deal to direct three pictures, but Hitchcock wouldn't release me from my contract.

Q: *How did you end up working for American–International?*

A: I knew Deke Heyward from Universal. Our offices were located near each other and we became friendly. Deke had moved over to American–International and my contract with Universal had ended. One day I got a call from Sam Arkoff, who asked me if I would be interested in producing a film about the Marquis de Sade for him in Germany. I was sent a copy of the Richard Matheson script and soon I was on my way to Munich. Michael Reeves was supposed to direct but time passed and nothing happened. Reeves became ill and was replaced by Cy Endfield, who didn't particularly like me and wanted me off the picture. I was summoned to England to produce *The Oblong Box* instead. Michael Reeves was set to direct but he thought that the script was terrible. He brought in Christopher Wicking to rewrite it. Originally *The Oblong Box* was going to be filmed in Ireland, but when Reeves' health became increasingly more unstable, it was decided to film it in England. After a few preproduction meetings with Reeves, he dropped out entirely and I was given the opportunity to direct as well as produce. Toward the end of production I was actually given extra money for the budget to give the picture a more impressive look. This was unheard of from AIP, who seldom gave extra money for anything.

Q: *Are you pleased with the way the film turned out?*

A: Apparently it was a big success with AIP as they gave me a contract to direct three more pictures for them. I would have liked to give Price and Lee more to do. Their parts seemed to have been written in for name value only. I did learn that you must hire the best technicians because they can make an inexpensive film look good.

Q: *Your next film was* Scream and Scream Again. *This was a coproduction between AIP and Amicus.*

A: Yes. Milton Subotsky had read the book and brought it to the attention of AIP. Amicus wanted another director but AIP insisted on using me. I think Chris Wicking's script really improved upon the original novel, which was total pulp stuff.

Chris added all of the political and scientific elements, which really set it apart from other horror films being made at that time. Rosenberg and Subotsky didn't understand the film at all and were continually trying to interfere. Deke finally had them barred from the set. I am very pleased with this film. We used lots of hand-held cameras and extended takes, which was a bit daring at the time. *Scream and Scream Again* got some terrific reviews and seems to have quite a cult following today.

Q: *How about* Cry of the Banshee?

A: The script for this came from the head office in Hollywood. Chris Wicking and I thought it was awful so we took off for Scotland to see if we could come up with something better. Deke Heyward and Sam Arkoff got impatient and we were told we could only rewrite ten percent of the original Tim Kelly story. Since most AIP films were pre-sold on the strength of the poster artwork, the scripts didn't matter that much to them anyway.

Q: *Would you talk about Elisabeth Bergner?*

A: She had been hired for name value. She hadn't made a movie in a number of years and seemed quite happy to be working again. Her scenes were all filmed in a very short amount of time — probably about three days.

Q: Any other comments about this film?
A: I chose not to show the Banshee to any great extent because I feel you should never show the object of horror as it will always be a disappointment. It can never live up to the imagination. I thought that the original background score by Wilfred Josephs elevated the movie to a higher level ... but then AIP replaced it with one by Les Baxter for the American release. I felt his was too modern for the film.

Q: You worked on three films in a row with Vincent Price. How did you find him to work with?
A: Vincent was a wonderful person. Unique. Although he was trapped in these B-pictures, he worked hard to make them believable. He never went on about himself or his films. When I was living in England, I always invited Vincent to my home before each picture to have cocktails and discuss the upcoming film. He was an extraordinary man.

Q: Your last film for AIP was Murders in the Rue Morgue.

A: I originally went to Nice, where we were going to use the sets from *Les Enfants Du Paradis*, which were still standing. AIP couldn't get French financial participation, so we ended up filming in Spain. Chris Wicking had written a very complex script. Rather than rehash the Poe story, which had already been filmed several times, Chris' script focused on an actress who is appearing in a play version of Poe's "Murders in the Rue Morgue." She is tormented by nightmares which are not flashbacks but flash-forwards. She does not perceive that these dreams are actually a glimpse into her future. The true horror is that her nightmare never ends. Jim Nicholson liked the finished film, but Sam Arkoff didn't. Despite pleading from Deke Heyward and myself, the movie was heavily reedited. At AIP's insistence, I had persuaded Lilli Palmer to appear in the film and then they proceeded to cut out most of her scenes. She was a pivotal character who was reduced to a bit player. This was the end of my association with AIP.

Q: They never approached you to direct for them again?
A: At one point Sam wanted to do a film called "Dante's Inferno" to be filmed in Germany. I had worked with a wonderful Canadian writer during my days with Hitchcock. His name was Lou Davidson and he had written several of the television episodes. Sam hired him to write a script, which turned out brilliantly. It dealt with a young boy's loss of innocence. Arkoff wanted to star Peter Fonda in the film and insisted that the script be rewritten to accommodate him. We refused and the picture was never made. We later tried to buy the script from Arkoff, but he refused to sell it to us.

Q: "The Golden Voyage of Sinbad" was a very different type of film for you to direct. How did this come about?
A: I had directed a film which Mel Ferrer produced called *Embassy*. Charles Schneer and Ray Harryhausen liked it and asked me to direct *The Golden Voyage of Sinbad*. Harryhausen is a genius and it was an honor to work with him. I tried to continually challenge him with new ideas. He told me we could do anything provided we had the time and the money. He worked wonders within the confines of the budget.

Q: I read recently that you were the original choice to direct Hammer's The Legend of the Seven Golden Vampires.
A: To my recollection, I was never asked to work on this film. I was, however, considered for *Blood from the Mummy's Tomb*.

Q: Of the films discussed, which do you prefer?

A: I think that *Scream and Scream Again* turned out the best. *Murders in the Rue Morgue* would have been better if it had been left in its original state. I would love to see it restored as it was intended to be.

Q: What is currently occupying your time?

A: Now that I am semi-retired, I am at last beginning to watch classic movies. I recently saw three Greta Garbo films and I thought they were brilliantly directed by Clarence Brown.

The Films

1. *The Abominable Dr. Phibes*

American–International (1971); 93 minutes; Color by Movielab

EXP: James H. Nicholson and Samuel Z. Arkoff; **P:** Louis M. Heyward and Ronald S. Dunas; **D:** Robert Fuest; **S:** James Whiton and William Goldstein; **M:** Basil Kirchin; **DP:** Norman Warwick; **E:** Tristam Cones; **PD:** Brian Eatwell; **AD:** Bernard Reeves; **Cast:** Vincent Price, Joseph Cotten, Virginia North, Hugh Griffith, Terry Thomas, Peter Jeffrey, Maurice Kaufmann, John Cater, Derek Godfrey, John Laurie, Barbara Keogh and Norman Jones.

In this art deco horror film, the wife of Dr. Anton Phibes (Vincent Price) dies on the operating table. Phibes, crazed with grief, vows to avenge her death by taking the lives of the people he feels are responsible: Dr. Vesalius (Joseph Cotten) and his team of associates who assisted with the operation. This revenge comes in the form of the ten Plagues of Egypt which Phibes recreates with fiendish ingenuity. He is assisted by the beautiful but mute Vulnavia (Virginia North).

The film consists of little more than a series of cleverly contrived murders, but it is all done so stylishly that you take little note of the plot deficiencies. Brian Eatwell and Bernard Reeves did wonders within the restrictions of the budget; the design of *The Abominable Dr. Phibes* is uniquely fanciful. Although AIP executive Samuel Z. Arkoff had little faith in the marketability of this movie, it was a big hit with both critics and audiences. Vincent Price said, "Actually, this was a mock-horror movie, and some say it was ridiculous when I had to speak out of an electric socket in my neck. But audiences loved the film." Popular "scream queen" Caroline Munro plays Phibes' wife Victoria, seen only in photographs and as a corpse at the conclusion.

Video: U.S.

2. *The Abominable Snowman*

A Hammer Film Production (1957); 91 minutes; HammerScope; U.S. (*The Abominable Snowman of the Himalayas*): 20th Century–Fox; 85 minutes; Regalscope

---

Credits Abbreviations

EXP	Executive Producer	DP	Director of Photography
P	Producer	E	Editor
D	Director	PD	Production Designer
S	Screenwriter	AD	Art Director
M	Composer	SVE	Special Visual Effects

Peter Cushing tries to comfort a distressed Maureen O'Connell in *The Abominable Snowman*.

EXP: Michael Carreras; **P:** Aubrey Baring; **D:** Val Guest; **S:** Nigel Kneale; **M:** Humphrey Searle **DP:** Arthur Grant; **E:** Bill Lenny; **PD:** Bernard Robinson; **AD:** Ted Marshall; **Cast:** Peter Cushing, Forrest Tucker, Maureen Connell, Richard Wattis, Robert Brown, Michael Brill, Wolfe Morris, Arnold Marle and Anthony Chin.

Dr. John Rollason (Peter Cushing) joins an expedition in search of the legendary Yeti. Rollason wishes only to conduct a scientific study, but the group's leader Tom Friend (Forrest Tucker) plans to capture the creature for monetary gain.

Anyone anticipating the horrorfest promised by Fox's advertising campaign ("The Superbeast Unleashes New Worlds of Terror!") may be disappointed in this thoughtful thriller. Nigel Kneale adapted the literate script from his teleplay "The Creature." This, combined with excellent performances and convincing production design, easily make it the best of a quartet of films about the Yeti produced in the Fifties (the inferior others are *The Snow Creature*, *Man Beast* and *Half Human*).

Video: U.K./U.S.

The Abominable Snowman of the Himalayas see ***The Abominable Snowman***

Alien Women see *Zeta One*

3. The Amazing Mr. Blunden

Hemisphere Productions Ltd. (1972); 100 minutes; Color; U.S.: Hemdale

P: Barry Levinson; **D/S:** Lionel Jeffries; **M:** Elmer Bernstein; **DP:** Gerry Fisher; **E:** Teddy Darvas; **PD:** Wilfred Shingleton; **AD:** Bryan Graves; **Cast:** Laurence Naismith, Lynne Frederick, Garry Miller, Marc Granger, Rosalyn Landor, Diana Dors, James Villiers, Madeline Smith, David Lodge, Deddie Davies, Dorothy Alison and Graham Crowden.

This is an amazing film, missing from many fantasy-horror filmographies. Based on "The Ghosts" by Antonia Barber and directed with style by Lionel Jeffries, it deserves to be seen.

In 1928, an impoverished widow and mother of three (Dorothy Alison) takes a job as caretaker of a neglected mansion. It is said to be haunted by the ghosts of two children who died there 100 years before. The ghosts (Rosalyn Landor and Marc Granger) appear to the widow's two oldest children, Lucy (Lynne Frederick) and James (Garry Miller). They beg them to return to the past and help save them from their untimely deaths at the hands of the evil housekeeper Mrs. Wickens (Diana Dors). *The Amazing Mr. Blunden* is a handsome production filled with "on the mark" performances, not the least of which is Diana Dors as one of the most vile shrews ever to appear on a motion picture screen. The end credits are particularly charming, a fitting ending to a unique movie.

Video: U.K./U.S.

4. And Now the Screaming Starts (a.k.a. *The Bride of Fengriffen*)

An Amicus Production (1973); 87 minutes; A Harbor Productions Inc.; Presentation Technicolor; U.S.: Cinerama Releasing

EXP: Gustave Berne; **P:** Max J. Rosenberg and Milton Subotsky; **D:** Roy Ward Baker; **S:** Roger Marshall; **M:** Douglas Gamley; **DP:** Denys Coop; **E:** Peter Tanner; **AD:** Tony Curtis **Cast:** Peter Cushing, Stephanie Beacham, Ian Ogilvy, Herbert Lom, Patrick Magee, Geoffrey Whitehead, Guy Rolfe, Rosalie Crutchley, Janet Key, Gillian Lind, Sally Harrison and Frank Forsyth.

In the year 1795, Charles Fengriffen (Ian Ogilvy) brings his virgin bride Catherine (Stephanie Beacham) to Fengriffen Estate (Oakley Court). On their wedding night, Catherine is raped by a malevolent spirit, beginning a series of macabre occurrences that are the result of a curse placed on the family two generations before. Charles' grandfather Henry (Herbert Lom) was a debauchee who not only raped the bride of his woodsman Silas (Geoffrey Whitehead) on his wedding night, but cut off the unfortunate man's hand as well. Silas cursed Henry Fengriffen and his descendants.

Based on the novel *Fengriffen* by David Case, this atmospheric Gothic horror film is the closest Amicus ever came to emulating the Hammer style. The cast is an exceptionally fine one, particularly Peter Cushing as Dr. Pope, a psychiatrist brought in to help unravel the mystery.

Video: U.K./U.S.

5. And Soon the Darkness

Associated British Productions Ltd. (1970); 94 minutes; Technicolor; U.S.: Levitt-Pickman

P: Albert Fennell and Brian Clemens; **D:** Robert Fuest; **S:** Brian Clemens and Terry Nation; **M:** Laurie Johnson; **DP:** Ian Wilson; **E:** Ann Chegwidden; **AD:** Philip Harrison; **Cast:** Pamela Franklin, Michele Dotrice, Sandor Eles, John Nettleton, Clare Kelly, Hana:Marie Pravda, John Franklyn, Claude Bertrand and Jean Carmet

A slow-moving suspense thriller from the creative team that was responsible for *The Avengers* television series. Jane (Pamela Franklin) and Cathy (Michele Dotrice) are two pretty English girls on a bicycling holiday in the French countryside. They attract the attention of a mysterious young man (Sandor Eles) who follows them. The girls have a disagreement and part company on a deserted stretch of road. Jane goes on, but has second thoughts and returns to discover that Cathy has vanished. Jane also learns that a young woman was found murdered along the same road the year before and the killer was never apprehended. The story takes place during one endless day in which Jane encounters all manner of suspicious characters as she searches for Cathy. This is definitely not the film to see if you are planning to go on a cycling tour in France.

Video: U.K./U.S.

6. *The Anniversary*

A Hammer/Seven Arts Production (1967); 95 minutes; Technicolor; U.S.: 20th Century–Fox; DeLuxe Color

P/S: Jimmy Sangster; **D:** Roy Ward Baker; **Music Supervisor:** Philip Martell; **DP:** Harry Waxman; **PD:** Reece Pemberton; **E:** James Needs and Peter Weatherley; **Cast:** Bette Davis, Sheila Hancock, Jack Hedley, James Cossins, Elaine Taylor, Christian Roberts, Timothy Bateson, Arnold Diamond, Albert Shepherd, Sally-Jane Spencer and Ralph Watson.

This black comedy may seem an odd choice for inclusion in a survey of horror films, but it fits comfortably into the "horror hag" subgenre established by Bette Davis and Joan Crawford in *What Ever Happened to Baby Jane?* (1962). The American distributors played up this horror angle with advertising catchlines such as "There Is No Name For Their Kind of Evil!"

Adapted from the stage play by Bill MacIlwraith, *The Anniversary* provided Bette Davis with one of the campiest (and nastiest) roles in her long career. No bit of scenery is left unchewed. To their credit, the rest of the cast is able to hold its own. Sheila Hancock is almost a match for the formidable Davis in the scenery-chewing sweepstakes.

Although her husband has been dead for a decade, every year Mrs. Taggart (Bette Davis) gathers her three grown sons around her to celebrate the anniversary of her wedding. She uses this occasion to reinforce her total domination of their lives.

Alvin Rakoff was the original director, but a week into shooting Davis insisted that he be replaced by Roy Ward Baker. Davis and Baker had become friends in the early 50s (during the Hollywood phase of Baker's career), and together they were able to finish the film amicably.

Video: U.S.

7. *The Asphyx* (a.k.a. *Spirit of the Dead*)

A Glendale Production (1972); 99 minutes; Eastman Color and Todd-AO 35; U.S.: Paragon Pictures

P: John Brittany; **D:** Peter Newbrook; **S:** Brian Comport; **M:** Bill McGuffie; **DP:** Freddie Young; **E:** Maxine Julius; **PD:** John Stoll; **Cast:** Robert Stephens, Robert Powell, Jane Lapotaire, Alex Scott, Ralph Arliss, Fiona Walker, Terry Scully, John Lawrence, David Grey, Tony Caunter and Paul Bacon

In the late 1800s, Sir Hugo Cunningham (Robert Stephens) inadvertently films the death of his son in a boating accident. Just before his son dies, a strange shape appears in the film. Sir Hugo has seen similar shapes in photographs taken of people as they are about to die. He concludes that this is a spirit which appears at the moment of death to capture the soul of the dying. In Greek mythology it was called the Asphyx. Sir Hugo succeeds in capturing the Asphyx of a guinea pig and seals it in an impenetrable receptacle, thereby making the animal immortal. He decides to do the same for himself, his daughter Christina (Jane Lapotaire) and her fiancée Giles (Robert Powell).

Robert Stephens and Robert Powell in *The Asphyx*.

Although Sir Hugo is successful with isolating his own Asphyx, Christina is killed when he attempts to capture hers. Distraught, Giles forms a plan to put an end to the experiments.

A highly original premise makes this worth watching. Acting and technical work are of a high caliber, although the direction is a bit pedestrian at times.

Video: U.K./U.S.

8. Assault

A Peter Rogers Production (1971); 88 minutes; Color; U.S. (*Tower of Terror* [a.k.a. *In the Devil's Garden*]): Hemisphere (1973)

P: George H. Brown; **D:** Sidney Hayers; **S:** John Kruse; **M:** Eric Rogers; **DP:** Ken Hodges; **E:** Anthony Palk; **AD:** Lionel Couch; **Cast:** Suzy Kendall, Frank Finlay, James Laurenson, Lesley-Anne Down, Freddie Jones, Tony Beckley, Dilys Hamlett, James Cosmo, Anthony Ainley, Patrick Jordon, Allan Cuthbertson and Anabel Littledale

Peter Rogers took time off from the "Carry On" comedies to produce this psychological thriller in which a rapist-killer terrorizes the students of a girls' school. Suzy Kendall is a pretty art instructor who puts her own life in jeopardy to try and trap the killer. Based on the novel *The Ravine* by Kendal Young, the film has little to recommend it other than a good cast which includes Lesley-Anne Down in her movie debut. Also watch for singer David Essex as the unfortunate victim of an explosion in a pharmacy.

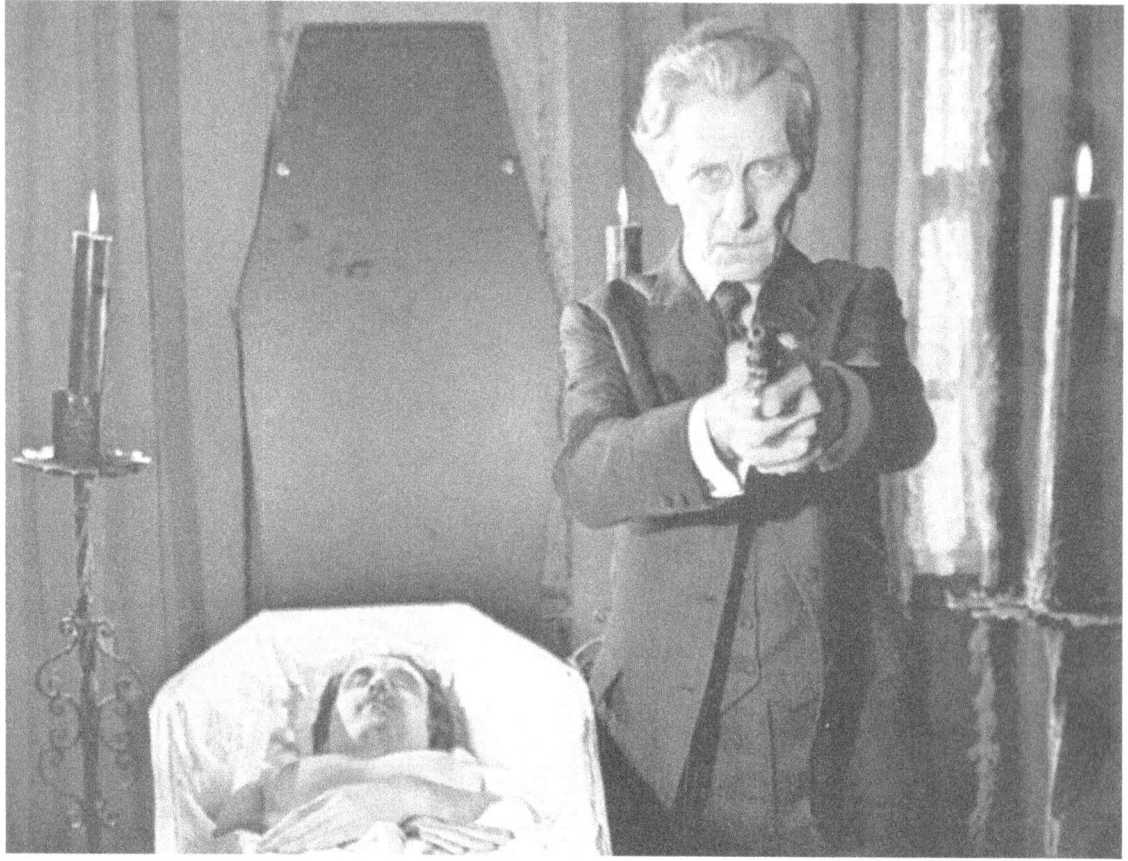

Peter Cushing was featured in *Asylum* as well as many other Amicus' productions.

Video: U.S. (alternate video title: *The Creepers*)

9. Asylum (a.k.a. *House of Crazies*)

An Amicus Production (1972); 88 minutes; Technicolor; U.S.: Cinerama Releasing

P: Max J. Rosenberg and Milton Subotsky; **D:** Roy Ward Baker; **S:** Robert Bloch; **M:** Douglas Gamley; **DP:** Denys Coop; **E:** Peter Tanner; **AD:** Tony Curtis; **Cast:** Peter Cushing, Britt Ekland, Herbert Lom, Patrick Magee, Barry Morse, Barbara Parkins, Robert Powell, Charlotte Rampling, Sylvia Sims, Richard Todd, James Villers and Geoffrey Bayldon

A doctor, applying for a position at an institute for the incurably insane, must interview four of the patients to try and ascertain which one is the former head of the hospital.

In the first story, Richard Todd murders his wife (Sylvia Sims) and dismembers her body. Unfortunately, her body parts come back to haunt Todd and his girlfriend (Barbara Parkins). In the next sequence, Barry Morse is a tailor hired by Peter Cushing to make a very unusual suit for his son. This Robert Bloch story was previously used as the basis for an episode of the Boris Karloff television series *Thriller*. The third, and least interesting, tale stars Charlotte Rampling as a disturbed woman who insists that the murders she is accused of were committed by her friend Lucy (Britt Ekland). The last story, which also incorporates the framing device, features Herbert Lom as a doctor

Two unconvincing monsters battle *At the Earth's Core*.

who has created a miniature being in his own image that he uses as an instrument to kill. A good script and a very strong cast helps to make this one of Amicus' most entertaining anthology films.

Video: U.K./U.S.

10. *At the Earth's Core*

A Samuel Z. Arkoff–Amicus Productions Presentation; A Max J. Rosenberg and Milton Subotsky Production (1976); 90 minutes; Technicolor; U.S.: American–International; Color by Movielab

EXP: Harry N. Blum; **P:** John Dark; **D:** Kevin Connor; **S:** Milton Subotsky; **M:** Mike Vickers; **DP:** Alan Hume; **E:** John Ireland and Barry Peterson; **DP:** Maurice Carter; **AD:** Bert Davey; **Cast:** Doug McClure, Peter Cushing, Caroline Munro, Cy Grant, Godfrey James, Sean Lynch and Keith Barron

Amicus' second Edgar Rice Burroughs fantasy is not as good as their first, *The Land That Time Forgot*. David Innes (Doug McClure) and Prof. Perry (Peter Cushing) are testing a burrowing device called the "Iron Mole" when it suddenly goes out of control. They end up in Pellucidar, a land located at the Earth's core and inhabited by fierce beasts and various primitive tribes. Innes and Perry are captured and taken to the city of the Mahars, the evil bird-like creatures who rule Pellucidar. The remainder of the film deals with Innes attempts to overthrow the Mahars and liberate the people of Pellucidar.

The original novel is one of Burroughs' most imaginative and spawned six sequels. In the books, Pellucidar is a land of vast oceans and towering mountains populated with animals which greatly resemble the fauna of the outer Earth's prehistoric past. The scope of Burroughs' work is all but lost in the claustrophobic production design of the film, which brings to mind the "Alice in Wonderland" ride at Disneyland. The monsters are mostly of the "man in a monster suit" variety and are totally unconvincing. Even the ever-reliable Peter Cushing is nearly defeated by a clichéd dotty professor role. The movie is filled with an endless collection of pyrotechnics which give it a sense of spectacle but do little to further the plot.

Video: U.K./U.S.

The Atomic Man see *Timeslip*

11. Battle Beneath the Earth

A Reynolds–Vetter Production (1967); 91 minutes; Technicolor; U.S.: Metro-Goldwyn–Mayer (1968)

EXP: Charles F. Vetter, Junior; **P:** Charles Reynolds; **D:** Montgomery Tully; **S:** Lance Z. Hargreaves; **M:** Ken Jones; **DP:** Kenneth Talbot; **E:** Sidney Stone; **AD:** Jim Morahan; **Cast:** Kerwin Mathews, Viviane Ventura, Martin Benson, David Spenser, Peter Elliott, Peter Arne, Robert Ayres, Edward Bishop, Bill Nagy, Al Mulock, Earl Cameron and Paula Li Shiu

In this Cold War fantasy, Commander Jonathan Shaw (Kerwin Mathews) discovers that the Red Chinese have dug tunnels under the major cities in the United States and are now tunneling under the Defense Centers. The leader of this operation is Gen. Chan Lu (Martin Benson). He and his men are using a tunnel-boring laser beam to plant nuclear bombs beneath strategic points in the U.S. This wild premise has promise and might have worked in a James Bond film but, unfortunately, it doesn't work here. If the direction and performances had just a touch of tongue-in-cheek, it would have helped; instead, the proceedings are played out with the utmost seriousness. The cheap production values give it the look of a low-grade made-for-TV movie.

Video: U.S.

12. The Beast in the Cellar (a.k.a. *The Cellar*)

A Tigon–British–Leander Films Ltd. Production (1970); 87 minutes; Color; U.S.: Cannon (1971)

EXP: Tony Tenser; **P:** Graham Harris; **D/S:** James Kelly; **M:** Tom Macaulay; **DP:** Harry Waxman and Desmond Dickinson; **E:** Nicholas Napier-Bell; **AD:** Roger King; **Cast:** Beryl Reid, Flora Robson, John Hamill, Tess Wyatt, T.P. McKenna, John Kelland, David Dodimead, Vernon Dobtcheff, Peter Craze, Dafydd Harvard, Gail Lidstone and Elisabeth Choice

Soldiers from a rural army camp are being slashed to death by some unknown creature with talons. This is cause for much alarm in the nearby household of the spinster Ballentyne sisters. Ellie (Beryl Reid) is excitable and perpetually overwrought. Joyce (Flora Robson) is more severe and tries to keep her cool, even though the body count continues to rise. In the end it turns out that the sisters did not want their only brother Steven to go off to World War II, so they walled him up in the cellar. Steven understandably went quite mad and now hates any man in uniform. This is all revealed in an endless expository monologue delivered by Reid. Slow-moving with some jarring gore effects, *The Beast in the Cellar* simply does not pay off after the extended build-up. When glimpsed at the climax, Steven resembles Howard Hughes in his final days with long hair, beard and fingernails.

Video: U.S.

13. The Beast Must Die

An Amicus Production (1974); 93 minutes; Technicolor; U.S.: Cinerama Releasing

EXP: Robert Greenberg; **P:** Max J. Rosenberg and Milton Subotsky; **D:** Paul Annett; **S:**

Michael Winder; **M:** Douglas Gamley; **DP:** Jack Hildyard; **E:** Peter Tanner; **AD:** John Stoll; **Cast:** Calvin Lockhart, Peter Cushing, Charles Gray, Anton Diffring, Marlene Clark, Ciaran Madden, Tom Chadbon, Michael Gambon, Sam Mansaray, Andrew Lodge, Carl Bohun and Eric Carte

"This film is a detective story in which you are the detective. The question is not 'Who is the murderer?' but 'Who is the werewolf?' After all the clues have been shown, you will get a chance to give your answer. Watch for the 'Werewolf Break.'"

Based on the above, you may well be wondering if this is a William Castle film. If only! Then it might have at least been some fun. Instead, what we have here is a most uninspiring offering from Amicus. Millionaire big game hunter Tom Newcliffe (Calvin Lockhart) brings six people to his remote estate. He is convinced that one of them is a werewolf and he intends to find out which one and then hunt it down. Peter Cushing is Dr. Lundgren, an expert on werewolves. Also in the cast are Anton Diffring and Charles Gray in roles which are a total waste of their talents. The werewolf seems to have been played by a large dog in a fur coat. A great title, but a mediocre film.

Video: U.K./U.S.

Beast of Morocco see *The Hand of Night*

14. *Bedazzled*

A Stanley Donen Production (1967); 107 minutes; DeLuxe Color and Panavision; U.S.: 20th Century–Fox

P/D: Stanley Donen; **S:** Peter Cook; **M:** Dudley Moore; **DP:** Austin Dempster; **E:** Richard Marder; **AD:** Terence Knight; **Cast:** Peter Cook, Dudley Moore, Eleanor Bron, Raquel Welch, Michael Bates, Barry Humphries, Bernard Spear, Evelyn Moore, Michael Trubshawe, Howard Goorney, Robin Hawdon and Charles Lloyd Pack

This frequently hilarious version of *Faust* features the brilliant comedy team of Peter Cook and Dudley Moore several years prior to Moore's solo international stardom. Moore plays the pitiful short-order cook Stanley Moon who secretly loves a waitress (Eleanor Bron). Distraught over his unrequited love, Moon tries to commit suicide. He bungles the attempt and along comes George Spiggot (Peter Cook), a.k.a. the Devil, to grant Moon seven wishes in return for his soul. The wishes propel Moon into a series of wild situations in which Spiggot always gets the better of him. Raquel Welch puts in a brief but memorable appearance as Lillian Lust.

Video: None

15. *Behemoth, The Sea Monster*

A David Diamond–Artistes Alliance Ltd. Production (1959); 79 minutes; U.S. (*The Giant Behemoth*): Allied Artists

P: Ted Lloyd; **D/S:** Eugene Lourie; **M:** Edwin Astley; **DP:** Ken Hodges; **E:** Lee Doig; **AD:** Harry White; **SVE:** Jack Rabin, Irving Block, Louis De Witt, Willis O'Brien and Pete Peterson; **Cast:** Gene Evans, Andre Morell, John Turner, Leigh Madison, Jack MacGowran, Henry Vidon, Maurice Kaufmann and Leonard Sachs

This movie gets off to a wonderfully ominous start when thousands of dead fish wash up on the Cornwall coast. A fisherman is found suffering from fatal burns and his last word is "behemoth." Two scientists (Gene Evans and Andre Morell) are called in to investigate and one of them comes to the conclusion that a gigantic radioactive sea beast may be responsible. Once this has been established, the Behemoth begins its inevitable rampage through the streets of London. The remainder of the film becomes a mere rehash of director Eugene Lourie's earlier (and better) dinosaur-on-the-loose effort *The Beast from 20,000 Fathoms* (1953). The special effects are of variable quality. The stop-motion animation sequences by Willis O'Brien and Pete Peterson are impressive, particularly given the minuscule effects budget for the entire film. The other effects, by Rabin, Block and De Witt, are second-rate and a poor match for the animation. Lourie would return to this sub-genre once again for *Gorgo*.

Video: U.S.

16. Berserk!

A Herman Cohen Production (1967); 96 minutes; Technicolor; U.S.: Columbia

P: Herman Cohen; **D:** Jim O'Connolly; **S:** Aben Kandel and Herman Cohen; **M:** Patrick John Scott; **DP:** Desmond Dickinson; **E:** Raymond Poulton; **AD:** Maurice Pelling; **Cast:** Joan Crawford, Ty Hardin, Diana Dors, Judy Geeson, Michael Gough, Robert Hardy, Geoffrey Keen, Sydney Tafler, Milton Reid, George Claydon, Philip Madoc and Marianne Stone

Yet another in the series of post–*Baby Jane* thrillers which headlined accomplished, but aging, actresses in leading roles. This one is a bit different as Joan Crawford is not cast as a "horror hag" but is indecorously showcased as the sexy romantic lead. Apparently the producer decided to ignore the fact that she was at least 63 years old at the time. The scenes where Crawford is drooled over by both Michael Gough and Ty Hardin are horrific indeed! In this outing, Crawford is Monica Rivers, owner of the Great Rivers Circus where a series of uninspiring acts are an excuse to pad the running time of the film. "Phyllis and Her Intelligent Poodles" are particularly grueling to sit through, as is an awful "in your face" musical number sung by members of the sideshow. The mundane circus acts turn lethal as performers are shockingly killed in a series of suspicious "accidents." Unfortunately, Phyllis and the Poodles survive. The revelation of the killer's identity is terribly contrived and completely illogical. Be sure to check out the obvious plug for Pepsi (Joan was a board member). Producer Herman Cohen and Crawford would team up again for *Trog*.

Video: U.S.

Beware the Brethren see ***The Fiend***

17. The Black Torment

A Compton–Cameo–Tekli Production (1964); 85 minutes; Color; U.S.: Governor Films

EXP: Michael Klinger and Tony Tenser; **P/D:** Robert Hartford-Davis; **S:** Donald and Derek Ford; **M:** Robert Richards; **DP:** Peter Newbrook; **E:** Alastair McIntyre; **AD:** Alan Harris; **Cast:** Heather Sears, John Turner, Ann Lynn, Peter Arne, Norman Bird, Raymond Huntley, Annette Whitely, Francis De Wolff, Edina Ronay, Patrick Troughton and Joseph Tomelty

Sir Robert Fordyke (John Turner) brings his new bride Elizabeth (Heather Sears) home to the ancestral mansion where she learns that the family closet has more than its share of skeletons. Sir Robert is suspected of the violent rape and murder of a local village girl, although he was in London at the time the crime occurred. Witnesses also swear that they have seen him riding his horse at night, pursued by the ghostly figure of his deceased first wife who shrieks "Murderer!" The promising story bogs down at the end when the supposedly supernatural elements turn out to be a rather conventional plot to drive the main character insane. John Turner, as twin brothers (one good, one mad), tends to overplay both roles. There are some interesting directorial touches such as one scene which is shown from the point of view of a stoke victim who is confined to a wheelchair. Set in eighteenth century England, this handsomely mounted production was Tony Tenser's first foray into the genre of horror movies.

Video: U.K./U.S. (U.S. video title: *Estate of Insanity*)

Blast-Off see ***Jules Verne's Rocket to the Moon***

Heather Sears and John Turner in *The Black Torment*, Tony Tenser's first horror film.

18. Blind Terror

Genesis Productions Ltd. (1971); 89 minutes; Eastman Color; U.S. *(See No Evil)*: Columbia/Filmways

P: Martin Ransohoff and Leslie Linder; **D:** Richard Fleischer; **S:** Brian Clemens; **M:** Elmer Bernstein; **DP:** Gerry Fisher; **E:** Thelma Connell; **AD:** John Hoesli; **Cast:** Mia Farrow, Dorothy Alison, Robin Bailey, Diane Grayson, Lila Kaye, Brian Rawlinson, Norman Eshley, Paul Nicholas, Scott Francis, Christopher Matthews, Reg Harding and Max Faulkner

Sarah (Mia Farrow) is blinded in a horseback riding accident. When she is released from the hospital, she comes to stay at the country estate of her aunt and uncle. One day while Sarah is out, her aunt, uncle and cousin are savagely murdered by a psychopath (we see only his cowboy boots). She returns home and does not realize she is in a house filled with corpses. The killer discovers that he has lost his ID bracelet and comes back to the scene of the crime to find it. Director Richard Fleischer really puts Mia Farrow through her paces in this tense thriller. Rather than have her trapped alone in the confines of the house with the killer, Fleischer moves the action to the outdoors where blind Sarah is even more vulnerable to dangers she cannot see. *Blind Terror* is a tense and sometimes grueling exercise in suspense.

Video: U.K./U.S.

Blood Beast from Outer Space see ***The Night Caller***

19. The Blood Beast Terror

A Tigon–British Production (1967); 81 minutes; Eastman Color; U.S. *(The Vampire-Beast Craves Blood)*: Pacemaker (1969); Color by Movielab

EXP: Tony Tenser; **P:** Arnold L. Miller; **D:** Vernon Sewell; **S:** Peter Bryan; **M:** Paul Ferris; **DP:** Stanley A. Long; **E:** Howard Lanning; **AD:** Wilfred Woods; **Cast:** Peter Cushing, Robert Flemyng, Wanda Ventham, Vanessa Howard, Roy Hudd, David Griffin, Kevin Stoney, Glynn Edwards, John Paul, Russell Napier and William Wild

An odd little film in which the daughter of a famed entomologist is inexplicably able to change into a giant Death's Head moth. Wanda Ventham is the lethal lady whose moth makeup makes her look like a close relative of *The Wasp Woman*. Peter Cushing plays a police inspector who is trying to solve a series of ghastly murders in which the victims, all male, have been drained of their blood.

Robert Flemyng, as the entomologist, keeps his daughter's horrible secret and even attempts to create a giant moth mate for her. In the end he comes to his senses and destroys the mate before it has fully developed in its cocoon. The female moth monster is seen only briefly and the hurried climax suffers badly due to shoddy special effects.

Video: U.S.

20. Blood from the Mummy's Tomb

A Hammer Film Production (1971); 94 minutes; Technicolor; U.S.: American–International (1972); 92 minutes; DeLuxe Color

P: Howard Brandy; **D:** Seth Holt; **S:** Christopher Wicking; **M:** Tristram Cary; **DP:** Arthur Grant; **E:** Peter Weatherley; **AD:** Scott MacGregor; **Cast:** Valerie Leon, Andrew Keir, James Villiers, Hugh Burden, George Coulouris, Mark Edwards, Rosalie Crutchley, Aubrey Morris, David Markham, James Cossins, David Jackson and Tamara Ustinov

A team of archeologists, led by Julian Fuchs (Andrew Keir), discovers the tomb of an ancient Egyptian sorceress named Tera and brings her corpse back to England. Twenty-one years later, her evil spirit begins to manifest itself in Fuchs' daughter Margaret (Valerie Leon).

This may seem like a routine "mummy" movie but there is very little of the conventional about this film. It had a particularly troubled production history. Peter Cushing had been cast in the part of Julian Fuchs but, when his wife became gravely ill and died, he withdrew from the production. Seth Holt died during the final week of shooting and Michael Carreras took over as director. Apparently Holt left behind an editing nightmare, and much trouble was taken to create order out of the material at hand. Based on Bram Stoker's *The Jewel of Seven Stars*, *Blood from the Mummy's Tomb* had its world premiere in London at the National Film Theatre's 1971 tribute to Hammer. When it was picked up for distribution in the U.S. by American–International, they edited out most of the blood and then chose to advertise the film in the most grisly of terms: "More gore than ever before...as the bloodiest butchers in history turn the screen into a slaughterhouse!" In 1980, Charlton Heston starred in *The Awakening*, which was based on the same material. Despite a big budget and location filming in Egypt, *The Awakening* is devoid of atmosphere and is not nearly as chilling as the Hammer film. A third version, *Bram Stoker's The Mummy* (1998) starred Louis Gossett and also featured Aubrey Morris, who was in *Blood from the Mummy's Tomb*.

Video: U.K.

Blood Island see **The Shuttered Room**

ANDREW KEIR AND VALERIE LEON ATTEMPT TO DESTROY THE EVIL QUEEN TERA (ALSO KNOWN AS VALERIE LEON) IN *BLOOD FROM THE MUMMY'S TOMB*.

21. *Blood of the Vampire*

An Eros Films Ltd. Production (1958); 85 minutes; Eastman Color; U.S.: Universal–International

P: Robert S. Baker and Monty Berman; **D:** Henry Cass; **S:** Jimmy Sangster; **M:** Stanley Black; **DP:** Monty Berman; **E:** Douglas Myers; **AD:** John Elphick; **Cast:** Donald Wolfit, Barbara Shelley, Vincent Ball, Victor Maddern, William Devlin, Andrew Faulds, John Le Mesurier, George Murcell, Bryan Coleman, Bernard Bresslaw, Cameron Hall and Milton Reid

In 1874 Transylvania, a doctor is thought to be a vampire because of his experiments involving blood. He is executed by having a stake driven through his heart. Six years later in Carlstadt, Dr. John Pierre (Victor Ball) is sentenced to be imprisoned for malpractice involving a blood transfusion. He is sent to a prison for the criminally insane run by Dr. Callistratus (Donald Wolfit). This is the same doctor who was executed years before; he has been restored to life by a heart transplant but left with a blood disease that requires constant transfusions. He hopes that Pierre's knowledge will help find a cure for his condition. Pierre's fiancee (Barbara Shelley) contrives to become Callistratus' housekeeper to be near to the man she loves and, as they say, the plot thickens. This was the first concentrated effort by another company to imitate Hammer's Gothic horror films. *Blood of the Vampire* has all of Hammer's colorful trap-

DONALD WOLFIT AND HIS VICTIM BARBARA SHELLEY IN *BLOOD OF THE VAMPIRE*.

pings but lacks their pacing and style, despite an interesting screenplay by Jimmy Sangster. The title is also a misnomer as the vampire reference is cursory, at best. Donald Wolfit, as the mad doctor, is made up to resemble Bela Lugosi and his performance is the equal of many given by that venerable ham. Victor Maddern is quite good as Callistratus' mute hunchback assistant Carl, and Barbara Shelley is a lovely damsel in distress.

Video: U.S.

The Blood on Satan's Claw see *Satan's Skin*

Blood Will Have Blood see *Demons of the Mind*

Bloodsuckers see *Incense for the Damned*

22. *Bluebeard's Ten Honeymoons*
Allied Artists (1960); 92 minutes

P: Roy Parkinson; **D:** W. Lee Wilder; **S:** Myles Wilder; **M:** Albert Elms; **P:** Stephen Dade; **E:** Tom Simpson; **AD:** Paul Sheriff; **Cast:** George Sanders, Corinne Calvet, Jean Kent, Patricia Roc, Greta Gynt, Maxine Audley, Ingrid Hafner, Selma Vaz Diaz, Peter Illing, George Coulouris and Sheldon Lawrence

Henri Landru (George Sanders) becomes enamored of a greedy nightclub singer named Odette (Corinne Calvet). In order to keep her in the manner she desires, Henri seeks out lonely, wealthy widows whom he captivates and then murders for their money.

John Carradine starred as *Bluebeard* in a memorable 1944 version and Richard Burton camped it up in the forgetable 1972 film of the same name. *Bluebeard's Ten Honeymoons* provided the fine character actor George Sanders with one of the best parts of his later career. His performance is both charming and sinister. Director W. Lee Wilder makes up for his previous British effort (the dreadful *The Man Without a Body*) with this wry look at murder and mayhem. James Bond author Ian Fleming has a small role as an attorney.

Video: None

23. The Body Stealers (a.k.a. Thin Air)

A Tigon–British–Sagittarius Film Production (1969); 90 minutes; Color; U.S.: Allied Artists (1970)

P: Tony Tenser; **D:** Gerry Levy; **S:** Mike St. Clair and Peter Marcus; **M:** Reg Tilsely; **DP:** John Coquillon; **E:** Howard Lanning; **AD:** Wilfred Arnold; **Cast:** George Sanders, Maurice Evans, Patrick Allen, Neil Connery, Robert Flemyng, Lorna Wilde, Allan Cuthbertson, Carl Rigg, Hilary Dwyer, Sally Faulkner, Michael Culver and Shelagh Fraser

It's films like this that tarnished the Golden Age of British Horror around the edges. Parachutists begin to disappear into thin air, so the government brings in arch womanizer Bob Meagan (Patrick Allen), a sort of poor man's James Bond, to try and solve the conundrum. During the course of his investigations, Meagan meets a mysterious woman named Lorna (Lorna Wilde). In no time at all, they are making passionate love on a very rocky and uncomfortable looking beach. The shocking denouement will come as a surprise to anyone who never seen another science fiction film: Aliens, of which Lorna is one, are abducting male earthlings to help repopulate their dying planet. Meagan tells Lorna that if she will release her captives, he will organize a group of self-sacrificing volunteers to return with her and start mating! George Sanders, top billed as Gen. Armstrong, spends most of his screen time talking on the telephone looking bewildered and/or exasperated. The cast also includes Neil Connery, brother of Sean, and the ever watchable Hilary Dwyer playing a lady scientist ("Beauty and brains," drools leering Bob Meagan upon meeting her, as if he had coined the phrase).

Video: U.S.

The Brain see *Vengeance*

The Bride of Fengriffen see *And Now the Screaming Starts*

24. The Brides of Dracula

A Hammer–Hotspur Production (1960); 86 minutes; Technicolor; U.S.: Universal-International

EXP: Michael Carreras; **P:** Anthony Hinds; **D:** Terence Fisher; **S:** Jimmy Sangster, Peter Bryan and Edward Percy; **M:** Malcolm Williamson; **DP:** Jack Asher; **E:** James Needs and Alfred Cox; **PD:** Bernard Robinson; **Cast:** Peter Cushing, Martita Hunt, Yvonne Monlaur, Freda Jackson, David Peel, Miles Malleson, Henry Oscar, Mona Washbourne, Andree Melly, Michael Ripper, Vera Cook and Marie Devereux

While on her way to join the staff of a girl's finishing school in Badstein, Marianne Danielle (Yvonne Monlaur) is invited to spend the night at Chateau Meinster. There, she inadvertently sets free the vampire Baron Meinster (David Peel). Van Helsing (Peter Cushing) comes to the rescue and eventually ends the vampire's reign of terror. This is one of the finest motion pictures produced by Hammer. Every aspect of the production deserves the highest of accolades. When Christopher Lee decided not to appear in a sequel to *Dracula*, Hammer went ahead and made one anyway, featuring the other main character, Van Helsing, as the link to the first film. *The Brides of Dracula* is a most

David Peel as the vampire Baron Meinster threatens Yvonne Monlaur in *The Brides of Dracula*.

Peel is an attractive and androgynous vampire. Full marks all around for this one.

Video: U.S.

25. The Brides of Fu Manchu

A Hallam Production (1966); 91 minutes; Color; U.S.: Seven Arts

P: Harry Alan Towers; **D:** Don Sharp; **S:** Peter Welbeck; **M:** Bruce Montgomery; **DP:** Ernest Steward; **E:** Allan Morrison; **AD:** Frank White; **Cast:** Christopher Lee, Douglas Wilmer, Marie Versini, Heinz Drache, Rupert Davies, Carole Gray, Tsai Chin, Howard Marion Crawford, Eric Young, Kenneth Fortescue and Joseph Furst

This second film in producer Harry Alan Towers' Fu Manchu series starring Christopher Lee is quite a comedown from its predecessor, *The Face of Fu Manchu*, but far superior to the sequels which followed. The story is an incredibly confused mess which has Fu Manchu kidnapping young girls to force their fathers or fiancés into assisting him in creating a death ray. The "brides" all sport typical 1960s hairdos and clothes; were it not for some vintage automobiles on view, one would never know that this is supposed to be a "period piece." Douglas Wilmer replaced Nigel Green as Fu Manchu's dauntless opponent Nayland Smith. The sets, particularly Fu Manchu's Egyptian underground hideaway, have an opulent look which is lacking in the subsequent entries in this inconsistent series.

Video: U.S.

worthy successor and, in some ways, improves upon the original. There are a number of unexpected plot twists and some excellent performances. Martita Hunt deserves special mention as the initially sinister Baroness Meinster who becomes a reluctant vampire after her own son drains her blood. Peter Cushing is as good as ever and David

26. Burke and Hare

A Kenneth Shipman Production (1971); 91 minutes; Eastman Color; U.S.: No theatrical release

EXP: Kenneth Shipman; **P:** Guido Coen; **D:** Vernon Sewell; **S:** Ernie Bradford; **M:** Roger Webb; **DP:** Desmond Dickinson; **E:** John Colville; **AD:** Scott MacGregor; **Cast:** Derren Nesbitt, Harry Andrews, Glynn Edwards, Yootha Joyce, Francoise Pascal, Dee Shenderey, Alan Tucker, Yutte Stensgaard, Duncan Lamont, James Hayter, Robin Hawdon and Katya Wyeth

A totally failed attempt at turning the horrific story of Burke and Hare into a ribald comedy with macabre overtones. It just doesn't work at all and the entire running time of this tedious effort seems to be spent with the film trying to decide what it wants to be.

The story of history's two most infamous body snatchers is intercut with ridiculous T & A sequences set in an Edinburgh brothel that have nothing at all to do with the central plotline until the very end. Halfway through, the horror elements seem to be taking over when suddenly the viewer is faced with a montage of murder scenes underscored by a terrible pop song sung by "The Scaffold."

The cast, filled with familiar faces, is wasted in thankless roles. Harry Andrews, as Dr. Knox, is a perfect example, as his character (which should be integral to this story) is reduced to near insignificance. The cast also includes two former "Mircalla Karnsteins," Yutte Stensgaard (*Lust for a Vampire*) and Katya Wyeth (*Twins of Evil*).

Video: U.S. (video title: *The Horrors of Burke and Hare*)

Burn Witch, Burn see *Night of the Eagle*

27. Captain Clegg

A Hammer–Major Production (1962); 82 minutes; Technicolor; U.S. *(Night Creatures)*: Universal–International; Eastman Color

P: John Temple-Smith; **D:** Peter Graham Scott; **S:** John Elder; **M:** Don Banks; **DP:** Arthur Grant; **E:** James Needs and Eric Boyd-Perkins; **PD:** Bernard Robinson; **AD:** Don Mingaye; **Cast:** Peter Cushing, Yvonne Romain, Patrick Allen, Oliver Reed, Michael Ripper, Martin Benson, David Dodge, Derek Francis, Milton Reid, Daphne Anderson, Jack MacGowran and Sydney Bromley

In addition to their horror films, Hammer also produced a series of "swashbucklers" which included, *Pirates of Blood River* (1962) and *Devil-Ship Pirates* (1964). This exciting period adventure is the best of Hammer's action films and it is the only one with conspicuous horror overtones. In the year 1792, Capt. Collier (Patrick Allen), an officer in the British Navy, comes with his crew to the village of Dymchurch to investigate reports of smuggling. Upon his arrival he discovers that his informer has died. Collier is told that the death may have been caused by an encounter with the legendary "Marsh Phantoms," apparitions whose fearsome appearance can cause a man to die of fight. Peter Cushing is outstanding as Dr. Blyss, a former pirate turned vicar, and Michael Ripper has one of his very best roles as coffin maker Jeremiah Mipps. The following year, Disney released a live-action feature based on the same source material, *Dr. Syn, Alias the Scarecrow*. It starred Patrick McGoohan and lacked any horror overtones.

Video: None

28. Captain Kronos: Vampire Hunter (a.k.a. *Kronos*)

A Hammer Film Production (1973); 91 minutes; Eastman Color; U.S.: Paramount (1974); Color by Movielab

"The Marsh Phantoms" of *Captain Clegg*.

EXP: Roy Skeggs; **P:** Albert Fennell and Brian Clemens; **D/S:** Brian Clemens; **M:** Laurie Johnson; **DP:** Ian Wilson; **E:** James Needs; **PD:** Robert Jones; **AD:** Kenneth McCallum Tait; **Cast:** Horst Janson, John Carson, Caroline Munro, Shane Briant, John Cater, Lois Daine, Ian Hendry, Wanda Ventham, William Hobbs, Brian Tully, Robert James and Perry Soblosky

Captain Kronos (Horst Janson) and his assistant Prof. Grost (John Cater) arrive in the village of Durward where several young girls have been depleted of their youth by a vampire.

Hammer attempted something a bit different with this unusual film which succeeds in combining swashbuckling and horror. Most of the credit should go to Albert Fennell and Brian Clemens, who adapted an *Avengers*–style formula to fit into the Hammer milieu. At this point in time, Hammer desperately needed a hit and they hoped that a new series could be built around the character of Kronos. Despite some better-than-average reviews (*Boxoffice* found it to be "leagues beyond the average 'bucket of blood' programmer"), the film was poorly distributed in England and failed to find much of an audience in the United States. The action highlight of the picture is a climactic duel between Kronos and a vampire played by swordsman William Hobbs, who also staged the fight sequences. An amusing bit of casting is worth noting in the end credits, where the part of the "Whore" is played by Penny Price.

Video: U.S.

29. Captain Nemo and the Underwater City

An Omnia Film Production (1969); 106 minutes; MetroColor and Panavision; U.S.: Metro-Goldwyn-Mayer (1970)

EXP: Steven Pallos; P: Bertram Ostrer; D: James Hill; S: Pip and Jane Baker and R. Wright Campbell; M: Wally Stott; DP: Alan Hume; E: Bill Lewthwaite; AD: Bill Andrews; Cast: Robert Ryan, Chuck Connors, Nanette Newman, Luciana Paluzzi, Bill Fraser, Kenneth Connor, John Turner, Allan Cuthbertson, Vincent Harding, Christopher Hartstone, Ralph Nasseck and Ann Patrice

Capt. Nemo returns again, this time in the person of Robert Ryan. Nemo uses his submarine, the *Nautilus*, to rescue a group of passengers who were on a ship which sank in a storm. He takes them to his fabulous underwater city Templemer. There he informs them that they can never leave as he is determined to keep the existence of Templemer a secret from the rest of the world. One of the captives is Robert Fraser (Chuck Connors), a U.S. Senator on a special mission for President Lincoln. His escape is imperative in order to fulfill this important obligation. There are two good reasons for watching this elaborate if somewhat prosaic family-oriented adventure fantasy: Ryan is quite good as Capt. Nemo and the underwater photography by Egil S. Woxholt is outstanding. Extensive sets were built and lowered into the Mediterranean Sea near Malta, where filming went on for eight weeks. The production later moved to the Red Sea near Hurghada, Egypt, for further underwater photography. It's too bad that all this effort couldn't have produced a better film.

Video: None

30. Carry on Screaming

A Peter Rogers Production (1966); 92 minutes; Eastman Color; U.S.: Audio Film Center

P: Peter Rogers; D: Gerald Thomas; S: Talbot Rothwell; M: Eric Rogers; DP: Alan Hume; E: Rod Keys; AD: Bert Davey; Cast: Harry H. Corbett, Kenneth Williams, Jim Dale, Charles Hawtrey, Fenella Fielding, Joan Sims, Angela Douglas, Bernard Bresslaw, Jon Pertwee, Tom Clegg, Michael Ward and Billy Cornelius

It was inevitable that the "Carry On" gang would get around to parodying horror films in general and Hammer films in particular. In this frantic farce, several young girls disappear and Police Inspector Bung (Harry H. Corbett) follows the trail of clues to the sinister Bide-A-Wee Rest Home. There, a mad scientist (Kenneth Willams) and his sexy sister (Fenella Fielding) are abducting women and turning them into dress shop mannequins. The expected mayhem ensues, complete with the usual corny jokes and double entendres. Elements from a variety of horror films are mixed into the stew, including references to *Frankenstein, Dr. Jekyll and Mr. Hyde, The Mummy* and *House of Wax*. Fielding plays a sex-crazed temptress very much like the character she portrayed in the William Castle–Hammer version of *The Old Dark House*. It can be fun, if you're not in a demanding mood.

Video: U.K.

31. The Cat and the Canary

A Grenadier Films Ltd. Production (1977); 98 minutes; Technicolor; U.S.: Quartet-Films Incorporated (1978); 90 minutes

P: Richard Gordon; D/S: Radley Metzger; M: Steven Cagan; DP: Alex Thomson; E: Roger Harrison; AD: Anthony Pratt; Cast: Honor Blackman, Michael Callan, Edward Fox, Wendy Hiller, Olivia Hussey, Beatrix Lehmann, Carol Lynley, Daniel Massey, Peter McEnery, and Wilfrid Hyde-White

In 1934, the remaining relatives of Cyrus West (Wilfrid Hyde-White) gather at the family home on the twentieth anniversary of his death. They have come to find out who will be the sole heir to his millions. The lucky person turns out to be Annabelle West (Carol Lynley), who only gets the loot if she survives the night. To complicate matters, the guests learn that a homicidal killer called "The Cat" has escaped from the local asylum and is lurking in the vicinity of the house. *The Cat and the Canary* is quite a change of pace from producer Richard Gordon's two previous bloodbaths, *Tower of Evil* and *Horror Hospital*. Inspired by the success of the all-star version of Agatha Christie's *Murder on the Orient Express*, Gordon attempted to emulate that movie with this filming of John Willard's play. It was the third screen version of this melodramatic chestnut, the first having been filmed in 1927 and the second in 1939. This time around, the performances range from very good (Wendy Hiller) to downright awful (Michael Callan). The director later turned to making hardcore sex films under the name of Henry Paris.

Video: U.S.

32. Cat Girl

Insignia Films Ltd. (1957); 69 minutes; U.S.: American–International

P: Lou Rusoff and Herbert Smith; **D:** Alfred Shaughnessy; **S:** Lou Rusoff; **DP:** Peter Hennessy; **E:** Jocelyn Jackson; **PD:** Jack Stevens; **AD:** Eric Saw; **Cast:** Barbara Shelley, Robert Ayres, Kay Callard, Ernest Milton, Lilly Kann, Jack May, Patricia Webster, John Lee, Edward Harvey, Martin Boddey and Jack Watson

This early AIP coproduction made in England is a pedestrian affair, memorable mainly for Barbara Shelley's performance. It was her introduction to the horror genre and she makes the most of the limited material at hand. The rest of the cast is dull, to put it mildly.

The plot is very derivative of *Cat People* (1942) but this film has none of the style or atmosphere of that Val Lewton classic. Leonora Brant (Shelley) suffers from a family curse which fuses her soul with that of a leopard. When her adulterous husband is torn to pieces on the family estate by a leopard, Leonora insists that she is responsible for his death. For a time she is committed to a mental institution, but then her doctor (Robert Ayers) pronounces her well enough to return with him and his wife to London. Soon Leonora is again dominated by her animal instincts and begins to stalk the doctor's wife.

Video: U.S.

33. Catacombs

A Parroch–McCallum Production (1964); 90 minutes; U.S. *(The Woman Who Wouldn't Die)*: Warner Bros. (1965); 84 minutes

P: Jack Parsons and Neil McCallum; **D:** Gordon Hessler; **S:** Daniel Mainwaring; **M:** Carlo Martelli; **DP:** Arthur Lavis; **E:** Robert Winter; **AD:** George Provis; **Cast:** Gary Merrill, Jane Merrow, Georgina Cookson, Neil McCallum, Rachel Thomas, Jack Train and Frederick Piper

While Gordon Hessler was a story editor for Alfred Hitchcock, he read a novel by Jay Bennett that he thought would interest the director. Although the property was rejected by Hitchcock, Hessler had enough faith in the material to try and stir up interest elsewhere. The end result was Hessler's first feature film as a director.

Raymond Garth (Gary Merrill) kills his invalid wife Ellen (Georgina Cookson). His accomplices in the murder are his wife's secretary Dick (Neil McCallum) and her niece Alice (Jane Merrow). To Raymond's horror, Ellen returns to haunt him and eventually drives him to his death. It all turns out to be a plot concocted by Alice and Dick to obtain Ellen's considerable fortune. Hessler's atmospheric direction already

indicates the sure-handedness he would exhibit in his later horror films. The plot is reminiscent of the suspense thrillers Jimmy Sangster scripted for Hammer.
Video: None

Child of Satan see *To the Devil...A Daughter*

34. Children of the Damned

A Lawrence P. Bachmann Production (1963); 90 minutes; U.S.: Metro–Goldwyn–Mayer (1964)

P: Ben Arbeid; **D:** Anton M. Leader; **S:** Jack Briley; **M:** Ron Goodwin; **DP:** David Boulton; **E:** Ernest Walter; **AD:** Elliot Scott; **Cast:** Ian Hendry, Alan Badel, Barbara Ferris, Clive Powell, Alfred Burke, Sheila Allen, Patrick Wymark, George Couloris, Martin Miller, Harold Goldblatt, Andre Mikhelson and Patrick White

In this sequel to *Village of the Damned*, six children of different nationalities (but identically developed super intelligence) gather in a deserted London church. The governments of their various countries wish to claim them in order to utilize their advanced intellects for military purposes. The children obviously have other ideas but their plans are never made clear. The story suffers from an overabundance of ambiguity and a lack of dramatic inspiration. There is no allusion made to the events of the first film. This time, rather than being the offspring of earth women and extraterrestrials, there is some hint that the children may be examples of human beings a million years hence. This plot device seems to have been included to create sympathy for the terrible tykes when they are finally blown to bits at the end.

Time magazine summed it up in their review: "The sequel pales in comparison, as do most sequels. But it is filmed with taste and acted in crisp style."
Video: U.S.

35. Circus of Fear

A Circus Film Ltd. Production (1966); 89 minutes; Eastman Color; U.S. *(Psycho Circus)*: American–International (1967); 65 minutes; Black-and-White

P: Harry Alan Towers; **D:** John Moxey; **S:** Peter Welbeck; **M:** Johnny Douglas; **DP:** Ernest Steward; **E:** John Trumper; **AD:** Frank White; **Cast:** Christopher Lee, Leo Genn, Anthony Newlands, Heinz Drache, Eddi Arent, Klaus Kinski, Margaret Lee, Suzy Kendall, Cecil Parker, Victor Maddern, Maurice Kaufmann and Skip Martin

A good cast is wasted in what is surely the worst entry in the "horror circus" sub-genre. *Circus of Fear* is so inept and tedious that even *Berserk!* seems like a masterpiece by comparison. The money from an armored car robbery ends up hidden in a circus. Leo Genn is the Scotland Yard inspector investigating the heist. Clues lead him to the circus, where he is confronted with a number of suspicious characters. Christopher Lee plays Gregor, a lion tamer who has been so badly scarred in an accident that he wears a black hood to conceal his disfigurement. When this film was released in the United States by American–International, they cut over 20 minutes from the running time, which relieved some of the agony of sitting through it but made for an even more confused plotline.
Video: U.K./U.S.

36. Circus of Horrors

A Lynx Films Ltd. Production (1960); 88 minutes; Eastman Color; U.S.: American–International; SpectaColor

P: Julian Wintle and Leslie Parkyn; **D:** Sidney Hayers; **S:** George Baxt; **M:** Franz Reizenstein and Muir Mathieson; **DP:** Douglas Slocombe; **E:** Reginald Mills; **AD:** Jack Shampan; **Cast:** Anton Diffring, Erika Remberg, Yvonne Monlaur, Yvonne Romain, Jane Hylton, Donald Pleasence, Kenneth Griffith, Conrad Phillips, Jack Gwillim, Vanda Hudson, Colette Wilde and John Merivale

In this perversely fascinating film, Anton Diffring stars as Dr. Rossiter, a brilliant plastic surgeon whose unconventional methods force him to leave England and assume a new identity. In France, as Dr. Schuler, he gains control of a run-down circus. Under Schuler's guidance the circus becomes a tremendous success. His beautiful star attractions are former thieves, murderesses and prostitutes whose appearances he has altered. Extremely possessive of his "creations," Schuler stages fatal accidents whenever one of his stars plans to leave the circus. These "accidents" cause it to become known as the "Jinx Circus."

Circus of Horrors is filled with warped images of beauty and disfigurement. Buxom women clad in sexy lingerie have scarred or bandaged faces and circus performers do not defy death but are claimed by it. Like the best circus acts, you can't look but you also can't look away. This is the first and the best in England's "horror circus" subgenre, which also includes *Berserk!* and *Circus of Fear*. Screenwriter George Baxt also coauthored the story for Hammer's *Vampire Circus*.

Video: U.S.

37. *City of the Dead*

A Vulcan Film Production (1960); 76 minutes; U.S. *(Horror Hotel)*: Trans-Lux (1963)

EXP: Milton Subotsky; **P:** Donald Taylor; **D:** John Moxey; **S:** George Baxt; **M:** Douglas Gamley and Ken Jones; **DP:** Desmond Dickinson; **E:** John Pomeroy; **AD:** John Blezard; **Cast:** Christopher Lee, Betta St. John, Patricia Jessel, Dennis Lotis, Venetia Stevenson, Valentine Dyall, Norman MacOwan, Ann Beach, Tom Naylor, Fred Johnson, James Dyrenforth, William Abney and Maxine Holden

This extremely effective thriller was filmed entirely in England but the setting is Massachusetts. Nan Barlow (Venetia Stevenson) is a student who is urged by her college instructor Prof. Driscoll (Christopher Lee) to go the village of Whitewood to research her term paper on witchcraft. Whitewood was once the scene of devil worship and witch burnings. She arrives in the dilapidated town and takes a room at the Raven's Inn. After Nan is secretly killed by devil cultists, her brother and boyfriend journey to Whitewood to find out what has happened to her. The uncomplicated plot is greatly enhanced by atmospheric black-and-white photography, taut direction and some very eerie performances. Patricia Jessel and Valentine Dyall are especially creepy as a witch and her consort. This was Milton Subotsky's initial foray into the horror genre. In addition to coproducing *City of the Dead*, he also wrote the original story on which the script was based.

Video: U.S.

38. *City Under the Sea*

An Anglo Amalgamated–Bruton Film Production (1965); 85 minutes; ColorScope; U.S. *(War Gods of the Deep)*: American-International

P: George Willoughby and Daniel Haller; **D:** Jacques Tourneur; **S:** Charles Bennett and Louis M. Heyward; **M:** Stanley Black; **DP:** Stephen Dade; **E:** Gordon Hales; **AD:** Frank White; **Cast:** Vincent Price, Tab Hunter, Susan Hart, David Tomlinson, John Le Mesurier, Henry Oscar, Derek Newark, Roy Patrick, Anthony Selby, Michael Heyland, Steven Brooke and William Hurndell

Suggested by Edgar Allan Poe's poem "City in the Sea," this was the first film in AIP's Poe series not directed by Roger Corman.

City Under the Sea is actually a pseudo–Jules Verne adventure fantasy with just a hint of Poe. Deep under the waters off the Cornish coast lies Lyonesse, a lost city ruled over by Sir Hugh Tregathion (Vincent Price), otherwise known as "The Captain." When pretty Jill Tregellis (Susan Hart) is kidnapped by one of Sir Hugh's Gill-Men,

JANE HYLTON IS ANTON DIFFERING'S DEVOTED ACCOMPLICE IN *CIRCUS OF HORRORS*.

Ben Harris (Tab Hunter) and Harold Tiffen-Jones (David Tomlinson) set out to find her. Ben and Harold are made prisoners but eventually they are able to rescue Jill and escape after a confused and seemingly endless underwater chase.

This was Jacques Tourneur's final film and it is difficult to believe that this was directed by the same man who did the splendid *Night of the Demon*. Susan Hart was the wife of AIP exec James Nicholson and she vies with Tab Hunter and Herbert the Rooster for the "worst performance" prize. Even the ever-watchable Vincent Price seems disinterested in the proceedings. To borrow a line from the script, the whole thing "smells like an overripe cheese." American prints list Daniel Haller as the producer but he is not mentioned in the British credits at all.

Video: U.K.

39. *A Clockwork Orange*

A Stanley Kubrick–Polaris Production (1971); 137 minutes; Color; U.S.: Warner Bros.

EXP: Max L. Raab and Si Litvinoff; **P/D/S:** Stanley Kubrick; **M:** Walter Carlos; **DP:** John Alcott; **E:** Bill Butler; **PD:** John Barry; **AD:** Russell Hagg and Peter Shields; **Cast:** Malcolm McDowell, Patrick Magee, Michael Bates, Adrienne Corri, Mariam Karlin, Warren Clarke, John Clive, Carl Duering, David Prowse, Aubrey Morris, Margaret Tyzack and Madge Ryan

In a super-violent futuristic society, Alex (Malcolm McDowell) is the leader of the "droogs," a gang of vicious juvenile delinquents. When one of their victims dies, Alex is sent to prison for murder. In the hope of an early release, he enlists himself as the human guinea pig in a government experiment which will attempt to condition him against committing any future acts of violence. The experiment works all too well and Alex is set free into a world which does not so easily forgive his past transgressions. Based on the novel by Anthony Burgess, the message of the book and film is "freedom of will at any cost." The slick production and smug tone of the movie often make it seem as though it is glamorizing the violence it should be condemning, and there is even a "happy" ending for its obnoxious anti-hero. It was praised by some and denounced by others; the controversy which greeted *A Clockwork Orange* upon its original release endures today. Watch for "Hammer girls" Gillian Hills, Katya Wyeth and Virginia Wetherell in various states of undress.

Video: U.K./U.S.

40. The Comeback

A Peter Walker–Heritage Ltd. Production (1977); 100 minutes; Color; U.S. *(The Day the Screaming Stopped)*: Bedford (1978)

P/D: Peter Walker; **S:** Murray Smith; **M:** Stanley Myers; **DP:** Peter Jessop; **E:** Alan Brett; **AD:** Mike Pickwood; **Cast:** Jack Jones, Pamela Stephenson, David Doyle, Bill Owen, Sheila Keith, Richard Johnson, Holly Palance, Peter Turner, Patrick Brock, June Chadwick, Penny Irving and Jeff Silk

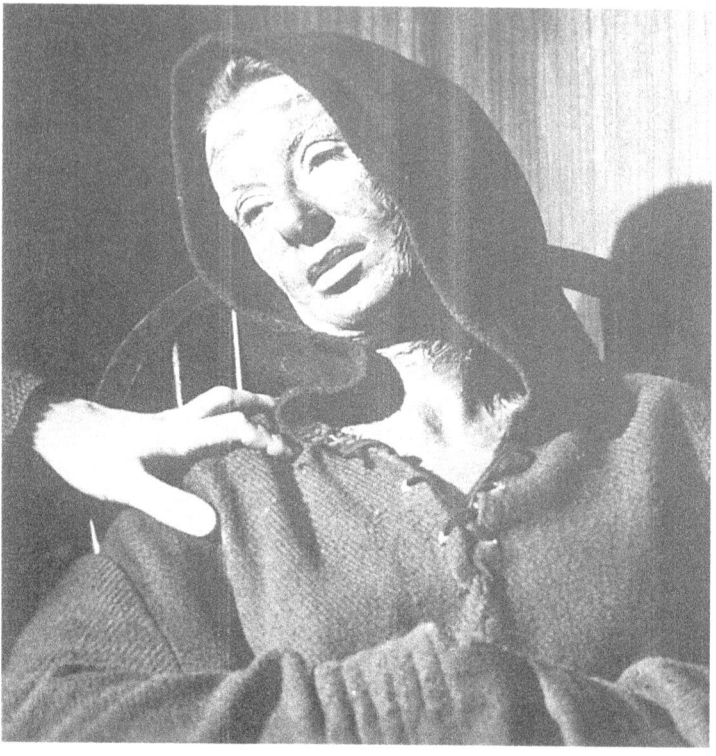

WITCH PATRICIA JESSEL MEETS HER DOOM IN *CITY OF THE DEAD*.

More gory mayhem from producer-director Peter Walker, who specialized in the type of bloody slasher films that would soon become an American horror staple. Pop singer Nick Cooper (Jack Jones) returns to England after a six-year absence from the recording industry. He has been recently divorced from his wife Gail (Holly Palance) and hopes to make a comeback with a new album. In the opening sequence, Gail is hacked to death in Nick's penthouse apartment as his airplane lands in England. For most of the rest of the film, the audience is treated to shots of Gail's putrefying, maggot-infested corpse. Nick does not return to the penthouse but instead leases a country estate where he can work on his music in peace. The caretakers of the estate are a weird but seemingly harmless old couple

VINCENT PRICE AND SUSAN HART IN *CITY UNDER THE SEA*.

(Bill Owen and Sheila Keith). Nick's peace of mind is short-lived as he hears screams and moans in the night and sees a rotting corpse in a wheelchair in the hall outside his bedroom. Driven to the brink of madness, Nick is hospitalized for nervous exhaustion. Is he insane or is it a terrible plot to drive him crazy? Jack Jones hoped to make the transition from singer to movie star with this ill-chosen vehicle. Although his acting isn't bad, the sight of his doormat chest, exposed at every opportunity, is tiresome. This was Peter Walker's final slasher-type horror film. After a hiatus of several years, he returned in 1983 to direct *House of the Long Shadows*. This remake of *Seven Keys to Baldpate* starred Vincent Price, Christopher Lee, Peter Cushing, John Carradine, Sheila Keith and Desi Arnaz, Jr.

Video: U.K./U.S. (alternate U.S. video title: *Encore*)

Computer Killers see **Horror Hospital**

The Confessional see ***House of Mortal Sin***

Conqueror Worm see ***Witchfinder General***

41. The Corpse (a.k.a. *Velvet House*)

A London Cannon–Abacus–May Films Ltd. Production (1969); 91 minutes; Color; U.S. (*Crucible of Horror*): Cannon (1971)

EXP: Dennis Friedland and Christopher Dewey; **P:** Gabrielle Beaumont; **D:** Viktors Ritelis; **S:** Olaf Pooley; **M:** John Hotchkis; **DP:**

John Mackey; **E:** Nicholas Pollock; **AD:** Peter Hampton; **Cast:** Michael Gough, Yvonne Mitchell, Sharon Gurney, Simon Gough, David Butler, Olaf Pooley, Nicholas Jones, Mary Hignett and Howard Goorney

Walter (Michael Gough) is the tyrannical head of the Eastwood household. Although he dotes on his priggish son Rupert (Simon Gough), he makes life hell for his wife Edith (Yvonne Mitchell) and his daughter Jane (Sharon Gurney). Edith and Jane finally have enough of his cruelty and decide to kill him. They follow him to their country cottage and poison him with barbiturates, making it appear to be a suicide. Later, his corpse inexplicably turns up in a packing crate which the two women dump into a lake.

Tormented by guilt, they return home to discover that they may not really have killed Walter after all. There are some clues to suggest that Rupert may be involved in Walter's resuscitation and subsequent reappearance. The film ends as it began, with Walter completely dominating the Eastwood family, Edith now having retreated into madness. Slow-moving and crudely made, *The Corpse* is not without interest, but the ending definitely needs a greater degree of clarification.

Video: U.S.

42. *Corridors of Blood* (a.k.a. *The Doctor from Seven Dials*)

A Producers Associates–Amalgamated Production (1958); 85 minutes; U.S.: Metro–Goldwyn–Mayer (1963)

EXP: Richard Gordon; **P:** John Croydon; **D:** Robert Day; **S:** Jean Scott Rogers; **M:** Buxton Orr; **DP:** Geoffrey Faithfull; **E:** Peter Musgrave; **AD:** Tony Masters; **Cast:** Boris Karloff, Betta St. John, Christopher Lee, Francis Matthews, Francis De Wolff, Adrienne Corri, Finlay Currie, Frank Pettingell, Basil Dignam, Marian Spencer, Nigel Green and Charles Lloyd Pack

Conceived as a follow-up to *Grip of the Strangler*, *Corridors of Blood* is long on atmosphere but short on horror. In 1840 London, Dr. Bolton (Boris Karloff) cannot reconcile himself to the pain suffered by his patients during surgery. He embarks on a series of experiments to find a drug which will serve as an anesthetic; in the process, he becomes an opium addict. Through his charity work in the London slums, Bolton comes into contact with Black Ben (Francis De Wolff) and Resurrection Joe (Christopher Lee), body snatchers who involve the good doctor in their heinous crimes. Karloff contributes his usual fine performance and, as in *Grip of the Strangler*, Robert Day evokes the seamy aspects of Victorian London with great success. Frequent Hammer heroine Yvonne Romain (billed as Yvonne Warren) has a supporting role as a prostitute named Rosa.

Video: U.K./U.S.

43. *Corruption*

A Titan Films–Peter Newbrook–Robert Hartford–Davis Production (1967); 91 minutes; Eastman Color; U.S.: Columbia (1968)

P/DP: Peter Newbrook; **D:** Robert Hartford-Davis; **S:** Donald and Derek Ford; **M:** Bill McGuffie; **E:** Don Deacon; **PD:** Bruce Grimes; **Cast:** Peter Cushing, Sue Lloyd, Noel Trevarthan, Kate O'Mara, David Lodge, Anthony Booth, Wendy Varnals, Bill Murray, Vanessa Howard, Jan Waters, Valerie Van Ost and Alexandra Dane

There's medical madness and murder galore after Jan (Sue Lloyd), the fiancee of famous surgeon Sir John Rowan (Peter Cushing), suffers facial disfigurement in an accident. Rowan perfects an operation using the pituitary gland to restore Jan's face, but the effect is only temporary. Jan goads him into killing women so that she can maintain her beauty. The early part of this movie is reminiscent of the Italian film *Atom Age Vampire* but the end goes off on a wildly divergent course when a gang of toughs invade the seaside home of Rowan and Jan. Despite his usual reliable performance, Cushing has never seemed more out of place than he does

BORIS KARLOFF, CHRISTOPHER LEE, ADRIENNE CORRI AND FRANCIS DE WOLFF IN *CORRIDORS OF BLOOD*.

in this trashy thriller. He has class, but the picture does not. The music by Bill McGuffie is a major contender for the worst background score ever!

Video: None

Cosmic Monsters see *The Strange World of Planet X*

Count Dracula and His Vampire Bride see *The Satanic Rites of Dracula*

44. *Countess Dracula*

A Hammer Film Production (1971); 93 minutes; Eastman Color; U.S.: 20th Century–Fox (1972); 90 minutes; DeLuxe Color

P: Alexander Paal; **D:** Peter Sasdy; **S:** Jeremy Paul; **M:** Harry Robinson; **DP:** Kenneth Talbot; **E:** Henry Richardson; **AD:** Philip Harrison; **Cast:** Ingrid Pitt, Nigel Green, Sandor Eles, Patience Collier, Maurice Denham, Peter Jeffrey, Lesley-Anne Down, Jessie Evans, Charles Farrell, Nike Arrighi, Andrea Lawrence and Susan Brodrick

Despite the title, *Countess Dracula* has nothing to do with the King of the Vampires. Instead it draws its inspiration from the exploits of the infamous Elisabeth Bathory, a real-life "vampire" who reputedly kept a youthful appearance by bathing in the blood of virgins. Director Peter Sasdy

Noel Trevarthan examines Sue Lloyd's face as Peter Cushing looks on in *Corruption*.

said, "The new idea behind this picture is that it will have a combination of horror, suspense and historical facts." Hammer had already explored this "new idea" a few years before with *Rasputin—The Mad Monk*. However, *Countess Dracula* has even less "historical facts" on view than the previous film. It does work on the level of the grimmest of fairy tales as a cautionary fable about mankind's obsession with youth. The elderly Countess Elisabeth (Ingrid Pitt) accidently discovers that she can restore her youthful beauty by bathing in the blood of a virgin. She poses as her own daughter and proceeds to fall in love with a young soldier, Imre Toth (Sandor Eles). Unfortunately, the effects of the blood bath are temporary. Elisabeth must kill again and again to retain her beauty, and with each murder, she descends deeper into madness. Pitt had considerable reason to be displeased by the finished film. Her dialogue was re-voiced by another actress without her knowledge, and one of her best scenes lost much of its impact in the final editing. Despite this, *Countess Dracula* is an outstanding production in every department, particularly the costume design by Raymond Hughes.

Video: U.K.

The Crawling Eye see **The Trollenberg Terror**

45. Craze

A Herman Cohen–Harbor Production (1974); 96 minutes; Technicolor; U.S.: Warner Bros.

EXP: Gustave Berne; **P:** Herman Cohen; **D:** Freddie Francis; **S:** Aben Kandel and Herman Cohen; **M:** John Scott; **DP:** John Wilcox; **E:** Henry Richardson; **AD:** George Provis; **Cast:** Jack Palance, Diana Dors, Trevor Howard, Julie Ege, Edith Evans, Hugh Griffith, Michael Jayston, Suzy Kendall, Martin Potter, Percy Herbert, David Warbeck and Kathleen Byron

The producer-director team of Herman Cohen and Freddie Francis strikes again, but while their previous opus, *Trog*, was entertainingly silly, *Craze* is unpalatable. The cast is filled with familiar names but they are mostly wasted on the vulgar material.

Neal Mottram (Jack Palance) is an antique store owner who has an idol of the African god Chuku in his basement. There, Mottram leads his coven of devil worshippers in pagan rites in praise of Chuku. When he accidently kills one of the coven and suddenly gains a large amount of money, Mottram believes that Chuku has rewarded him. This drives him to commit more murders as blood sacrifices to his god. Mottram's live-in boyfriend, Ronnie (Martin Potter), finally has enough of this and takes an axe to Chuku, which succeeds in driving Mottram completely bonkers!. Palance plays the entire film at a fever pitch, chewing the scenery to bits and the cast along with it. Suzy Kendall, as a giddy prostitute, does manage to hold her own in a scene with Palance but, unfortunately, he kills her anyway.

Video: U.S. (alternate video title: *The Demon Master*)

46. *Creatures the World Forgot*

A Hammer Film Production (1971); 95 minutes; Technicolor; U.S.: Columbia

INGRID PITT AS ELISABETH BATHORY A.K.A. *COUNTESS DRACULA*.

P/S: Michael Carreras; **D:** Don Chaffey; **M:** Mario Nascimbene; **DP:** Vincent Cox; **E:** Chris Barnes; **PD:** John Stoll; **AD:** Roy Taylor and Josie MacAvin; **Cast:** Julie Ege, Tony Bonner, Brian O'Shaughnessy, Robert John, Marcia Fox, Rosalie Crutchley, Don Leonard, Beverly Blake, Doon Baide, Ken Hare, Sue Wilson and Derek Ward

In this final installment of Hammer's trio of prehistoric films, twin brothers fight against the elements and each other for a position of tribal leadership and possession of a beautiful girl. This is a far grittier representation of stone age life than Hammer's previous efforts. It is also the least entertaining. The French title of the film sums up the contents perfectly: *Violence et Sexe aux*

The Creepers see *Assault*

47. The Creeping Flesh

A Tigon–British–World Film Services Ltd. Production (1972); 91 minutes; Color; U.S.: Columbia

EXP: Tony Tenser and Norman Priggen; **P:** Michael Redbourn; **D:** Freddie Francis; **S:** Peter Spenceley and Jonathan Rumbold; **M:** Paul Ferris; **DP:** Norman Warwick; **E:** Oswald Hafenrichter; **AD:** George Provis; **Cast:** Peter Cushing, Christopher Lee, Lorna Heilbron, George Benson, Kenneth J. Warren, Duncan Lamont, Michael Ripper, Catherine Finn, Hedger Wallace, Robert Swann, Maurice Bush and Jenny Runacre

Dr. Emmanuel Hildern (Peter Cushing) returns from an expedition to New Guinea with what he believes is the skeleton of a primitive man. Experiments reveal that contact with water causes living flesh to grow on the bones. Dr. Hildern somehow comes to the conclusion that this is the skeleton of a creature who was the incarnation of pure evil. Fearing that his repressed and simpering daughter Penelope (Lorna Heilbron) may inherit her mother's insanity, Hildern injects her with an anti-evil serum made from blood extracted from the flesh that has formed on the skeleton. And this is only the beginning! Penelope loses all of her inhibitions and becomes a gin-swilling wanton who cuts a man's throat with a broken bottle. She ends up in an insane asylum run by her father's half-brother, James (Christopher Lee). When James gets wind of Emmanuel's experiments he plots to steal the skeleton. Unfortunately he picks a night when there is a rainstorm and, consequently, the skeleton is soaked with water.

The Creeping Flesh is filled with almost

JACK PALANCE IS ABOUT TO GO OFF THE DEEP END IN *CRAZE*.

Temps Prehistoriques (Violence and Sex in Prehistoric Times).

This time around, there are no dinosaurs in sight and South-West African locations, instead of the Canary Islands, were used for the prehistoric terrain. Once again Hammer conducted a worldwide talent hunt, this time in conjunction with Columbia Pictures, to find a new sex symbol to play the female lead, Nala. The winner was Julie Ege, a former Miss Norway, who managed to forge a brief career in British cinema over the next few years. Her handsome leading man in *Creatures the World Forgot* was blonde and bronzed Australian actor Tony Bonner as Toomak, the less savage of the quarreling twins.

Video: U.K./U.S.

Tony Bonner and Julie Ege relax on the South African location for *Creatures the World Forgot*.

as many plot twists as *Horror Express*, a film it resembles in many ways. This is one of director Freddie Francis' very best efforts and it is to his credit that the wild premise becomes almost plausible. Lorna Heilbron should be given special mention. Her performance is the personification of liberated Victorian repression gone wild.

Video: U.K./U.S.

The Creeping Unknown see *The Quatermass Xperiment*

48. Crescendo

A Hammer Film Production (1970); 95 minutes; Technicolor; U.S.: Warner Bros. (1972); 83 minutes

P: Michael Carreras; **D:** Alan Gibson; **S:** Jimmy Sangster and Alfred Shaughnessy; **M:** Malcolm Williamson; **DP:** Paul Beeson; **E:** Chris Barnes; **AD:** Scott MacGregor and Don Picton; **Cast:** Stefanie Powers, James Olson, Margaretta Scott, Jane Lapotaire, Joss Ackland and Kirsten Betts

Music student Susan Roberts (Stefanie Powers) goes to the south of France to do research for her thesis on the late composer Henry Ryman. She is welcomed into the home of his widow Danielle (Margaretta Scott) and their crippled son Georges (James Olson). Susan is not told that Georges has a twin brother named Jacques who is hopelessly insane but has inherited his father's musical genius. Danielle hopes

FREDDIE FRANCIS DIRECTS PETER CUSHING IN *THE CREEPING FLESH*.

to mate Susan with Jacques and produce an offspring to carry on the family's musical heritage. This psychological thriller from Hammer took several years to make it to the United States. It finally showed up as the cofeature to *Dracula A.D. 1972*, with most of the nudity and violence cut out. At one time it had been hinted that Joan Crawford was interested in playing the part of Danielle. It would have been a perfect vehicle for Crawford, and a far more fitting finale to her screen career than the misguided *Trog*.

Video: None

The Crimson Cult see ***Curse of the Crimson Altar***

Crucible of Horror see ***The Corpse***

49. *Crucible of Terror*

A Peter Newbrook–Glendale Production (1971); 91 minutes; Color; U.S.: Scotia/Barber (1972); 79 minutes

EXP: Peter Newbrook; **P:** Tom Parkinson; **D:** Ted Hooker; **S:** Ted Hooker and Tom Parkinson; **M:** Paris Rutherford; **DP:** Peter Newbrook; **E:** Maxine Julius; **AD:** Arnold Chapkis; **Cast:** Mike Raven, Mary Maude, James Bolam, Ronald Lacey, Melissa Stribling, John Arnatt, Judy Matheson, Beth Morris, Betty Alberge and Kenneth Keeling

This was another attempt by Mike Raven, a former radio deejay, to become a major horror movie star. The film is unpleasant and unmemorable and contains much footage of the characters running around with little or no motivation. An art

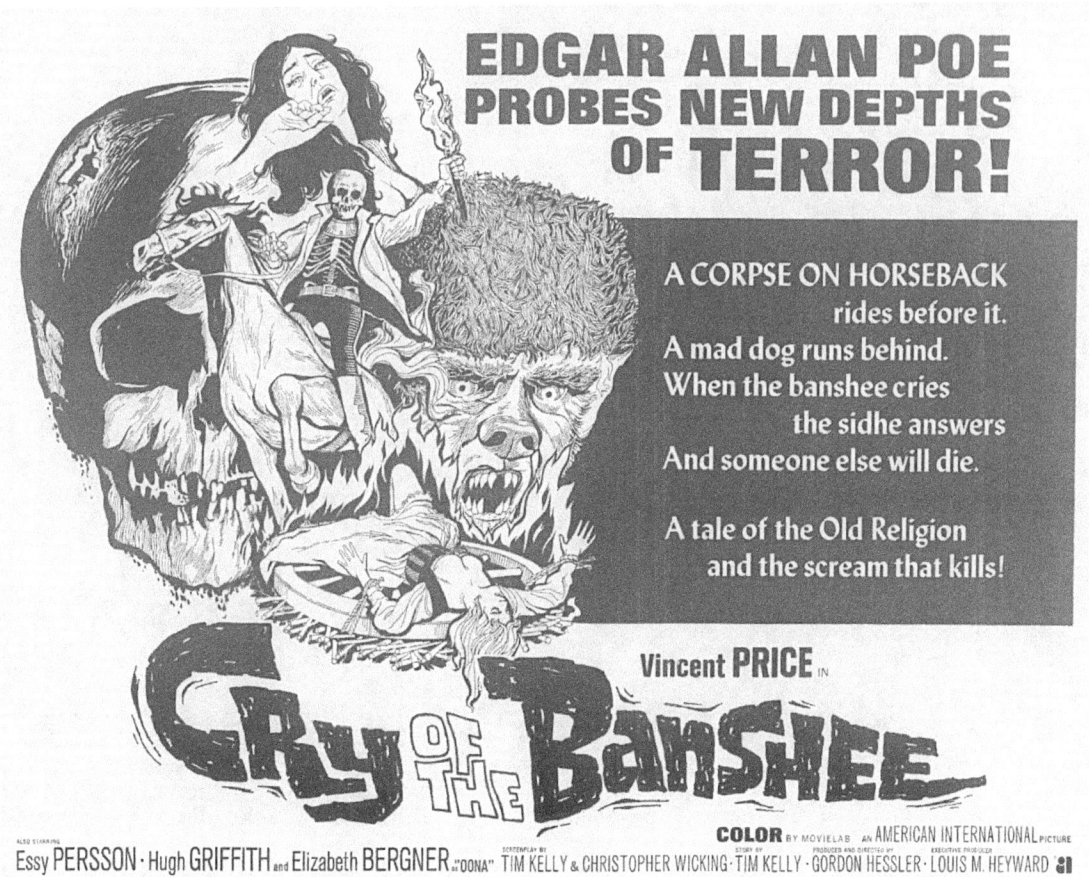

CRY OF THE BANSHEE

dealer (James Bolam) and his girlfriend Millie (Mary Maude) go to the house of an eccentric artist named Victor Clare (Mike Raven). The house is in a remote area on the Cornwall coast near an abandoned tin mine which Clare has converted into a forge for sculpting bronze statues. Years before, Clare had been infatuated with a beautiful Japanese model and, to forever preserve her beauty, he covered her with molten bronze. The house is filled with a collection of weird characters, several of whom end up being mysteriously murdered (although no one else seems to take any notice). As it turns out, Millie bought a used kimono which once belonged to the dead Japanese woman. Her spirit has returned to possess Millie, who is committing the murders. Eventually she revenges herself on Clare by pushing him into a vat of boiling bronze. Melissa Stribling appears briefly as a patron of the arts.

Video: U.S.

50. Cry of the Banshee

American–International (1970); 87 minutes; Color by Movielab; U.S.: American–International

EXP: Louis M. Heyward; **P/D:** Gordon Hessler; **S:** Tim Kelly and Christopher Wicking; **M:** Wilfred Josephs (U.K.)/Les Baxter (U.S.); **DP:** John Coquillon; **E:** Oswald Hafenrichter; **AD:** George Provis; **Cast:** Vincent Price, Hugh Griffith, Elisabeth Bergner, Essy Persson, Hilary Dwyer, Patrick Mower, Robert Hutton, Stephen Chase, Marshall Jones, Sally Geeson, Pamela Farbrother and Carl Rigg

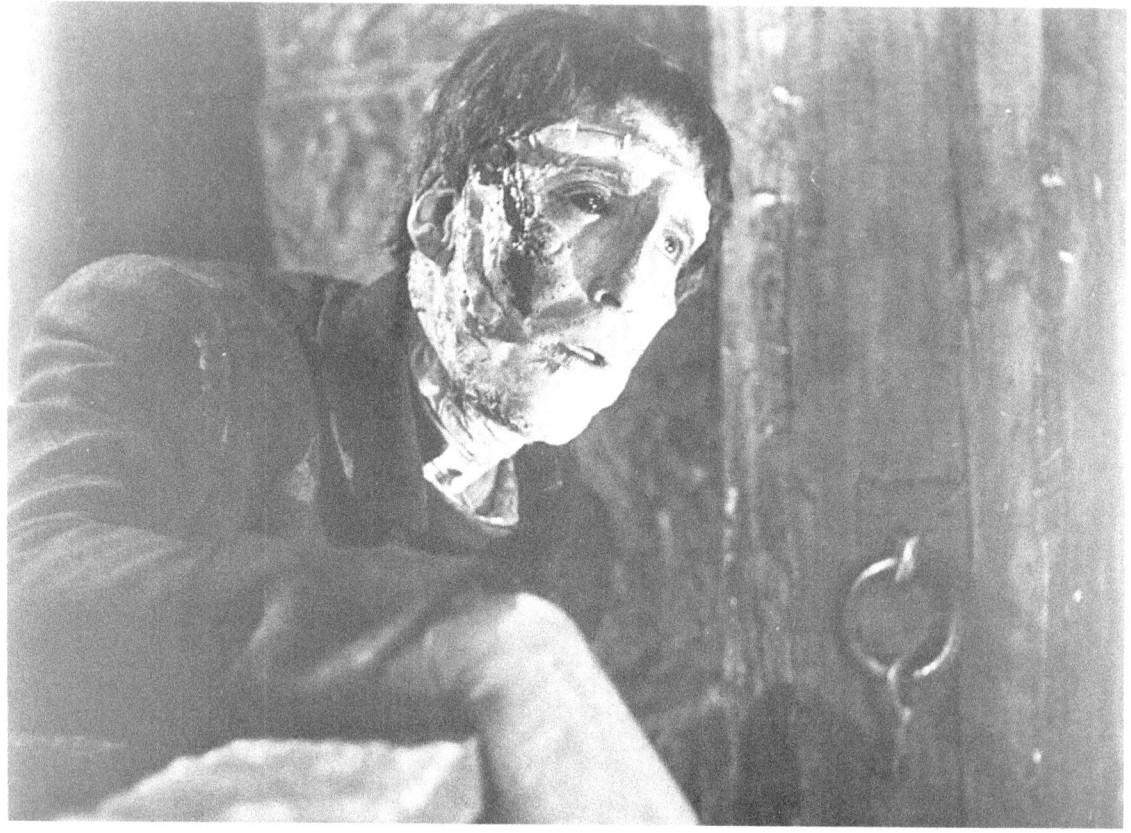

CHRISTOPHER LEE AS "THE CREATURE" IN HAMMER'S *THE CURSE OF FRANKENSTEIN*.

Lord Edward Whitman (Vincent Price) is the cruel magistrate of a rural village in sixteenth century England. When he causes the massacre of the followers of a witch named Oona (Elisabeth Bergner), she curses him and his family. Oona prays to Satan and conjures up an avenger in the form of a young man named Roderick (Patrick Mower). Roderick ingratiates himself into the Whitman household because he has a calming effect on Lord Edward's near-mad wife, Lady Patricia (Essy Persson). When Oona's satanic influence turns Roderick into a werewolf-like demon called a "Sidhe," he begins to slaughter the members of the Whitman family. The film opens with a quote from Poe and his name is invoked in the advertising but, as usual, the story has nothing to do with his writings. Vincent Price is given little to do here, other than to act unpleasant, but his presence is always welcome. The production is "well mounted" due in no small part to the use of opulent costumes which were left over from the big-budget historical film *Anne of the Thousand Days*.

Video: U.S.

51. *The Curse of Frankenstein*

A Hammer/Clarion Films Ltd. Production (1957); 82 minutes; Eastman Color; U.S.: Warner Bros.; WarnerColor

EXP: Michael Carreras; **P:** Anthony Hinds; **D:** Terence Fisher; **S:** Jimmy Sangster; **M:** James Bernard; **DP:** Jack Asher; **E:** James Needs; **PD:** Bernard Robinson; **AD:** Ted Marshall; **Cast:** Peter Cushing, Christopher Lee, Hazel Court, Robert Urquhart, Valerie Gaunt, Noel Hood, Marjorie Hume, Melvyn Hayes, Sally Walsh, Paul Hardtmuth, Fred Johnson and Henry Caine

The Quartermass Xperiment opened the door to international success for Hammer, but it was this film that firmly established the style for which the company became famous. The winning formula included humorist Joe Bob Briggs' three key ingredients for cinematic success: boobs, beasts and blood. In addition to these important components, Hammer also incorporated color, top-notch actors and outstanding production values. *The Curse of Frankenstein* was about as far from the Universal Frankenstein movies as you could possibly get and still tell the same basic story.

Baron Frankenstein (Peter Cushing) attempts to create a man from parts of various dead bodies. The brain he acquires is damaged and the resulting creature (Christopher Lee) is not only hideously disfigured but deranged as well. Moviegoers had seldom seen anything quite as graphic as some of the scenes depicted in this film...and in color no less! Audience attendance records were broken, causing *Variety* to declare, "*The Curse of Frankenstein* is a box office blessing!" Hammer never looked back. In 1964, Seven Arts Pictures successfully re-released *The Curse of Frankenstein* and *Horror of Dracula* on a double bill, using the catchline "Frankenstein spills it!... Dracula drinks it! in the screen's greatest double creature feature." For once the ads didn't exaggerate as this pairing was a horror film fans' dream.

Video: U.K./U.S.

52. *Curse of Simba*

A Galaworldfilm Ltd/Gordon Films Production (1964); 77 minutes; U.S. *(Curse of the Voodoo)*: Allied Artists (1965)

EXP: Richard Gordon; **P:** Kenneth Rive; **D:** Lindsay Shonteff; **S:** Tony O'Grady; **M:** Brian Fahey; **DP:** Gerald Gibbs; **E:** Barrie Vince; **AD:** Tony Inglis; **Cast:** Bryant Haliday, Dennis Price, Lisa Daniely, Mary Kerridge, Ronald Leigh-Hunt, Jean Lodge, Dennis Alaba Peters, Danny Daniels, John Witty, Tony Thawnton, Michael Nightingale and Andy Myers

Big-game hunter Mike Stacey (Bryant Haliday) tracks a wounded lion into an area of Africa inhabited by a tribe of lion worshippers. He kills the lion and the chief of the tribe curses him for his transgression. Shortly thereafter, Stacey's wife leaves him and takes their son back to London. Stacey follows, hoping for a reconciliation. While in London, he continually imagines that he is being pursued by natives who are bent on killing him. He learns that to break the spell, he must return to Africa and kill the person who cursed him. The most terrifying thing in this film is Mary Kerridge as Stacey's dreadful mother-in-law. *Curse of Simba* greatly resembles many of the cheesy black-and-white horror films that were cranked out in the United States during the late 50s and early 60s. In the United States it was released as the cofeature to one of the worst of these, the infamous *Frankenstein Meets the Spacemonster*.

Video: U.S.

53. *Curse of the Crimson Altar*

A Tigon–British/American–International Production (1968); 89 minutes; Color by Movielab; U.S. *(The Crimson Cult)*: American–International (1970); 87 minutes

EXP: Tony Tenser; **P:** Louis M. Heyward; **D:** Vernon Sewell; **S:** Mervyn Haisman and Henry Lincoln; **M:** Peter Knight; **DP:** John Coquillon; **E:** Howard Lanning; **AD:** Derek Barrington; **Cast:** Boris Karloff, Christopher Lee, Mark Eden, Barbara Steele, Michael Gough, Rupert Davies, Virginia Wetherell, Rosemarie Reede, Derek Tansley, Michele Warren, Nicholas Head and Vivienne Carlton

In this uncredited adaptation of H.P. Lovecraft's story "Dreams in the Witch House," Robert Manning (Mark Eden) goes to the town of Greymarsh in search of his missing brother Peter (Denys Peek). At Craxton Lodge he questions the owner, Mr.

Morley (Christopher Lee), a descendant of witch Lavinia Morley (Barbara Steele), who was burned 300 years before. Morley denies having seen Manning's brother, but his niece Eve (Virginia Wetherell) is sympathetic to Robert's plight. Together, Robert and Eve attempt to unravel the mystery of Peter's disappearance. Boris Karloff plays Prof. Marshe, an occult expert who is initially menacing but rescues Robert and Eve from a fiery demise at the end. In a very peculiar plot twist, it is revealed that Morley is actually Lavinia in disguise. Seeing Lee tranform into Barbara Steele is odd, to say the least. A "swinging" party sequence and some kinky torture scenes have dated badly and now come across as extremely silly attempts to be controversial. Karloff gives a delightfully wry performance. Tragically, he came down with a case of double pneumonia because of the cold weather he had to endure during the making of this film. He never fully recovered and died in 1969. Vincent Price was originally to have played Mr. Morley but, when script revisions delayed the filming, he was forced to bow out owing to a prior commitment. Despite the potentially powerful combination of Karloff, Lee, Steele and Gough, *Curse of the Crimson Altar* is poorly directed and never attains any true heights of horror.

Video: U.S.

The Curse of the Demon see *Night of the Demon*

54. The Curse of the Fly

A Lippert Films Ltd. Production (1965); 86 minutes; CinemaScope

P: Robert L. Lippert and Jack Parsons; **D:** Don Sharp; **S:** Harry Spalding; **M:** Bert Shefter; **DP:** Basil Emmott; **E:** Robert Winter; **AD:** Harry White; **Cast:** Brian Donlevy, George Baker, Carole Gray, Michael Graham, Jeremy Wilkins, Charles Carson, Burt Kwouk, Yvette Rees, Rachel Kempson, Mary Manson, Stan Simmons and Arnold Bell

This second sequel to *The Fly* (1958) tells of the further misfortunes of the Delambre family as they once again attempt to perfect their "matter teleporter." Patricia Stanley (Carole Gray) is an escaped mental patient who marries Martin Delambre (George Baker) and finds herself in a worse madhouse than the one she left. Martin's father (Brian Donlevy) is obsessed with proving that the teleporter can be used safely, although his gallery of mutated human guinea pigs proves otherwise. Rather than rehashing the original film, as the previous sequel had done, *The Curse of the Fly* takes the original premise and develops the story along different lines. The script is involving and Don Sharp directs with his usual expertise; this combination creates a fascinating, but underrated, motion picture.

Video: None

55. The Curse of the Mummy's Tomb

A Hammer/Swallow Production (1964); 80 minutes; Technicolor and Techniscope; U.S.: Columbia

P/D: Michael Carreras; **S:** Henry Younger; **M:** Carlo Martelli; **DP:** Otto Heller; **E:** James Needs and Eric Boyd-Perkins; **PD:** Bernard Robinson; **Cast:** Terence Morgan, Fred Clark, Ronald Howard, Jeanne Roland, George Pastell, Jack Gwillim, John Paul, Dickie Owen, Bernard Rebel, Michael McStay, Vernon Smythe and Michael Ripper

An ancient curse strikes the members of an archaeological expedition when an American promoter plans to exhibit the mummy of Ra-Antef as a sideshow attraction. Although this second entry in Hammer's "Mummy" series is certainly not as good as their first, it does not deserve its reputation as a lamentable misfire. As usual, the production values alone set it above many of the other horror movies that were being produced at the time. It also boasts two very good performances. Fred Clark manages to

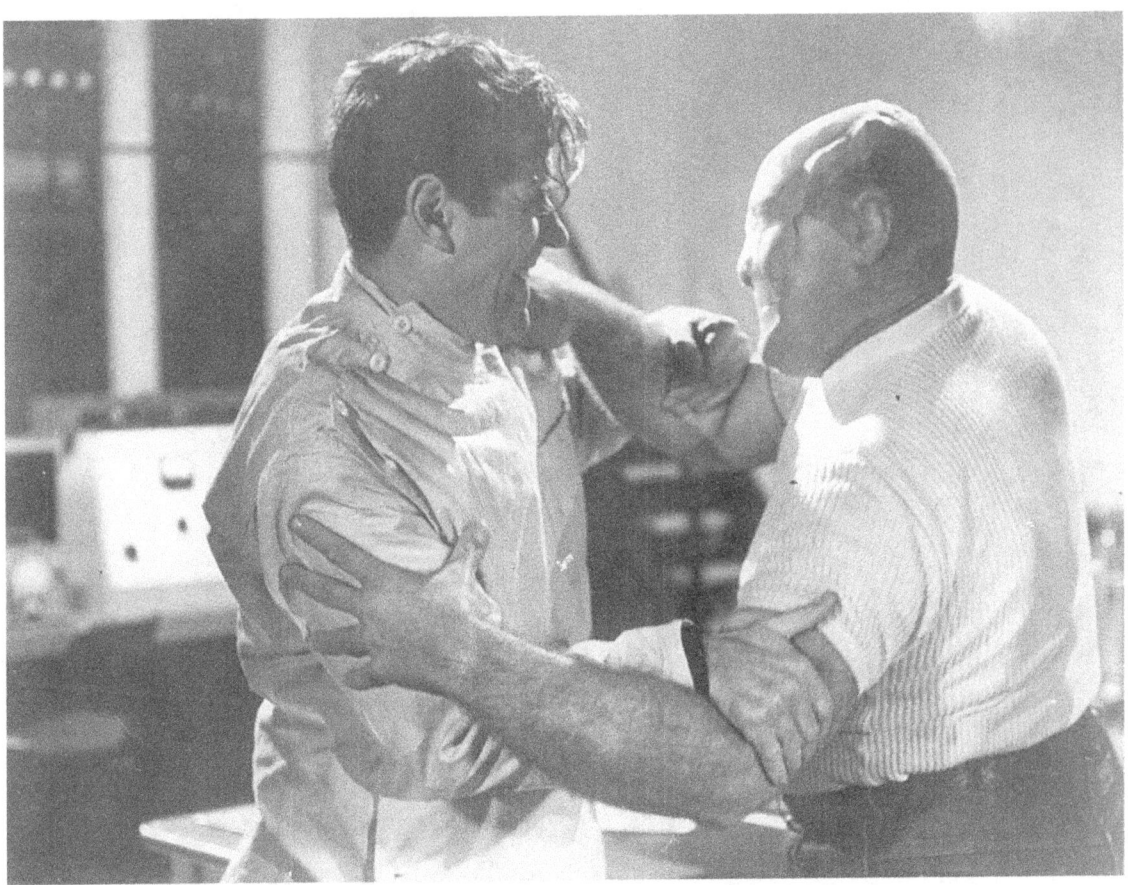

Martin Delambre (George Baker) fights against one of his father's hideous mutations in *The Curse of the Fly*.

be both annoying and likable as the brash American showman, Alexander King. His death at the hand of the living mummy is the film's most frightening sequence. Terence Morgan is also impressive as Adam Beauchamp, a mysterious gentleman who befriends the archaeologists. It is revealed that Beauchamp is actually Be, the treacherous sibling of Ra-Antef, cursed by his father to everlasting life for the death of his brother. It was released as the companion feature to *The Gorgon*, and this duo made for a particularly entertaining double-bill.

Video: U.K.

Curse of the Voodoo see *Curse of Simba*

56. *The Curse of the Werewolf*

A Hammer/Hotspur Production (1961); 91 minutes; Technicolor; U.S.: Universal–International; 88 minutes; Eastman Color

EXP: Michael Carreras; **P:** Anthony Hinds; **D:** Terence Fisher; **S:** John Elder; **M:** Benjamin Frankel; **DP:** Arthur Grant; **E:** James Needs and Alfred Cox; **PD:** Bernard Robinson; **AD:** Don Mingaye; **Cast:** Oliver Reed, Clifford Evans, Yvonne Romain, Catherine Feller, Anthony Dawson, Hira Talfrey, Richard Wordsworth, George Woodbridge, John Gabriel, Warren Mitchell, Michael Ripper and Ewen Solon

Loosely based on Guy Endore's 1933 novel *The Werewolf of Paris*, Hammer's version is set in Spain to make use of sets left over from an unrealized production about the Spanish Inquisition.

OLIVER REED AS THE TRAGIC LEON IN *THE CURSE OF THE WEREWOLF*.

Whatever the locale, this is one of Hammer's finest films. A mute servant girl (Yvonne Romain) is raped by a crazed beggar (Richard Wordsworth) and the child she conceives grows up to become a werewolf. This story is told in three "acts." The opening section chronicles the events leading up to the birth of the baby, Leon. The second part deals with Leon's tormented childhood. In the final third of the film, the adult Leon (Oliver Reed) falls in love and then learns the terrible truth about his affliction. Roy Ashton's imaginative and frightening werewolf makeup is complemented by Reed's savage performance. Reed later made a successful transition to big-budget international stardom in such diverse films as *Oliver* (1968), *Women in Love* (1970) and *The Three Musketeers* (1974).

Video: U.K./U.S

57. Daleks' Invasion Earth 2150 A.D.

An AARU/Amicus Production (1966); 84 minutes; Technicolor and Techniscope; U.S.: Continental

EXP: Joe Vegoda; **P:** Milton Subotsky and Max J. Rosenberg; **D:** Gordon Flemyng; **S:** Milton Subotsky; **M:** Bill McGuffie; **DP:** John Wilcox; **E:** Ann Chegwidden; **AD:** George Provis; **Cast:** Peter Cushing, Bernard Cribbins, Ray Brooks, Jill Curzon, Roberta Tovey, Andrew Keir, Roger Avon, Geoffrey Cheshire, Peter Reynolds, Bernard Spear, Keith Marsh and Philip Madoc

This is the second of two theatrical movies based on the popular BBC television series *Doctor Who*. While not a particularly good film, this is still considerably better than *Dr. Who and the Daleks*, owing to some decent special effects and far better production design. Dr. Who (Peter Cushing) and three companions take the time machine TARDIS to the year 2150 A.D. Once there, they find that London has been reduced to ruins by the dreaded Daleks and their army of "Robomen." Dr. Who and his friends join an underground resistance force in hopes of destroying the invaders. This film does manage to convey a sense of scope entirely lacking in its predecessor.

Video: U.S.

58. *The Damned*

A Hammer/Swallow Production (1961); 87 minutes; HammerScope; U.S. *(These Are the Damned)*: Columbia (1965); 77 minutes

EXP: Michael Carreras; **P**: Anthony Hinds; **D**: Joseph Losey; **S**: Evan Jones; **M**: James Bernard; **DP**: Arthur Grant; **E**: James Needs; **PD**: Bernard Robinson; **AD**: Don Mingaye; **Cast**: Macdonald Carey, Shirley Anne Field, Viveca Lindfors, Alexander Knox, Oliver Reed, Walter Gotell, Brian Oulton, Kenneth Cope, James Villers, Thomas Kempinski, James Maxwell and Edward Harvey

This complex and compelling movie, based on the novel *Children of Light* by H.L. Lawrence, was one of Hammer's big box office failures on both sides of the Atlantic. The story opens as a gang of leather-clad Teddy Boys, led by King (Oliver Reed), rob an American named Simon (Macdonald Carey). Joan (Shirley Anne Field), King's sister, participated in the crime and goes to Simon to apologize. King and his gang follow her, and Joan and Simon must flee. Attempting to hide in some caves in the cliffs overlooking the ocean, the couple discover a hidden government installation in which nine radioactive children are being held captive. They are being prepared to survive nuclear disaster.

The film's original running time was 100 minutes, and neither Hammer or Columbia seemed to know what to do with it except cut it; this resulted in more confusion in an already complicated plot. The British release was held up until 1963 and the American release was two years later. Despite critical praise, the film was deemed to be uncommercial and was given a "throwaway" release by the distributors. Years later, when James Carreras was asked about *The Damned*, he replied, "No, it's not our cup of tea at all. Losey is a very eminent director and he has a great following among the critics and the film, I'm sure, was a good film. But unfortunately, you know, we can only judge it on results. Did it get its money back? And the answer is, no, it didn't."

Video: U.K.

59. *Dance of the Vampires*

A Cadre Films/Filmways Ltd. Production (1967); 107 minutes; MetroColor and Panavision; U.S. *(The Fearless Vampire Killers)*: Metro–Goldwyn–Mayer; 98 minutes

EXP: Martin Ransohoff; **P**: Gene Gutowski; **D**: Roman Polanski; **SP**: Gerard Brach and Roman Polanski; **M**: Christopher Komeda; **DP**: Douglas Slocombe; **E**: Alastair McIntyre; **PD**: Wilfred Shingleton; **AD**: Fred Carter; **Cast**: Jack MacGowran, Roman Polanski, Alfie Bass, Sharon Tate, Jessie Robbins, Ferdy Mayne, Iain Quarrier, Terry Down, Fiona Lewis, Ronald Lacey, Sydney Bromley and Matthew Walters

Daffy Prof. Abronsius (Jack MacGowran) and his ineffectual sidekick Alfred (Roman Polanski) go vampire hunting in Transylvania. When Sarah (Sharon Tate), an innkeeper's lovely daughter, is abducted by the local vampire, Abronsius and Alfred go to the castle of Count Von Krolock (Ferdy Mayne) to rescue her.

In their 1971 tribute to Hammer Films, the National Film Theatre of London chose

BEAUTIFUL SHARON TATE ABOUT TO BE BITTEN BY FERDY MAYNE AT THE *DANCE OF THE VAMPIRES*.

to show *Dance of the Vampires* as the final program in the series. The program notes state: "Polanski's film has been included in this tribute because of this director's affection for the Hammer films, and because the film in itself can be regarded as the highest tribute one could pay to Hammer Productions." His "affection" for Hammer did not prevent Polanski from disparaging the studio in his autobiography. In discussing this film, he said, "I realized what the setting for a picture of this type should be: not a tatty rural location situated conveniently near a film studio — the rule with most Hammer productions." Obviously highly regarded in some circles, *Dance of the Vampires* is, nevertheless, a somewhat strained mixture of comedy and horror. The comedy is mostly of the "slapstick" variety, with endless pratfalls and accelerated action. The plot features a Jewish vampire ("Oy! Oy!") and a gay vampire. Both are stereotypical in the extreme. There are some hauntingly beautiful visuals and Sharon Tate (in a role originally intended for Jill St. John) never looked more gorgeous, but as a whole it is an overlong, misguided affair. In 1997, Polanski directed a musical stage version of *Dance of the Vampires* which had its world premiere in Vienna. *Variety* found it to be an improvement on the original.

Video: U.S.

The Dark see *The Haunted House of Horror*

60. Dark Eyes of London

A John Argyle Production Ltd (1939); 76 minutes; U.S. *(The Human Monster)*: Monogram (1940)

P: John Argyle; **D:** Walter Summers; **S:** Patrick Kirwan, Walter Summers and J.F. Argyle; **M:** Guy Jones; **DP:** Bryan Langley; **E:** E.G. Richards; **AD:** Duncan Sutherland; **Cast:** Bela Lugosi, Greta Gynt, Hugh Williams, Edmond Ryan, Wilfrid Walter, Arthur E. Owen, Alexander Field, Julie Suedo, Gerald Pring, Bryan Herbert, May Hallett and Charles Penrose

Death by drowning is the preferred method of murder in this impressive film version of the Edgar Wallace thriller. Over a very short period of time, six heavily insured men are found drowned in the Thames. Scotland Yard is called in and the investigation leads to an insurance agency run by Dr. Orloff (Bela Lugosi). Orloff is a benefactor for a charity home for blind men run by kindly Mr. Dearborn (also Lugosi). Diane Stuart (Greta Gynt), the daughter of one of the drowned men, goes to work as a secretary for Mr. Dearborn and discovers that the home is being used by Orloff as a front for his insurance frauds. Orloff is assisted in his murderous mayhem by the blind and hideously deformed Jake (Wilfrid Walter). In addition to being a very good film, *Dark Eyes of London* is noteworthy for several of reasons. It was the first movie to receive the "H" for Horrific certification and it features two uncharacteristically fine performances by Bela Lugosi. As it turned out, this was the last chance for Lugosi to shine before his descent into the maelstrom of mediocrity that typified his later career.

Video: U.K./U.S.

61. Dark Places

A James Hannah, Jr./Glenbeigh Production (1972); 91 minutes; Eastman Color; U.S.: Cinerama Releasing (1974)

P: James Hannah Jr.; **D:** Don Sharp; **S:** Ed Brennan and Joseph Van Winkle; **M:** Wilfred Josephs; **DP:** Ernest Steward; **E:** Teddy Darvas; **AD:** Geoffrey Tozer; **Cast:** Robert Hardy, Christopher Lee, Joan Collins, Herbert Lom, Jane Birkin, Jean Marsh, Jennifer Thanisch, Roy Evans, Carlton Hobbs, Martin Boddey, Roger Glyn Jones and Michael McVey

On his deathbed in a mental institution, Andrew Marr bequeaths his country mansion to his friend Edward Foster (Robert Hardy). Upon his arrival in the village, Foster is warned that "bad things" have happened at the Marr house and he also learns that there may be a fortune hidden away somewhere within. He is quickly befriended by Dr. Ian Mandeville (Christopher Lee) and his slutty sister Sarah (Joan Collins), who have designs on the missing money. Foster takes possession of the house but the dire events that once occurred there seem to take possession of him. Foster goes into trances and has glimpses of the Marr family's sordid past, which result in terrible consequences in the present. This neglected film has the advantage of a good cast and Don Sharp's usual perceptive direction.

Video: U.S.

62. The Day of the Triffids

A Security Pictures Ltd. Production (1963); 94 minutes; Eastman Color and CinemaScope; U.S.: Allied Artists

EXP: Philip Yordan; **P:** Bernard Glasser and George Pitcher; **D:** Steve Sekely; **S:** Bernard Gordon; **M:** Ron Goodwin; **DP:** Ted Moore; **E:** Spencer Reeve; **AD:** Cedric Dawe; **SVE:** Wally Veevers; **Cast:** Howard Keel, Nicole Maurey, Janette Scott, Kieron Moore, Mervyn Johns, Janina Faye, Alison Leggatt, Ewan Roberts, Colette Wilde, Carole Ann Ford, Geoffrey Matthews and Gilgi Hauser

The dazzling light of a meteorite shower blinds most of the Earth's population. Concurrently, a species of man-sized, carnivorous plants, called Triffids, becomes ambulatory and begins to prey on the blinded humans.

ARTIST JOE SMITH'S CONCEPT OF *THE DAY OF THE TRIFFIDS*.

John Wyndham's thoughtful novel of mankind's struggles within a new society is reduced to a standard sci-fi thriller here. Sequences showing the populace panicked by their sudden blindness are far more horrifying than attacks by the walking plants. Director Steve Sekely originally brought in the film at well under a feature-length running time, so Freddie Francis was hired to film additional scenes with Kieron Moore and Janette Scott trapped in a lighthouse by the Triffids. In typical monster movie fashion, the antidote for destroying the Triffids is discoverd by accident and consists of a simple element: sea water. The film provides a number of chills and has some effective special effects but, given the source material, it could have been so much more.

Video: U.K./U.S.

63. The Day the Earth Caught Fire

A British Lion–Pax Picture; A Val Guest Production (1961); 94 minutes; U.S.: Universal–International

P/D: Val Guest; **S:** Wolf Mankowitz and Val Guest; **M:** Stanley Black; **DP:** Harry Waxman; **E:** Bill Lenny; **AD:** Tony Masters; **SVE:** Les Bowie; **Cast:** Edward Judd, Janet Munro, Leo McKern, Michael Goodliffe, Bernard Braden, Reginald Beckwith, Gene Anderson, Arthur Christiansen, Austin Trevor, Renee Asherson, Peter Butterworth and Robin Hawdon

The coincidental detonation of nuclear test bombs at each of the poles causes the Earth to shift on its axis. Thermometers soar in London as an unprecedented heat wave heralds the indisputable fact that the Earth is moving towards the Sun. As extreme weather conditions panic the world's populace, scientists scramble to correct the error by setting off four strategically placed H-Bombs in Siberia. An inconclusive finale leaves viewers to speculate on the fate of mankind. A forerunner to the disaster film, *The Day the Earth Caught Fire* combines a hard-hitting documentary style with some remarkably eerie visuals of a dehydrated London,

EDWARD JUDD (FAR RIGHT) STROLLS THROUGH A CHAOTIC LONDON ON *THE DAY THE EARTH CAUGHT FIRE*.

convincingly realized by special effects ace Les Bowie.

Video: U.S.

64. The Day the Fish Came Out

A Michael Cacoyannis Production (1967); 109 minutes; DeLuxe Color; U.S.: 20th Century–Fox

P/D/S: Michael Cacoyannis; **M:** Mikis Theodorakis; **DP:** Walter Lassally; **E:** Vassilis Syropoulos; **AD:** Spyros Vassiliou; **Cast:** Tom Courtenay, Sam Wanamaker, Colin Blakely, Candice Bergen, Ian Ogilvy, Nicos Alexiou, Dimitris Nicolaidis, Patricia Burke, Tom Klunis, Paris Alexander, Arthur Mitchell and William Berger

The story is set in 1972 in a small Greek seaport village. A NATO bomber carrying two atomic bombs and a new kind of weapon in a sealed box crashes into the nearby ocean. The pilot (Colin Blakely) and navigator (Tom Courtenay) survive and make their way to shore. In an attempt to cover up the incident, a group of military personnel arrive in the village disguised as hotel experts and tourists. They plan to recover the bombs and secret weapon without attracting too much attention.

The plan backfires and the formerly sleepy village suddenly becomes a hot tourist spot. In the meantime, a goatherd (Nicos Alexiou) finds the box and opens it, exposing the populace to a deadly virus which blackens the waters and kills all the fish. This was a British-Greek coproduction beautifully filmed in the Greek village of

Galaxidion, located on the Gulf of Corinth. Although sometimes interesting, the many disparate elements and moods involved never quite gel into a homogenous whole. The film must be classifed as a curiosity piece, at best.

In addition to producing, writing and directing this bizarre opus, Michael Cacoyannis also designed the camp costumes.

Video: None

65. Dead of Night

An Ealing Studios Production (1945); 102 minutes; U.S.: Universal (1946); 77 minutes

P: Michael Balcon; D: Basil Dearden, Alberto Cavalcanti, Robert Hamer and Charles Crichton; S: John Baines and Angus MacPhail; M: Georges Auric; DP: Stanley Pavey and Douglas Slocombe; E: Charles Hasse; AD: Michael Relph; Cast: Mervyn Johns, Frederick Valk, Antony Baird, Miles Malleson, Sally Ann Howes, Michael Allen, Googie Withers, Ralph Michael, Basil Radford, Naughton Wayne, Michael Redgrave and Hartley Power

This somewhat overrated movie is the "granddaddy" of the British omnibus horror films. What sets it apart from later productions is that the five stories are realized by different directors. In the framing device, an architect (Mervyn Johns) is invited to a country house where he meets a group of strangers who have been in his nightmares. Each of these people relates a personal story that deals with a supernatural occurrence. The worst of these is the droll but dull "Golf Story," wisely trimmed from the American theatrical release prints. "The Ventriloquist's Dummy" segment has received the most attention and inspired a mini-genre of its own. It features a splendidly deranged performance by Michael Redgrave as a ventriloquist pathologically obsessed with his dummy. The best of the bunch is "The Haunted Mirror," in which Googie Withers buys fiancé Ralph Michael an antique mirror that mysteriously reflects a room from a past century. Staid and talky, *Dead of Night* is important nevertheless as the first major British horror film of the postwar era.

Video: U.K./U.S.

66. The Deadly Bees

An Amicus Production (1966); 83 minutes; Technicolor; U.S.: Paramount (1967)

P: Max J. Rosenberg and Milton Subotsky; D: Freddie Francis; S: Robert Bloch and Anthony Marriott; M: Wilfred Josephs; DP: John Wilcox; E: Oswald Hafenrichter; AD: Bill Constable; Cast: Suzanna Leigh, Frank Finlay, Guy Doleman, Catherine Finn, Michael Ripper, Katy Wild, John Harvey, Anthony Bailey, Tim Barrett, James Cossins, Frank Forsyth and Maurice Good

Overworked pop-singer Vicki Robbins (Suzanna Leigh) suffers a nervous breakdown. Her doctor recommends that she convalesce on the farm of his friend on Seagull Island. Shortly after arriving, Vicki discovers that there is a heated rivalry between her host, Mr. Hargrove (Guy Doleman), and his neighbor Mr. Manfred (Frank Finlay). Both are beekeepers and one of them has bred a strain of killer bees. Soon the deadly bees are killing everyone in sight. As the population of Seagull Island dwindles, Vicki begins to realize that this may actually be more stressful than the music industry! For some reason these bee movies (no pun intended) never seem to work (remember Irwin Allen's *The Swarm?*). Outside of everyone's normal aversion to being stung, the bees just aren't that frightening, especially when they are so obviously superimposed over actors wildly waving their arms.

Video: None

67. Death Line

A Jay Kanter–Alan Ladd, Jr. Production (1972); 87 minutes; Technicolor; U.S. (*Raw Meat*): American–International (1973)

P: Paul Maslansky; D: Gary Sherman; S: Ceri Jones; M: Jeremy Rose and Wil Mallone; DP: Alex Thomson; E: Geoffrey Foot; AD: Denis Gordon-Orr; Cast: Donald Pleasence, Norman Rossington, David Ladd, Sharon Gurney, Christopher Lee, Clive Swift, Hugh Armstrong, June Turner, James Cossins, Heather Stoney, Hugh Dickson and Jack Woolgar

Police investigate the disappearances of several people who were last seen at the Russell Square underground station. The malefactor is one of two surviving descendants of a group of workers who were trapped when the tunnel they were digging collapsed in 1892. They, and their progeny, lived by eating human flesh. When this pathetic creature's wife dies, he abducts a young girl from the station to be his new mate.

The premise of *Death Line* is original and almost plausible. The creepy atmosphere of a deserted subway station late at night seems the perfect place for such frightful occurrences. Hugh Armstrong is both terrifying and pitiable as the cannibal whose only intelligible words are "mind the doors." Christopher Lee appears in only one very brief scene.

Video: U.K.

The Demon Master* see *Craze

68. Demons of the Mind (a.k.a. Blood Will Have Blood)

A Hammer Film Production (1972); 89 minutes; In Association with Frank Godwin Productions Ltd.; Technicolor; U.S.: International Co-Productions (1974)

P: Frank Godwin; D: Peter Sykes; S: Christopher Wicking; M: Harry Robinson; DP: Arthur Grant; E: Chris Barnes; PD: Michael Stringer; Cast: Paul Jones, Patrick Magee, Yvonne Mitchell, Robert Hardy, Gillian Hills, Michael Hordern, Kenneth J. Warren, Shane Briant, Virginia Wetherell, Robert Brown, Deidre Costello and Barry Stanton

In 1850 Bavaria, the forest surrounding Castle Zorn is believed to be the home of a demon. Actually, the real "demon" to fear is the demented Count Zorn (Robert Hardy), who keeps his children Emil (Shane Briant) and Elizabeth (Gillian Hills) locked away in the castle and bleeds them into submission. He is fearful that the incest and insanity which are prevalent in the family have been passed on in the blood of his offspring. Zorn has power over Emil's mind and drives him to murder the local village girls who resemble Elizabeth. Carl Richter (Paul Jones) is a medical student who has fallen in love with Elizabeth and comes to the castle to rescue her. This is a complex and unusual film which is sometimes confusing but always compelling. Paul Jones was the lead singer in the rock band Manfred Mann and later created the role of Juan Peron in the original concept album of *Evita*. Shane Briant made his film debut in *Demons of the Mind* and would go on to appear in three other movies for Hammer.

Video: U.S.

69. Devil Doll

A Galaworldfilm Ltd. Gordon Films Production (1963); 80 minutes; U.S.: Associated Film Distributors (1964); 70 minutes

EXP: Kenneth Rive and Richard Gordon; P/D: Lindsay Shonteff; S: George Barclay and Lance Z. Hargreaves; DP: Gerald Gibbs; E: Ernest Bullingham; AD: Stan Shields; Cast: Bryant Haliday, William Sylvester, Yvonne Romain, Sandra Dorne, Nora Nicholson, Alan Gifford, Karl Stepanek, Francis De Wolff, Pamela Law, Heidi Erich, Antony Baird and Ray Landor

The Great Vorelli (Bryant Haliday) is a master hypnotist and ventriloquist who keeps the soul of a former assistant, Hugo, trapped inside a wooden dummy. When Vorelli meets the beautiful and very wealthy Marianne (Yvonne Romain), he forms a plan to steal her fortune. He will hypnotically force her to marry him and then transfer her

Yvonne Romain falls under the hypnotic spell of the Great Vorelli (Bryant Haliday) in *Devil Doll*.

soul into another dummy. Unlike other demonic dummy movies such as *Dead of Night* (1945) and *Magic* (1978), this time around the pitiful puppet is a victim of his evil master. Although the overall production is rather cheap and sleazy, there are a number of genuinely creepy moments. Sadly, the overall effect is damaged by a hurried and unsatisfying climax. This is the only film where Bryant Haliday's weird screen persona really works. Haliday was a particular favorite of producer Richard Gordon. He had originally trained for the priesthood but abandoned this to become a stage actor. He was a cofounder of Janus Films, one of the earliest foreign film distributors in the United States.

Video: U.S./U.K.

70. Devil Girl from Mars

A Danzinger Production (1954); 75 minutes; U.S.: DCA Pictures (1955)

P: Harry and Edward Danziger; **D:** David Macdonald; **S:** John Mather and James Eastwood; **M:** Edwin Astley; **DP:** Jack Cox; **E:** Brough Taylor; **AD:** Norman Arnold; **Cast:** Hugh McDermott, Hazel Court, Patricia Laffan, Peter Reynolds, Adrienne Corri, John Laurie, Joseph Tomelty and Sophie Stewart

Eight people are held prisoner in an inn on the Scottish moors by Nyah, a pernicious woman from Mars. She explains that the final war on Mars was a "war of the sexes" from which the women emerged the victors with the men as their slaves. Their men have become impotent so she has come to Earth to round up healthy male specimens to take

CHRISTOPHER LEE ATTEMPTS TO PROTECT PATRICK MOWER, PAUL EDDINGTON AND SARAH LAWSON FROM THE POWERS OF DARKNESS IN *THE DEVIL RIDES OUT*.

back to Mars in order to perpetuate her race. Most of the action takes place in the inn's pub, where the captives plot to get the better of Nyah (with no success). Patricia Laffan (so memorable as the wicked empress Poppaea in *Quo Vadis*) is the "Devil Girl," clad in a black leather spacesuit and giving a wonderfully high-camp performance. The technical effects are surprisingly well executed, given the obvious low budget of this production. The film's message is clearly stated by one of the characters: "Nothing like a good cup of tea in a crisis."

Video: U.K./U.S.

71. The Devil Rides Out

A Hammer–Seven Arts Production (1968); 95 minutes; Technicolor; U.S. *(The Devil's Bride)*: 20th Century–Fox; DeLuxe Color

P: Anthony Nelson-Keys; **D:** Terence Fisher; **S:** Richard Matheson; **M:** James Bernard; **DP:** Arthur Grant; **E:** James Needs and Spencer Reeve; **AD:** Bernard Robinson; **Cast:** Christopher Lee, Charles Gray, Nike Arrighi, Leon Greene, Patrick Mower, Sarah Lawson, Gwen Ffrangcon-Davies, Rosalyn Landor, Russell Waters and Paul Eddington

This is one of Hammer's finest productions and it is Terence Fisher's ultimate depiction of the conflict between the forces of good and the powers of evil. Based on the novel by Dennis Wheatley, *The Devil Rides Out* relates the story of the Duc de Richleau (Christopher Lee) and his fight to save the soul of his friend Simon (Patrick Mower) from the evil warlock Mocata

(Charles Gray). It is set in the 1920s, and the production design reflects Hammer's usual attention to period detail. For once, Hammer seems to have chosen a leading lady for her acting ability rather than her measurements. Nike Arrighi is notable as Tanith, a pawn in this conflict of good versus evil. The film was well-received by the critics. Even the usually uncharitable *Films and Filming* found *The Devil Rides Out* to be "a chilling and frightening film which is vastly entertaining." Unfortunately, this movie appeared near the end of Hammer's association with 20th Century–Fox. Fox had become increasingly dissatisfied with the box office returns on the Hammer–Seven Arts productions and, after re-titling the film *The Devil's Bride*, gave it a very poor release. In an attempt to cash in on the success of *Rosemary's Baby*, the U.S. trade ads declared, "There has never been so much interest in the Devil's sex life as there is today!"

Video: U.K./U.S.

The Devil Within Her see *I Don't Want to Be Born*

72. The Devils

Russo Productions Ltd. (1971); 111 minutes; Technicolor and Panavision; U.S.: Warner Bros. 109 minutes

P: Robert H. Solo and Ken Russell; **D/S:** Ken Russell; **M:** Peter Maxwell Davies; **DP:** David Watkins; **E:** Michael Bradsell; **AD:** Robert Cartwright; **Cast:** Oliver Reed, Vanessa Redgrave, Dudley Sutton, Max Adrian, Gemma Jones, Murray Melvin, Michael Gothard, Georgina Hale, Christopher Logue, Andrew Faulds, Catherine Willmer and Edith Paris

Excessive...self-indulgent...over the top. These terms could be applied to most of Ken Russell's works but in discussing *The Devils* they are particularly apt. Taken from an actual historical incident, Russell's screenplay is based on the play *The Devils* by John Whiting and the book *The Devils of Loudun* by Aldous Huxley. In seventeenth century France, Father Grandier (Oliver Reed) is a priest in open opposition to the growing political power of Cardinal Richelieu (Christopher Logue). When Sister Jeanne (Vanessa Redgrave), a nun driven to madness by her sexual frustration, accuses Grandier and a host of devils of raping her and the other sisters in her order, Richelieu's men seize this opportunity to destroy Grandier. They attempt to torture a confession out of Grandier to no avail and eventually he is burned to death at the stake. Given the wild excesses of this film, it is interesting to note that Reed gives a surprisingly subdued performance. Michael Gothard, as a priest who is brought in to exorcise the evil spirits from the nuns, plays his part with no restraint whatsoever. He completely devours the rest of the cast and Derek Jarman's imaginative sets as well.

Video: U.K./U.S.

The Devil's Bride see *The Devil Rides Out*

73. The Devil's Men

A Getty Pictures/Poseidon Films Production (1976); 94 minutes; Color; U.S. (*Land of the Minotaur*): Crown International (1977); 88 minutes

P: Frixos Constantine; **D:** Costa Carayiannis; **S:** Arthur Rowe; **M:** Brian Eno; **DP:** Ari Stavrou; **E:** Barry Reynolds; **Cast:** Peter Cushing, Donald Pleasence, Luan Peters, Nikos Verlekis, Costas Skouras, Bob Behling, Vanna Revilli, Jane Lyle and Fernando Bislani

The catchline on the American poster for this film reads: "Trapped in a world forgotten by time." That is exactly how you may feel while watching this dull and incoherent film which seems to go on forever. In a Greek village, Baron Corofax (Peter Cushing) leads a satanic cult that worships the stone image of the Minotaur. The cult skulks around in what look like Ku Klux Klan

COUNT SINISTRE (HUBERT NOEL) ABDUCTS TRACY REED IN *DEVILS OF DARKNESS*.

robes, sacrificing any handy strangers to their fire-breathing idol. When a trio of amateur archaeologists disappears, an Irish priest (Donald Pleasence) decides to investigate. This was a British-American coproduction shot entirely on location in Greece.

Video: U.S.

74. *Devils of Darkness*

A Planet Films Ltd Production (1965); 88 minutes; Eastman Color; U.S.: 20th Century–Fox; DeLuxe Color

P: Tom Blakeley; **D:** Lance Comfort; **S:** Lyn Fairhurst; **M:** Bernie Fenton; **DP:** Reg Wyer; **E:** John Trumper; **AD:** John St. John Earl; **Cast:** William Sylvester, Hubert Noel, Carole Gray, Diane Decker, Tracy Reed, Rona Anderson, Peter Illing, Gerald Heinz, Victor Brooks, Avril Angers, Eddie Byrne and Brian Oulton

Devils of Darkness is a tale of black magic and vampirism set in contemporary times. This was a departure for the British vampire movie as, prior to this, all had been period costume dramas. Unfortunately, any originality the picture has begins and ends there. Perhaps the most interesting aspect of this effort is the unsuccessful attempt to imitate the Hammer vampire mythos within a modern setting. As it turned out, this was a feat even Hammer couldn't pull off.

A brief prologue shows a marriage ceremony in a gypsy encampment; it turns tragic when the bride (Carole Gray) is mysteriously struck down and dies. She is later revived from the dead to become the immortal bride of Count Sinistre (Hubert Noel), a vampire. Flash forward several hundred years to a small village in France where Paul Baxter (William Sylvester) and a group of friends are on holiday. When his friends are killed, Paul is left with a strange golden amulet as his only clue to their deaths. He returns to England and Count Sinistre follows him there to try and reclaim the amulet, a symbol of his satanic powers. Count Sinistre finally meets his abrupt end when he is trapped in daylight and decomposes into a skeleton.

Video: U.K.

The Devil's Own see *The Witches*

The Devil's Undead see *Nothing But the Night*

75. *The Devil's Widow*

A Jerry Gershwin–Elliott Kastner/Winkast Films Ltd. Production (1969); 106 minutes; Technicolor and Panavision; U.S. (*The Ballad of Tam Lin* [a.k.a. *Tam Lin*]): A Commonwealth United Presentation; American-International (1971)

EXP: Henry T. Weinstein and Anthony B. Unger; **P:** Alan Ladd, Jr., and Stanley Mann; **D:** Roddy McDowall; **S:** William Spier; **M:** Stanley Myers; **DP:** Billy Williams; **E:** John Victor Smith; **PD:** Don Ashton; **AD:** Jon Graysmark; **Cast:** Ava Gardner, Ian McShane, Stephanie Beacham, Cyril Cusack, Richard Wattis, Madeline Smith, David Whitman, Sinead Cusack, Jenny Hanley, Joanna Lumley, Fabia Drake and Bruce Robinson

Roddy McDowall's sole directorial effort took several years to make it to the screen and then it received only limited release. Made in 1969, the film was first tied up in financial litigation and then underwent extensive reworking by the director, at the insistance of the distributors, prior to its 1971 release. The end result is a sometimes uneven but often mesmerizing modern allegory of Robert Burns' poem about a powerful fairy queen and her enchanted lover.

Ava Gardner plays Michaela Cazaret, a wealthy middle-aged woman who has retained her beauty and surrounds herself with a cultish gang of sybaritic youths. When her current paramour, Tom Lynn (Ian McShane), falls in love with a young woman (Stephanie Beacham), Michaela attempts to make his life a living hell. Striking photography and an excellent cast (which includes four future Hammer heroines) are just two of the many good reasons for watching this neglected gem. *The Devil's Widow* was virtually a lost film until Martin Scorsese championed a 1998 restoration for video.

Video: U.S.

Die! Die! My Darling! see *Fanatic*

Die, Monster, Die! see *Monster of Terror*

76. *Die Screaming, Marianne*

A Peter Walker Production (1971); 99 minutes Eastman Color; U.S.: No theatrical release

P/D: Peter Walker; **S:** Murray Smith; **M:** Cyril Ornadel; **DP:** Norman Langley; **E:** Tristam Cones; **Cast:** Susan George, Barry Evans, Christopher Sandford, Judy Huxtable, Leo Genn, Kenneth Hendel, Paul Stassino, Alan Curtis, Anthony Sharp, John Laurimore and Martin Wyldeck

Sebastian (Christopher Sandford) picks up Marianne (Susan George) on a road in Portugal and takes her back to London with him. After only two weeks of living together, Sebastian asks Marianne to marry him. She reluctantly agrees but, because of a glitch in the paperwork, she ends up married to "Best Man" Eli (Barry Evans) instead. This all turns out to be part of a plot to return Marianne to her father (Leo Genn) in Portugal. He is desperate to get the number to a Swiss bank account that only Marianne knows.

Peter Walker previously filmed softcore

sex films; this was his first thriller. *Die Screaming, Marianne* received a surprising amount of critical attention, with some reviewers actually suggesting that Walker might be a fledgling Hitchcock. There are some effective sequences but overall this is a fairly cheesy affair. An unintentional comic highlight is the main title with Susan George wildly go-go dancing in a chainmail bikini.

Video: U.S.

77. *Disciple of Death*

A Chromage/Allan King Associates Ltd. Production (1972); 84 minutes; Color; U.S.: Avco Embassy

P/S: Tom Parkinson and Churton Fairman; **D:** Tom Parkinson; Music Arranged by Robert Cornford; **DP:** William Brayne; **E:** Richard Key; **AD:** Denys Pavitt; **Cast:** Mike Raven, Ronald Lacey, Stephen Bradley, Marguerite Hardiman, Virginia Wetherell, Nick Amer, George Belbin, Betty Alberge, Rusty Goffe, Louise Jameson, Joe Dunlop and Daisika

This was the last attempt by Mike Raven to achieve horror stardom. After two inoffensive supporting roles in films for Hammer and Amicus, Raven teamed with producer Tom Parkinson in *Crucible of Terror*. In that largely forgettable movie, Raven gave a mildly effective performance. *Disciple of Death* is an entirely different matter. Raven had originally taken the script to Hammer and it was put on their production schedule for 1971. They evidently came to their senses and decided against making it. Raven and Tom Parkinson went ahead and made it themselves. Shot in 16mm on a minuscule budget, the film is amateurish and Raven is dreadful in the extreme. Ronald Lacey comes in a close second as a badly bewigged parson.

In eighteenth century England, a mysterious stranger (Raven) appears in a rural village to claim an abandoned mansion as his inheritance. This stranger is actually the evil spirit of a suicide victim come from hell to recruit new souls for the devil and thereby gain everlasting peace for himself.

Laughably overacted by everyone involved, the ritual sacrifice scenes are especially hilarious. Needless to say, this film did not elevate Raven to the pantheon of horror stars. He retired from films shortly thereafter.

Video: U.S.

78. *Doctor Blood's Coffin*

A Caralan Production (1960); 92 minutes; Eastman Color; U.S.: United Artists (1961)

P: George Fowler; **D:** Sidney J. Furie; **S:** Jerry Juran; **M:** Buxton Orr; **DP:** Stephen Dade; **E:** Anthony Gibbs; **AD:** Scott MacGregor; **Cast:** Kieron Moore, Hazel Court, Ian Hunter, Gerald Lawson, Kenneth J. Warren, Fred Johnson, Paul Stockman, Andy Alston and Paul Hardtmuth

Dr. Peter Blood (Kieron Moore) is a medical research scientist who is forced to leave his position in Vienna because of his unconventional experiments. He returns to his home in England, a small village on the Cornwall coast. Dr. Blood continues his experiments in some abandoned mines, diminishing the already tiny population of the village. Blood becomes attracted to his father's widowed nurse Linda (Hazel Court), but when she finds out about his experiments and rejects him, he plans a terrible revenge. Using the living heart of one of the villagers, Blood succeeds in resurrecting the moldering corpse of Linda's dead husband with predictably dire results.

A fairly indifferent film without much to recommend it outside of some nice color photography. Even this attribute was lost on American audiences as most of the theatrical showings there were in black and white.

Video: U.S.

79. *Dr. Crippen*

A John Clein–Torchlight Production (1962); 97 minutes; U.S.: Warner Bros. (1964)

PAUL STOCKMAN IS BROUGHT BACK FROM THE DEAD IN *DR. BLOOD'S COFFIN*.

P: John Clein; **D:** Robert Lynn; **S:** Leigh Vance; **M:** Ken Jones; **DP:** Nicolas Roeg; **E:** Lee Doig; **AD:** Robert Jones; **Cast:** Donald Pleasence, Samantha Eggar, Coral Browne, Donald Wolfit, James Robertson Justice, John Arnatt, Oliver Johnston, Paul Carpenter, Geoffrey Toone, John Lee, Edward Underdown and Douglas Bradley-Smith

Donald Pleasence portrays real-life convicted murderer Dr. Hawley Harvey Crippen, whose trial shocked Edwardian England. Dr. Crippen is a timid, quiet man and his wife Belle (Coral Browne) is a vulgar, blowsy dance hall singer with a gluttonous sexual appetite. Crippen and his secretary Ethel (Samantha Eggar) fall deeply in love and he decides to leave his wife for her. When Belle disappears, Scotland Yard suspects that Crippen may have done away with her. The film has two performances that should be cited. Donald Pleasence plays Dr. Crippen with such reserve and humility that, at times, he seems barely to be there at all. Coral Browne, on the other hand, plays Belle at full tilt, creating a truly monsterous characterization. The story is told with restraint but the sexual aspects are treated quite frankly for the time.

Video: U.K.

80. Doctor Faustus

An Oxford University Screen Production (1967); 93 minutes; In Association with Nassau Films and Venfilms, Rome; Technicolor; U.S.: Columbia (1968)

P: Richard Burton and Richard McWhorter; **D:** Richard Burton and Neville Coghill; Adapted by Neville Coghill; **M:** Mario Nascimbene/**DP:** Gabor Pogany; **E:** John Shirley; **PD:** John De Cuir; **AD:** Boris Juraga; **Cast:** Richard Burton, Elizabeth Taylor, Andreas Teuber, Elizabeth O'Donovan, Jeremy Eccles, David McIntosh, Ian Marter, Adrian Benjamin, Richard Carwardine, Ram Chopra, Richard Heffer and Richard Harrison

In those golden days when the Burtons were cinema royalty, they attempted, on two occasions, to bring "culture" to the masses. Their first such attempt was a very successful movie version of Shakespeare's *The Taming of the Shrew*. Their second cultural endeavor was the considerably less successful *Doctor Faustus*.

In 1966, Burton returned to his alma mater, Oxford University, to star in a stage production of Christopher Marlowe's sixteenth century morality play *The Tragical History of Doctor Faustus*. The success of the play prompted Burton to undertake a film version which would be filmed in England and Rome. In addition to Burton in the title role, the film also starred the Oxford University Dramatic Society. Elizabeth Taylor appeared, *sans* dialogue, as Helen of Troy, whose beauty is used by Mephistopheles (Andreas Teuber) to tempt Dr. Faustus in the battle for his soul. Oddly, for this wordless part, Elizabeth Taylor received some of the unkindest reviews of her entire career. The film was met with vicious critical attacks and audience indifference. In truth, *Doctor Faustus* is a decidedly uncommercial undertaking and an obvious "vanity piece" for Burton, but it is not the affront to mankind that many critics seemed to suggest.

Video: U.S.

HELEN OF TROY (ELIZABETH TAYLOR) IS ONE OF THE TEMPTATIONS USED BY THE DEVIL TO LURE *DR. FAUSTUS*.

The Doctor from Seven Dials see **Corridors of Blood**

81. Dr. Jekyll and Sister Hyde

A Hammer Film Production (1971); 97 minutes; Technicolor; U.S.: American–International (1972); 94 minutes

P: Albert Fennell and Brian Clemens; D: Roy Ward Baker; S: Brian Clemens; M: David Whitaker; DP: Norman Warwick; E: James Needs; PD: Robert Jones; Cast: Ralph Bates, Martine Beswick, Gerald Sim, Lewis Fiander, Dorothy Alison, Susan Brodrick, Ivor Dean, Tony Calvin, Virginia Wetherell, Philip Madoc, Dan Meaden and Paul Whitsun-Jones

In this clever variation on the Robert

Gerald Sim is about to become a victim of seductive Martine Beswick in *Dr. Jekyll and Sister Hyde*.

Louis Stevenson story, Dr. Jekyll (Ralph Bates) is searching for the "elixir of life" and inadvertently transforms himself into the beautiful, but murderous, Sister Hyde (Martine Beswick). When Hammer first made the announcement that Dr. Jekyll and Sister Hyde was on their production schedule, Sir James Carreras said he was looking for a new girl for the lead: "We want one who looks like Ursula Andress, with the fire and sex appeal of Raquel Welch. Whoever gets the part will get the full Hammer treatment." Caroline Munro was under consideration, but she balked at the brief nudity required by the script. Hammer wisely picked Martine Beswick, who had previously appeared in two of their movies.

Both she and Ralph Bates give their finest performances for Hammer in this superior film. Brian Clemens' shrewd screenplay is filled with just the right amounts of humor and horror, and the dramatic climax has a truly tragic impact. David Whitaker's haunting score is also a plus factor. When this gem was imported for distribution in the United States by American–International, they decided to promote it with the most lurid advertising campaign imaginable. "Victim after victim dies horribly in throat cutting orgy!…Unnatural laboratory experiments performed behind barred doors!…Once again he will change sexes and kill, kill, kill!" The real irony in all of this is that AIP cut out all of the nudity and blood letting to get a PG rating!

Video: U.K./U.S.

82. Dr. Phibes Rises Again

American–International (1972); 89 minutes; Color by Movielab; U.S.: American–International

EXP: James H. Nicholson and Samuel Z. Arkoff; **P:** Louis M. Heyward; **D:** Robert Fuest; **S:** Robert Fuest and Robert Blees; **M:** John Gale; **DP:** Alex Thomson; **E:** Tristam Cones; **PD:** Brian Eatwell; **Cast:** Vincent Price, Robert Quarry, Valli Kemp, Fiona Lewis, Peter Cushing, Beryl Reid, Terry Thomas, Hugh Griffith, Peter Jeffrey, John Cater, Gerald Sim, Lewis Fiander and Milton Reid

Three years after the events which took place in *The Abominable Dr. Phibes*, the diabolical doctor (Vincent Price) is revived. This time his plan is to journey to Egypt where he will use an elixir of life to restore his dead wife Victoria (once again played by a comatose Caroline Munro). Unfortunately he has a rival, Biederbeck (Robert Quarry), who is also seeking the elixir for reasons of his own. Once again, Phibes is assisted in his mayhem by the faithful Vulnavia, inexplicably restored after her acid bath in the previous film. This time around she is played by Valli Kemp, a former "Miss Australia." Peter Cushing is on hand, very briefly, in the role of a ship's captain. Although *The Hollywood Reporter* thought "this sequel is even better than the original," it is not nearly as stylish or engaging as the first film. Despite an ending that seemed to pave the way for yet another sequel, Dr. Phibes did not rise again; when last seen, he was sailing down the River of Life with his beloved, but still dead, Victoria.

Video: U.S.

Dr. Anton Phibes (Vincent Price) causes more havoc in Dr. Phibes Rises Again.

83. Dr. Terror's House of Horrors

An Amicus Production (1964); 98 minutes; Technicolor and Techniscope; U.S.: Paramount (1965)

P: Milton Subotsky and Max J. Rosenberg; **D:** Freddie Francis; **S:** Milton Subotsky; **M:** Elisabeth Lutyens; **DP:** Alan Hume; **E:** Thelma Connell; **AD:** Bill Constable; **Cast:** Peter Cush-

ARTIST MICHAEL GOUGH PLAYS A TRICK ON ART CRITIC CHRISTOPHER LEE IN *DR. TERROR'S HOUSE OF HORRORS*.

ing, Christopher Lee, Roy Castle, Donald Sutherland, Neil McCallum, Max Adrian, Jennifer Jayne, Michael Gough, Bernard Lee, Alan Freeman, Ursula Howells and Katy Wild

Five men sharing a train compartment are joined by the mysterious Dr. Schreck (Peter Cushing), who proceeds to tell their fortunes using a deck of Tarot cards. The five stories all deal with conventional horror elements and the titles say it all: "Werewolf," "Creeping Vine," "Voodoo," "Disembodied Hand" and "Vampire." In the end we learn that the men have all died in a train crash and Dr. Schreck is actually Death come to claim them. This was Amicus' initial entry in the horror market and it was so successful that they continued to mine that vein, often using a multi-story format. They eventually became Hammer's closest competitor.

Video: U.S.

84. Dr. Who and the Daleks

An AARU–Amicus Production (1965); 85 minutes; Technicolor and Techniscope; U.S.: A Walter Reade–Sterling Presentation; Continental (1966)

EXP: Joe Vegoda; **P:** Milton Subotsky and Max J. Rosenberg; **D:** Gordon Flemyng; **SP:** Milton Subotsky; **M:** Malcolm Lockyer; **DP:** John Wilcox; **E:** Oswald Hafenrichter; **AD:** Bill Constable; **Cast:** Peter Cushing, Roy Castle, Jennie Linden, Roberta Tovey, Barrie Ingham, Geoffrey Toone, Michael Coles, John Bown, Yvonne Antrobus, Mark Petersen, Ken Garady and Michael Lennox

Peter Cushing gets his turn to play the famous doctor in *Dr. Who and the Daleks*, a big screen version of the popular television series.

This was the first of a pair of theatrical films adapted from the long-running British television series created by Terry Nation. The main interest here is the presence of Peter Cushing as the venerable Dr. Who. Beyond that, there is little effort made on the part of the producers to expand the television program to fit the broader canvas offered by motion pictures. The sets are unbelievably chintzy (the corridors of the Dalek city seem to be hung with pink vinyl shower curtains) and the special effects are all but non-existent. There is much talk of the horribly mutated monsters which inhabit the forbidden swamp, but we never even get a glimpse of one. What we do see are a tribe of aliens wearing bad wigs, false eyelashes and lots of green eyeshadow...and these are the men! The most monstrous things in the film are the irritating electronic voices of the villainous Daleks, certain to drive any audience mad. For laughs, watch as Jennie Linden's hairstyle gives new meaning to the phrase "big hair" and also check out the Daleks' lava lamp collection.

Video: U.K./U.S.

85. *Dominique* (a.k.a. *Dominique Is Dead*)

A Sword and Sorcery Production (1978); 98 minutes; Color; U.S.: No theatrical release

EXP: Melvin Simon; **P:** Milton Subotsky and Andrew Donally; **D:** Michael Anderson; **S:** Edward and Valerie Abraham; **M:** David Whitaker; **DP:** Ted Moore; **E:** Richard Best; **PD:** David Minty; **Cast:** Cliff Robertson, Jean Simmons, Jenny Agutter, Simon Ward, Ron Moody, Judy Geeson, Michael Jayston, Flora Robson, Jack Warner, David Tomlinson, Leslie Dwyer and Brian Hayes

Milton Subotsky's first motion picture independent of Amicus was a British-Canadian coproduction entitled *The Uncanny* (1977), an anthology film featuring Peter Cushing and Ray Milland. Subotsky then formed Sword and Sorcery Productions and returned to England to produce *Dominique*. Dominique Ballard (Jean Simmons) is a mentally fragile woman who is convinced that her husband David (Cliff Robertson) is trying to drive her mad. Tormented by disturbing visions, Dominique eventually commits suicide. After her funeral, David begins to experience some fairly disturbing visions himself and comes to the conclusion that the ghost of Dominique has returned to haunt him. It is, of course, yet another convoluted plan designed to drive the main character insane and thereby inherit his money. The script was adapted from Harold Lawlor's story "What Beckoning Ghost," which had already been filmed more effectively for the Boris Karloff television series *Thriller*. The action of the movie advances at a snail's pace and the "twist" ending had by now become all too familiar. The film's greatest fault is that it is an utter waste of Jean Simmons' talents. Simmons is a highly accomplished performer who, if given half a chance, might even have made something out of this unlikely material.

Video: U.S.

86. *Don't Look Now*

A Casey–Eldorado Films Production (1973); 110 minutes; Technicolor and Panavision; U.S.: Paramount

P: Peter Katz; **D:** Nicolas Roeg; **S:** Allan Scott and Chris Bryant; **M:** Pino Donaggio; **DP:** Anthony Richmond; **E:** Graeme Clifford; **AD:** Giovanni Soccol; **Cast:** Julie Christie, Donald Sutherland, Hilary Mason, Clelia Matania, Massimo Serato, Renato Scarpa, Giorgio Trestini, Leopoldo Trieste, David Tree, Ann Rye, Nicholas Salter and Adelina Poerio

Following the accidental drowning of their daughter, John (Donald Sutherland) and Laura Baxter (Julie Christie) leave England for Venice. John has been contracted to do some restoration work on a church there and both feel the change of locale may help to ease their grief. John begins to experience psychic visions and believes he sees the figure of his daughter dressed in her red raincoat scurrying around Venice. Based on a story by Daphne du Maurier, this atmospheric film is filled with haunting images but the climax (Sutherland is bloodily slain by a knife-wielding dwarf [Adelina Poerio] in a red raincoat) is at odds with the tone of the rest of the movie. An odd footnote in film history is the hiring of Pino Donaggio to compose the score. Donaggio already had a successful career as a pop songwriter. One day he was spotted in Venice by associate producer Ugo Mariotti, who had a "vision" that this was the man who must compose the score to *Don't Look Now*. This was the start of a new career for Donaggio and he has since composed many excellent scores, particularly those he has written for director Brian DePalma.

Video: U.S./U.K.

87. *Doomwatch*

A Tigon–British Production (1972); 92 minutes; Color; U.S.: No theatrical release

P: Tony Tenser; **D:** Peter Sasdy; **S:** Clive Exton; **M:** John Scott; **DP:** Kenneth Talbot; **E:** Keith Palmer; **AD:** Colin Grimes; **Cast:** Ian Bannen, Judy Geeson, George Sanders, John Paul, Simon Oates, Jean Trend, Joby Blanshard, Percy Herbert, Shelagh Fraser, Geoffrey Keen, Joseph O'Connor and George Woodbridge

This film was adapted from a successful British television series created by Kit

Pedler and Gerry Davis about a governmental organization (Doomwatch) devoted to anti-pollution. Dr. Del Shaw (Ian Bannen) goes to Balfe Island to study the effects of a tanker oil spill. The island's inhabitants are unfriendly and uncooperative and Shaw suspects there is some deep, dark secret the islanders are hiding. Shaw discovers that radioactive pollution is causing advanced cases of the disease Acromegaly, resulting in severe deformities and madness among the villagers.

Doomwatch is well directed and has an interesting first half, but the second half doesn't hold up. Ian Bannen makes an unlikely hero and the main characters of the television series are reduced to supporting parts. Producer Tony Tenser's failure to find an American distributor for this film heralded the eventual downfall of Tigon.

Video: U.S.

88. *Doppelganger*

A Gerry Anderson–Universal Pictures Ltd. Production; (1969); 99 minutes; Technicolor; U.S. *(Journey to the Far Side of the Sun)*: Universal

P: Gerry and Sylvia Anderson; **D:** Robert Parrish; **S:** Gerry and Sylvia Anderson and Donald James; **M:** Barry Gray; **DP:** John Read; **E:** Len Walter; **AD:** Bob Bell; **SVE:** Derek Meddings; **Cast:** Roy Thinnes, Lynn Loring, Herbert Lom, Patrick Wymark, Ian Hendry, George Sewell, Loni Von Friedl, Franco Derosa, Edward Bishop, Philip Madoc, Vladek Sheybal and George Mikell

The European Space Exploration Council (a.k.a. Eurosec) has sent an unmanned rocket (Sun Probe One) into space. When it returns, it shows evidence of a tenth planet in our solar system with the same orbit as Earth but on the opposite side of the Sun. Plans to send astronauts (Roy Thinnes and Ian Hendry) to this planet are immediately put into motion. The spaceship crash-lands on the new planet and one of the astronauts is badly burned. The other awakens to find himself back on Earth. As he recovers, he begins to realize that this is actually a mirror image of the Earth he knew. This is a surprisingly well-done film with a fascinating storyline and impressive special effects. Herbert Lom appears as a spy in a brief pre-credits sequence, but he is a red herring who has little or nothing to do with the remainder of the movie.

Video: U.S.

89. *Dorian Gray* (a.k.a. *The Secret of Dorian Gray*)

A Towers of London/Regal Film/Terra Film Production (1970); 93 minutes; Eastman Color; U.S.: A Commonwealth United Presentation; American–International (1971); in Color by Movielab

P: Harry Alan Towers; **D:** Massimo Dallamano; **S:** Massimo Dallamano, Marcello Coscia and Gunter Ebert; **M:** Peppino De Luca and Carlo Pes; **DP:** Otello Spila; **E:** Nicholas Wentworth; **AD:** Mario Ambrosino; **Cast:** Helmut Berger, Richard Todd, Herbert Lom, Marie Liljedahl, Margaret Lee, Maria Rohm, Beryl Cunningham, Isa Miranda, Renato Romano, Stewart Black and Eleonora Rossi Drago

Oscar Wilde's classic *The Picture of Dorian Gray* is given the Harry Alan Towers treatment in this British-Italian-German coproduction. Helmut Berger is ideal physical casting as the beautiful and innocent young man who turns to a life of dissolute experiences. It is difficult to judge his acting as he is dubbed throughout. Performance doesn't seem to count for much here and it is obvious Berger wasn't chosen for his thespian abilities anyway. Handsome Dorian Gray has his portrait painted by an artist friend, Basil (Richard Todd). Dorian is so entranced by his own effigy that he says he would give his soul to stay young and have the figure in the portrait age instead. His wish is granted and he spends the next several decades indulging in every imaginable

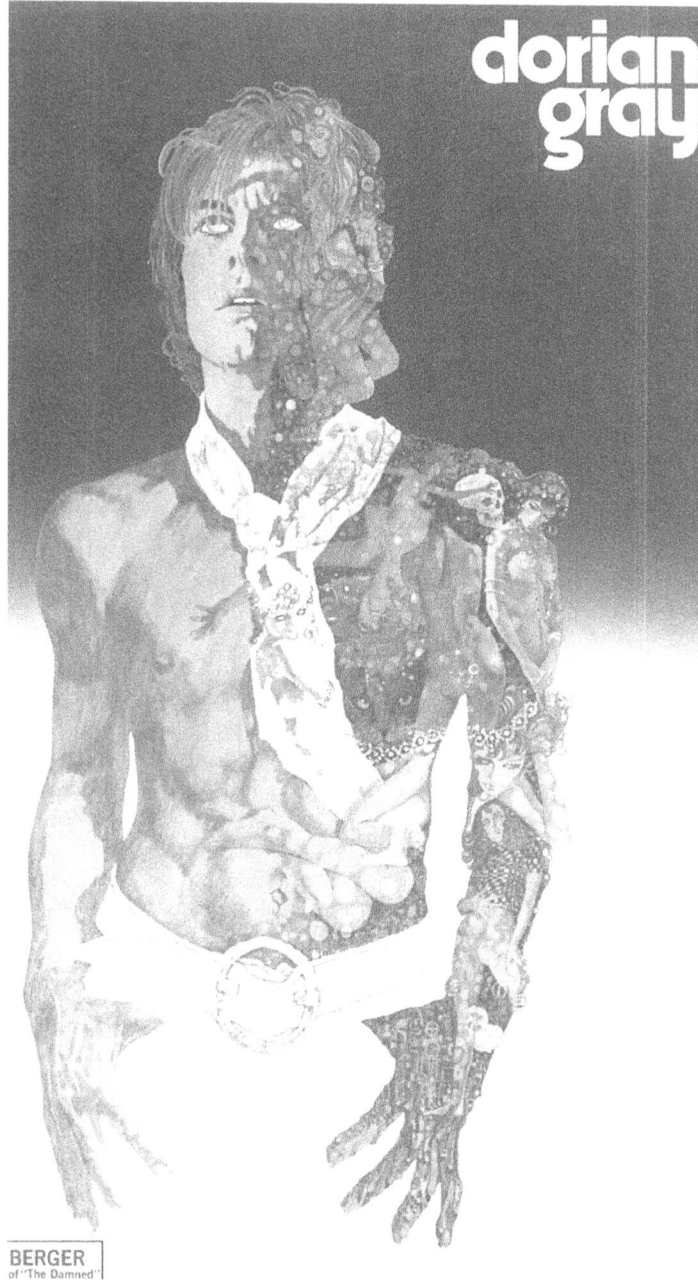

BERGER of "The Damned"

Dorian Gray

"swinging London" of the 70s. The new permissive attitude in the cinema at that time is exercised to great extent. Berger and most of the rest of the cast constantly shed their clothes and have sex with whomever happens to be at hand, regardless of gender. This might have been terribly daring in 1970 but now it merely looks silly. Shortly before the release of this film, Hammer announced their forthcoming production *The Ecstasy of Dorian Gray*. The poor reception given to Towers' version cancelled any plans Hammer had in that direction.

Video: U.S.

90. Dracula

A Hammer Film Production (1958); 82 minutes; Eastman Color; U.S. *(Horror of Dracula)*: Universal–International; Technicolor

EXP: Michael Carreras; **P:** Anthony Hinds; **D:** Terence Fisher; **S:** Jimmy Sangster; **M:** James Bernard; **DP:** Jack Asher; **E:** James Needs and Bill Lenny; **AD:** Bernard Robinson; **Cast:** Christopher Lee, Peter Cushing, Michael Gough, Melissa Stribling, Carol Marsh, John Van Eyssen, Miles Malleson, Valerie Gaunt, Olga Dickie, Janina Faye, George Woodbridge and Charles Lloyd Pack

This is one of a handful of motion pictures which changed the face of horror films forever. All vampire movies made since owe a debt to this version of *Dracula* and its director Terence Fisher, who not only gave his vampires fangs but sex appeal as well. In the Dracula films of the 30s and 40s, the infamous Count was always portrayed as an

vice, while the painted image ages in his attic. One of the major flaws in this greatly flawed motion picture is that there is absolutely no sense of any passage of time. Sure, some of the characters do get gray hair, but the background always remains the

urbane gentleman — creepy perhaps, but not particularly frightening. Christopher Lee's Dracula is a ferocious, fanged monster who still manages to exude a great deal of sexual magnetism. The plot is basically that of the Bram Stoker novel scaled down somewhat due to budgetary restrictions but retaining the essential elements of the source. Every facet of the production is outstanding with a special mention for the superlative cast, Bernard Robinson's exquisite sets and the outstanding score by James Bernard. Lee appeared as Dracula in six sequels for Hammer but none had the impact of the original.

Video: U.K./U.S.

91. *Dracula*

A Dan Curtis/Latglen Ltd. Production (1973); 100 minutes; Color; U.S.: television release

P/D: Dan Curtis; **S:** Richard Matheson; **M:** Robert Cobert; **DP:** Oswald Morris; **E:** Richard A. Harris, Anthony Palk and Jack Davies; **PD:** Trevor Williams; **Cast:** Jack Palance, Nigel Davenport, Simon Ward, Pamela Brown, Fiona Lewis, Penelope Horner, Murray Brown, George Pravda, Sarah Douglas, Virginia Wetherell and Barbara Lindley

Following the success of his daytime television series *Dark Shadows*, producer Dan Curtis fancied himself a real "horrormeister" and went on to adapt a number of classic horror stories for American television. This production of *Dracula*, filmed in

VAMPIRE WOMAN VALERIE GAUNT AND THE DESICCATED CORPSE OF JONATHAN HARKER IN A PUBLICITY SHOT FROM HAMMER'S *DRACULA*.

England and Yugoslavia, is far more ambitious than Curtis' other TV adaptations and it did have a theatrical release in England.

On the plus side, Richard Matheson's script is fairly faithful to the original novel. Two major exceptions are the inclusion of a superfluous plot device in which Dracula (Jack Palance) believes that Lucy (Fiona Lewis) is the reincarnation of his lost love from centuries before. A very similiar idea was also used by James V. Hart in his screenplay for Francis Ford Coppola's 1992 *Dracula. The other exception is that Jonathan Harker (Murray Brown) is turned into a vampire who is destroyed by Arthur Holmwood (Simon Ward) and Dr. Van Helsing (Nigel Davenport) at Castle Dracula. Curtis tries to make this Dracula a tragic and heroic figure but Palance overplays the part so wildly that there is little room left for sympathy.

To his credit, Curtis was daring to cast Palance in the role at a time when Christopher Lee was so closely identified with the character. The film's major drawback is a lack of atmosphere.

Many of the exteriors are photographed in glaring daylight and the interiors are often too brightly illuminated. The theatrical version has a great deal more bloodletting than its television counterpart.

Video: U.K./U.S.

92. Dracula A.D. 1972 (a.k.a. Dracula Today)

A Hammer Film Production (1972); 95 minutes; Eastman Color; U.S.: Warner Bros.

EXP: Michael Carreras; **P:** Josephine Douglas; **D:** Alan Gibson; **S:** Don Houghton; **M:** Mike Vickers; **DP:** Dick Bush; **E:** James Needs; **PD:** Don Mingaye; **Cast:** Christopher Lee, Peter Cushing, Stephanie Beacham, Christopher Neame, Michael Coles, William Ellis, Marsha Hunt, Janet Key, Caroline Munro, Philip Miller, Michael Kitchen and Lally Bowers

Hammer's disastrous first attempt to bring Dracula into the present day somehow seems better now than it did at the time of its release. Perhaps this is because there are no high expectations and also because it now seems almost as much of a "period piece" as the Gothics. The film opens promisingly enough with a Hyde Park confrontation between Dracula and Van Helsing set in Victorian London. Both Dracula and his pursuer are killed and the story shifts to the year 1972. Dracula is resurrected in "mod" London and sets out to take revenge on the descendants of his enemy Van Helsing. It's great to see Lee and Cushing together in their first Dracula film since the 1958 original, but their talents are mostly squandered here. Christopher Neame fares better as Dracula's devoted disciple, Johnny Alucard. His performance is a deft combination of the sinister and the flamboyant. The film's greatest liabilities are the terrible score by Michael Vickers and a dreadful musical interlude featuring the San Francisco rock band Stoneground.

When *Dracula A.D. 1972* failed to produced the expected box office results, Warner Bros. executives in the United States decided to shelve the sequel, *The Satanic Rites of Dracula*.

Video: U.K./U.S.

Dracula and the 7 Golden Vampires see ***The Legend of the 7 Golden Vampires***

93. Dracula Has Risen from the Grave

A Hammer Film Production (1968); 92 minutes; Technicolor; U.S.: Warner Bros–Seven Arts (1969)

P: Aida Young; **D:** Freddie Francis; **S:** John Elder; **M:** James Bernard; **DP:** Arthur Grant; **E:** James Needs and Spencer Reeve; **AD:** Bernard Robinson; **Cast:** Christopher Lee, Rupert Davies, Veronica Carlson, Barry Andrews, Barbara Ewing, Ewan Hooper, Michael Ripper, George A. Cooper, Marion Mathie, John D. Collins, Christopher Cunningham and Norman Bacon

A monsignor (Rupert Davies) performs the rite of exorcism at Castle Dracula, thereby making it impossible for the vampire to enter his abode. An understandably livid Dracula (Christopher Lee) goes to the town of Keinenburg to enact his revenge on Maria (Veronica Carlson), the monsignor's beautiful niece.

DRACULA (CHRISTOPHER LEE) IS PREVENTED FROM BITING MARIA (VERONICA CARLSON) BY THE MONSIGNOR (RUPERT DAVIES) IN *DRACULA HAS RISEN FROM THE GRAVE*.

This was Hammer's third Dracula film and it established the plot pattern of the next three: The romance of a young couple is threatened when Dracula attempts to "vampirize" the woman. *Dracula Has Risen from the Grave* is neither the best nor the worst of the Hammer Dracula series but it was the most financially successful. In 1969, *Films and Filming* listed it as Hammer's third biggest moneymaker, following behind *One Million Years B.C.* and *She*. Obviously, it was in the right place at the right time as there is nothing particularly special to set it apart from the other films in the series. However, it can boast the introduction of lovely Veronica Carlson into the Hammer fold. She was one of the few Hammer glamour girls to have staying power and appeared in two more films for the company. The American release of this movie was accompanied by some controversy. The American motion picture rating system had recently gone into effect and *Dracula Has Risen* was awarded a "G" (Suggested for General Audiences) rating. Parental groups objected stongly — not too surprising considering the film's violent content.

Video: U.K./U.S.

Dracula Is Dead and Well and Living in London see ***The Satanic Rites of Dracula***

CHRISTOPHER LEE AS *DRACULA—PRINCE OF DARKNESS*.

94. Dracula — Prince of Darkness

A Hammer/Seven Arts Production (1966); 90 minutes; Technicolor and Techniscope; U.S.: 20th Century–Fox; DeLuxe Color and Techniscope

P: Anthony Nelson-Keys; D: Terence Fisher; S: John Sansom (Jimmy Sangster); M: James Bernard; DP: Michael Reed; E: James Needs and Chris Barnes; PD: Bernard Robinson; AD: Don Mingaye; Cast: Christopher Lee, Barbara Shelley, Andrew Keir, Francis Matthews, Suzan Farmer, Charles Tingwell, Thorley Walters, Philip Latham, Walter Brown, George Woodbridge, Jack Lambert and John Maxim

Four English travelers, on holiday in the Carpathian Mountains, take refuge at Castle Dracula. One of them is murdered by Dracula's servant and his blood is used in a grisly ritual to resurrect the Count. Christopher Lee, who was reluctant to reprise his most famous role, was finally persuaded to star in this sequel to *Dracula* (1958). Lee, *sans* dialogue, plays the part with demonic fury but it is Barbara Shelley who steals the show. As Helen, she is the very picture of prim, Victorian repression but, after she is bitten by Dracula, she turns into one of filmdom's most rapacious female vampires. Her death scene is a high point of Hammer horror. Andrew Keir is also memorable in the pseudo–Van Helsing role of Father Sandor.

Video: U.K./U.S.

Dracula Today see *Dracula A.D. 1972*

95. The Earth Dies Screaming

A Lippert Films Ltd. Production (1964); 62 minutes; U.S.: 20th Century–Fox

EXP: Robert L. Lippert; P: Jack Parsons; D: Terence Fisher; S: Henry Cross; M: Elisabeth Lutyens; DP: Arthur Lavis; E: Robert Winter; AD: George Provis; Cast: Willard Parker, Virginia Field, Dennis Price, Vanda Godsell, Thorley Walters, David Spenser and Anna Palk

This is the first of three science fiction films directed by Terence Fisher in between assignments for Hammer. A mysterious force has destroyed most of the life on Earth. The few surviving humans are being hunted by robots from another planet whose mere touch causes death. The victims later come back as blank-eyed zombies who are controlled by the aliens. Given the obviously paltry budget he had to work with, Fisher still manages to stage some effectively eerie end-of-the-world sequences in the tiny Surrey village of Shere. Despite his admitted disdain for SF subjects, this is by far Fisher's best work in that particular genre.

Video: None

The Electronic Monster see **Escapement**

96. Endless Night

A Frank Launder and Sidney Gilliat Production (1972); 95 minutes; Color; U.S.: no theatrical release

P: Leslie Gilliat; **D/S:** Sidney Gilliat; **M:** Bernard Herrmann; **DP:** Harry Waxman; **E:** Thelma Connell; **PD:** Wilfred Shingleton; **AD:** Fred Carter; **Cast:** Hywel Bennett, Hayley Mills, Britt Ekland, George Sanders, Per Oscarsson, Aubrey Richards, Peter Bowles, Lois Maxwell, Madge Ryan, David Bauer, Patience Collier and Leo Genn

Based on a somewhat uncharacteristic Agatha Christie novel, *Endless Night* is a story of love, murder and madness. Michael Rogers (Hywel Bennett), an unemployed chauffeur, meets Ellie (Hayley Mills), a pretty young American, at a beautiful spot on the South Devon coast called Gipsy's Acre. Michael tells Ellie of his dream to build a house there. A mysterious old lady appears and warns them that any plans involving Gipsy's Acre can only end in disaster. Michael and Ellie fall in love and only later does he discover that she is heiress to a fortune. They marry and build Michael's dream house. Despite the interference of her family, they live an idyllic life until Ellie's dominating friend Greta (Britt Ekland) comes to visit them. To say any more would spoil the twists and turns of the plot.

Teamed for the third time, Hywel Bennett and Hayley Mills are an engaging and attractive couple. Bernard Herrmann contributed a haunting, melancholy score.

Video: U.S.

Enemy from Space see **Quatermass II**

97. Escapement

An Amalgamated Production (1957); 72 minutes; U.S. *(The Electronic Monster)*: Columbia (1960)

P: Alec C. Snowden; **D:** Montgomery Tully; **S:** Charles Eric Maine; **M:** Soundrama; **DP:** Bert Mason; **E:** Geoffrey Muller; **AD:** Wilfred Arnold; **Cast:** Rod Cameron, Mary Murphy, Meredith Edwards, Peter Illing, Carl Jaffe, Kay Callard, Carl Duering, Robert Huby, Felix Felton, Larry Cross, Carlo Borelli and John McCarthy

When film star Claude Denver (John McCarthy) dies in an automobile accident, insurance investigator Jeff Keenan (Rod Cameron) is sent to Europe to examine the situation. He discovers that Denver was a patient at a psychiatric clinic where new methods of electronic hypnosis are being used as treatment. Patients are fitted with an apparatus which induces bizzare dreams. Paul Zakon (Peter Illing), the director of the clinic, devises a plan to dominate the patients by forcing them to experience horrific nightmares. Some of these "treatments" have resulted in the deaths of the patients. The brief dream sequences, directed by David Paltenghi, are the only fascinating aspect of an otherwise mundane film. Interestingly, the therapy foreshadows the idea of "virtual reality" decades before it became a fact. Originally the American release was to have been called *Zex*.

Video: U.S.

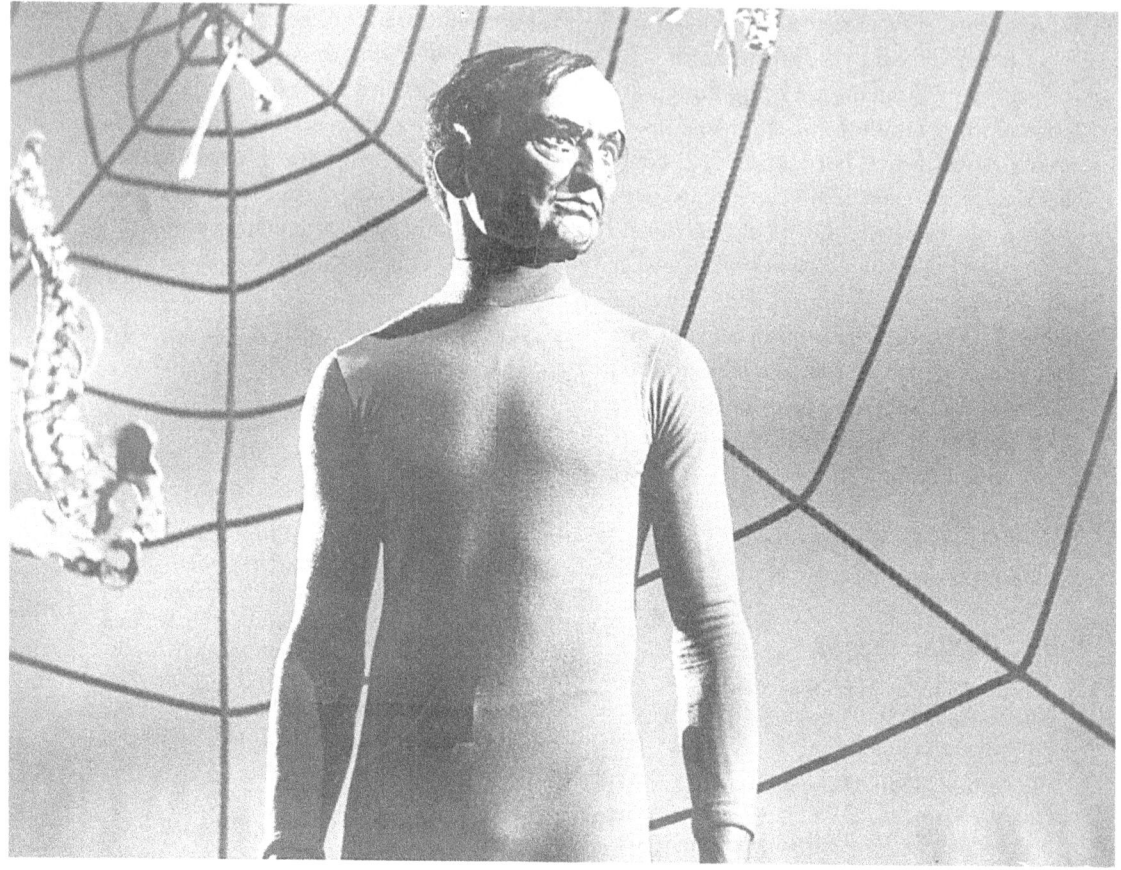

A SCENE FROM ONE OF THE WEIRD DREAM SEQUENCES IN *ESCAPEMENT*.

Estate of Insanity see ***The Black Torment***

98. *The Evil of Frankenstein*

A Hammer Film Production (1964); 84 minutes; Eastman Color; U.S.: Universal–International

P: Anthony Hinds; **D:** Freddie Francis; **S:** John Elder; **M:** Don Banks; **DP:** John Wilcox; **E:** James Needs; **AD:** Don Mingaye; **Cast:** Peter Cushing, Peter Woodthorpe, Sandor Eles, Katy Wild, Duncan Lamont, Kiwi Kingston, David Hutcheson, Caron Gardner, Tony Arpino, James Maxwell, Frank Forsyth and Howard Goorney

The third entry in Hammer's Frankenstein series is not a sequel to the previous films, but a self-contained story which reinvents the creation of the original monster in a flashback. When Baron Frankenstein's attempts to revive his creation prove unsuccessful, he enlists the services of a seedy hypnotist to help reactivate the creature's damaged brain. Since this picture was made for Universal, the design of the Creature (Kiwi Kingston) was allowed to be closer to the original Universal concept. Peter Cushing again plays Baron Frankenstein but his character is far more sympathetically presented here than it is in the two previous films. The production values are of a very high standard and the film features the most elaborate laboratory set of the entire Hammer series.

Video: U.S.

Exorcism at Midnight see ***Naked Evil***

99. Expose

Norfolk International Pictures Ltd. (1975); 82 minutes; Technicolor; U.S. *(The House on Straw Hill)*: New World Pictures (1976)

P: Brian Smedley-Aston; **D/S:** James Kenelm Clarke; **M:** Steve Gray; **DP:** Denis Lewiston; **E:** Jim Connock; **Cast:** Udo Kier, Linda Hayden, Fiona Richmond, Patsy Smart, Vic Armstrong and Karl Howman

Paul Martin (Udo Kier) is a successful, self-centered and highly neurotic author who is busy writing his second novel at an isolated house in the English countryside. He hires a pretty typist named Linda (Linda Hayden) to assist him with his work. Linda is a conscientious worker who spends much of her spare time masturbating. This weirdly fascinating sex thriller was heavily edited (the original running time was 117 minutes) but what remains is still fairly explicit for a non-porno movie. The vast amounts of blood and nudity would almost put Peter Walker to shame. Despite the questionable material, Linda Hayden not only strips un–self-consciously but manages to turn in a very good performance as well.

Video: U.S.

100. Eye of the Devil (a.k.a. *13*)

A Filmways Picture (1966); 92 minutes; U.S.: Metro-Goldwyn-Mayer (1967)

P: Martin Ransohoff and John Calley; **D:** J. Lee Thompson; **S:** Robin Estridge and Dennis Murphy; **M:** Gary McFarland; **DP:** Erwin Hillier; **E:** Ernest Walter; **AD:** Elliot Scott; **Cast:** Deborah Kerr, David Niven, Donald Pleasence, Flora Robson, Emlyn Williams, Sharon Tate, David Hemmings, Edward Mulhare and John Le Mesurier

This attempt at a "sophisticated" horror film starring a cast of top-flight performers is mostly a failure due, in part, to pretentious direction and artless editing. In all fairness, the original intentions may have been good and the production did have more than its share of problems. Originally it was to have been called *Day of the Arrow*, which was the title of the source novel by Philip Loraine. Shortly after filming began, director Michael Anderson was forced to withdraw because of illness. He was replaced by J. Lee Thompson who was, perhaps, not the wisest choice to direct a subtle thriller.

During production the title was changed to *13*. Two weeks before filming was scheduled to be completed, star Kim Novak was thrown from a horse while on location in France. Thompson shot around her as best he could, but it soon became apparent that Novak had suffered a back injury that would not allow her to resume filming for quite awhile. The decision was made to reshoot all of Novak's scenes with Deborah Kerr. Kerr is certainly put through her paces as the plot calls for her to run wildly throughout the chateau of her husband (David Niven), attempting to unravel a family mystery involving devil worship and failed vineyards. Just prior to release, the title was changed to *Eye of the Devil* and the film was heavily re-edited. These last-ditch efforts could not save it from being a $3 million fiasco. Sharon Tate is "introduced" in the film and she is lovingly, and lingeringly, photographed throughout.

Video: None

101. The Eyes of Annie Jones

A Parroch–McCallum/Associated Producers Inc. Production; (1963); 71 minutes; U.S.: 20th Century–Fox

P: Jack Parsons; **D:** Reginald LeBorg; **S:** Louis Vittes; **M:** Buxton Orr; **DP:** Peter Hennessy; **E:** Robert Winter; **AD:** George Provis; **Cast:** Richard Conte, Francesca Annis, Joyce Carey, Myrtle Reed, Shay Gorman, Victor Brooks, Jean Lodge, Alan Haines and Mara Purcell

When wealthy Geraldine Wheeler (Jean Lodge) goes missing, Aunt Helen (Joyce Carey) enlists the aid of a young

DEBORAH KERR PLEADS WITH HER HUSBAND DAVID NIVEN IN *EYE OF THE DEVIL*.

orphan to help locate her niece. This teenage girl is Annie Jones (Francesca Annis) and she possesses extrasensory perception. Geraldine's brother David (Richard Conte) is suspected of murdering his sister to gain control of her mills. Annie goes into a trance but the results are inconclusive and she is sent back to the orphanage. When the mystery is finally solved, it becomes apparent that Annie was on the right track after all.

Francesca Annis made her movie debut as Cleopatra's handmaiden Erias in the 1963 film *Cleopatra*. She is now one of England's leading stage actresses. Director Reginald LeBorg's horror output also includes *The Mummy's Ghost* (1944), *Jungle Woman* (1944), *The Black Sleep* (1956) and *Diary of a Madman* (1963).

Video: None

102. Eyewitness

An Irving Allen Production Ltd. (1971); 95 minutes; An Anglo–EMI Film; Technicolor; U.S. *(Sudden Terror)*: National General Pictures

EXP: Irving Allen; **P:** Paul Maslansky; **D:** John Hough; **S:** Ronald Harwood; **M:** David Whitaker; **DP:** David Holmes; **E:** Geoffrey Foot; **PD:** Herbert Westbrook; **Cast:** Mark Lester, Lionel Jeffries, Susan George, Tony Bonner, Jeremy Kemp, Peter Vaughan, Peter Bowles, Betty Marsden, Anthony Stamboulieh, John Allison, Joseph Furst and Jonathan Burn

The island of Malta is the setting for this suspenseful chase thriller. Ziggy (Mark Lester) is an 11-year-old with a highly active imagination. His older sister Pippa (Susan George) is fed up with his prevarications so, when he actually witnesses the assassination of a visiting dignitary, she refuses to believe him. Unfortunately, the killers (Peter Vaughan and Peter Bowles) have seen Ziggy and they decide to eliminate the only person who can positively identify them. This variation on "The Boy Who Cried Wolf" is fast-moving and tautly directed by John Hough (his feature film debut).

Video: U.S.

103. The Face of Fu Manchu

A Hallam Production (1965); 96 minutes; Technicolor and Techniscope; U.S.: Seven Arts

EXP: Oliver A. Unger; **P:** Harry Alan Towers; **D:** Don Sharp; **S:** Peter Welbeck; **M:** Christopher Whelen; **DP:** Ernest Steward; **E:** John Trumper; **AD:** Frank White; **Cast:** Christopher Lee, Nigel Green, James Robertson Justice, Joachim Fuchsberger, Karin Dor, Howard Marion Crawford, Tsai Chin, Walter Rilla, Harry Brogan and Poulet Tu

This is the first and best in Harry Alan Towers' series of films featuring Christopher Lee as Sax Rohmer's oriental mastermind.

Nayland Smith (Nigel Green) witnesses the execution of Fu Manchu (Christopher Lee), but somehow he cannot convince himself that the evil doctor's reign of terror has ended. Smith's supposition is correct; he discovers that Fu Manchu lives and is attempting to obtain an extremely lethal poison, capable of killing the populations of entire cities. Nayland's pursuit of his nemesis comes to a climax at Fu Manchu's Tibetian stronghold.

Production values, which rapidly deteriorated as the series progressed, are of a high caliber in this outing. Nigel Green is by far the best of the three actors who would portray Nayland Smith opposite Lee.

Video: U.S./U.K.

104. Fahrenheit 451

An Enterprise–Vineyard Film Production (1966); 112 minutes; Technicolor; U.S.: Universal

P: Lewis M. Allen; **D:** Francois Truffaut; **S:** Francois Truffaut and Jean-Louis Richard; **M:** Bernard Herrmann; **DP:** Nicolas Roeg; **E:** Tom Noble; **PD:** Tony Walton; **AD:** Sydney Cain; **Cast:** Oscar Werner, Julie Christie, Cyril Cusack, Anton Diffring, Jeremy Spenser, Alex Scott, Bee Duffell, Anna Palk and Mark Lester

Francois Truffaut's first English language film was an adaptation of Ray Bradbury's novel of a futuristic society controlled by total censorship. Montag (Oscar Werner) is a "fireman" whose job is to burn books, the possession of which is a crime against the state. His wife Linda is a victim of society-induced apathy and drug dependency. As Montag begins to question his profession, he turns from Linda to Clarisse, a nonconformist book reader.

Linda and Clarisse are both played by Julie Christie, who succeeds in making them distinctly different personalities. Despite some rather heavy-handed symbolism, *Fahrenheit 451* is both fascinating and moving. Much of the film's effectiveness can be attributed to the Bernard Herrmann's score and Nicolas Roeg's color cinematography.

Video: U.S.

105. Fanatic

A Hammer Film Production (1965); 97 minutes; Technicolor; U.S. *(Die! Die! My Darling!)*: Columbia; Eastman Color

EXP: Michael Carreras; **P:** Anthony Hinds; **D:** Silvio Narizzano; **S:** Richard Matheson; **M:** Wilfred Josephs; **DP:** Arthur Ibbetson; **E:** James Needs and John Dunsford; **PD:** Peter Proud; **Cast:** Tallulah Bankhead, Stefanie Powers, Maurice Kaufmann, Peter Vaughan, Yootha Joyce, Donald Sutherland, Gwendolyn Watts, Robert Dorning, Philip Gilbert, Diane King and Winifred Dennis

Hammer's first entry into the "horror hag" catagory is this top notch thriller based on Anne Blaisdell's novel *Nightmare*. Somehow Hammer was able to lure Tallulah Bankhead back to the screen (she had not made a film since 1953) and her presence, combined with Richard Matheson's wry script, made this a highly entertaining offering. A young American girl (Stefanie Powers), in England, visits Mrs. Trefoile (Bankhead), the mother of her dead fiancé. It soon becomes all too apparent that the old lady is mad as a hatter and has no intention of letting her would-be daughter-in-law leave. By turns humorous and frightening, Bankhead pulls out all stops and gives an extraordinary performance in what was to be her last film. Stefanie Powers is also quite effective as the recalcitrant victim.

Video: U.S.

106. Fear in the Night

A Hammer Film Production (1972); 94 minutes; Technicolor; U.S.: International Co-Productions (1974)

EXP: Michael Carreras; **P/D:** Jimmy Sangster; **S:** Jimmy Sangster and Michael Syson; **M:** John McCabe; **DP:** Arthur Grant; **E:** Peter Weatherley; **AD:** Don Picton; **Cast:** Judy Geeson, Joan Collins, Peter Cushing, Ralph Bates, Gillian Lind, James Cossins, John Bown and Brian Grellis

Robert Heller (Ralph Bates) takes his new bride Peggy (Judy Geeson) to the remote country school for boys where he is employed. Prior to their departure from London, Peggy was attacked by an unknown person with an artificial arm. Shortly after her arrival at the school, she suffers a similar attack. To her horror, Peggy discovers that the sinister headmaster, Michael (Peter Cushing), also has an artificial arm.

This was the last in a series of psychological thrillers scripted by Jimmy Sangster for Hammer. A good cast makes the most of a fairly standard "plot to drive the girl insane" scenario. *Fear in the Night* was released in the United Kingdom with *Straight on Till Morning* under the heading "Women In Fear." Michael Carreras' concept was to produce two films linked by a similar motif and release them on a double bill. Carreras said at the time: "My original concept was to have two properties by the same author on a central theme, being made into two films both directed by the same person."

Video: U.K./U.S (alternate U.S. video title: *Honeymoon of Fear*)

The Fearless Vampire Killers see Dance of the Vampires

107. The Fiend

A World Arts Media (U.K.) Ltd. Production (1971); 87 minutes; Color; U.S. *(Beware the Brethren)*: Cinerama Releasing (1972)

EXP: John Lightfoot; **P/D:** Robert Hartford-Davis; **S:** Brian Comport; **M:** Tony Osborne and Richard Kerr; **DP:** Desmond Dickinson; **E:** Alan Pattillo; **AD:** George Provis; **Cast:** Ann Todd, Patrick Magee, Tony Beckley, Madeline Hinde, Suzanna Leigh, Percy Herbert, David Lodge, Ronald Allen, Maxine Barrie, Jeanette Wild, Diane Chappell and Susanna East

Birdy Wemys (Ann Todd) and her son Kenny (Tony Beckley) belong to a fanatical religious cult called "Christ's Children Evangelical Crusade," otherwise know as "The Brethren." Birdy and the Minister (Patrick Magee) have so throughly "enlightened" Kenny about the evils of sex that he has become a twisted psychopath who murders young women. A nurse (Madeline Hinde) comes to attend the ailing Birdy and she suspects that the Brethren are up to no good. She asks her sister (Suzanna Leigh), who is a reporter, to investigate by posing as a potential convert. The least of her discoveries turns out to be Kenny's bra and panty collection in the basement.

This is a well-acted thriller with good production values. The material would have been perfect for Peter Walker and it is easy to imagine Sheila Keith in the Ann Todd part. Watch for the scene where Kenny picks up one of his victims at a cinema showing the double feature *Scars of Dracula/Horror of Frankenstein*, and try to ignore the two terribly out-of-place musical numbers performed by the church congregation.

Video: U.S.

108. Fiend Without a Face

Eros/Producers Associates Production (1957); 75 minutes; U.S.: Metro-Goldwyn-Mayer (1958)

EXP: Richard Gordon; **P:** John Croyden; **D:** Arthur Crabtree; **S:** Herbert J. Leder; **M:** Buxton Orr; **DP:** Lionel Banes; **E:** R.Q. McNaughton; **AD:** John Elphick; **SVE:** Puppel Nordhoff and Peter Nielson; **Cast:** Marshall Thompson, Terence Kilburn, Kim Parker, Kynaston Reeves, Michael Balfour, Gil Winfield, Shane Cordell, Stanley Maxted, James Dyrenforth, Kerrigan Prescott, Peter Madden and Lala Lloyd

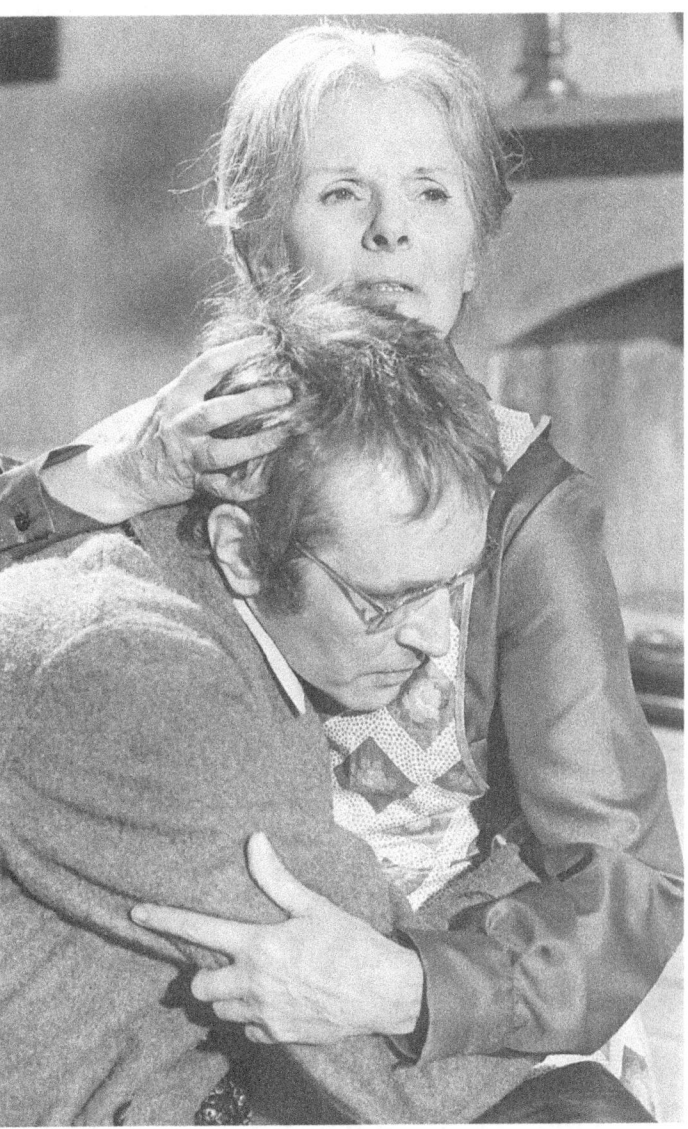

ANN TODD COMFORTS HER INSANE SON TONY BECKLEY IN *THE FIEND*.

When a U.S. Army anti-missile project bases its operation near a small Canadian village, the local inhabitants are distressed that the close proximity of an atomic reactor is causing problems with the milk production of their cattle. As if this wasn't bad enough, a number of the townspeople have turned up dead, their brains sucked out of their skulls through two holes on the back of the neck. The blame eventually falls on an eccentric, kindly professor who has been tapping the atomic power for his experiments in thought materialization. He has unwittingly created invisible "mental vampires" which survive by feeding on human brains. A power boost in the reactor makes the fiends visible and they are nauseating sights, resembling a human brain with spinal cord and tentacles attached. The finale of the film is a gruesome special effects extravaganza in which the creatures are shot,

Marshall Thompson (right) starred in the Richard Gordon productions *Fiend without a Face* and *First Man Into Space*.

axed and eventually melted down into pools of putrification. Quite a nifty little film and strong stuff for its day.

Video: U.S.

109. The Final Programme

A Goodtimes Enterprises/Gladiole Production (1973); 89 minutes; An Anglo–EMI Ltd Film; Technicolor; U.S. *(The Last Days of Man on Earth)*: New World Pictures (1974); 78 minutes

EXP: Roy Baird and David Puttnam; **P:** John Goldstone and Sandy Lieberson; **D/S/PD:** Robert Fuest; **M:** Paul Beaver and Bernard Krause; **DP:** Norman Warwick; **E:** Barrie Vince and Barbara Pokras; **AD:** Philip Harrison; **Cast:** Jon Finch, Jenny Runacre, Sterling Hayden, Patrick Magee, Hugh Griffith, Harry Andrews, Graham Crowden, Derrick O'Connor, George Coulouris, Julie Ege, Basil Henson and Sarah Douglas

An unsuccessful attempt to bring the oblique visions of author Michael Moorcock to the screen. Jerry Cornelius (Jon Finch) lives in a futuristic London which is part of a world poised for global destruction. He is chosen by a trio of scientists to be the human guinea pig in an experiment. Their purpose is to create a new messiah who will rescue mankind from annihilation.

This incoherent film tries hard to be clever and camp but really doesn't succeed with either. Director Robert Fuest had better luck with these elements in the *Dr. Phibes* films and episodes of *The Avengers* television series, but the material here just isn't of the same caliber.

Video: U.S.

110. Fire Maidens of Outer Space

A Saturn Films Presentation; A Cy Roth/Criterion Production (1956); 80 minutes; U.S.: Topaz Films

P: George Fowler; **D/S:** Cy Roth; **M:** Adapted from Alexander Borodin, Monia Liter and Trevor Duncan; **DP:** Ian Struthers; **E:** A.C.T. Clair; **AD:** Scott MacGregor; **Cast:** Anthony Dexter, Paul Carpenter, Susan Shaw, Harry Fowler, Sydney Tafler, Jacqueline Curtis, Rodney Dark, Maya Koumani, Richard Walter, Owen Berry, Norma Arnould and Jan Holden

If *The Quatermass Xperiment* was the apex of British science fiction films in 1956, then *Fire Maidens of Outer Space* is surely the nadir. The governments of the United States and Great Britain join forces for "Plan 13;" a manned space flight to the newly discovered thirteenth moon of Jupiter. The five astronauts brave the dangerous flight (which includes the inevitable shower of meteorites) and arrive at their destination to discover a lost civilization of scantily clad young women. The lone male is an old man who tells the explorers that this is "New Atlantis." When the continent of Atlantis sank, the survivors used their advanced technology to go to this moon of Jupiter. There is also a terrible monster which continually menaces the inhabitants of New Atlantis. The monster is a tall, skinny man in a black leotard with makeup by Roy Ashton. As if seeing Ashton's name in the credits wasn't a big enough surprise, it is a total shock to see that Scott MacGregor was responsible for the cardboard sets. This idiotic film is part of that absurd "planet of lost women" sub-genre which includes such treasures as *Cat Women of the Moon* and *Queen of Outer Space*.

Video: None

111. First Man into Space

A Producers Associates/Amalgamated Production (1959); 77 minutes; U.S.: Metro-Goldwyn-Mayer

EXP: Richard Gordon; **P:** John Croydon and Charles F. Vetter; Robert Day; **S:** John C. Cooper and Lance Z. Hargreaves; **M:** Buxton Orr; **DP:** Geoffrey Faithfull; **E:** Peter Mayhew; **Cast:** Marshall Thompson, Marla Landi, Bill Edwards, Robert Ayers, Bill Nagy, Carl Jaffe, Helen Fores, Roger Delgado, Michael Bell, Richard Shaw, Bill Nick and John McLaren

Marshall Thompson is the beleaguered brother of a daredevil Navy test pilot (Bill Edwards) who can't seem to obey orders, even if his life depends on it. On a test flight into outer space, Edwards takes his rocket beyond the limits of safety and returns to Earth encrusted with meteorite dust and with an insatiable thirst for blood. The film is slow-moving and seems much longer than its 77-minute running time. Not badly done but not terribly thrilling either. One contemporary reviewer wrote, "You have to be really mad about all movie monsters to enjoy this not very-scientific bit of science fiction." A similiar plot was even less successfully presented in *The Incredible Melting Man* (1978).

Video: U.K./U.S.

112. First Men in the Moon

A Charles H. Schneer Production (1964); 105 minutes; An Ameran Film; LunaColor by Pathe, Panavision and Dynamation; U.S.: Columbia

P: Charles H. Schneer; **D:** Nathan Juran; **S:** Nigel Kneale and Jan Read; **M:** Laurie Johnson; **DP:** Wilkie Cooper; **E:** Maurice Rootes; **AD:** John Blezard; **SVE:** Ray Harryhausen; **Cast:** Edward Judd, Martha Hyer, Lionel Jeffries, Eric Chitty, Betty McDowall, Miles Malleson, Lawrence Herder, Gladys Henson, Marne Maitland, Hugh McDermott, Gordon Robinson and Sean Kelly

A United Nations spaceship lands on the Moon and discovers a Union Jack and a paper dated 1899 which claims the Moon for England in the name of Queen Victoria. Back on Earth, authorities are able to trace the document to Arnold Bedford (Ed-

Professor Cavor (Lionel Jeffries) is surrounded by Selenites in *First Men in the Moon*.

ward Judd), an old man living in a nursing home. He tells them the story of his journey to the Moon with his fiancée Katherine (Martha Hyer) and a daft inventor named Cavor (Lionel Jeffries). Cavor had invented a anti-gravity substance that, when coated on a sphere, enabled them to fly to the Moon. On the Moon, the trio discovered an underground city populated by insect-like creatures called Selenites. The screenplay is loosely adapted from the H. G. Wells novel and takes a definitely lighthearted approach to the material. Nearly half the film's running time is spent on build-up but the last half is so good that it's worth the wait. Harryhausen's visual effects, shot for the first time in widescreen, are sensational. Watch for Peter Finch in a cameo role as the bailiff. Video: U.K./U.S.

Five Million Years to Earth see *Quatermass and the Pit*

113. The Flesh and Blood Show

A Peter Walker/Heritage Ltd. Production (1972); 91 minutes; Color; U.S.: Entertainment Ventures Inc (1974)

P/D: Peter Walker; **S:** Alfred Shaughnessy; **M:** Cyril Ornadel; **DP:** Peter Jessop; **E:** Ron Pope; **Cast:** Ray Brooks, Jenny Hanley, Luan Peters, David Howey, Penny Meredith, Robin Askwith, Patrick Barr, Judy Matheson, Tristan Rogers, Candace Glendenning and Elizabeth Bradley

Another murder and mammaries fest from the fevered brain of Peter Walker. A group of young actors goes to a seaside community to join an improvisational theatrical company called Theatre Group 40.

A PROSTITUTE (BILLIE WHITELAW) IS STALKED BY HARE (DONALD PLEASENCE) IN *THE FLESH AND THE FIENDS*.

Rehearsals are being held in an abandoned theater located on a derelict pier. Short on cash, they all decide to sleep at the theater as well. Since this is a slasher horror film, the characters all behave in a typically illogical manner. They wander off alone into the dark recesses of the theater and, even though several of them turn up dead, they continue to stay at the theater anyway! The denouement is revealed in a sepia-toned, 3-D flashback in which the killer declares that all actors are "excrement."

Video: U.S./U.K.

114. The Flesh and the Fiends

A Triad Production (1959); 97 minutes; Dyaliscope; U.S. *(Mania* [1961]*)*: Valiant Films

P: Robert S. Baker and Monty Berman; **D:** John Gilling; **S:** John Gilling and Leon Griffths; **M:** Stanley Black; **DP:** Monty Berman; **E:** Jack Slade; **AD:** John Elphick; **Cast:** Peter Cushing, June Laverick, Dermot Walsh, Donald Pleasence, George Rose, Renee Houston, Billie Whitelaw, John Cairney, Melvin Hayes, June Powell and George Woodbridge

"This is a story of lost men and lost souls. It is a story of vice and murder. We make no apologies to the dead. It is all true." With these ominous words begins one of the most impressive thrillers to come out of Britain. In their brief career as horror film producers, Robert Baker and Monty Berman were responsible for two genre classics; this is one. The year is 1828 and the city is Edinburgh, Scotland. Dr. Knox (Peter Cushing) is an professor of anatomy at the med-

JAMES HAYTER ASSISTS STEPHEN MURRAY IN AN UNORTHODOX EXPERIMENT IN *FOUR SIDED TRIANGLE*.

ical university. In his zeal to obtain anatomical specimens for the edification of his students, Knox enlists grave robbers Burke (George Rose) and Hare (Donald Pleasence) to supply cadavers. Although Knox suspects that they are committing murders to keep him supplied, he turns a blind eye to their crimes. Well-written, with just the right touches of black humor, the story of Burke and Hare has never been filmed more effectively. Peter Cushing is splendid as Dr. Knox. In his capable hands, the character never comes across as evil, just misguided. The scene when he finally realizes the extent of his misdeeds is very convincingly played. Special mention should also be made of Billie Whitelaw. As Mary, a prostitute who becomes involved with one of the medical students, she gives a moving performance with the perfect balance of pathos and sexuality.

The film was cut to 84 minutes and reissued in the United States in 1965 under the title *The Fiendish Ghouls*. In 1985, Freddie Francis directed a virtual remake entitled *The Doctor and the Devils* starring Timothy Dalton and Jonathan Pryce.

Video: U.S.

115. *Four Sided Triangle* (a.k.a. *The Monster and the Woman*)

An Alexander Paal–Hammer Film Production (1953); 81 minutes; U.S.: Astor Pictures

P: Alexander Paal and Michael Carreras; **D:** Terence Fisher; **S:** Paul Tabori and Terence Fisher; **M:** Malcolm Arnold; **DP:** Reg Wyer;

E: Maurice Rootes; AD: J. Elder Wills; Cast: Barbara Payton, James Hayter, Stephen Murray, John Van Eyssen, Percy Marmont, Jennifer Dearman, Glyn Dearman, Sean Barrett, Kynaston Reeves, John Stuart and Edith Saville

This is an early example of British science fiction courtesy of Hammer Films and director Terence Fisher. Although it is an interesting movie, there is little here to indicate the heights of horror both would achieve in a few short years. What it does have in common with the later Hammer films directed by Fisher is that it essentially a "morality play." However, here the antagonist is not evil but sadly misguided.

Lena (Barbara Payton), Bill (Stephen Murray) and Robin (John Van Eyssen) have been close friends since childhood. Lena grows up into a blonde bombshell and the two men become brilliant scientific inventors. Bill and Robin invent an apparatus which can duplicate any matter exactly. For Bill, the triumph of their successful invention is short-lived because Lena and Robin announce that they are going to be married. Bill has secretly loved Lena, so he asks her if he can create a duplicate of her for himself. For some insane reason, she agrees. The duplicating process is a success and Bill names the twin Helen. Unfortunately, Bill didn't take into consideration that Helen's feelings would be the same as Lena's; Helen is also in love with Robin. Bill attempts to correct the situation with a further experiment which has tragic consequences.

Video: U.S.

116. *Fragment of Fear*

Columbia (1970); 95 minutes; Color

P: John R. Sloan; D: Richard C. Sarafian; S: Paul Dehn; M: Johnny Harris; DP: Oswald Morris; E: Malcolm Cooke; AD: Ray Simm; Cast: David Hemmings, Gayle Hunnicutt, Flora Robson, Wilfrid Hyde-White, Daniel Massey, Roland Culver, Adolfo Celi, Mona Washbourne, Mary Wimbush, Yootha Joyce, Bernard Archard and Glynn Edwards

When his Aunt Lucy (Flora Robson) is murdered in Pompeii, Tom Brett (David Hemmings) attempts to find out why. Because of Tom's past history of drug addiction, the authorities refuse to take him seriously. His suspicions entangle him in a web of complications which eventually lead to a nervous breakdown and an inconclusive ending. Based on a novel by John Bingham, the taut script was by Paul Dehn, who also served as associate producer. When director Richard Sarafian became indisposed, Dehn was also forced to take over as director on a number of scenes. Sarafian also tampered with Dehn's original finale, which accounts for the unsatisfying end result.

Video: None

117. *Frankenstein and the Monster from Hell*

A Hammer Film Production (1973); 99 minutes; Technicolor; U.S.: Paramount (1974); 93 minutes; Color by Movielab

P: Roy Skeggs; D: Terence Fisher; S: John Elder; M: James Bernard; DP: Brian Probyn; E: James Needs; AD: Scott MacGregor; Cast: Peter Cushing, Shane Briant, Madeline Smith, John Stratton, Bernard Lee, Clifford Mollison, David Prowse, Patrick Troughton, Charles Lloyd Pack, Christopher Cunningham, Peter Madden and Andrea Lawrence

This is the last of the Hammer films made in their true classic style and it is also Terence Fisher's final film. The cast and credits are a veritable "Who's Who" of Hammer alumni. Peter Cushing returns for his final turn as Baron Frankenstein, herein known as Dr. Victor, the supervising doctor of a lunatic asylum. Dr. Simon Heller (Shane Briant) is committed to the asylum for his unorthodox medical experiments but he is immediately engaged by Dr. Victor as an assistant. Heller quickly realizes the true identity of his benefactor and together they create Frankenstein's greatest botch job. Using

CHRISTINA (SUSAN DENBERG) TAKES HER REVENGE ON JOHANN (DEREK FOWLDS) IN *FRANKENSTEIN CREATED WOMAN*.

the body of a "neolithic throwback," the hands of a skilled woodcarver and the brain of a violin-playing mathematical genius, the result almost makes Frankenstein's first effort look good by comparison. Worst of all, Frankenstein then plans to have this grotesque brute mate with his pretty assistant, Sarah (Madeline Smith). Of course his plans go wildly wrong and the film ends with the ever-undaunted Baron speculating on future experiments. These would never come to pass as this turned out to be the finale to Hammer's Frankenstein series. In an attempt to keep up with then current trends, the film features some "grossout" gore effects and a fair amount of gallows humor.

Video: U.K./U.S.

118. Frankenstein Created Woman

A Hammer/Seven Arts Production (1967); 86 minutes; Technicolor; U.S.: 20th Century–Fox; DeLuxe Color

P: Anthony Nelson-Keys; **D:** Terence Fisher; **S:** John Elder; **M:** James Bernard; **DP:** Arthur Grant; **E:** James Needs and Spencer Reeve; **PD:** Bernard Robinson; **AD:** Don Mingaye; **Cast:** Peter Cushing, Susan Denberg, Thorley Walters, Robert Morris, Duncan Lamont, Peter Blythe, Barry Warren, Derek Fowlds, Peter Madden, Alan MacNaughton, Philip Ray and John Maxim

Baron Frankenstein's young assistant Hans (Robert Morris) loves Christina (Susan Denberg), the crippled and disfigured daughter of the local innkeeper. When Christina's father is murdered by a trio of obnoxious dandies, Hans is accused of the crime and executed. Distraught, Christina commits suicide. Frankenstein brings Christina back to life as a ravishingly beautiful blonde and transfers the soul of Hans into her body. Hans' soul drives Christina to take

Peter Cushing as Dr. Frankenstein in *Frankenstein Must Be Destroyed*.

revenge on the three men who caused his death.

This film was a title on Hammer's production schedule as far back as July 1958 when a *Variety* ad announced *The Hound of the Basskervilles* and *Frankenstein Created Woman* "in preparation." It took the project nearly a decade to come to fruition, but the end result turned out to be well worth the lengthy wait. Peter Cushing is excellent in his signature role, if a trifle more benevolent than usual. Susan Denberg, a former *Playboy* Playmate of the Year, is a stunning beauty who turns in a highly sympathetic performance as the tragic Christina. Contemporary reviews were mixed. *Variety* said, "The visual aspects of the film are considerably superior to the script," and *Films and Filming* stated, "Terence Fisher directs with his usual expertise, but in future let's have a token attempt at credibility, even in horror." The years have been kind and *Frankenstein Created Woman* is now one of the most venerated films from Britain's "Golden Age."

Video: U.K./U.S.

119. Frankenstein Must Be Destroyed

A Hammer Film Production (1969); 101 minutes; Technicolor; U.S.: Warner Bros–Seven Arts (1970); 97 minutes

P: Anthony Nelson-Keys; D: Terence Fisher; S: Bert Batt; M: James Bernard; DP: Arthur

Grant; **E:** Gordon Hales; **AD:** Bernard Robinson; **Cast:** Peter Cushing, Veronica Carlson, Simon Ward, Freddie Jones, Thorley Walters, Maxine Audley, George Pravda, Geoffrey Bayldon, Colette O'Neil, Harold Goodwin, Frank Middlemass and George Belbin

This is director Terence Fisher's most bleak and tragic vision of horror. It is also one of his greatest achievements and a high point in Hammer's Frankenstein series. Baron Frankenstein (Peter Cushing) blackmails a young couple (Veronica Carlson and Simon Ward) into assisting him with experiments involving brain transplants. Bert Batt, a Hammer assistant director, contributed an intricate and engrossing screenplay based on an original story that he coauthored with producer Anthony Nelson-Keys. Cushing plays the most cold-blooded Frankenstein of the entire series. His work is exemplary, as is that of the entire cast. Maxine Audley, in particular, is outstanding as the tormented wife of Frankenstein's latest victim-creation.

This was art director Bernard Robinson's final film for Hammer.

Video: U.K./U.S.

120. *Frankenstein: The True Story*

Universal Pictures Ltd. (1973); 122 minutes; Technicolor; U.S.: Television release; 180 minutes

P: Hunt Stromberg, Jr.; **D:** Jack Smight; **S:** Christopher Isherwood and Don Bachardy; **M:** Gil Melle; **DP:** Arthur Ibbetson; **E:** Richard Marder; **PD:** Wilfred Shingleton; **AD:** Fred Carter; **Cast:** James Mason, Leonard Whiting, David McCallum, Michael Sarrazin, Jane Seymour, Nicola Pagett, Michael Wilding, Clarissa Kaye, Agnes Moorehead, Margaret Leighton, Ralph Richardson and John Gielgud

This elaborate version of Mary Shelley's classic novel was released as a theatrical feature in Britain and was telecast as a two-part mini-series on NBC–TV in the United States. Touted at the time of its release as the most faithful adaptation of the book, it is actually no closer than previous versions, despite the Arctic finale.

There is a definite homosexual subtext, not too surprising considering that the script was written by Christopher Isherwood and his longtime companion Don Bachardy. Victor Frankenstein (Leonard Whiting) meets Henry Clerval (David McCallum) and the two doctors share lodgings while trying to work out the secrets of life. Victor's fiancée Elizabeth (Nicola Pagett) is understandably upset and tells him that he must choose between them. When Clerval dies of a heart attack, Victor decides to carry on their work alone. He creates an incredibly handsome man (Michael Sarrazin) and promptly moves him into his apartments. The two men share an idyllic life, looking for all the world like a couple of young lovers as they attend the opera and stroll in the park. Unfortunately, the features of the poor creature begin to deteriorate and Victor, disgusted, rejects him. The analogy to our modern world where physical appearance is of such major importance is not lost here. Victor's creation continues to love him nevertheless and in the end the two move toward each other for a final embrace before dying together in an avalanche. Jane Seymour deserves a mention for her chilling performance as the evil female creation Prima.

Video: U.S.

The Freak Maker see *The Mutations*

121. *Frenzy*

Universal (1972); 116 minutes; Technicolor

P/D: Alfred Hitchcock; **S:** Anthony Shaffer; **M:** Ron Goodwin; **DP:** Gilbert Taylor; **E:** John Jympson; **PD:** Sydney Cain; **AD:** Robert Laing; **Cast:** Jon Finch, Alec McCowen, Barry Foster, Billie Whitelaw, Anna Massey, Bernard Cribbins, Barbara Leigh-Hunt, Vivien Merchant, Clive Swift, Michael Bates, Jean Marsh and Gerald Sim

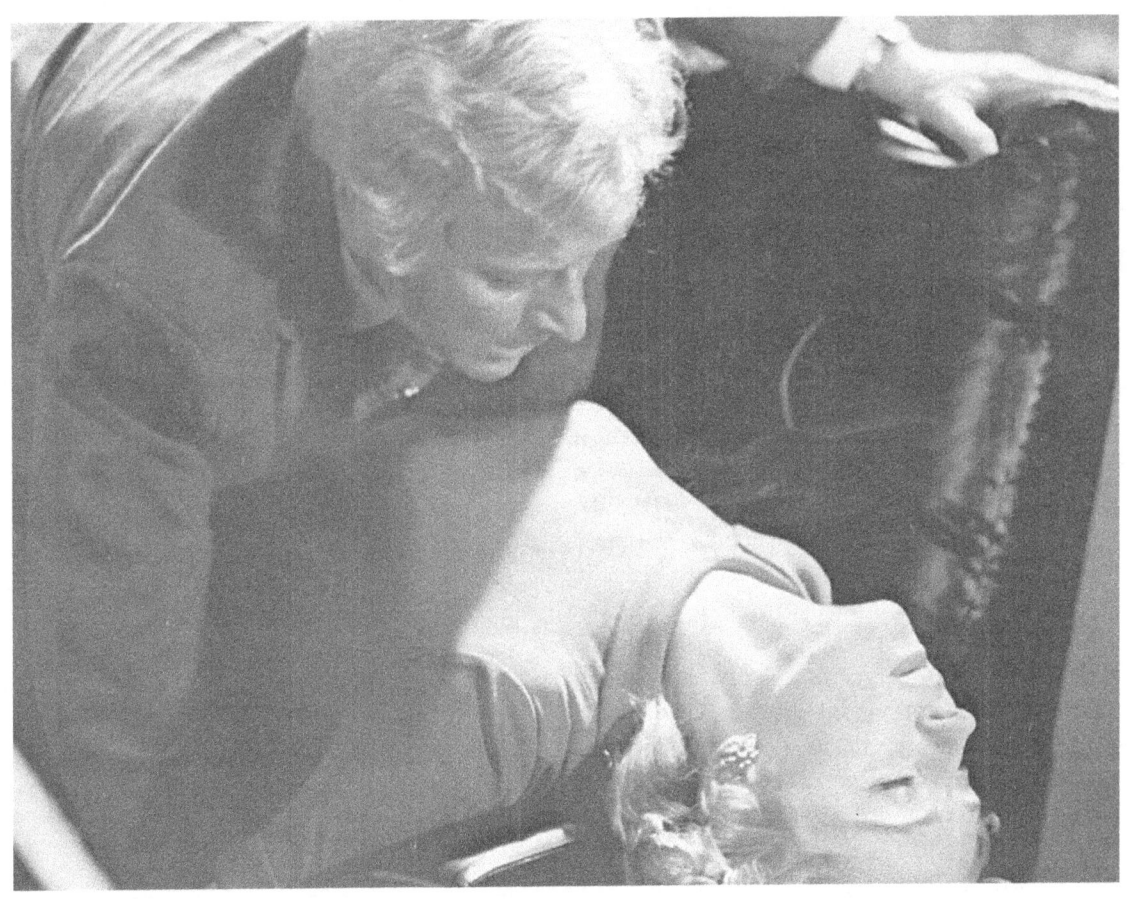

ONE OF THE MOST GHASTLY MURDER SCENES EVER FILMED: BARRY FOSTER AND BARBARA LEIGH-HUNT IN HITCHCOCK'S *FRENZY*.

For his fifty-second feature film, Alfred Hitchcock returned to the country of his birth. He had not made a motion picture in England for over 20 years. Once again Hitchcock uses the theme of an innocent man trapped by circumstances which make him appear to be guilty. In *Frenzy*, the "hero" (Jon Finch) is a surly fellow who is initially unsympathetic. On the other hand, the "villain" (Barry Foster) is an affable gent who just happens to be a sexual psychopath.

Eschewing a star cast of familiar faces, Hitchcock assembled a very talented group of ensemble performers (carefully chosen from the London stage) who more than do justice to Anthony Shaffer's clever script. There is a great deal of black humor but there is also one of the most grueling rape-murder scenes ever put on film. This scene is all the more shocking because of an extremely affecting performance by Barbara Leigh-Hunt as the unfortunate victim.

Henry Mancini was hired to compose the background music, but Hitchcock did not agree with Mancini's approach and the score was rejected. Ron Goodwin supplied the rather innocuous music that was finally used. With Hitchcock's two prior films, critics had suggested that the famous director had gone into decline, but *Frenzy* turned out to be a notable critical and financial success.

Video: U.K./U.S.

122. Fright

A Fantale Production (1971); 87 minutes; Eastman Color; U.S.: Allied Artists

P: Harry Fine and Michael Style; **D:** Peter Collinson; **S:** Tudor Gates; **M:** Harry Robinson; **DP:** Ian Wilson; **E:** Raymond Poulton; **PD:** Disley Jones; **Cast:** Susan George, Ian Bannen, Honor Blackman, John Gregson, George Cole, Dennis Waterman, Tara Collinson, Maurice Kaufmann, Michael Brennan and Roger Lloyd Pack

Fright is a precursor to the babysitter-in-peril movies which became prevalent in the late 70s with films such as *Halloween* (1978) and *When A Stranger Calls* (1979).

Susan George is Amanda, the mini-skirted babysitter who comes to a remote country house to take care of Tara (Tara Collinson) while his parents (Honor Blackman and George Cole) go out for a night on the town. Amanda doesn't know that Tara's real father is a homicidal maniac (Ian Bannen) who has just escaped from a mental institution. You can easily imagine the rest. *Fright* is a step down for the producing-writing team responsible for Hammer's excellent Karnstein series.

And why is Susan George always such an unsympathetic heroine?

Video: U.S.

123. Frightmare

A Peter Walker/Heritage Ltd. Production (1974); 86 minutes; Eastman Color; U.S.: Joseph Brenner Associates

EXP: Tony Tenser (uncredited); **P/D:** Peter Walker; **S:** David McGillvray; **M:** Stanley Myers; **DP:** Peter Jessop; **E:** Robert Dearberg; **AD:** Chris Burke; **Cast:** Rupert Davies, Sheila Keith, Deborah Fairfax, Paul Greenwood, Kim Butcher, Fiona Curzon, Jon Yule, Tricia Mortimer, Pamela Farbrother, Edward Kalinski, Leo Genn and Gerald Flood

In a black-and-white prologue set in 1957, a husband and wife are committed to an insane asylum for perpetrating a series of heinous murders. Fifteen years later, Dorothy Yates (Sheila Keith) and her husband Edmund (Rupert Graves) are pronounced sane and released. They move into an isolated farmhouse where Dorothy begins to show signs of reverting to her previous mental condition, which is Pathological Cannibalism. Edmund's daughter by a previous marriage attempts to help and keeps their daughter Debbie (the aptly named Kim Butcher) ignorant of her parents' existence. Dorothy's compulsions drive her to kill again and again to obtain the human flesh she craves and it becomes increasingly difficult for all involved to conceal her crimes. This time around Peter Walker directs with no bare breasts in sight but gallons of Kensington gore on view. Sheila Keith is wonderful in her most deranged role ever.

Video: U.S. (video title: *Frightmare II*)

Frightmare II see *Frightmare*

124. From Beyond the Grave

An Amicus Production (1973); 98 minutes; Technicolor; U.S.: Howard Mahler Films Inc. (1975)

P: Max J. Rosenberg and Milton Subotsky; **D:** Kevin Connor; **S:** Robin Clarke and Raymond Christodoulou; **M:** Douglas Gamley; **DP:** Alan Hume; **E:** John Ireland; **PD:** Maurice Carter; **AD:** Bert Davey; **Cast:** Peter Cushing, Ian Bannen, Ian Carmichael, Diana Dors, Margaret Leighton, Donald Pleasence, Nyree Dawn Porter, David Warner, Angela Pleasence, Ian Ogilvy, Lesley-Anne Down and Wendy Allnutt

Peter Cushing is the proprietor of an antique shop called Temptations Ltd. Four seperate stories show the fates of the customers who sometimes try to cheat him. The basis for these stories is the work of author R. Chetwynd-Hayes.

In the first, David Warner purchases a mirror which imprisons an evil spirit who demands blood sacrifices. The second has

IAN OGLIVY AND LESLEY-ANNE DOWN PURCHASE AN ANTIQUE DOOR WITH TERRIFYING CONSEQUENCES IN *FROM BEYOND THE GRAVE*.

Ian Bannen as an unhappy husband who becomes involved with a young woman who practices witchcraft. The standout is the third tale featuring a hilarious performance by Margaret Leighton as a medium who tries to remove the invisible spirit of a malevolent demon from Ian Carmichael's shoulder. In the final episode, Ian Ogilvy buys a seventeeth century door which, when installed in his flat, leads to a mysterious blue room in the past. This was the last omnibus film to be produced by Amicus. Warner Bros. was originally set to distribute it in 1973 but instead it was shelved until an independent company picked it up for release two years later.

In 1980, Milton Subotsky produced *The Monster Club*, another anthology film based on the works of R. Chetwynd-Hayes.

Video: U.S.

125. *The Frozen Dead*

A Goldstar Production (1966); 95 minutes; Eastman Color; U.S.: Seven Arts (1967); Black-and-White

P/D/S: Herbert J. Leder; **M:** Don Banks; **DP:** David Boulton; **E:** Tom Simpson; **AD:** Scott MacGregor; **Cast:** Dana Andrews, Anna Palk, Philip Gilbert, Kathleen Breck, Karl Stepanek, Alan Tilvern, Basil Henson, Tom Chatto, Oliver McGreevy, John Moore, Charles Wade and Edward Fox

A totally weird film which is yet another entry in the "living head" subgenre.

Dr. Norberg (Dana Andrews) is a Nazi scientist who is attempting to revive frozen Nazis in a plan to restore the Third Reich. Although he has been able to resuscitate his subjects, they all suffer from severe brain damage. Enter Norberg's niece Jean (Anna Palk) and her friend Elsa (Kathleen Breck). Norberg's overzealous assistant murders Elsa and the doctor keeps her severed head alive. He removes the top of the skull and replaces it with a plastic dome in order to observe the brain. Jean becomes suspicious of her friend's disappearance and begins to snoop around the mansion. She discovers a veritable chamber of horrors which includes a gallery of frozen Nazis, a wall of living dismembered arms and the head of Elsa. The head, bathed in a hideous blue light and whispering "Bury me," is a truly chilling sight. A young Edward Fox plays one of the doctor's unsuccessful experiments.

Video: None

126. *Full Circle*

A United Kingdom/Canadian Official Co-Production; Fetter Productions/Classic Film Industries Ltd. (1976); 96 minutes; Technicolor and Panavision; U.S. *(The Haunting of Julia)*: Discovery Films (1981)

EXP: Julian Melzack; **P:** Peter Fetterman and Alfred Pariser; **D:** Richard Loncraine; **S:** Dave Humphries; **M:** Colin Towns; **DP:** Peter Hannon; **E:** Ron Wisman; **AD:** Brian Morris; **Cast:** Mia Farrow, Keir Dullea, Tom Conti, Robin Gammell, Jill Bennett, Cathleen Nesbitt, Peter Sallis, Mary Morris, Pauline Jameson, Anna Wing, Sophie Ward and Nigel Havers

A dark and depressing "art house" horror film adapted from the novel *Julia* by Peter Straub. When her young daughter Kate dies tragically, Julia (Mia Farrow) suffers a nervous breakdown and must be hospitalized. Upon her release, Julia leaves her unfeeling husband (Keir Dullea) and buys an old house in Kensington. Shortly after moving in, Julia allows a séance to be held in her new home and the medium tells her that she senses the presence of a dead child. Julia at first believes it is the spirit of Kate but she learns that 30 years before an evil little girl named Olivia died in the house. Most everyone Julia comes into contact with dies, but it is inconclusive at the end whether Julia or Olivia is the killer. Is Julia insane or is there really a malevolent ghost? Does anybody really care?

Video: U.S.

127. *The Full Treatment*

A Falcon Film Production (1961); 109 minutes; MegaScope; U.S. *(Stop Me Before I Kill!)*: Columbia 93 minutes

P/D: Val Guest; **S:** Val Guest and Ronald Scott Thorn; **M:** Stanley Black; **DP:** Gilbert Taylor; **E:** Bill Lenny; **AD:** Tony Masters; **Cast:** Claude Dauphin, Diane Cilento, Ronald Lewis, Francoise Rosay, Bernard Braden, Katya Douglas, Barbara Chilcott, Ann Tirard, Edwin Styles and George Merritt

While on their honeymoon, Denise (Diane Cilento) and Alan (Ronald Lewis) Colby have an automobile accident. After the accident, Alan begins to experience murderous impulses directed toward his wife. Following his attempt to strangle Denise, Alan enlists the help of Dr. Prade (Claude Dauphin), a psychiatrist. Prade subjects Alan to "the full treatment" and eventually convinces him that he did indeed murder his wife. Alan runs away but later discovers that Denise is alive and Prade is her lover.

Falcon Films was a subsidiary of Hammer and, like *The Snorkel*, this film anticipates their series of "mini–Hitchcocks" which began with *Taste of Fear* the same year. Ronald Lewis was a very fine but extremely underrated actor. He also appeared for Hammer in *Taste of Fear* and *The Brigand of Kandahar* (1965) as well as such diverse films as William Castle's *Mr. Sardonicus* and Robert Wise's *Helen of Troy*.

Video: None

128. The Gamma People

Warwick Films (1955); 79 minutes; U.S.: Columbia (1956)

P: John Gossage; **D:** John Gilling; **S:** John Gilling and John Gossage; **M:** George Melachrino; **DP:** Ted Moore; **E:** Alan Osbiston and Jack Slade; **AD:** John Box; **Cast:** Paul Douglas, Eva Bartok, Leslie Phillips, Walter Rilla, Philip Leaver, Martin Miller, Michael Caridia, Pauline Drewett, Jackie Lane, Olaf Pooley, Rosalie Crutchley and Leonard Sachs

A reporter (Paul Douglas) and photographer (Leslie Phillips), en route to the Salzburg Music Festival, are sidetracked when their railway coach ends up in the tiny country of Gudavia. A scientist named Boronski (Walter Rilla) is conducting experiments on the Gudavian children which alter their intelligence, for better or worse. As a result, many of the youngsters are either precocious and super-intelligent or mindless zombies called Goons. The two intruders take it upon themselves to assist the townspeople in overthrowing the dictatorship of Boronski and attempt to return Gudavia to the quaint European locale it once was.

The Gamma People is a second-rate effort, mainly of interest as an early example of British science fiction and Communist paranoia. Douglas and Phillips overplay their parts badly, making much of the film seem like a parody.

Video: U.S.

129. Ghost Ship

An Abtcon Pictures–Merton Park Studios Ltd. Production (1952); 69 minutes; U.S.: A Herman Cohen Presentation; A Lippert Pictures Release (1953)

P/D: Vernon Sewell; **S:** Vernon Sewell and Philip Thornton; **M:** Eric Spear; **DP:** Stanley Grant; **E:** Francis Bieber; **AD:** George Haslam; **Cast:** Dermot Walsh, Hazel Court, Hugh Burden, John Robinson, Joss Ambler, Joan Carol, Hugh Latimer, Mignon O'Doherty, Joss Ackland, Ian Carmichael, Ewen Solon, Patricia Owens, Laidman Browne and Melissa Stribling

This was director Vernon Sewell's fourth of five screen adaptations of the same narrative. His first version was *The Medium* in 1934 and the last was *House of Mystery* in 1961. This rendition takes place aboard a haunted ship, presumably because Sewell owned the yacht which provided an inexpensive location for filming. A young couple (real-life husband-and-wife Dermot Walsh and Hazel Court) buy a yacht but are warned that the ship has an unpleasant reputation. The original owner and two other people vanished mysteriously and subsequent owners have complained of strange disturbances.

The husband dismisses the stories as nonsense but, despite his skepticism, he witnesses a ghostly manifestation in the engine room. His wife contacts a psychic investigator (Hugh Burden) who brings in a spiritual medium. Through the medium, they learn that the original owner murdered his wife and her lover and hid their bodies aboard the ship. Although the acting is good, the film suffers from the restraint common to most British horror films in this pre–Hammer period. The best reason for watching is to see lovely Hazel Court in the first of many genre appearances.

Video: U.S.

130. Ghost Story

Stephen Weeks Company Ltd (1974); 89 minutes; Fujicolor; U.S.: No theatrical release

P/D: Stephen Weeks; **S:** Philip Norman, Rosemary Sutcliff and Stephen Weeks; **M:** Ron Geesin; **DP:** Peter Hurst; **E:** John Costelloe; **AD:** Peter Young; **Cast:** Marianne Faithfull, Leigh Lawson, Larry Dann, Anthony Bate, Sally Grace, Penelope Keith, Vivian Mackerell, Murray Melvin and Barbara Shelley

In 1930, three young gentlemen go to a huge country estate for a holiday. One of

story goes but director Weeks manages to stretch it out for nearly 90 minutes and still hold your interest. Unfortunately, that wonderful actress Barbara Shelley is totally wasted in her thankless role as the asylum matron.

Video: U.S. (video title: *Madhouse Mansion*)

131. The Ghoul

A Gaumont–British Production (1933) 80 minutes; U.S.: Gaumont–British Pictures

P: Michael Balcon; **D:** T. Hayes Hunter; **S:** Roland Pertwee and John Hastings Turner; **Musical Director:** Louis Levy; **DP:** Gunther Krampf; **E:** Ian Dalrymple; **AD:** Alfred Junge; **Cast:** Boris Karloff, Cedric Hardwicke, Ernest Thesiger, Anthony Bushell, Ralph Richardson, Dorothy Hyson, Kathleen Harrison, Harold Huth, Jack Raine and D.A. Clarke-Smith

Prof. Morlant (Boris Karloff) is an Egyptologist who has surrounded himself with artifacts of ancient Egypt. On his deathbed he makes his butler (Ernest Thesiger) promise that he will be buried with a jewel called "The Eternal Light" in his hand. Morlant believes that at the first full moon after his death, he will be revived and that the jewel will give him immortality if he places it in the hand of a statue of the god Anubis. Morlant dies and the butler steals the jewel. Morlant does come back from the dead and is less than happy to find the jewel gone.

Boris Karloff returned his homeland as a star and appeared in this mixture of elements from *The Mummy* and *The Old Dark House*, which was based on a novel by Frank King. Director T. Hayes Hunter was an

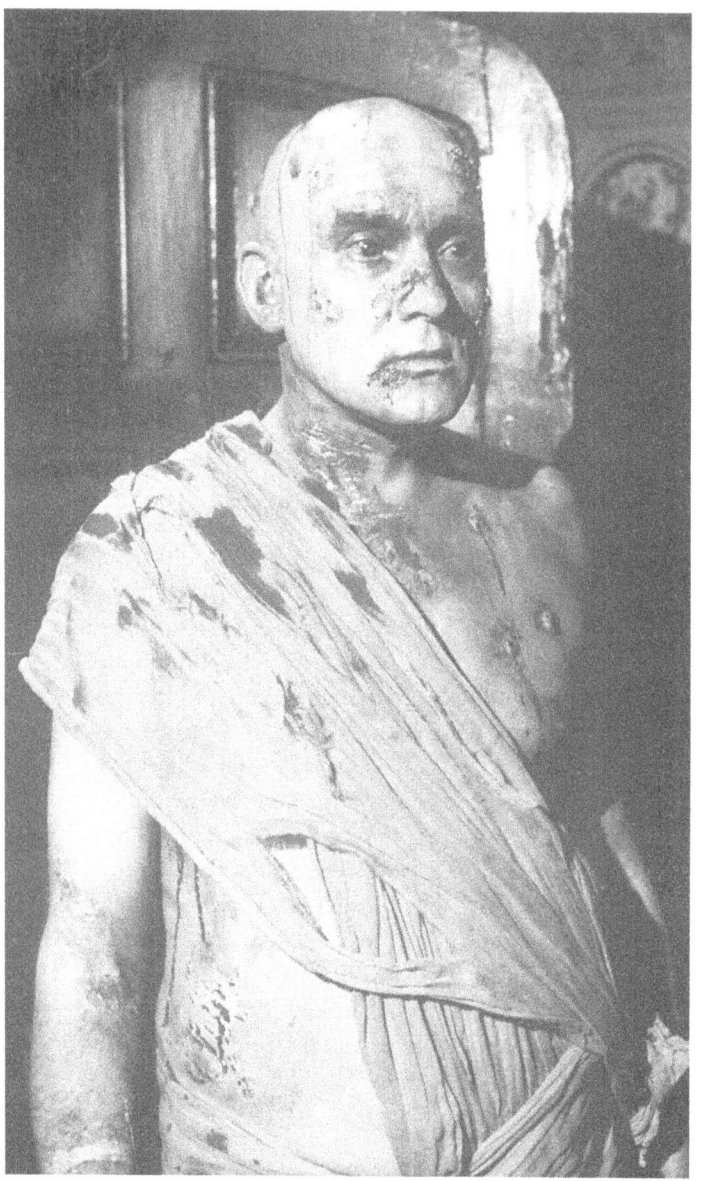

DON HENDERSON AS *THE GHOUL*.

them is Mr. Talbot (Larry Dann), who begins to have glimpses of events that happened in the house many years before. A young girl named Sophy (Marianne Faithfull) was wrongfully committed by her brother (Leigh Lawson) to an insane asylum. When the asylum inmates escape, Sophy returns to the house and stabs her brother to death. That's about all there is as far as

American who had gone to Britain following an undistinguished Hollywood career. Considered the first British horror movie of the sound era, *The Ghoul* was thought to be a lost film for many years. A 35mm print was eventually found in Prague and restored for video release.

Video: U.K./U.S.

132. The Ghoul

A Tyburn Film Production (1975); 88 minutes; Eastman Color; U.S.: No theatrical release

P: Kevin Francis; **D:** Freddie Francis; **S:** John Elder; **M:** Harry Robinson; **DP:** John Wilcox; **E:** Henry Richardson; **AD:** Jack Shampan and Peter Williams; **Cast:** Peter Cushing, John Hurt, Veronica Carlson, Alexandra Bastedo, Gwen Watford, Stewart Bevan, Ian McCulloch and Don Henderson

Tyburn's second production is marginally better than their first, *Persecution*. The story is set in the 1920s, for no apparent reason other than to make use of sets, props and costumes left over from *The Great Gatsby*. Madcap flapper Daphne (Veronica Carlson) instigates a car race which leaves her and her companion stranded and in need of gas. Daphne ends up at the house of Dr. Lawrence (Peter Cushing), a former clergyman who offers her shelter. That night she is stabbed to death by Dr. Lawrence's son, the victim of a Hindu curse which has turned him into a ghoul who lives on human flesh. Despite the involvement of so many Hammer personnel, Tyburn's productions always somehow seem to miss the mark. The story is reminiscent of Hammer's *The Reptile*, but far less effective in every instance.

Video: U.K./U.S.

The Giant Behemoth see ***Behemoth, the Sea Monster***

Girly see ***Mumsy, Nanny, Sonny and Girly***

133. The Golden Voyage of Sinbad

A Charles H. Schneer Production (1973); 105 minutes; Color and Dynarama; U.S.: Columbia

P: Charles H. Schneer and Ray Harryhausen; **D:** Gordon Hessler; **S:** Brian Clemens; **M:** Miklos Rozsa; **DP:** Ted Moore; **E:** Roy Watts; **PD:** John Stoll; **AD:** Fernando Gonzalez; **SVE:** Ray Harryhausen; **Cast:** John Phillip Law, Caroline Munro, Tom Baker, Douglas Wilmer, Martin Shaw, Gregorie Aslan, Kurt Christian, Takis Emmanuel, John D. Garfield, Aldo Sambrel and Fernando Poggi

After the failure of their 1969 dinosaur film *The Valley of Gwangi*, Charles Schneer and Ray Harryhausen decided to return to an early source of inspiration. In 1958, *The Seventh Voyage of Sinbad* had been a big success. It had led them down the path to producing the color fantasies that became their trademark.

Although *The Golden Voyage* of Sinbad lacks the charm of the earlier film, it is an exciting adventure filled with memorable stop-motion sequences. In the best of these, a six-armed statue of the goddess Kali comes to life to duel with Sinbad. The plot is similar to that of the previous Sinbad movie. Once again an evil magician fights against Sinbad to possess a powerful talisman (in the first film it is a magic lamp, here it is a golden amulet). Obviously, the story doesn't count for all that much in a film of this type. The special effects are what everyone wants to see and Harryhausen certainly doesn't disappoint. Reviews were somewhat unenthusiastic. *Variety* called it "a potboiler for the kids" and further stated, "As anachronistic entertainment…the Columbia release could prove a sales challenge in some areas." They couldn't have been more wrong. Two months later, in the article "Schneer's *Sinbad* Features Help Ferry Columbia to Gold Mines," it was stated that *The Golden Voyage of Sinbad* had already grossed more than

STOP-MOTION ANIMATION BY WILLIS O'BRIEN AND PETE PETERSON IS THE HIGHLIGHT OF *BEHEMOTH, THE SEA MONSTER* (A.K.A. *THE GIANT BEHEMOTH*).

$12,000,000. It was so successful that another Sinbad adventure was planned. *Sinbad and the Eye of the Tiger* was released in 1977 but it did not duplicate the fortunes of its predecessors. The script is uninvolving and even Ray Harryhausen's creations lack his usual inspiration.

Video: U.K./U.S.

134. Gorgo

A King Brothers Production (1961); 76 minutes; Technicolor; U.S.: Metro-Goldwyn-Mayer

P: Frank King and Maurice King; **D:** Eugene Lourie; **S:** John Loring and Daniel Hyatt; **M:** Angelo Francisco Lavagnino; **DP:** F.A. Young; **E:** Eric Boyd-Perkins; **AD:** Elliot Scott; **SVE:** Tom Howard; **Cast:** Bill Travers, William Sylvester, Vincent Winter, Bruce Seton, Joseph O'Connor, Martin Benson, Berry Keegan, Dervis Ward, Christopher Rhodes, Basil Dignam and Maurice Kaufmann

Britain's answer to Godzilla is a colorful and exciting motion picture featuring what is arguably the best "man in a dinosaur suit" monster on film.

Searching for sunken treasure off the coast of Ireland, Joe Ryan (Bill Travers) and Sam Slade (William Sylvester) find an enormous amphibious dinosaur instead. Reasoning that this may be even more profitable than gold, they capture the beast and transport it back to London. They name the monster Gorgo and put it on display in the Battersea Park fun fair. Scientists study Gorgo and come to the conclusion that it is an infant (albeit a large one) whose parents would be over 200 feet tall. Concurrently, Gorgo's mother surfaces and cuts a path of destruction through London in search of her baby. Two unique elements set *Gorgo* apart from other films of this type; there is no superfluous love interest, and the monsters triumph over man, returning to the sea unharmed in the end.

Video: U.K./U.S.

135. The Gorgon

A Hammer Film Production (1964); 83 minutes; Technicolor
U.S.: Columbia; Eastman Color by Pathe

P: Anthony Nelson-Keys; **D:** Terence Fisher; **S:** John Gilling; **M:** James Bernard; **DP:** Michael Reed; **E:** James Needs and Eric Boyd-Perkins; **PD:** Bernard Robinson; **AD:** Don Mingaye; **Cast:** Peter Cushing, Christopher Lee, Barbara Shelley, Richard Pasco, Michael Goodliffe, Patrick Troughton, Jack Watson, Jeremy Longhurst, Toni Gilpin, Redmond Phillips, Michael Peake and Prudence Hyman

THE GODDESS KALI COMES TO LIFE COURTESY OF RAY HARRYHAUSEN'S SPECIAL EFFECTS MAGIC IN *THE GOLDEN VOYAGE OF SINBAD*.

The village of Vandorf is haunted by the evil spirit of Magaera, a Gorgon whose gaze turns people into stone. When his brother and father die mysteriously, Paul Heitz (Richard Pasco) goes to Vandorf to discover the actual cause of their deaths. Paul meets a beautiful woman named Carla (Barbara Shelley) who is jealously guarded by the local doctor, Namaroff (Peter Cushing). After Paul sees a reflection of the Gorgon and is hospitalized, his friend Prof. Meister (Christopher Lee) comes to Vandorf to help unravel the mystery.

Terence Fisher made a triumphant return to Hammer with this stylish production. The company added a new monster to their inventory, this time turning to Greek mythology for their inspiration. By now, Hammer had become a recognized name in the film industry. Critic Dave McIntyre, reviewing for the *San Diego Evening Tribune* wrote: "*The Gorgon* is the work of the Hammer Film Company, which in England seem to be to horror what the Old Vic is to Shakespeare."

Video: U.K./U.S.

The Graveyard see **Persecution**

An irate parent destroys London as she searches for her baby *Gorgo*.

136. *Grip of the Stangler*

A Producers Associates/Amalgamated Production (1957); 81 minutes; U.S. *(The Haunted Strangler)*: Metro-Goldwyn-Mayer (1958)

EXP: Richard Gordon; **P:** John Croydon; **D:** Robert Day; **S:** Jan Read and John C. Cooper; **M:** Buxton Orr; **DP:** Lionel Banes; **E:** Peter Mayhew; **AD:** John Elphick; **Cast:** Boris Karloff, Jean Kent, Elizabeth Allan, Anthony Dawson, Derek Birch, Vera Day, Tim Turner, Diane Aubrey, Dorothy Gordon, Peggy Ann Clifford, Leslie Perrins and Roy Russell

This was the first film to come out of Richard Gordon's newly formed company, Producers Associates. Boris Karloff brought the project to Gordon. It was originally entitled *Stranglehold*, and had been specifically written for Karloff by Jan Read. In 1880, a London novelist (Karloff) becomes obsessed with his research into a 20-year-old series of murders committed by a vicious killer known as the Haymarket Strangler. His discoveries become the catalyst for another killing spree in a shockingly similar mode. Karloff gives one of the finest (and most energetic) performances of his later career and director Robert Day skillfully recreates the more unpleasant aspects of Victorian England, particularly in the asylum sequences.

Video: U.S.

137. *The Hand of Night*

Associated British Pathe Ltd. (1966); 73 minutes; Technicolor; U.S. *(Beast of Morocco)*: American–International

P: Harry Field; **D:** Frederic Goode; **S:** Bruce

Stewart; **M:** Joan Shakespeare; **DP:** William Jordan; **E:** John Blair and Frederick Ives; **AD:** Peter Moll; **Cast:** William Sylvester, Diane Clare, Alizia Gur, Edward Underdown, Terence de Marney, William Dexter, Sylvia Marriott, Avril Sadler, Angela Lovell, Maria Hallowi and the Boscoe Holder Dancers

After the deaths of his wife and children in an automobile accident, Paul Carver (William Sylvester) journeys to Morocco to try and forget his anguish. There he becomes involved with a beautiful woman named Marisa (Alizia Gur). She uses his death wish to draw him into the Servants of the Night, the cult of mystical vampires which she leads. Fighting to save his soul is Chantal (Diane Clare), who tries to lead him out of the darkness and back to the world of the living. This extremely surrealistic film attempts to provide new angles on the vampire legend and occasionally succeeds.

Video: U.K.

138. The Hands of Orlac (a.k.a. Hands of the Strangler)

A Pendennis Film Production (1960); 95 minutes; U.S.: Continental (1961); 77 minutes

PRUDENCE HYMAN AS MEGERA *THE GORGON* WHO CAN TURN PEOPLE INTO STONE WITH A GLANCE.

P: Steven Pallos and Donald Taylor; **D:** Edmond T. Greville; **S:** John Baines and Edmond T. Greville; **M:** Claude Bolling; **DP:** Desmond Dickinson; **E:** Oswald Hafenrichter; **AD:** John Blezard; **Cast:** Mel Ferrer, Christopher Lee, Dany Carrel, Lucile Saint Simon, Felix Aylmer, Basil Sydney, Donald Wolfit, Donald Pleasence, David Peel, Peter Reynolds, Campbell Singer and Janina Faye

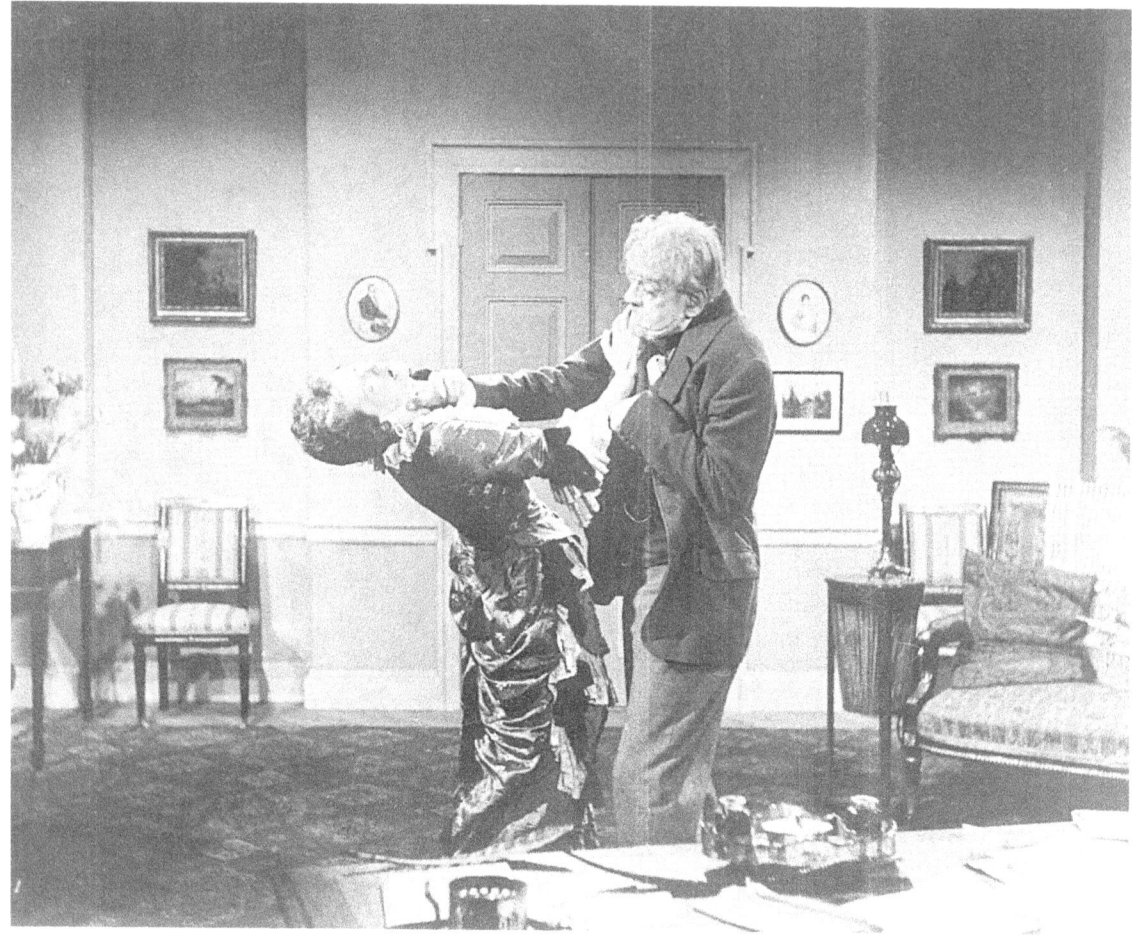

Boris Karloff has the *Grip of the Strangler* on Elizabeth Allen.

Stephen Orlac (Mel Ferrer) is a famous concert pianist. After his hands are badly burned in an airplane crash, he suspects that the hands of an executed strangler have been grafted onto him. Christopher Lee is a standout as Nero, a would-be extortionist who preys on Orlac's fears that the hands have a will of their own. David Peel (Hammer's "Baron Meinster") is glimpsed, all too briefly, as the airplane pilot. This uninspired third filming of Maurice Renard's novel in no way approaches the delirious heights achieved in the 1935 MGM version, *Mad Love*. A French–language version was shot simultaneously and runs 105 minutes.

Video: U.S.

139. Hands of the Ripper

A Hammer Film Production (1971); 85 minutes; Technicolor; U.S.: Universal (1972); 82 minutes

P: Aida Young; D: Peter Sasdy; S: L.W. Davidson; M: Christopher Gunning; DP: Kenneth Talbot; E: Chris Barnes; AD: Roy Stannard; Cast: Eric Porter, Angharad Rees, Jane Merrow, Keith Bell, Derek Godfrey, Dora Bryan, Marjorie Rhodes, Lynda Baron, Marjie Lawrence, Norman Bird, Margaret Rawlings and Katya Wyeth

Dr. Prichard (Eric Porter), a psychiatrist, rescues a young woman named Anna (Angharad Rees) from an unscrupulous medium and takes her into his home. A hor-

Frankie Avalon and friends make an unpleasant discovery in *The Haunted House of Horror*.

rifying chain of events leads him to suspect that she may be the daughter of the infamous killer Jack the Ripper. Peter Sasdy's final feature for Hammer is also his best, a near-perfect combination of pathos and horror. Anna commits the most gruesome murders but, because of Angharad Rees' sensitive performance, she never loses the sympathy of the audience. Porter is also excellent as the well-intentioned (but essentially misguided) doctor. The tragic finale is set in the Whispering Gallery of St. Paul's Cathedral, an effective set piece for the climax to a superior motion picture.
Video: U.K./U.S.

Hands of the Strangler see *The Hands of Orlac*

140. The Haunted House of Horror (a.k.a. *The Dark*)

A Tigon–British Film Production (1969); 92 minutes; Color by Movielab; U.S. *(Horror House)*: American–International (1970); 79 minutes

EXP: Tony Tenser; **D/S:** Michael Armstrong; **M:** Reg Tilsely; **DP:** Jack Atchelor; **E:** Peter Pitt; **AD:** Hayden Pearce; **Cast:** Frankie Avalon, Jill Haworth, Dennis Price, George Sewell, Mark Wynter, Gina Warwick, Richard O'Sullivan, Carol Dilworth, Julian Barnes, Veronica Doran, Robin Stewart and Jan Holden

A short film starring David Bowie brought young director Michael Armstrong to the attention of Tigon executive Tony Tensor, who hired him to direct his first feature for the company. Armstrong wrote and

JULIE HARRIS AS THE TORMENTED ELEANOR IN *THE HAUNTING*.

directed a haunted house thriller called *The Dark*. When the results were shown to AIP's top man in England, Louis M. Heyward, he was unhappy with what he saw. Heyward brought in Frankie Avalon and then rewrote the script to accommodate him as the lead. He then turned the project over to director Gerry Levy, who shot the new material. Heyward may have been unhappy with the original version, but the end product seems to please no one, least of all Michael Armstrong. A gang of bored swingers decide to visit an old haunted house located outside of London. Once there, they hold the inevitable séance and then, in typical horror movie fashion, go their separate ways to stay in rooms throughout the house. One of the young men is brutally slashed to death. After discovering the body, the survivors hide the corpse and flee the house. When the dead man is reported as a missing person, the group discovers that they are still very much enmeshed in the events surrounding the murder.

Video: None

The Haunted Strangler see ***Grip of the Strangler***

141. *The Haunting*

An Argyle Enterprises Picture; A Robert Wise Production (1963); 112 minutes; Panavision; U.S.: Metro–Goldwyn–Mayer

P/D: Robert Wise; **S:** Nelson Gidding; **M:** Humphrey Searle; **DP:** David Boulton; **E:** Ernest Walter; **PD:** Elliott Scott; **SVE:** Tom Howard;

Cast: Julie Harris, Claire Bloom, Richard Johnson, Russ Tamblyn, Fay Compton, Rosalie Crutchley, Lois Maxwell, Valentine Dyall, Diane Clare, Ronald Adam, Howard Lang and Paul Maxwell

Anthropologist Dr. John Markway (Richard Johnson) assembles a research team to investigate Hill House, a reportedly haunted Gothic New England mansion. The interactions and personal dramas of the group's members become enmeshed with the psychic phenomena they experience, suggesting that their own troubled psyches are the catalyst for the evil forces within the house. At the time of its release, this adaptation of Shirley Jackson's classic novel *The Haunting of Hill House* was the ultimate example of the "sophisticated" horror film. By today's standards it is a bit plodding and short on thrills, but still manages to evoke some uneasy sensations.

Video: U.K./U.S.

The Haunting of Julia see *Full Circle*

142. The Headless Ghost

A Merton Park Studios Ltd. Production (1959); 63 minutes; DyaliScope; U.S.: American–International

EXP: Herman Cohen; P: Jack Greenwood; D: Peter Graham Scott; S: Kenneth Langtry and Herman Cohen; M: Gerard Schurmann; DP: John Wiles; E: Bernard Gribble; AD: Wilfred Arnold; Cast: Richard Lyon, Liliane Sottane, David Rose, Clive Revill, Jack Allen, Alexander Archdale, Carl Bernard, Josephine Blake, John Stacy, Donald Bisset and Janina Faye

Three foreign exchange students in England go on a tour of Ambrose Castle. Intrigued by the castle's reputation for being haunted, they decide to hide away and spend the night to try and discover if there really are any ghosts. The trio get more than they bargained for when they are recruited into aiding the ghost of a decapitated nobleman who wishes to be reunited with his head. The opening cartoon credits are a tip-off that this is not going to be the fright fest implied by the advertising.

Actually, this was a hastily assembled production made to comply with American–International's demand for a companion feature to the truly terrifying *Horrors of the Black Museum*. With a running time of only 63 minutes, *The Headless Ghost* is too brief to be offensive.

Video: U.S.

Honeymoon of Fear see *Fear in the Night*

143. Horror Express (a.k.a. Panic in the Trans-Siberian Train)

A Granada/Benmar Production (1972); 88 minutes; Eastman Color; U.S.: Scotia International (1973)

P: Bernard Gordon; D: Gene (Eugenio) Martin; S: Arnaud D'Usseau and Julian Halevy; M: John Cacavas; DP: Alejandro Ulloa; E: Ramiro Gomez; AD: Robert Dearberg; Cast: Christopher Lee, Peter Cushing, Telly Savalas, Alberto de Mendoza, Silvia Tortosa, Jorge Riguad, Helga Line, Angel de Pozo, Julio Pena and Jose Jaspe

This Spanish-British coproduction has enough plot elements for five motion pictures but manages to bring them all together successfully. In 1906, Prof. Alex Caxton (Christopher Lee) leads an expedition to a remote area of China. There he discovers the body of a prehistoric man-like creature frozen in ice. He attempts to transport it back to England aboard the Trans-Siberian Express, but the creature thaws out and returns to life. When it causes the bizzare deaths of several passengers, Caxton and a rival scientist (Peter Cushing) deduce that an alien life form arrived on Earth millions of years ago and inhabited the body of the neanderthal. Telly Savalas makes a mercifully brief appearance as a crazed Cossack who tries to take over the train. The claustrophobic feeling of being trapped aboard a moving train with a deadly monster is used effectively. The miniature train effects are generally quite good (the train was left over from the big-budget film *Nicholas and Alexandra*).

Video: U.K./U.S.

144. Horror Hospital

A Richard Gordon–Antony Balch–Noteworthy Films Ltd. Production (1973); 91 minutes; Eastman Color; U.S.: Hallmark; 88 minutes

P: Richard Gordon; **D:** Antony Balch; **S:** Antony Balch and Alan Watson; **M:** De Wolfe; **DP:** David McDonald; **E:** Robert Dearberg; **AD:** David Bill; **Cast:** Michael Gough, Robin Askwith, Vanessa Shaw, Ellen Pollock, Skip Martin, Kurt Christian, Barbara Wendy, Kenneth Benda, Martin Grace, Colin Skeaping, George Herbert and Dennis Price

Jason (Robin Askwith), a young songwriter, decides to take a vacation from the music industry at a rest clinic in the country. During the train ride there, Jason meets Judy (Vanessa Shaw). She is going to the clinic to visit her Aunt Harris (Ellen Pollock), a former brothel keeper who is now married to Dr. Storm (Michael Gough), the head of the clinic.

Upon arrival, it is quite obvious to Jason and Judy that all is not quite right. At dinner they are surrounded by speechless zombies; later, blood flows from the tap in their sink. This is only the beginning of a series of strange incidents that culminate with the revelation that Dr. Storm is performing brain operations on humans, turning them into robots who obey his every whim. A gory, dreary affair that only Michael Gough manages to rise above, *Horror Hospital* tries for a combination of laughs and terror but misses the mark on both counts. With his long hair, sideburns, scrawny physique and hip-hugging bell bottom trousers, Robin Askwith is the epitome of 70s cool. Dennis Price does a memorable comic turn as a lecherous travel agent.

Video: U.K./U.S. (alternate U.S. video title: *Computer Killers*)

Horror Hotel see *City of the Dead*

Horror House see *The Haunted House of Horror*

Horror of Dracula see *Dracula*

145. The Horror of Frankenstein

A Hammer Film Production (1970); 95 minutes; Technicolor; U.S.: American Continental (1971)

P/D: Jimmy Sangster; **S:** Jeremy Burnham and Jimmy Sangster; **M:** Malcolm Williamson; **DP:** Moray Grant; **E:** Chris Barnes; **AD:** Scott MacGregor; **Cast:** Ralph Bates, Kate O'Mara, Veronica Carlson, Graham James, Bernard Archard, Dennis Price, Joan Rice, David Prowse, Jon Finch, James Hayter, Stephen Turner and James Cossins

It's back to the beginning as young Baron Frankenstein (Ralph Bates) attempts to bring life to a man he has created from corpses. This is a rather ill-advised "black comedy" remake of *The Curse of Frankenstein*, featuring Jimmy Sangster's debut as a director for Hammer. Realizing that Peter Cushing couldn't go on playing Frankenstein forever, Hammer attempted to launch a new series starring Ralph Bates as the Baron. Many Hammer fans were put off by the movie's cynical approach to the material while the film critics were divided. *The New York Times* thought it was "something special" but *The Los Angeles Times* said, "The changes, unfortunately, are not for the better." The film features some prime examples of "Hammer Glamour" with both Kate

AT LEAST HE GOT THE BODY RIGHT THIS TIME ... DAVID PROWSE AS THE MONSTER IN *THE HORROR OF FRANKENSTEIN*.

O'Mara and Veronica Carlson displaying a very high quotient of cleavage.

However, the best reason for watching *The Horror of Frankenstein* is Ralph Bates. Bates came to the attention of Hammer when he appeared as Caligula in the television series *The Caesars*. After he made an impressive debut in a supporting role in *Taste the Blood of Dracula*, Hammer decided to groom him for stardom. Bates starred in a number of horror films but his greatest success came on television, first as the villianous George Warleggen in *Poldark* and later in the series *Penmarric* and *Dear John*. His untimely death of cancer at age 50 in 1991 left behind a memorable legacy of stage, screen and television performances.

Video: U.K./U.S.

ANDREE MELLY IS THE BEST REASON FOR WATCHING *THE HORROR OF IT ALL*.

146. The Horror of It All

A Lippert Films Ltd./Associated Producers Inc. Production (1964); 75 minutes; U.S.: 20th Century–Fox

P: Robert L. Lippert; **D:** Terence Fisher; **S:** Ray Russell; **M:** Douglas Gamley; **DP:** Arthur Lavis; **E:** Robert Winter; **AD:** Harry White; **Cast:** Pat Boone, Erica Rogers, Andree Melly, Valentine Dyall, Dennis Price, Jack Bligh, Eric Chitty, Archie Duncan and Oswald Lawrence

This disappointing film was directed by Terence Fisher during his brief exile from Hammer. In yet another "old dark house"–style comedy-horror movie, former teen idol Pat Boone is the guileless American who finds himself in a house full of bizarre characters. The cast of British supporting players is good (as it is in other films of this type) but Boone is fairly awful. Andree Melly is definitely worth watching as the resident vampire, Natalia. The rest of this unfunny mess is well deserving of its reputation as Fisher's least favorite film. Fisher would return to form with his next Hammer effort, *The Gorgon*.

Video: None

Horror on Snape Island see *Tower of Evil*

The Horrors of Burke and Hare see *Burke and Hare*

147. Horrors of the Black Museum

A Merton Park Studios Ltd. Production (1959); 94 minutes; Eastman Color and CinemaScope; U.S.: American–International

EXP: Herman Cohen; **P:** Jack Greenwood; **D:** Arthur Crabtree; **S:** Aben Kandel and Herman Cohen; **M:** Gerard Schurmann; **DP:** Desmond Dickinson; **E:** Geoffrey Muller; **AD:** Wilfred Arnold; **Cast:** Michael Gough, Graham Curnow, June Cunningham, Shirley Anne Field, Geoffrey Keen, Gerald Anderson, Beatrice Varley, Nora Gordon, John Warwick, Malou Pantera, Hilda Barry and Austin Trevor

"Lurid" is the word that first comes to mind when contemplating *Horrors of the Black Museum*. Lurid plot, lurid performances, lurid color…lurid! And who could ever forget the opening sequence featuring the infamous death by binoculars?

By 1959, American–International Pictures began to realize that the cheap black-and-white features that they had been cranking out were less and less successful at the box office. Herman Cohen, one of their top

MICHAEL GOUGH MENACES MALOU PANTERA IN THIS PUBLICITY SHOT FOR *HORRORS OF THE BLACK MUSEUM*.

producers, made *Horrors* as a joint venture between Britain's Anglo-Amalgamated Pictures and AIP. Crazed crime writer Edmund Bancroft (Michael Gough) is perpetrating a series of gruesome homicides to give himself material to write about. The murder weapons come from his personal "Black Museum," which is lovingly cared for by Bancroft and his young assistant Rick (Graham Curnow). These instruments of death include a "Jekyll and Hyde" formula which turns Rick into a disfigured killer. With the character of Rick, Cohen was able to incorporate the teenage angst element he had exploited in his previous AIP films (*I Was a Teenage Werewolf*, *Blood of Dracula*, etc.). For the U.S. release, AIP tacked on a prologue explaining the wonderous screen process "HypnoVista," which would supposedly achieve new heights in audience participation.

Video: U.K./U.S.

148. The Hound of the Baskervilles

A Hammer Film Production (1959); 84 minutes; Technicolor; U.S.: United Artists

EXP: Michael Carreras; **P:** Anthony Hinds; **D:** Terence Fisher; **S:** Peter Bryan; **M:** James Bernard; **DP:** Jack Asher; **E:** James Needs and Alfred Cox; **AD:** Bernard Robinson; **Cast:** Peter Cushing, Christopher Lee, Andre Morell, Marla Landi, Francis De Wolff, Ewen Solon, John Le Mesurier, Sam Kydd, Judi Moyens, Helen Goss, David Birks, David Oxley, Miles Malleson and Michael Hawkins

The great detective Sherlock Holmes is called upon to investigate the death of Sir

Charles Baskerville, who is believed to have been the victim of a family curse. Sir Arthur Conan Doyle's classic story is given the full Hammer treatment here, complete with typically macabre touches. Peter Cushing as Holmes and Andre Morell as Watson are as memorable a pair of sleuths as ever graced the screen. It is difficult to imagine more flawless casting. Christopher Lee, uncharacteristically cast as a romantic lead, makes the most of his part as Henry Baskerville. *The Hound of the Baskervilles* was Hammer's attempt to begin a series of Sherlock Holmes films starring Cushing. Although United Artists stressed the more horrific aspects of the story in the advertising campaign, the film failed to draw the expected audiences. This ended any further plans by Hammer to continue a Holmes series. In 1984, Cushing played an aged Holmes in the Tyburn TV movie *Sherlock Holmes and the Masks of Death*.

Video: U.S.

149. The House in Marsh Road

Eternal Films (1960); 70 minutes; U.S. (a.k.a. *Invisible Creature*): American–International (1964)

P/S: Maurice J. Wilson; **D:** Montgomery Tully; **M:** John Veale; **DP:** James Harvey; **E:** Jim Connock; **AD:** John G. Earl; **Cast:** Tony Wright, Patricia Dainton, Sandra Dorne, Derek Aylward, Sam Kydd, Llewellyn Rees, Anita Sharp Bolster, Roddy Hughes, Oliver Sloane, Geoffrey Denton and Harry Hutchinson

When her aunt dies, Jean Lynton (Patricia Dainton) inherits an old country mansion, and with it a poltergeist named Patrick. When Jean and her handsome miscreant husband David (Tony Wright) move in, the ghostly disturbances are minor. When David takes up with the local tart (Sandra Dorne) and decides to murder his wife, the poltergeist protects Jean at every turn. After the second attempt on her life, Jean flees the house. David wastes no time in inviting his mistress over for some hanky panky. As they are upstairs getting heated up in bed, Patrick sets fire to the house downstairs. The trapped lovers are burned to death for their misdeeds. Although this is a well-acted and rather interesting film, it is also very old-fashioned in its execution. At times you would swear that it was made in the 40s rather than 1960.

Video: None

150. The House in Nightmare Park

An Associated London Films–Extonation Production (1973); 96 minutes; Technicolor; U.S.: No theatrical release

P/S: Clive Exton and Terry Nation; **D:** Peter Sykes; **M:** Harry Robinson; **DP:** Ian Wilson; **E:** Bill Blunden; **AD:** Maurice Carter; **Cast:** Frankie Howerd, Ray Milland, Rosalie Crutchley, Hugh Burden, Kenneth Griffith, John Bennett, Ruth Dunning, Elizabeth MacLennan, Peter Munt, and Aimee Delamain

This variation on *The Old Dark House* is an excuse to showcase the sophomoric talents of British comic Frankie Howerd. Imagine the William Castle–Hammer version of J.B. Priestley's classic story with Howerd instead of Tom Poston and you've just about got the whole picture. Tenth-rate actor Foster Twelvetrees (Howerd) is hired to entertain at a remote country estate. (Could it be Oakley Court? Why, yes, I believe it is.) Ray Milland is the head of the loony Henderson clan and Twelvetrees is the unknowing heir to the family fortune. After many murders and even more bad jokes, the mystery is finally revealed for anyone who is still awake. Harry Robinson contributes a score far better than the film it accompanies.

Video: U.K.

House of Crazies see *Asylum*

House of Fright see *The Two Faces of Dr. Jekyll*

151. House of Mortal Sin

A Peter Walker/Heritage Ltd. Production (1975); 104 minutes; Color; U.S. (*The Confessional*): Atlas Films

P/D: Peter Walker; **S:** David McGillvray; **M:** Stanley Myers; **DP:** Peter Jessop; **E:** Matt McCarthy; **AD:** Chris Burke; **Cast:** Anthony Sharp, Susan Penhaligon, Stephanie Beacham, Norman Eshley, Sheila Keith, Hilda Barry, Stewart Beven, Julia McCarthy, Jon Yule, Mervyn Johns, Victor Winding and Kim Butcher

Insane priest Xavier Meldrum (Anthony Sharp) uses the confessions of his flock to blackmail them. When they refuse to cooperate, he kills them with a variety of religious paraphernalia. The fabulous Sheila Keith is back once again, this time as Meldrum's housekeeper who is secretly in love with him. This time around, Peter Walker's excesses seem to exist merely for the sake of excess. *Frightmare* and *House of Whipcord* are lurid to be sure, but there is something beyond the sensationalism that *House of Mortal Sin* sorely lacks. It difficult to imagine a more vitriolic condemnation of organized religion.

Video: U.S.

152. House of Mystery (a.k.a. The Unseen)

Independent Artists (1961); 56 minutes; U.S.: Allied Artists

P: Julian Wintle and Leslie Parkyn; **D/S:** Vernon Sewell; **M:** Stanley Black; **DP:** Ernest Steward; **E:** John Trumper; **AD:** Jack Shampan; **Cast:** Jane Hylton, Peter Dyneley, Nanette Newman, Maurice Kaufmann, Colin Gordon, Molly Urquhart, John Merivale, Ronald Hines and Colette Wilde

Director Vernon Sewell apparently "had a thing" for ghost stories in general...and one in particular! Beginning with 1934's *The Medium*, which was based on a French play by Pierre Mills and C. Vylars, he adapted this same material five times during his career. This is the last of these adaptations and probably the best. A young couple are seeking to buy a house. While they are examining it, an old lady appears who relates to them the unsavory history of the previous residents. This is an outstanding supernatural thriller that, despite its obvious economies (the feature runs less than an hour), manages to make a considerable impact and induce some genuine chills.

Video: None

153. House of Whipcord

A Peter Walker/Heritage Ltd. Production (1974); 101 minutes; Eastman Color; U.S.: American–International; 94 minutes; Color by Movielab

P/D: Peter Walker; **S:** David McGillvray; **M:** Stanley Myers; **DP:** Peter Jessop; **E:** Matt McCarthy; **AD:** Mike Pickwood; **Cast:** Barbara Markham, Patrick Barr, Ray Brooks, Ann Michelle, Penny Irving, Sheila Keith, Dorothy Gordon, Robert Tayman, Ivor Salter, David McGillvray, Karen David and Celia Quicke

House of Whipcord opens with these "noble" sentiments: "This film is dedicated to those who are disturbed by today's lax moral codes and who eagerly await the return of corporal and capital punishment." Dim-witted French model Ann-Marie (Penny Irving) meets a rather sinister young man named Mark E. Desade (Robert Tayman) and falls for him. One weekend he takes her to his remote country home, ostensibly to meet Mother. The home turns out to be a former prison which is being run as a private "House of Correction" for young women by Mark's insane parents. Mark is the tool they use to lure prospective inmates. The harsh regime of the prison is gleefully enforced by a pair of cruel female guards (Sheila Keith and Dorothy Gordon). Errant prisoners are given only three chances. For the first offense, they are put in solitary confinement for two weeks; the second is punishable by whipping; and the third is death by hanging. There are many of the typical

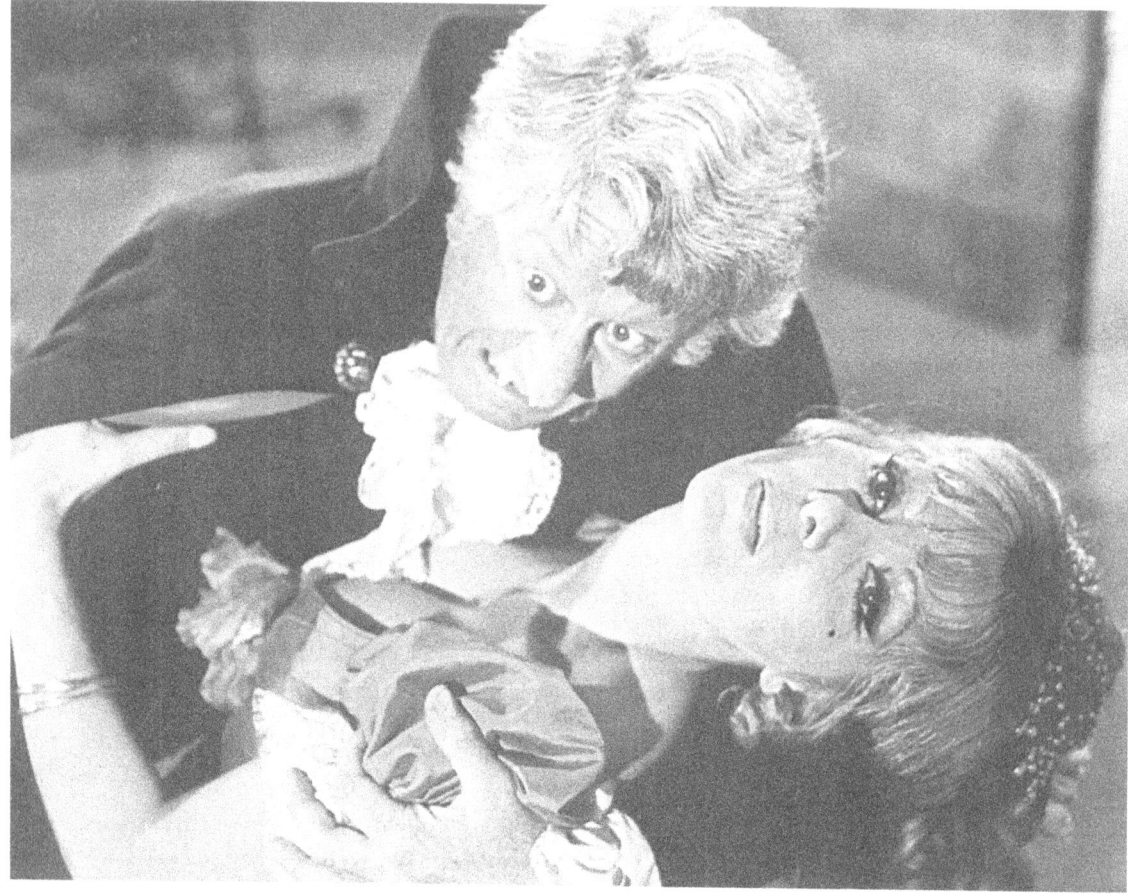

IN THIS SCENE FROM *THE HOUSE THAT DRIPPED BLOOD*, JON PERTWEE IS AN ACTOR WHO GETS CARRIED AWAY WITH HIS ROLE OPPOSITE INGRID PITT.

"women in prison" plot devices used here but there are also several interesting twists in the story and the performances are quite good. *House of Whipcord* is possibly Peter Walker's most demented film and it is also his most accomplished. It well deserves its status as one of his best efforts.

Video: U.K./U.S.

The House on Straw Hill see *Expose*

154. The House that Dripped Blood

An Amicus Production (1971); 102 minutes; Eastman Color; U.S.: Cinerama Releasing
EXP: Paul Ellsworth and Gordon Wescourt; **P:** Max J. Rosenberg & Milton Subotsky; **D:** Peter Duffell; **S:** Robert Bloch; **M:** Michael Dress; **DP:** Ray Parslow; **E:** Peter Tanner; **AD:** Tony Curtis; **Cast:** Christopher Lee, Peter Cushing, Nyree Dawn Porter, Denholm Elliott, Jon Pertwee, Ingrid Pitt, Tom Adams, Joanna Dunham, Joss Ackland, John Bennett, Wolfe Morris and Geoffrey Bayldon

Amicus' second omnibus film is, perhaps, their best. The framing story involves a house where all of the occupants come to ghastly ends. In the first story, "Method for Murder," Denholm Elliott plays a writer of horror stories. His latest creation, a demented strangler called Dominick (Tom Adams), appears to have come to life from the pages of his manuscript. In "Waxworks," Peter

THE ENTIRE CAST ASSEMBLES FOR THE SURPRISE DENOUEMENT OF *HYSTERIA*.

Cushing and Denholm Elliott are former romantic rivals who discover that the image of Salome in a wax museum is the double for their dead love. "Sweets to the Sweet" finds a father (Christopher Lee) tormented by his eight-year-old daughter (Chloe Franks). It seems that she is a witch, just like her dead mother, and already adept at practicing witchcraft. The last story is "The Cloak," featuring Jon Pertwee as a famous horror film actor who buys a cloak which turns him into a vampire. Ingrid Pitt is his delectable co-star, who turns out to have a few surprises of her own.

Director Peter Duffell proficiently handles the various moods of the stories, from the straightforward suspense of the first to the tongue-in-cheek nature of the last.

Video: U.S.

The House That Vanished see *Scream and Die*

155. *Hysteria*

A Hammer Film Production (1965); 85 minutes; U.S.: Metro–Goldwyn–Mayer

P/S: Jimmy Sangster; **D:** Freddie Francis; **M:** Don Banks; **DP:** John Wilcox; **E:** James Needs; **PD:** Edward Carrick; **Cast:** Robert Webber, Lelia Goldoni, Anthony Newlands, Jennifer Jayne, Maurice Denham, Sandra Boize, Peter Woodthorpe, Sue Lloyd, John Arnatt, Marianne Stone, Irene Richmond and Kiwi Kingston

Christopher Smith (Robert Webber) awakens in hospital after an automobile crash and realizes that he has no memory of anything prior to the accident. A mysterious benefactor pays his hospital bills and provides him with a luxurious flat in a new building where he is apparently the only tenant. The ensuing story involves a shower bath, a butcher knife and blood. The plot is extremely convoluted and Robert Webber is rather unsympathetic as the hero/victim. This was the last in Hammer's series of black-and-white "mini–Hitchcock" psychological thrillers. Former "Frankenstein's Monster" Kiwi Kingston has a very brief scene *sans* makeup, but the cleft in his chin is unmistakable.

Video: U.S.

156. I Don't Want to Be Born

A Unicapital Production (1975); 94 minutes; Color by Movielab; U.S. *(The Devil Within Her)*; American–International (1976); 90 minutes

EXP: Nato DeAngeles; **P:** Norma Corney; **D:** Peter Sasdy; **S:** Stanley Price; **M:** Ron Grainer; **DP:** Kenneth Talbot; **E:** Keith Palmer; **AD:** Roy Stannard; **Cast:** Joan Collins, Ralph Bates, Eileen Atkins, Caroline Munro, Hilary Mason, Donald Pleasence, John Steiner, Janet Key, George Claydon, Derek Benfield, Stanley Lebor and Judy Buxton

"Not since Rosemary's Baby!" screamed the advertising for this film, leaving little doubt as to what movie they were trying to capitalize on. There are also liberal chunks of *The Exorcist* thrown in for good measure. Lucy and Gino Carlesi (Joan Collins and Ralph Bates) have their first child, a strapping son. The delivery is an especially difficult one and Lucy is understandably upset when the first thing her baby does is scratch her face, drawing blood. As the infant begins to exhibit increasingly aggressive behavior, Lucy thinks her child might be possessed. Lucy was once an exotic dancer in a London strip joint. One night she rebuffed the amorous advances of Hercules (George Claydon), a dwarf who also worked in the night club. For revenge, he cursed her firstborn child. Fortunately for Lucy, her husband's sister Albana (Eileen Atkins) is a nun. Unfortunately, by the time Sister Albana decides to perform an exorcism, the evil infant has already killed off most of the cast. The stylish direction exhibited by Peter Sasdy in his three films for Hammer is nowhere in evidence here. The background score by Ron Grainer is especially dire and would have been better suited to a porno movie.

Video: U.S.

157. I, Monster

An Amicus Production (1970); 75 minutes; Eastman Color; U.S.: Cannon (1974)

P: Max J. Rosenberg and Milton Subotsky; **D:** Stephen Weeks; **S:** Milton Subotsky; **M:** Carl Davis; **DP:** Moray Grant; **E:** Peter Tanner; **AD:** Tony Curtis; **Cast:** Christopher Lee, Peter Cushing, Mike Raven, Richard Hurndall, George Merritt, Susan Jameson, Kenneth J. Warren, Marjie Lawrence, Aimee Delamain and Michael Des Rarres

Dr. Charles Marlowe (Christopher Lee) develops a serum which sets free the feelings buried deep within a person's psyche. He experiments on one of his patients and the repressed young woman becomes sexually aggressive. He tries the drug on himself and he turns into Edward Blake, an evil alter ego who begins to lurk around the seamier districts of London. Does the plot sound a bit familiar? Small wonder, as this is the umpteenth screen version of Robert Louis Stevenson's *Dr. Jekyll and Mr. Hyde*. Why Milton Subotsky, chose to change the names of the main characters is anybodys guess. Little else has been changed, however, and the only novel aspect of this version of the story is that it was shot for potential show-

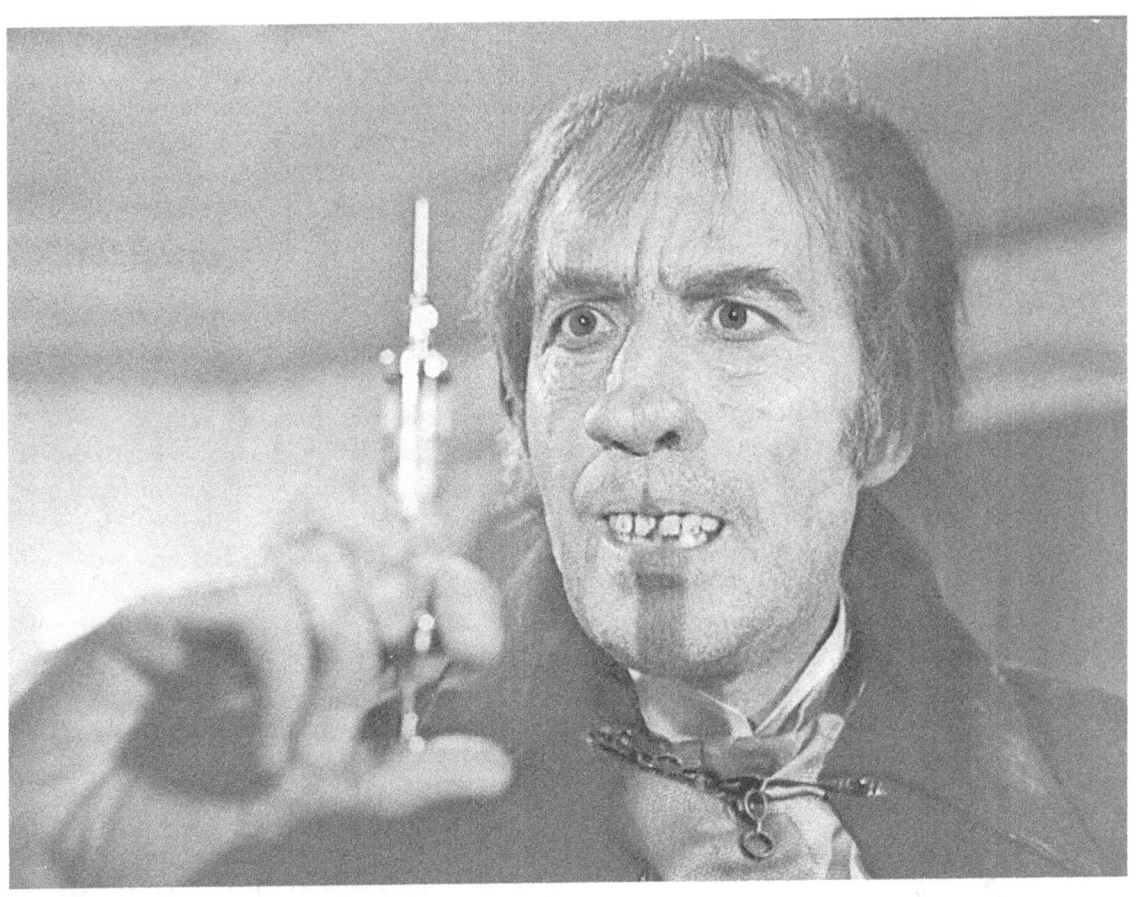

CHRISTOPHER LEE TRANSFORMS FROM DR. MARLOWE INTO THE EVIL EDWARD BLAKE IN *I, MONSTER*, AMICUS' THINLY VEILED VERSION OF "DR. JEKYLL AND MR. HYDE."

ings in 3-D, but it was released flat. The 3-D effects are fairly obvious as the camera continually prowls around the sets and occasionally something is thrust at the audience. Lee is very good in the dual role and does his best to make the most out of the uninspired screenplay, a feat he was often required to perform throughout his career. In his autobiography, Lee states that the film was originally offered to Peter Duffell to direct, but he turned it down because he didn't want to shoot it in 3-D. Says Lee: "The producers Milton Subotsky and Max Rosenberg pressed on with their caprice, and eventually persuaded the brave Stephen Weeks to undertake the venture. It was a nightmare for everybody, most of all for one of the best camera operators in Britain, Bob Kindred."

Video: U.K.

In the Devil's Garden see *Assault*

158. Incense for the Damned

A Lucinda/Titan International Production (1970); 87 min; Color By Movielab; U.S. (*Bloodsuckers*): Chevron Pictures (1971)

EXP: Peter Newbrook; **P:** Graham Harris; **D:** Robert Hartford-Davis; **S:** Julian More; **M:** Bobby Richards; **DP:** Desmond Dickinson; **AD:** George Provis; **Cast:** Alexander Davion, Patrick Mower, Johnny Sekka, Patrick Macnee, Peter Cushing, Imogen Hassall, Madeline Hinde, Edward Woodward, David Lodge and Valerie Van Ost

On sabbatical in Greece, Oxford academic Richard Fountain (Patrick Mower) falls in with a cult of blood-drinking devil worshippers led by the seductive Chriseis (Imogen Hassall). Richard's fiancée and friends track him down and he is presumably freed from Chriseis' evil influence when she dies in a fall. Back at Oxford, Chriseis' control over Richard continues with tragic consequences.

The screenplay is based on Simon Raven's novel *Doctors Wear Scarlet*. An unusual story performed by an interesting cast somehow just misses the mark of being a truly good film. Post-production tampering by the producers, including voice-over narration and a tacked-on ending, caused the director to ask that his name be removed from the credits. The location photography in Greece and at Oxford is a definite attribute, but a lengthy psychedelic orgy sequence is an unfortunate liability.

Video: U.K./U.S.

Inn of the Frightened People see ***Revenge***

159. The Innocents

A Jack Clayton/Achilles Production (1961); 99 minutes; CinemaScope; U.S.: 20th Century–Fox

EXP: Albert Fennell; **P/D:** Jack Clayton; **S:** William Archibald and Truman Capote; **M:** Georges Auric; **DP:** Freddie Francis; **E:** James Clark; **AD:** Wilfred Shingleton; **Cast:** Deborah Kerr, Martin Stephens, Pamela Franklin, Megs Jenkins, Michael Redgrave, Peter Wyngarde, Clytie Jessop, Isla Cameron and Eric Woodburn

Miss Giddens (Deborah Kerr) is hired as governess for two children, Miles (Martin Stephens) and Flora (Pamela Franklin), who live on a lonely country estate. She begins to suspect that they are being haunted by the spirits of the former governess (Clytie Jessop) and the groom (Peter Wyngarde), who were illicit lovers and died tragically.

Are the children prey to a genuine haunting or is Miss Giddens the victim of her own repressed sexuality? Much of the ambiguity of Henry James' *The Turn of the Screw* is retained in the screen adaptation for this classic film. The production is outstanding in every aspect, particulary Freddie Francis' black-and-white widescreen cinematography. Martin Stephens gives one of the finest performances by any child actor ever. The lyrics to Flora's lullaby were written by famed screenwriter Paul Dehn. The subtle approach of *The Innocents* did not deter the Fox advertising department from luridly touting the film as being based on "Henry James' evil masterpiece of macabre love."

Video: U.S.

160. Invasion

A Merton Park Studios Ltd. Production (1966); 82 minutes; U.S.: American–International

P: Jack Greenwood; **D:** Alan Bridges; **S:** Roger Marshall; **M:** Bernard Ebbinghouse; **DP:** James Wilson; **E:** Derek Holding; **AD:** Scott MacGregor; **Cast:** Edward Judd, Valerie Gearon, Yoko Tani, Lyndon Brook, Tsai Chin, Eric Young, Anthony Sharp, Stephanie Bidmead, Jean Lodge, Barrie Ingham, Glyn Houston and Peter Sinclair

A spacecraft from the planet Lystria makes a forced landing near an English village. One of the occupants is injured and Dr. Vernon (Edward Judd) takes him to the hospital. He does not realize that this alien was a prisoner and the other his captor. More aliens arrive and surround the hospital with an invisible force field in an attempt to make Vernon give up his patient. Although it was produced on a minuscule budget this is a highly effective movie which relies not on special effects but on a fine script and solid acting to make its impact.

Video: None

Invisible Creature see ***The House in Marsh Road***

PETER CUSHING IS CAUGHT BY THE TENTACLE OF A DEADLY "SILICATE" ON THE *Island of Terror*.

161. Island of Terror (a.k.a. Night of the Silicates)

A Protelco/Planet Films Ltd. Production (1966); 87 minutes; Eastman Color; U.S.: Universal (1967)

EXP: Richard Gordon and Gerald A. Fernback; **P:** Tom Blakeley; **D:** Terence Fisher; **S:** Edward Andrew Mann and Alan Ramsen; **M:** Malcolm Lockyer; **DP:** Reg Wyer; **E:** Thelma Connell; **AD:** John St. John Earl; **Cast:** Peter Cushing, Edward Judd, Carole Gray, Niall MacGinnis, Eddie Byrne, Sam Kydd, James Caffrey, Shay Gorman, Liam Caffney, Peter Forbes-Robertson, Roger Heathcott and Keith Bell

This is one of three science fiction films of varying quality which were directed by Terence Fisher during the 60s. The other films are *The Earth Dies Screaming* (1964) and *Night of the Big Heat* (1967). *Island of Terror* is better than average but it is still far below the level of Fisher's fine work at Hammer. Fisher stated that he had a greater affinity for the Gothic horror genre than science fiction and it shows. The story takes place on a small island off the Irish coast, where scientists are attempting to find a cure for cancer. One of the experiments goes wrong, resulting in the creation of a number of mutated Silicates which feed on the bones of living animals. These tentacled monsters are also capable of duplicating themselves every six hours. Soon the already tiny population of the island is being reduced to a mass of boneless corpses. Doctors Stanley (Peter Cushing) and West (Edward Judd) are called in from the mainland to investigate. *Night of the Big Heat* borrows many of the same plot elements, but uses them even less effectively.

Video: U.K./U.S.

Island of the Burning Damned see *Night of the Big Heat*

Island of the Burning Doomed see *Night of the Big Heat*

162. It!

A Goldstar Production (1966); 97 minutes; Eastman Color; U.S.: Seven Arts (1967); 95 minutes

P/D/S: Herbert J. Leder; **M:** Carlo Martelli; **DP:** David Boulton; **E:** Tom Simpson; **AD:** Scott MacGregor; **Cast:** Roddy McDowall, Jill Haworth, Paul Maxwell, Noel Trevarthen, Ian McCulloch, Ernest Clark, Aubrey Richards, Oliver Johnson, Alan Sellers, Richard Goolden, Tom Chatto and Russell Napier

A fire in a museum warehouse destroys all of the contents except for a curious statue which turns out to be the legendary Golem of Prague. Ineffectual assistant museum curator Arthur Pimm (Roddy McDowall) discovers the secret of bringing the Golem to life and proceeds to use its power for his own selfish ambitions. The film begins promisingly enough but soon bogs down in a mire of idiotic plot devices. For some unknown reason, Pimm lives with the decayed corpse of his mother (à la Norman Bates). This seems to have no purpose except to create a lame connection to *Psycho*. McDowall, so good as Octavian in the 1963 version of *Cleopatra*, gives an utterly hopeless performance as Pimm. This was released as the companion feature to the much-better *The Frozen Dead*.

Video: None

163. Jack the Ripper

A Mid-Century Film Production (1958); 88 minutes; U.S.: A Joseph E. Levine–Embassy Pictures Presentation; A Paramount Release (1960)

P/D/DP: Robert S. Baker and Monty Berman; **S:** Jimmy Sangster; **M:** Stanley Black (U.K.); Jimmy McHugh and Pete Rugolo (U.S.); **E:** Peter Benzencent; **AD:** William Kellner; **Cast:** Lee Patterson, Eddie Byrne, Betty McDowall, Ewen Solon, John Le Mesurier, George Rose, Barbara Burke, Philip Leaver, George Woodbridge, Anne Sharpe, Andre Mueller and Bill Shine

There is little to be learned about the true facts in the case of Jack the Ripper from this almost totally fictionalized account, but this is still the most effective rendering on film. A black-cloaked man is murdering the prostitutes of Whitechapel, first asking them "Are you Mary Clarke?" The staff of the nearby Mercy Hospital for Women is filled with suspicious characters, including the obligatory mute hunchback assistant. An American detective (Lee Patterson) is brought into the case but he has as little effect as the local police. The savage murders continue to occur. The finale finds the Ripper trapped in an elevator shaft in the hospital as his latest victim in being brought down to the morgue. As the elevator crushes him, the film suddenly turns to color with bright red blood oozing up through the floorboards (an unnecessary bit of sensationalism, but effective nevertheless). In the film's one true moment of conscience, one of the characters discusses the murders, saying, "It's a social problem as well as a criminal one...it's a matter of class distinction." This very concisely states one of the great real issues of the case. Joseph E. Levine bought the American distribution rights to *Jack the Ripper* and released it with a vast amount of publicity, hoping to duplicate the success he had with *Hercules* the previous year. Typical ad copy for the film read: "The swinging

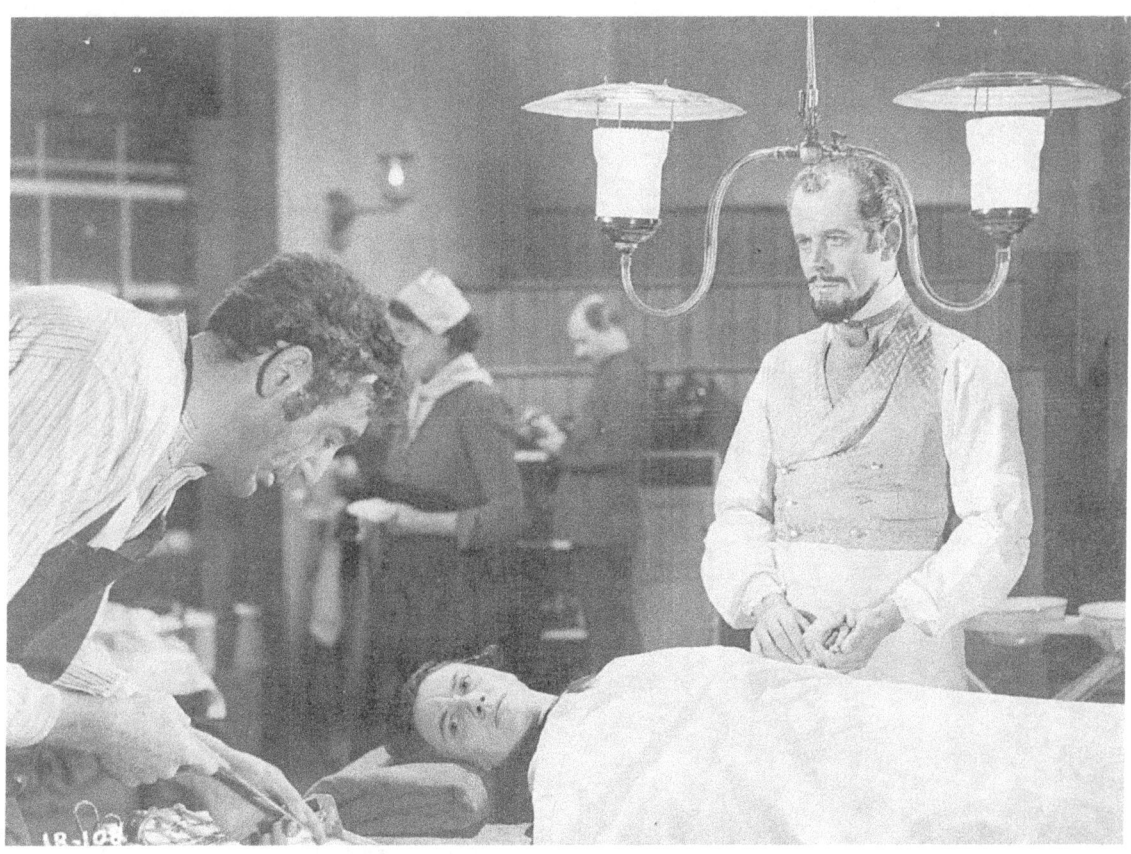

DIRE GOINGS ON AT THE MERCY HOSPITAL FOR WOMEN IN *JACK THE RIPPER*.

purse...the swaying hips...the sensuous body against the lamp-post...then, the sudden glint of a knife...a choked scream! This lady of the night has taken her last walk!" Who could resist?

Video: None

164. *Jason and the Argonauts*

A Charles H. Schneer Production; A Morningside Worldwide Film (1963); 104 minutes; Technicolor; U.S.: Columbia; Eastman Color by Pathe

P: Charles H. Schneer; **D:** Don Chaffey; **S:** Jan Read and Beverly Cross; **M:** Bernard Herrmann; **DP:** Wilkie Cooper; **E:** Maurice Rootes; **PD:** Geoffrey Drake; **AD:** Herbert Smith, Jack Maxsted and Tony Sarzi Braga; **SVE:** Ray Harryhausen; **Cast:** Todd Armstrong, Nancy Kovack, Gary Raymond, Laurence Naismith, Niall MacGinnis, Michael Gwynn, Douglas Wilmer, Jack Gwillim, Honor Blackman, John Cairney, Patrick Troughton and Nigel Green

This exciting and colorful version of the legend of Jason and his quest for the Golden Fleece is the highpoint of the Charles H. Schneer–Ray Harryhausen collaboration. Columbia invested three and a half million dollars in this special effects extravaganza. Some of the exteriors were shot in southern Italy at Palinuro, near Naples. Other location filming was done in the extensive Greek ruins at Paestum, south of Salerno. The film contains some of Ray Harryhausen's most spectacular stop-motion animation sequences, which include a seven-headed Hydra and an army of skeletons. Unfortunately, timing is everything and *Jason and the Argonauts* was released at a time when

Niall MacGinnis as Zeus and Honor Blackman as Hera control the destiny of *Jason and the Argonauts* from Mt. Olympus.

the movie market was flooded with scores of dubbed European "sword and sandal" films. There had already been two Italian versions of the Jason myth, *Hercules* (1959) and *Giants of Thessaly* (1961). Although *Jason and the Argonauts* is vastly superior to either of these films, critics and audiences failed to recognize its considerable merits and it was not the big success that Columbia had hoped for during its original release. Fortunately, the passage of time has conferred upon the film the very deserved status of "classic."

Video: U.K./U.S.

Journey to the Far Side of the Sun see ***Doppelganger***

165. Jules Verne's Rocket to the Moon

American–International (1967); 95 minutes; Color and Panavision; U.S. (*Those Fantastic Flying Fools* [a.k.a. *Blast-Off*])

P: Harry Alan Towers; **D:** Don Sharp; **S:** Dave Freeman; **M:** Patrick John Scott; **DP:** Reg Wyer; **E:** Ann Chegwidden; **AD:** Frank White; **Cast:** Burl Ives, Troy Donahue, Gert Frobe, Hermione Gingold, Lionel Jeffries, Dennis Price, Terry-Thomas, Daliah Lavi, Stratford Johns, Graham Stark, Jimmy Clitheroe and Edward de Souza

The great showman P.T. Barnum (Burl Ives) goes to England and joins forces with a group of eccentric inventors who plan to

REHEARSING THE CLIMACTIC SCENE FOR *KISS OF THE VAMPIRE* (NOTE CAMERA POSITION MARKED ON THE FLOOR).

send a manned rocket to the moon. The film tries hard to be a madcap romp but fails badly. It is difficult to believe that a director as talented as Don Sharp was involved in this fiasco. The original story by Peter Welbeck (pseudonym for producer Harry Alan Towers) claims to have been "Inspired by the writings of Jules Verne," but there is little Verne, or inspiration, in evidence. The cast is filled with competent performers (Troy Donahue and Daliah Lavi are not to be counted among them) but none can overcome the terrible material. Always quick to capitalize on a previous success, AIP changed the title of the film to resemble *Those Magnificent Men in Their Flying Machines*. When this failed to generate much interest, AIP changed the title to *Blast-Off*. No matter what it's called, this film is still a stinker.

Video: U.S. (as *Blast-Off*)

166. The Kiss of the Vampire

A Hammer Film Production (1963); 88 minutes; Eastman Color; U.S.: Universal-International

P: Anthony Hinds; D: Don Sharp; S: John Elder; M: James Bernard; DP: Alan Hume; E: James Needs; PD: Bernard Robinson; AD: Don Mingaye; Cast: Clifford Evans, Noel Willman, Edward de Souza, Jennifer Daniel, Barry Warren, Jacquie Wallis, Isobel Black, Peter Madden, Vera Cook, Noel Howlett, Brian Oulton and Olga Dickie.

In this classic Hammer vampire tale, Gerald and Marianne Harcourt (Edward de Souza and Jennifer Daniel) are a British couple on their honeymoon in Bavaria. When their motorcar runs out of gas, they are forced to stay at an inn which is no longer frequented by the villagers. Dr. Ravna (Noel Willman), a local aristocrat, invites the couple to attend a masked ball at his chateau. The seemingly dignified Ravna is actually the leader of a cult of vampires and he wants to initiate Marianne into the fold. When Gerald discovers the truth, he enlists the aid of Prof. Zimmer (Clifford Evans) to help save his wife.

When this stylish and perverse thriller was shown on NBC-TV, the original content was considerably altered. Some scenes were edited out, new sequences filmed in America by Universal were added and the title was changed to *Kiss of Evil*. The end result was a total bastardization of the original. Fortunately, the original version is now available on video.

Video: U.S.

167. Konga

A Merton Park/Herman Cohen Production (1961); 90 minutes; Eastman Color and SpectaMation; U.S.: American–International

P: Herman Cohen; **D:** John Lemont; **S:** Aben Kandel & Herman Cohen; **M:** Gerard Schurmann; **DP:** Desmond Dickinson; **E:** Jack Slade; **AD:** Wilfred Arnold; **Cast:** Michael Gough, Margo Johns, Jess Conrad, Claire Gordon, Austin Trevor, Jack Watson, George Pastell, Vanda Godsell, Stanley Morgan, Grace Arnold, Leonard Sachs and Kim Tracy.

This was another in producer Herman Cohen's long line of British productions. Once again he utilizes the talents of Michael Gough, who provides an even more crazed characterization than he did in Cohen's *Horrors of the Black Museum*. Dr. Charles Decker (Gough) returns to London after having been missing for a year in Africa. With him is a small chimpanzee named Konga. He has also brought cuttings from giant carnivorous plants which he plans to cultivate to help prove his theory of a link between plant life and animals. His long-suffering assistant Margaret (Margo Johns) loves him blindly and soon becomes an accomplice in his wild experiments, which involve extracting serum from the plants and injecting it into Konga. The first injection turns him from a tiny chimpanzee into a much larger one. The second injection, inexplicably, turns him into a gorilla! Decker then uses the gorilla to murder anyone he thinks is trying to keep him from realizing his ambitions. When Margaret realizes that Decker's interest in studious school sexpot Sandra (Claire Gordon) is more than that of a teacher to a student, she gives Konga yet another injection, turning him into a gigantic gorilla who goes on a rampage through London. The outlandish plot, wildly excessive performance by Gough and some truly terrible "special effects" make this tremendous fun to watch.

Video: U.K.

Kronos see *Captain Kronos: Vampire Hunter*

Land of the Minotaur see *The Devil's Men*

168. The Land That Time Forgot

An Amicus Productions Presentation; A Max J. Rosenberg and Milton Subotsky Production (1974); 90 minutes; Technicolor; U.S.: American–International (1975); Color by Movielab

P: John Dark/**D:** Kevin Connor; **S:** James Cawthorn and Michael Moorcock; **M:** Douglas Gamley; **DP:** Alan Hume; **E:** John Ireland; **PD:** Maurice Carter; **AD:** Bert Davey; **Cast:** Doug McClure, John McEnery, Susan Penhaligon, Keith Barron, Anthony Ainley, Declan Mulholland, Godfrey James, Roy Holder, Ben Howard, Brian Hall, Andrew McCullogh and Colin Farrell.

This was the first, and best, in a trio of Edgar Rice Burroughs adventure fantasies produced by Amicus and starring Doug McClure.

In 1916, a German U-Boat sinks a

REYNOLD BROWN'S POSTER ART FOR *KONGA*.

British passenger ship. The few survivors manage to overcome the crew of the U-Boat and take command of the vessel. Bowen Tyler (Doug McClure), an American who has considerable knowledge of submarines, sets out for a neutral port, but one of the German officers tampers with the navigation equipment and sends them off course. They eventually come upon the forgotten, ice-bound continent of Caprona. Tyler maneuvers the submarine through a narrow underwater tunnel, surfacing in the lagoon of a tropical jungle. They discover that they are stranded in a prehistoric world where all the early stages of evolution exist in microcosm. *The Land That Time Forgot* is an action-packed adventure yarn with some passable special effects. Roger Dicken's rod-puppet dinosaurs are no substitute for stop-motion animation but they are far superior to any of the effects in the two subsequent Burroughs adaptations. There is a wide variety of creatures on display and some of the dinosaur sequences are very impressive. John McEnery played the German U-Boat captain but his dialogue was completely re-voiced by Anton Diffring. In 1977, the same creative team produced an inferior sequel, *The People That Time Forgot*.

Video: U.K./U.S.

169. The Legacy

A Turman-Foster Production (1979); 100 minutes; Technicolor; U.S.: Universal

EXP: Arnold Kopelson; **P:** David Foster; **D:** Richard Marquand; **S:** Jimmy Sangster, Patrick Tilley and Paul Wheeler; **M:** Michael J. Lewis; **DP:** Dick Bush and Alan Hume; **E:** Anne V. Coates; **PD:** Disley Jones; **Cast:** Katherine Ross, Sam Elliott, John Standing, Ian Hogg, Margaret Tyzack, Charles Gray, Lee Montague, Hildegard Neil, Roger Daltry, Marianne Broome, William Abney and Patsy Smart.

Architect Maggie Walsh (Katherine Ross) is hired by Jason Mountolive (John Standing), an ailing British millionaire, to work on a project for him in England. She goes there with her dumb hunk boyfriend Pete (Sam Elliott) and they promptly have a motorcycle accident while on a drive in the country. The couple are rushed off to a nearby mansion where they are invited to stay until the motorcycle can be repaired. The mansion turns out to be the home of none other than Jason Mountolive! While the other house guests are dying in a variety of gruesome ways, Pete discovers that Maggie is the reincarnation of a witch who has been lured home to reclaim her legacy. This clunker's only claim to fame is that it is Jimmy Sangster's last British horror movie to date. Even this was unintentional as Sangster had written the script while living in America and his original story was set in a Detroit hospital. *The Legacy* is a prime example of the unfortunate trend in horror movies where a slight storyline becomes merely an excuse to show a series of elaborately staged and extremely grisly death scenes.

Video: U.S./U.K.

The Last Days of Man on Earth see *The Final Programme*

170. The Legend of Hell House

An Academy Pictures Production (1973); 94 minutes; Color by DeLuxe; U.S.: 20th Century–Fox

EXP: James H. Nicholson; **P:** Albert Fennell and Norman T. Herman; **D:** John Hough; **S:** Richard Matheson; **M:** Brian Hodgson and Delia Derbyshire; **DP:** Alan Hume; **E:** Geoffrey Foot; **AD:** Robert Jones; **Cast:** Pamela Franklin, Clive Revill, Roddy McDowall, Gayle Hunnicutt, Roland Culver, Peter Bowles and Michael Gough.

An ailing millionaire wishes to know if there is life after death, and he hires four people to spend a week in a notorious haunted house. Richard Matheson's perversely terrifying novel *Hell House* is so watered down for this screen adaptation that it barely holds your interest. Nothing much happens and there isn't a scare to be had. The climax, such as it is, has Roddy McDowall overacting to the hilt as he literally insults the ghost into extinction. It seems the original owner of the house suffered from a bad case of "short man's complex." Michael Gough makes a brief "guest" appearance as the corpse of this culprit, exorcised of his evil spirit at last.

Video: U.S.

The Legend of Spider Forest see *Venom*

171. The Legend of the 7 Golden Vampires

A Hammer/Shaw Production (1974); 89 minutes; Technicolor and Panavision; U.S. (*The Seven Brothers Meet Dracula*): Dynamite Entertainment (1979); 85 minutes

P: Don Houghton and Vee King Shaw; **D:** Roy Ward Baker; **S:** Don Houghton; **M:** James Bernard; **DP:** John Wilcox and Roy Ford; **AD:** Johnson Tsau; **E:** Chris Barnes and Larry Richardson; **Cast:** Peter Cushing, David Chiang,

Julie Ege, Robin Stewart, Shih Szu, John Forbes-Robertson, Robert Hanna, Chan Shen, James Ma, Liu Chia Yung, Feng Ko An, Chen Tien Loong and Wong Han Chan.

Prof. Van Helsing (Peter Cushing) journeys to Chungking, China, in the year 1904. His purpose is to educate the people on the possibilities of vampirism in the Far East. Following a lecture at the Chinese University, Van Helsing is approached by a young man named Hsi Ching (David Chiang) who offers proof of the legend of the Seven Golden Vampires. He aspires to lead an expedition to his village of Ping Kuei to free it from the curse of these vampires. Vanessa Buren (Julie Ege) is a wealthy widow who agrees to finance the venture...if they will take her with them. Along the way, the group is attacked by the vampires and their army of zombies. The final confrontation takes place at the temple of the Seven Golden Vampires where Van Helsing learns that Count Dracula (John Forbes-Robertson) is behind the reign of terror.

This was another attempt by Michael Carreras to diversify Hammer's product. He negotiated a deal with Hong Kong's prolific producers, the Shaw Brothers, to make two films in conjuction with Hammer (the other was the non-horror *Shatter*). *The Legend of the 7 Golden Vampires* was the last Gothic Hammer film and it utilizes a number of Hammer regulars. In one case this was not the producers' original intent. Background music by Wang Fu-Ling was deemed unacceptable so, at the last minute, Hammer's music director Philip Martell brought in James Bernard to compose a rousing new score. Unfortunately, the film's unusual mixture of kung fu and horror did not set well with audiences and, despite a promising London opening, it was not a popular success. Warner Bros. shelved the film in the U.S. but it was eventually released in 1979 by Max Rosenberg's company, Dynamite Entertainment. This version was retitled and severely reedited, eliminating most of the characterization and plot exposition. When *Variety* reviewed the film, it was a Chinese theatrical version entitled *Dracula and the 7 Golden Vampires*, with a running time of 110 minutes.

Video: U.K./U.S.

172. Legend of the Werewolf

A Tyburn Film Production (1975); 90 minutes
Eastman Color; U.S.: No theatrical release

P: Kevin Francis; **D:** Freddie Francis; **S:** John Elder; **M:** Harry Robinson; **DP:** John Wilcox; **E:** Henry Richardson; **AD:** Jack Shampan; **Cast:** Peter Cushing, David Rintoul, Ron Moody, Hugh Griffith, Roy Castle, Lynn Dalby, Renee Houston, Norman Mitchell, Patrick Holt, Mark Weavers, Marjorie Yates and Michael Ripper.

Tyburn's third theatrical feature is a definite improvement over its predecessors. The peasant parents of an infant boy are killed by a pack of wolves in the forest. The wolves take the child and raise it as one of their own. Years later, a sideshow caravan captures the wolf boy, names him Etoile and puts him on exhibition. When he grows to manhood, Etoile (David Rintoul) turns into a werewolf and kills a member of the troupe. Horrified by what he has done, he runs away to Paris. He is hired as a keeper at a rundown zoo and there he becomes attracted to Christine (Lynn Dalby), a young girl who works nearby. She neglects to tell Etoile that she works as a prostitute in a brothel. When he eventually finds this out, he again turns into a werewolf and savagely slaughters several of the brothel's clients. Enter Prof. Paul Cataflanque (Peter Cushing), the Judiciary Surgeon at the city morgue, who assists in police cases. It is Cataflanque who unravels the mystery surrounding the murders, but not before the werewolf goes on another bloody killing spree. In many ways this film is reminiscent of Hammer's excellent *The*

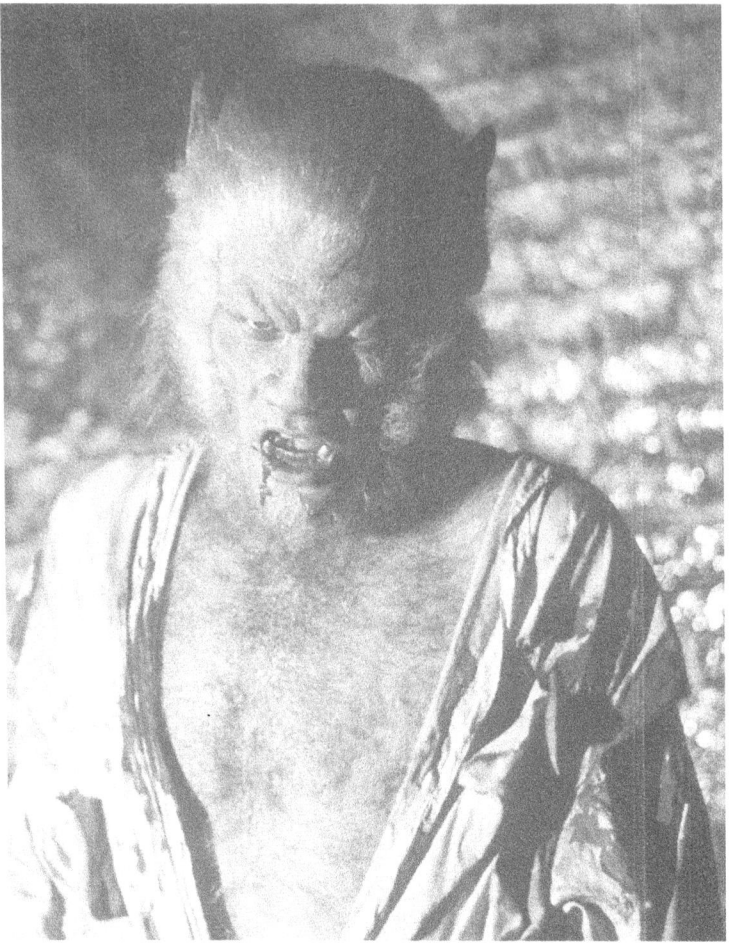

David Rintoul is the unfortunate title character of *Legend of the Werewolf*.

Curse of the Werewolf, particulary Graham Freeborn's werewolf makeup (very close to that created by Roy Ashton for the Hammer film). David Rintoul is sympathetic as Etoile and Peter Cushing is a total delight as the meddlesome Prof. Cataflanque. On the negative side, the cheap-looking sets are decidedly un–Parisian, as is Ron Moody's overdone Cockney zookeeper.

Video: U.K./U.S.

173. The Lost Continent

A Hammer/Seven Arts Production (1968); 98 minutes; Technicolor; U.S.: 20th Century–Fox; 89 minutes; DeLuxe Color

P/D: Michael Carreras; **S:** Michael Nash (Michael Carreras); **M:** Gerard Schurmann; **DP:** Paul Beeson; **E:** James Needs and Chris Barnes; **AD:** Arthur Lawson and Don Picton; **Cast:** Eric Porter, Hildegard Knef, Suzanna Leigh, Tony Beckley, Nigel Stock, Neil McCallum, Benito Carruthers, Jimmy Hanley, James Cossins, Dana Gillespie, Victor Maddern and Michael Ripper.

This Hammer "spectacular" is adapted from the novel *Uncharted Seas* by Dennis Wheatley. A collection of desperate characters book passage on a dilapidated steamer leaving South Africa and bound for Caracas. A storm drives the ship into the Sargasso Sea, where the passengers and crew encounter a lost civilization and gigantic monsters. This was one of Hammer's bigger-budgeted productions and it had more than its share of problems. Leslie Norman was the original director, but Michael Carreras took over the direction shortly after filming began. Benjamin Frankel composed the background score, but Carreras rejected it and commissioned a new score composed by Gerard Schurmann. The end result was that the picture did go over budget, a rarity for a Hammer film. Robert A. Mattey, who created the giant squid for Disney's *20,000 Leagues Under the Sea* (1954), was brought over from America to design the full-size mechanical monsters. His creations are imaginative and impressive, but in this film it's the characters that count. This was succinctly stated in a review by Michael Armstrong in *Films and Filming* magazine: "One becomes so fascinated by the charac-

SUZANNA LEIGH IN THE TENTACLES OF AN ENORMOUS JELLYFISH ON *THE LOST CONTINENT*.

ters that, for once, one is not sitting patiently waiting for the monsters — in fact, I was rather upset whenever they appeared, as they seemed quite an intrusion upon a rather interesting set of people." Hildegard Knef is especially convincing as the ex-mistress of a former South American dictator who is sailing to Caracas to find her young son. An outstanding ensemble cast and ingenious visuals are combined into a highly entertaining mixture.

Video: U.S.

The Love Factor see *Zeta One*

174. *Lust for a Vampire* (a.k.a. *To Love a Vampire*)

A Hammer Film Production (1970); 95 minutes; Technicolor; U.S.: American Continental/Levitt-Pickman (1971)

P: Harry Fine and Michael Style; **D:** Jimmy Sangster; **S:** Tudor Gates; **M:** Harry Robinson; **DP:** David Muir; **E:** Spencer Reeve; **AD:** Don Mingaye; **Cast:** Yutte Stensgaard, Ralph Bates, Barbara Jefford, Suzanna Leigh, Michael Johnson, Mike Raven, Pippa Steele, Helen Christie, David Healy, Eric Chitty, Luan Peters, Harvey Hall and Christopher Cunningham.

The second entry in Hammer's Karnstein trilogy was originally to have been directed by Terence Fisher and feature Peter Cushing in an important supporting role. Fisher was hit by an automoblie while crossing a street and Cushing's wife became ill, so both were unable to participate in the

GILES BARTON (RALPH BATES) CONFRONTS MIRCALLA KARNSTEIN (YUTTE STENSGAARD) IN *LUST FOR A VAMPIRE*.

project. The finished product, while not as good as the other two films in the series, has much to recommend it and does not deserve the invectives which have been hurled at it. Even the much criticized song "Strange Love" is fairly inoffensive and contains one of Harry Robinson's loveliest melodies.

In many respects, the plot is closer to the spirit of a Gothic romance novel than a horror story. Vampire Carmilla Karnstein (Yutte Stensgaard) is resurrected from the grave by her undead parents. She is then enrolled in an exclusive finishing school for girls, located near Karnstein Castle. There, she finds easy victims among the pupils and staff but eventually falls in love with teacher

Vincent Price and Linda Hayden pose for a publicity shot for *Madhouse*.

Richard Lestrange (Michael Johnson). The inevitable band of irate villagers set fire to the castle and Carmilla is destroyed when a burning timber pierces her heart. The film contains many hauntingly beautiful moments and Stensgaard is certainly the screen's most angelic-looking vampire. Ralph Bates replaced Peter Cushing in the role of Giles Barton, an eccentric student of the occult who falls prey to Carmilla's deadly charms. Christopher Neame, who later played Johnny Alucard in *Dracula A.D. 1972*, has a small part as one of the villagers who storms Castle Karnstein.

Video: U.K./U.S.

175. Madhouse

An American–International/Amicus Co-Production (1973); 92 minutes; Eastman Color; U.S.: American–International (1974); 89 minutes; Color by Movielab

EXP: Samuel Z. Arkoff; **P:** Max J. Rosenberg and Milton Subotsky; **D:** Jim Clark; **S:** Greg Morrison and Ken Levison; **M:** Douglas Gamley; **DP:** Ray Parslow; **E:** Clive Smith; **AD:** Tony Curtis; **Cast:** Vincent Price, Peter Cushing, Robert Quarry, Adrienne Corri, Natasha Pyne, Linda Hayden, Barry Dennen, Ellis Dale, Catherine Willmer, John Garrie, Ian Thompson and Julie Crosthwait.

The story begins in "Hollywood ... some years ago" at a New Year's Eve party celebrating the engagement of famed horror movie star Paul Toombes (Vincent Price) to beautiful young starlet Ellen (Julie Crosthwait). Toombes and Ellen quarrel and later she is found decapitated. Toombes suffers a mental breakdown and retires from acting. The story resumes in present-day London, where sleazy TV producer Oliver Quayle (Robert Quarry) has hired Toombes to recreate his most famous characterization, Dr. Death, for a new television series. Shortly after Toombes' arrival, several murders occur — imitations of scenes from the old Dr. Death movies. Based on the novel *Devilday* by Angus Hall, *Madhouse* was originally announced as *The Revenge of Dr. Death*. This was Vincent Price's final film for AIP and it is a fitting end to his association with that company. There are a number of sequences which showcase scenes from the Corman–Poe films, sometimes making *Madhouse* seem like a tribute to Price's career.

Price gives a sympathetic performance as the faded horror star. You can sense his earnestness in a scene where he tells Peter Cushing, "In our day in Hollywood, the monsters didn't need makeup...they just came as themselves." Could he possibly have been thinking of Sam Arkoff when he delivered this line? Linda Hayden gives a brief but canny performance as an overly ambitious actress who ends up as one of Dr. Death's victims.

Video: U.K./U.S.

Madhouse Mansion see *Ghost Story*

176. The Man Who Could Cheat Death

A Hammer Film Production (1959); 83 minutes; Technicolor; U.S.: Paramount

P: Michael Carreras; **D:** Terence Fisher; **S:** Jimmy Sangster; **M:** Richard Rodney Bennett; **DP:** Jack Asher; **E:** James Needs and John Dunsford; **AD:** Bernard Robinson; **Cast:** Anton Diffring, Hazel Court, Christopher Lee, Arnold Marle, Delphi Lawrence, Francis De Wolff, Charles Lloyd Pack, John Harrison and Dennis Shaw.

Paramount enlisted Hammer's services to remake their 1944 film *The Man in Half Moon Street*, which was based on a play by Barré Lyndon. One hundred four years old, Dr. Georges Bonnet (Anton Diffring) owes his youthful appearance to an experimental gland operation. In his desperation to replace this vital gland every ten years, he must resort to deception and murder. When he falls in love with beautiful Janine Dubois (Hazel Court), complications arise which lead to his downfall. This film is long on talk and short on action but the compensations are a well-written script and excellent performances from the cast. The previous year, Anton Diffring had starred as Dr. Frankenstein Hammer's ill-fated television pilot *Tales of Frankenstein*. Diffring played the lead in only two feature horror films, but his screen presence is so commanding in these that he became closely identified with the genre.

Video: None

177. The Man Who Fell to Earth

British Lion Films Ltd. (1976); 138 minutes; Color and Panavision; U.S.: Columbia; 118 minutes

EXP: Si Litvinoff; **P:** Michael Deeley and Barry Spikings; **D:** Nicolas Roeg; **S:** Paul Mayersberg; **M:** John Phillips; **DP:** Anthony Richmond; **E:** Graeme Clifford; **PD:** Brian Eatwell; **Cast:** David Bowie, Candy Clark, Buck Henry, Rip Torn, Bernie Casey, Jackson D. Kane, Rick Riccardo, Linda Hutton, Adrienne Larussa, Hilary Holland, Tony Mascia and Lillybelle Crawford.

The presence of David Bowie, perfectly cast as alien Thomas Newton, is the best reason for watching this intermittently fascinating film. An alien from a parched planet lands on Earth in search of water. He uses his powers to become a business tycoon in order to secure the money to finance the construction of a spaceship. His ambition is to rescue his family from their dying planet. This plan is shattered as he is exploited and

Hazel Court with Anton Differing in *The Man Who Could Cheat Death*.

betrayed by the people who surround him. Magnificent location photography in New Mexico adds greatly to this sometimes dazzling but often heavy-handed screen adaptation of Walter Tevis' novel.

Video: U.S./U.K.

178. The Man Who Haunted Himself

A Michael Relph–Basil Dearden/Excalibur Films Ltd. Production for Associated British Productions Ltd. (1970); 94 minutes; Technicolor; U.S.: Levitt-Pickman

P: Michael Relph; **D:** Basil Dearden; **S:** Michael Relph and Basil Dearden; **M:** Michael J. Lewis; **DP:** Tony Spratling; **E:** Teddy Darvas; **AD:** Albert Witherick; **Cast:** Roger Moore, Hildegard Neil, Anton Rogers, Olga Georges-Picot, Thorley Walters, John Welsh, Freddie Jones, Charles Lloyd Pack, Gerald Sim, Edward Chapman, John Carson and Ruth Trouncer.

Harold Pelham (Roger Moore) has an automobile accident and dies on the operating table. The doctors manage to resuscitate him and for a moment the monitor registers two heartbeats. Later, a fully recovered Mr. Pelham resumes his daily routine, but he soon has reason to believe he has a doppelganger who is trying to take over his life.

After *The Saint* and before James Bond, Roger Moore starred in this interesting thriller which successfully conveys the confusion and frustration of the main character by providing the audience with no more information than he has. *Cue* magazine thought, "When the mystery is finally unraveled, it isn't worth the effort," but the film is actually quite riveting, with a tense denouement. Unfortunately, *The Man Who Haunted Himself* received very poor distribution in the United States, usually as the lower half of a double bill with Hammer's *Lust for a Vampire*.

Video: U.S.

179. The Man Without a Body

Eros/Filmplays Ltd. (1957); 80 minutes; U.S.: Budd Rogers Distribution

P: Guido Coen; **D:** W. Lee Wilder and Charles Sanders; **S:** William Grote; **M:** Albert Elms; **DP:** Brendan Stafford; **E:** Tom Simpson; **AD:** Harry White; **Cast:** George Coulouris, Robert Hutton, Julia Arnall, Nadja Regin, Michael Golden, Kim Parker, Sheldon Lawrence, Peter Copley, Norman Shelley, William Sherwood, Tony Quinn and Maurice Kaufmann.

An unscrupulous millionaire (George Coulouris), dying of a brain tumor, decides that he wants the brain of Nostradamus. His doctor (Robert Hutton) succeeds in resurrecting the head of the famous philosopher, but it simply refuses to cooperate with the plan they have in mind. The finale finds the unfortunate head transplanted onto another body and held in place with a huge square plaster cast. It wanders around London, arms outstretched, like some bad parody of Frankenstein's Monster. This is not as delightfully bad as *The Brain That Wouldn't Die*, but it is right up there. One of the directors, W. Lee Wilder, scored a modest success earlier in the 50s with a trio of low-budget science fiction films (*Phantom from Space*, *Killers from Space* and *The Snow Creature*). His considerably more talented brother is the great director Billy Wilder.

Video: None

Mania see *The Flesh and the Fiends*

180. Maniac

A Hammer Film Production (1963); 86 minutes; MegaScope

P/S: Jimmy Sangster; **D:** Michael Carreras; **M:** Stanley Black; **DP:** Wilkie Cooper; **E:** James Needs and Tom Simpson; **AD:** Edward Carrick; **Cast:** Kerwin Mathews, Nadia Gray, Donald Houston, Liliane Brousse, Norman Bird, George Pastell, Jerold Wells, Arnold Diamond, Leon Peers and Justine Lord.

In the Camargue district of France, Annette Beynat (Liliane Brousse) is raped by one of the local men. Her father kills the man with an acetylene torch and is committed to a mental institution for his crime. Four years later, Geoff Farrell (Kerwin Mathews), an American artist, comes to stay at the inn run by Annette and her stepmother Eve (Nadia Gray). Geoff is attracted to both women and becomes involved in a plan to help Eve's husband escape from the asylum.

This is another in Hammer's series of psychological thrillers scripted by Jimmy Sangster, and it one of the best of the lot. Kerwin Mathews took time off from "swashbuckling" to be cast against type as the womanizing heel who romances a woman and her stepdaughter and almost ends up getting killed for it. Mathews got his start as a Columbia contract player in the 1955 film *5 Against the House* starring Kim Novak. That same year, the studio cast him as the lead in *Joseph and His Brethren*, a big-budget Biblical extravaganza starring Rita Hayworth. Due to endless production problems, the film was never completed and Mathews lost his bid for superstardom. Starting with *The Seventh Voyage of Sinbad*, he found his niche as the sword-wielding hero of adventure fantasies. *Maniac* gave him the chance to show his versatility in a very different kind of role and he made the most of the opportunity.

Video: U.S.

181. The Masque of the Red Death

An Alta Vista Production (1964); 89 minutes; Pathecolor and Panavision; U.S.: American–International

Michael Carreras directs his *Maniac* stars Kerwin Mathews and Nadia Gray.

P/D: Roger Corman; **S:** Charles Beaumont and R. Wright Campbell; **M:** David Lee; **DP:** Nicolas Roeg; **E:** Ann Chegwidden; **PD:** Daniel Haller; **AD:** Robert Jones; **Cast:** Vincent Price, Hazel Court, Jane Asher, Patrick Magee, David Weston, Nigel Green, Skip Martin, John Westbrook, Gay Brown, Julian Burton, Doreen Dawn and Verina Greenlaw.

This is the seventh in the series of Poe adaptations directed by Roger Corman and the first to be filmed in England. Vincent Price plays the wicked Prince Prospero, who is barricaded in his castle with his followers while a deadly plague, the Red Death, ravages the countryside without. This movie is less horrific and far more esoteric than any of the other films in the series. The story is essentially a contest of faiths with good represented by the Christian peasant girl Francesca (Jane Asher) and evil being Prospero, who is a Satanist. The spectacular color photography is the work of Nicolas Roeg, who has since become a highly respected director. Harvey Hall, who appeared in all three films in Hammer's Karnstein series, has a small role as one of the courtiers in Prospero's palace. The film, which has scenes reminiscent of Ingmar Bergman's *The Seventh Seal*, was particularly well received by critics at the time of its release.

Video: U.K./U.S.

The Million Eyes of Su-Muru see *Sumuru*

182. *The Mind Benders*

A Michael Relph–Basil Dearden/Novus Production (1963); 99 minutes; U.S.: American–International

P: Michael Relph; **D:** Basil Dearden; **S:** James Kennaway; **M:** Georges Auric; **DP:** Denys Coop; **E:** John Guthridge; **AD:** Jim Morahan; **Cast:** Dirk Bogarde, Mary Ure, John Clements, Michael Bryant, Wendy Craig, Harold Goldblatt, Geoffrey Keen, Terry Palmer, Norman Bird, Roger Delgado, Edward Fox and Robin Hawdon.

Prof. Sharpey (Harold Goldblatt) commits suicide by throwing himself under a train. The large amount of money he was carrying leads investigators to suspect that he had been selling state secrets to a foreign party. Despite evidence to the contrary, his friend and assistant Henry (Dirk Bogarde) refuses to accept that Sharpey would voluntarily commit any crime against the government. Henry believes that Sharpey was the victim of a brainwashing experiment which uses a sensory deprivation technique. The investigator (John Clement) is skeptical, so Henry subjects himself to the procedure, nearly loosing his mind in the process. This is an interesting film which is carried by the strength of Dirk Bogarde's performance. The sequence involving his immersion in the sensory deprivation tank is extremely disturbing.

Video: None

183. *The Mind of Mr. Soames*

An Amicus Production (1970); 95 minutes; Color by Movielab; U.S.: Columbia

P: Max J. Rosenberg and Milton Subotsky; **D:** Alan Cooke; **S:** John Hale and Edward Simpson; **M:** Michael Dress; **DP:** Billy Williams; **E:** Bill Blunden; **PD:** Bill Constable; **AD:** Don Mingaye; **Cast:** Terence Stamp, Robert Vaughn, Nigel Davenport, Christian Roberts, Donal Donnelly, Norman Jones, Dan Jackson, Vickery Turner, Judy Parfitt, Scott Forbes, Jon Croft and Billy Cornelius.

An important medical advancement in brain surgery awakens John Soames (Terence Stamp), a 30-year-old who has been in a coma since birth. With the mind of an infant and the body of a man, Soames must be trained to be an adult. He runs away from the clinic into the outside world, where his presence is a possible danger as he has no concept of right or wrong. *Mr. Soames* was a definite departure from the norm for Amicus, who were fortunate to secure Terence Stamp and Robert Vaughn for the leading roles. Both actors were drawn to the offbeat script and realized its dramatic potential, turning in fine performances as a result.

Video: None

184. *Monster of Terror*

An Alta Vista Production (1965); 80 minutes; Pathecolor and Pathescope; U.S. *(Die, Monster, Die!)*: American–International; ColorScope

EXP: James H. Nicholson and Samuel Z. Arkoff; **P:** Pat Green; **D:** Daniel Haller; **S:** Jerry Sohl; **M:** Don Banks; **DP:** Paul Beeson; **E:** Alfred Cox; **AD:** Colin Southcott; **Cast:** Boris Karloff, Nick Adams, Freda Jackson, Suzan Farmer, Terence de Marney, Patrick Magee, Paul Ferrell, George Moon, Gretchen Franklin, Sydney Bromley, Leslie Dwyer and Billy Milton.

American scientist Steven Reinhart (Nick Adams) comes to the rural English town of Arkham to see his fiancée Susan Witley (Suzan Farmer). He is greeted with hostility by Susan's father Nahum (Boris Karloff), who immediately asks him to leave. Steven stays at the insistence of Susan's ailing mother (Freda Jackson) and he eventually unravels the terrifying facts involving a radioactive meteorite which landed on the Witley estate years before. This adaptation of H.P. Lovecraft's story *The Colour Out of Space* marked the directorial debut of art

SUZAN FARMER, NICK ADAMS AND BORIS KARLOFF IN *MONSTER OF TERROR*.

director Daniel Haller (and moved Lovecraft's town of Arkham to rural England from New England). Confined to a wheelchair for most of the film, Boris Karloff turns in another memorable performance as the sinister Nahum Witley. In 1987, the same story was filmed as *The Curse*, with inferior results.

Video: U.K./U.S.

185. Moon Zero Two

A Hammer Film Production (1969); 100 minutes; Technicolor; U.S.: Warner Bros. (1970)

P/S: Michael Carreras; **D:** Roy Ward Baker; **M:** Don Ellis; **DP:** Paul Beeson; **E:** Spencer Reeve; **AD:** Scott MacGregor; **SVE:** Les Bowie; **Cast:** James Olson, Catherina Von Schell, Warren Mitchell, Adrienne Corri, Ori Levy, Bernard Bresslaw, Dudley Foster, Neil McCallum, Joby Blanshard, Michael Ripper, Robert Tayman and Chrissie Shrimpton.

Hammer lavished a great deal of money on this ill-conceived "space western" set in the year 2021. Obviously inspired by the success of *2001: A Space Odyssey*, Hammer failed to foresee how puerile their film would look in comparison. Spaceman Bill Kemp (James Olson) is a freelance trouble-shooter who uses his derelict spaceship, Moon 02, for various questionable enterprises. He is approached by Clementine Taplin (Catherina Von Schell) to help her find her brother, who was prospecting for minerals on the far side of the Moon. The two stumble onto a plot in which business tycoon J.J. Hubbard (Warren Mitchell) plans to hijack a 6,000-

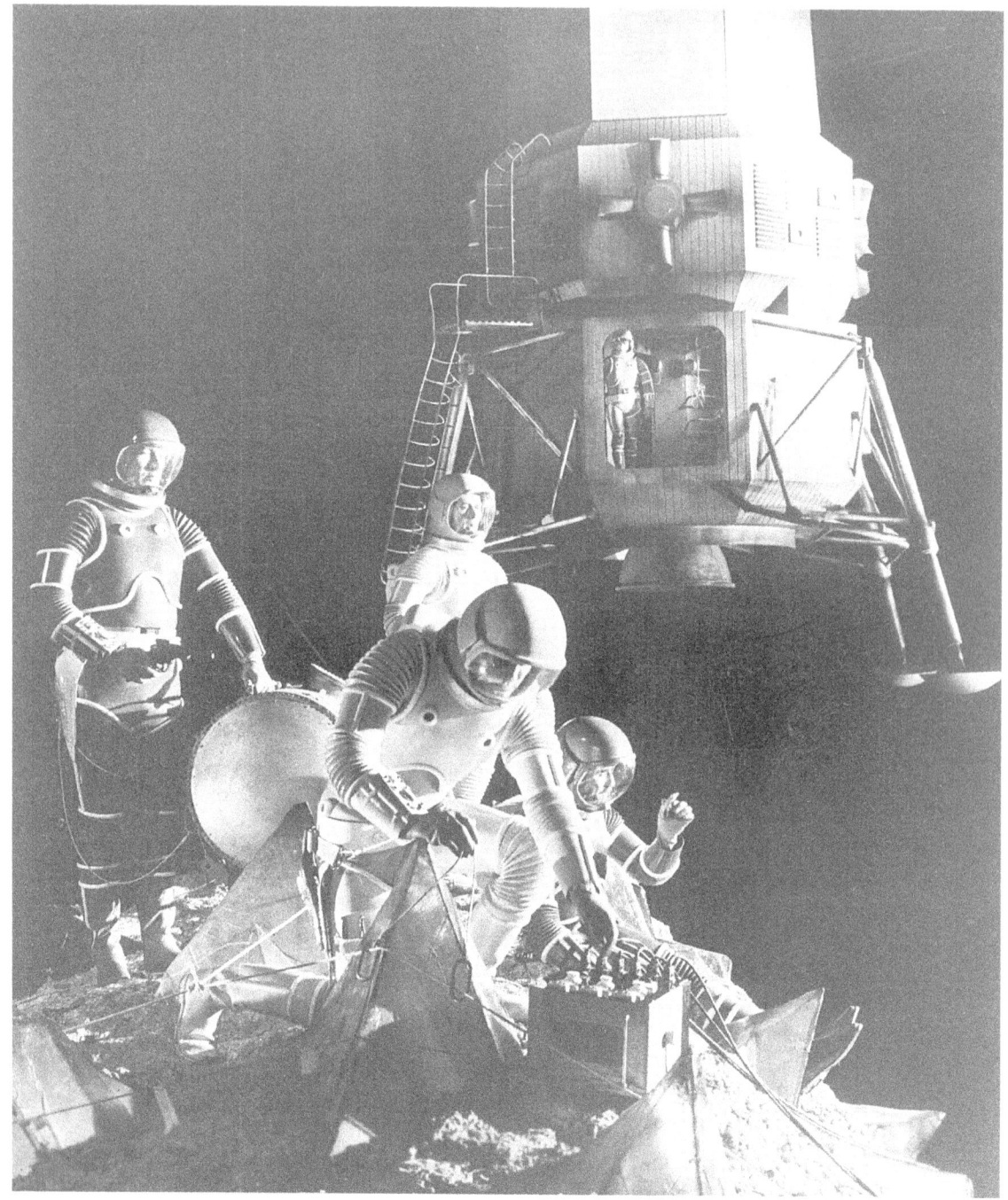

Moon Zero Two was one of Hammer's most costly productions.

ton sapphire asteroid and land it on the Moon. To its credit, the film does not take itself too seriously, but even the usually forgiving *Boxoffice* magazine found *Moon Zero Two* to be "naive and full of cliches." It lost a bundle for Hammer. A proposed sequel, entitled *Disaster in Space*, was never made.

Video: None

186. Mother Riley Meets the Vampire (a.k.a. *Vampire Over London*)

A Renown Pictures Corp. Ltd. Production (1952); 74 minutes; U.S. (*My Son the Vampire* [1963]): Jack H. Harris Enterprises

P/D: John Gilling; **S:** Val Valentine; **M:** Lindo Southworth; **DP:** Stan Davey; **E:** Len Trumm; **AD:** Bernard Robinson; **Cast:** Arthur Lucan, Bela Lugosi, Dora Bryan, Philip Leaver, Richard Wattis, Graham Moffat, Maria Mercedes, Roderick Lovell, David Hurst, Judith Furse, Ian Wilson and Charles Lloyd Pack.

Just what is it about the British and drag? Before Benny Hill and Barry Humphries there was Arthur Lucan, a popular music hall performer who created the character of the Irish washer woman Mother Riley. Lucan, as Mother Riley, starred in a series of films, of which this is the last. Bela Lugosi had come to England to star in a stage revival of *Dracula*; the show closed before it got to the West End and Lugosi and his wife were stranded in London with no money. Richard Gordon persuaded Lugosi to star in this film which, although terrible, isn't any worse than most of the other movies Lugosi appeared in during the 50s. Master criminal Dr. Van Hoosen (Lugosi), a.k.a. "The Vampire," plans to take over the world with 50,000 robots powered by uranium. Unfortunately, his prototype robot is delivered to Mother Riley (Lucan) instead. The robot's retrieval and Mother Riley's abduction cause no end of trouble for Van Hoosen. Lugosi plays his part as straight as possible, considering the circumstances. The film remained unreleased in the United States until 1963 when it appeared under the title *My Son the Vampire*, with a title song by humorist Allan Sherman.

Video: U.S.

187. The Mummy

A Hammer Film Production (1959); 88 minutes; Technicolor; U.S.: Universal–International

P: Michael Carreras; **D:** Terence Fisher; **S:** Jimmy Sangster; **M:** Franz Reizenstein; **DP:** Jack Asher; **E:** James Needs and Alfred Cox; **PD:** Bernard Robinson; **AD:** Don Mingaye; **Cast:** Peter Cushing, Christopher Lee, Yvonne Furneaux, Eddie Byrne, Felix Aylmer, George Pastell, Raymond Huntley, John Stuart, Harold Goodwin, Dennis Shaw, Michael Ripper and George Woodbridge.

In 1895, a team of British Egyptologists discover the tomb of the Princess Ananka. When her body is taken to England, Kharis, the mummy who guards over her, follows to kill the desecrators.

Instead of being a remake of the 1932 classic starring Boris Karloff, this excellent Hammer production is a distillation of ideas from the series of Kharis films of the 40s. It is, however, a vast improvement over those films. While the original Kharis was slow and shambling, Christopher Lee's interpretation is a fast-moving, relentless killing machine, but with a touch of pathos nevertheless. *The Mummy* is a perfect example of what Hammer was all about, with splendid direction, a fine cast and superb production values. Franz Reizenstein's grandiose score provides a truly epic quality and the painstakingly authentic flashback sequence to Ancient Egypt is a highlight. Horror films don't get much better than this.

Video: U.K./U.S.

188. The Mummy's Shroud

A Hammer/Seven Arts Production (1967); 84 minutes; Technicolor; U.S.: 20th Century–Fox; DeLuxe Color

P: Anthony Nelson-Keys; **D/S:** John Gilling; **M:** Don Banks; **DP:** Arthur Grant; **E:** James Needs and Spencer Reeve; **PD:** Bernard Robinson; **AD:** Don Mingaye; **Cast:** John Phillips, Andre Morell, David Buck, Elizabeth Sellers, Maggie Kimberley, Michael Ripper, Tim Barrett, Catherine Lacey, Roger Delgado, Eddie Powell, Dickie Owen and Richard Warner.

CHRISTOPHER LEE AS KHARIS MAKES HIS FIRST APPEARANCE IN *THE MUMMY*.

A prologue set in ancient Egypt relates the misfortunes of Kah-to-Bey, son of the Pharaoh Men-tah. In 1920, an expedition finds the tomb of Kah-to-Bey and takes his remains to the city of Mezzera. They soon have reason to regret their actions as the mummy of Prem, devoted slave of the young prince, comes to life to enact a terrible revenge on the tomb's desecrators. The script, based on an original story by John Elder, is fairly standard mummy movie fare but director John Gilling manages to infuse it with some inventive touches. The cast is quite good and Michael Ripper, as the hapless character Longbarrow, gives a performance that could have garnered a Best Supporting Actor Oscar in a more mainstream film. Special note should also be made of the authentic appearance of the mummy. The prototype for this costume is on display in the British Museum. This was the last motion picture produced by Hammer at Bray Studios.

Video: U.K./U.S.

189. *Mumsy, Nanny, Sonny and Girly*

A Ronald J. Kahn/Brigitte Films Ltd/Fitzroy Films Ltd. Production (1970); 101 minutes; Color; U.S. *(Girly)*: Cinerama Releasing

P: Ronald J. Kahn; **D:** Freddie Francis; **S:** Brian Comport; **M:** Bernard Ebbinghouse; **DP:**

David Muir; **E:** Tristam Cones; **AD:** Maggie Pinhorn; **Cast:** Vanessa Howard, Michael Bryant, Ursula Howells, Pat Heywood, Howard Trevor, Hugh Armstrong, Robert Swann, Imogen Hassall and Michael Ripper.

Based on a play by Masie Mosco, the confused narrative follows the exploits of a demented family consisting of the four title characters, who bring "new friends" into the fold and then kill them off. Michael Bryant is their latest acquisition and he proceeds to pit the female members against each other as they vie for his sexual attentions. Director Freddie Francis' affection for this film is almost as incomprehensible as the movie itself. The most interesting aspect of this black comedy is the extensive location work done at Oakley Court. This Gothic mansion, located adjacent to Bray Studios, was used in many horror films but seldom more effectively than it is in *Mumsy, Nanny, Sonny and Girly*. Today it is a luxury resort hotel, restored to its former glory.

Video: U.S.

190. *Murders in the Rue Morgue*

American–International Ltd. (1971); 86 minutes; Color by Movielab; U.S.: American–International

EXP: James H. Nicholson and Samuel Z. Arkoff; **P:** Louis M. Heyward; **D:** Gordon Hessler; **S:** Christopher Wicking and Henry Slesar; **M:** Waldo de los Rios; **DP:** Manuel Berenguer; **E:** Max Benedict; **PD:** Jose Luis Galicia; **Cast:** Jason Robards, Herbert Lom, Christine Kaufmann, Adolfo Celi, Michael Dunn, Lilli Palmer, Maria Perschy, Jose Calvo, Peter Arne, Luis Rivera, Werner Umburg and Marshall Jones.

AIP's British production team went to Spain to film this version of the Edgar Allan Poe story. Actually this movie has even less to do with the original Poe tale than Universal's 1932 version starring Bela Lugosi. The plot owes more to *Phantom of the Opera* than anything by Poe, complete with the actor who played Hammer's Phantom, Herbert Lom, as an acid-scarred, masked killer. Cesar Charron (Jason Robards) is the head of a Grand Guignol-style troupe performing Poe's *Murders in the Rue Morgue* at the Rue Morgue Theatre in Paris. Charron's wife Madeleine (Christine Kaufmann) is haunted by disturbing nightmares in which she is pursued by a masked man wielding an axe. Life begins to imitate art when past and present members of the troupe are murdered and disfigured by acid. The person responsible for this mayhem is Marot (Herbert Lom), a former actor who was in love with Madeleine's mother (Lilli Palmer). It was thought that he had committed suicide years before, but he has returned to take revenge on the people who betrayed him. Marot "dies" at least three times during the course of the story but, like that Energizer bunny, he just keeps on going. *Murders in the Rue Morgue* has been lavishly overpraised in some circles and, although it does have some interesting visuals, the story line is a bit of a muddle. Part of the blame for this is due to post-production tampering by Sam Arkoff; this ended Gordon Hessler's association with American–International once and for all.

Video: U.S.

191. *The Mutations*

A Getty Pictures Corporation Ltd. Film (1973); 92 minutes; A Robert D. Weinbach Production; Eastman Color; U.S.: Columbia (1974)

EXP: J. Ronald Getty; **P:** Robert D. Weinbach; **D:** Jack Cardiff; **S:** Edward Andrew Mann and Robert D. Weinbach; **M:** Basil Kirchin; **DP:** Paul Beeson; **E:** Russell Weelnough and David Beesley; **AD:** Herbert Smith; **Cast:** Donald Pleasence, Tom Baker, Brad Harris, Michael Dunn, Julie Ege, Scott Antony, Jill Haworth, Olga Anthony, Lisa Collings, Toby Lennon, Richard Davis and Tony Mayne.

Dr. Nolte (Donald Pleasence) is a crazed scientist attempting to cross-breed humans

Director Gordon Hessler and his star Christine Kaufmann on the set of *Murders in the Rue Morgue*.

and plants...with disastrous results. The monstrous mutations he creates are put on display in a "Freak Show" run by the hideously deformed Mr. Lynch (Tom Baker). Lynch assists Dr. Nolte because he hopes the perfected experiments will help to cure him of his deformity. A subplot involves the real-life freaks who appear in Lynch's carnival show and the cruelty he inflicts upon them. This part of the film is very derivative of Tod Browning's *Freaks* and elicits the same queasy feelings as these unfortunates are exploited because of their physical handicaps. Actor Brad Harris, who was also an associate producer on this movie, was the star of many Italian "sword and sandal" films as well as being the one-time husband of Hammer sex goddess Olinka Berova.

Video: U.K./U.S. (alternate U.S. video title: *The Freak Maker*)

192. Mysterious Island

A Charles H. Schneer Production (1961); 101 minutes; An Ameran Film; Technicolor and Superdynamation; U.S.: Columbia; Eastman Color by Pathe and SuperDynamation

P: Charles H. Schneer; **D:** Cy Endfield; **S:** John Prebble, Daniel Ullman and Crane Wilbur; **M:** Bernard Herrmann; **DP:** Wilkie Cooper; **E:** Frederick Wilson; **AD:** Bill Andrews; **SVE:** Ray Harryhausen; **Cast:** Michael Craig, Joan Greenwood, Michael Callan, Gary Merrill, Beth Rogan, Herbert Lom, Percy Herbert and Dan Jackson.

A GIANT CRAB THREATENS THE CASTAWAYS ON JULES VERNE'S *MYSTERIOUS ISLAND*.

In the tradition of Disney's *20,000 Leagues Under the Sea* and Fox's *Journey to the Center of the Earth*, this adventure-fantasy is based on a novel by Jules Verne. During the American Civil War, a group of Yankee captives escape from a Confederate prison an observation balloon. A terrible storm blows them to the "mysterious island" of the title. This island is populated by gigantic beasts which, it turns out, are the result of experiments conducted by the infamous Capt. Nemo (Herbert Lom).

Ray Harryhausen admitted, "We took certain liberties by altering the story to include gigantism for more visual excitement." A wise decision, Harryhausen's special effects are the highlights of the film. This is not to suggest that the rest of the movie is lacking. The small cast turns in excellent ensemble performances and Wilkie Cooper's color photography is splendid. Once again the Schneer–Harryhausen collaboration produced a winner. *Mysterious Island* became the number one boxoffice attraction in the United Kingdom in 1961.

Video: U.K./U.S.

193. Naked Evil

Gibraltar/Protelco Films (1966); 80 minutes; U.S. *(Exorcism at Midnight)*: Independent International (1973); MultiColor

EXP: Richard Gordon and Steven Pallos; **P:** Michael Johnson; **D/S:** Stanley Goulder; **M:** Bernard Ebbinghouse; **DP:** Geoffrey Faithfull; **E:** Peter Musgrave; **AD:** George Provis; **Cast:** Anthony Ainley, Basil Dignam, Brylo Ford, Richard Coleman, George A. Saunders, Suzanne Neve, Olaf Pooley, Ronald Bridges, Pearl Prescod, Carmen Munroe, Dan Jackson and Bari Johnson.

Naked Evil is the closest thing to a "blaxploitation" horror film to come out of England. Based on a play called *The Obi* which had been on British television, the story tells of some black university students in a small English town who become involved with voodoo. Shot on a shoestring budget in black-and-white and financed by the British division of Columbia Pictures, it proved to be a tough sell to American distributors. It was finally picked up by Independent International and, since the plot did feature an exorcism, it was retitled to capitalize on *The Exorcist*. New scenes featuring American actor Lawrence Tierney were shot in color as a framing device and the original black-and-white footage was tinted amber.

Video: None

194. The Nanny

A Hammer–Seven Arts Production (1965); 93 minutes; U.S.: 20th Century–Fox

P/S: Jimmy Sangster; **D:** Seth Holt; **M:** Richard Rodney Bennett; **DP:** Harry Waxman; **PD:** Edward Carrick; **E:** James Needs and Tom Simpson; **Cast:** Bette Davis, Wendy Craig, Jill Bennett, James Villiers, William Dix, Pamela Franklin, Jack Watling, Maurice Denham, Alfred Burke, Nora Gordon, Sandra Power and Harry Fowler.

Blamed for the death of his younger sister, Joey Fain (William Dix) is sent to an institution for disturbed children. Two years later, he returns home where he treats his family and his Nanny (Bette Davis) with increasing hostility. Joey contends that Nanny killed his sister and now wants to murder him as well. Based on the novel by Evelyn Piper, *The Nanny* showcases Bette Davis in one of the most subdued and effective performances of her later career. Her characterization shifts with seeming effortlessness from benevolent to menacing to pitiable. As her precocious accuser, William Dix is more than a match for Davis. In fact, the film is filled with top-notch performances by all involved. This is one of Hammer's most uncharacteristic productions and it also proved to be one of their most profitable.

Video: U.K./U.S.

195. Neither the Sea Nor the Sand

A Tigon–British Production (1972); 94 minutes; Eastman Color; U.S.: International Amusement Corp. (1974)

EXP: Tony Tenser and Peter J. Thompson; **P:** Jack Smith and Peter Fetterman; **D:** Fred Burnley; **S:** Gordon Honeycombe; **M:** Nachum Heiman; **DP:** David Muir; **E:** Norman Wanstall; **AD:** Michael Bastow; **Cast:** Susan Hampshire, Michael Petrovitch, Frank Finlay, Michael Craze, Jack Lambert, David Garth, Betty Duncan and Anthony Booth.

This was Tigon's final genre effort. Gordon Honeycombe adapted his novel in which a young man named Hugh (Michael Petrovitch) suffers a fatal heart attack but is kept on the edge of life by the love of his girlfriend Anna (Susan Hampshire). Hugh's brother George (Frank Finley) accuses Anna of practicing witchcraft and dies in an automobile accident shortly thereafter, suggesting that perhaps he was right. Although the power of Anna's love may be able to sustain Hugh's life, it cannot prevent him from decomposing and the movie ends on a downbeat and bittersweet note. The director chose to approach the material as a romantic melodrama, rather than stress the horror elements. This doesn't always work in the films favor and, despite the interesting premise, the overall result is less than it could have been.

Video: None

Never Take Candy from a Stranger see *Never Take Sweets from a Stranger*

196. Never Take Sweets from a Stranger

A Hammer Film Production (1960); 81 minutes; MegaScope; U.S. *(Never Take Candy from a Stranger* [1961]*)*: A Howard J. Beck Presentation; An Omat Release

EXP: Michael Carreras; **P:** Anthony Hinds; **D:** Cyril Frankel; **S:** John Hunter; **M:** Elisabeth Lutyens; **DP:** Freddie Francis; **E:** James Needs and Alfred Cox; **PD:** Bernard Robinson; **Cast:** Gwen Watford, Patrick Allen, Felix Aylmer, Niall MacGinnis, Alison Leggatt, Bill Nagy, Frances Green, Janina Faye, Michael Gwynn, Macdonald Parke, Bud Knapp and Vera Cook.

Peter Carter (Patrick Allen) moves his family to a small town Canada where he has taken a position as a school principal. They are beginning to settle in when their young daughter Jean (Janina Faye) tells them that an old man gave her and her friend Lucille (Frances Green) candy to take their clothes off in front of him. Understandably upset, the Carters go to the police and discover that the old man is Mr. Olderberry (Felix Aylmer), a respected pillar of the community. A trial ensues and Olderberry is acquitted and released. The Carters decided to leave town but, before they can go, Olderberry strikes again with far more dire consequences. This was extremely strong material in 1960 and, despite Hammer's declarations of the highest intentions in making the film, *Never Take Sweets from a Stranger* was disliked by most critics and ignored by the public at large. By way of explanation, James Carreras said, "People just don't want messages." The film is well-made

A PENSIVE BETTE DAVIS PLANS HER NEXT MAYHEM AS *THE*

and solidly acted but at times, particularly during Felix Aylmer's pursuit of the girls through the forest, it veers uncomfortably towards Hammer horror territory. Actually, it works far better when viewed as a psychological thriller instead of a public service film.

Video: None

197. Night, After Night, After Night

Dudley Birch Films Ltd. (1969); 87 minutes; Color; U.S.: No theatrical release

P: James Mellor; **D:** Lewis J. Force (Lindsay Shonteff); **S:** Dial Ambler; **M:** Douglas Gamely; **DP:** Douglas Hill; **E:** John Rushton; **AD:** Wilfred Arnold; **Cast:** Jack May, Justine Lord, Gilbert Wynne, Linda Marlowe, Gary Hope, Terry Scully, Donald Sumpter, Peter Forbes-Robert-

Janina Faye swears to tell the whole truth as Michael Gwynn looks on in *Never Take Sweets from a Stranger*.

son, Jack Smethurst, Michael Nightingale, April Harlow, Jacqueline Clerk and Carol Haddon.

This trashy thriller was directed by Lindsay Schonteff, who demanded that his name be removed from the finished product. It's easy to understand why. A modern-day "Jack the Ripper" is attempting to rid the mod London streets of loose women. The prime suspect is a self-proclaimed "banger of birds" (Donald Sumpter) who is mercilessly hounded by the police. Judge Lomax (Jack May) is a magistrate who inflicts harsh sentences on the evil scum that he deems to be a cancer on society. It isn't much of a surprise to discover who the killer really is. In the prolonged climax, the murderer eludes the police by dressing up in very bad drag. He then goes completely bonkers in his secret room, the walls of which are covered with photos of naked, large-breasted women. To call his performance over-the-top at this point would be a considerable understatement.

Video: U.S.

198. The Night Caller

Armitage Films (1965); 84 minutes; U.S. *(Blood Beast from Outer Space)*: A Harris Accociates Inc. Presentation; A World Entertainment Release (1966)

EXP: John Phillips; **P:** Ronald Liles; **D:** John Gilling; **S:** Jim O'Connolly; **M:** Johnny Gregory; **DP:** Stephen Dade; **E:** Philip Barnikel; **AD:** Harry White; **Cast:** John Saxon, Maurice Denham, Patricia Haines, John Carson, Alfred Burke, Jack Watson, Warren Mitchell, Aubrey Morris,

JOHN SAXON, PATRICIA HINES AND MAURICE DENHAM RECEIVE A MESSAGE FROM *THE NIGHT CALLER*.

Anthony Wager, Ballard Berkeley, Marianne Stone and Barbara French.

A luminous sphere comes out of the sky and lands outside of London, causing baffled scientists to speculate about its origins. The sphere is actually a matter transmitter which transports an alien from Ganymede, the third moon of Jupiter, to Earth. The alien is named Medra and he attempts to pass himself off as an Earthling. He then places an advertisement for models in a cheesecake magazine called *Bikini Girl*. His objective is to abduct young women and return them to his world for breeding purposes. The high number of female disappearances sparks a manhunt by the police which culminates in a showdown with Medra in a derelict building. An interesting film which has its share of surprises, not the least of which is the totally unexpected demise of leading lady Patricia Haines at the hands of the alien. Also worth noting is the unintentionally hilarious "Night Caller Theme" written by Albert Hague and sung by Mark Richardson over the opening credits.

Video: U.S. (video title: *Night Caller from Outer Space*)

Night Caller from Outer Space see **The Night Caller**

Night Creatures see **Captain Clegg**

199. The Night Digger (a.k.a. The Road Builder)

Yongestreet Films/Tacitus Productions Ltd. (1970); 100 minutes; MetroColor; U.S.: Metro–Goldwyn–Mayer (1971)

EXP: William O. Harbach; P: Alan D. Courtney and Norman S. Powell; D: Alastair Reid; S: Roald Dahl; M: Bernard Herrmann; DP: Alex Thomson; AD: Anthony Pratt; Cast: Patricia Neal, Pamela Brown, Nicholas Clay, Jean Anderson, Graham Crowden, Yootha Joyce, Peter Sallis, Brigit Forsyth, Sebastian Breaks, Dian Patrick, Jenny McCracken and Bruce Myles.

Maura (Patrica Neal) is a middle-aged spinster who has wasted her youth taking care of her demanding invalid mother (Pamela Brown). Enter Billy Jarvis (Nicholas Clay), an attractive 20-year-old who inveigles his way into their household in the capacity of handyman. Maura at first resents his presence but soon finds herself falling in love with him. Unfortunately, Billy is a psychopath who rapes and murders young women and then buries their bodies where roads are being paved. Roald Dahl adapted Joy Crowley's novel *Nest in a Fallen Tree* as a vehicle for his wife Patricia Neal who, like the character she played, was a recovering stroke victim. The film has many effective moments, enhanced by Bernard Herrmann's poignant music.

Video: None

200. *Night Hair Child*

Leander Films/Leisure-Media (1971); 89 minutes; Color by Movielab; U.S. *(What the Peeper Saw)*: Avco Embassy (1972)

EXP: Oliver A. Unger; P: Graham Harris; D: James Kelly; S: Trevor Preston; M: Stelvio Cipriani; DP: Harry Waxman and Luis Cuadrado; E: Nicholas Wentworth; Cast: Mark Lester, Britt Ekland, Hardy Kruger, Lilli Palmer, Harry Andrews, Conchita Montez and Colette Jack.

Twelve-year-old Marcus Bezant (Mark Lester) comes to live with his father Paul (Hardy Kruger) and his stepmother Elise (Britt Ekland). He tells them that he has been sent home from boarding school because of a chicken pox epidemic, but Elise learns that he has been expelled because of deleterious behavior. Elise comes to realize that Marcus is a malevolent child who is determined to cause a rift between her and his father. It is also possible that he may have caused the "accidental" death of his mother. The first half of the film, which is a cat-and-mouse game between Marcus and Elise, is absorbing. Unfortunately, the latter portion develops into an incoherent psychological thriller with a distinctly unpleasant surprise ending. The Spanish location photography is the one true asset of this movie.

Video: U.S.

201. *Night Must Fall*

Metro–Goldwyn–Mayer (1964); 101 minutes

EXP: Lawrence P. Bachmann; P: Albert Finney and Karel Reisz; D: Karel Reisz; S: Clive Exton; M: Ron Grainer; DP: Freddie Francis; E: Philip Barnikel; AD: Lionel Couch; Cast: Albert Finney, Mona Washbourne, Susan Hampshire, Sheila Hancock, Michael Medwin, Joe Gladwin, Martin Wyldeck and John Gill.

The advertising catchline says it all: "The lusty, brawling star of *Tom Jones* goes psycho in *Night Must Fall*." Director Karel Reisz stated that for this second screen version of Emlyn Williams' play, "We left only the bare bones of the original story." Unfortunately, those "bare bones" did not include any of the subtleties of the original material. Albert Finney, who provided much of financial backing for this film, uses every tic, twitch and facial grimace he can muster in his portrayal of Danny, a psychotic killer who charms his way into the household of a foolish old lady. Mona Washbourne gives a terrific performance as his employer, Mrs. Bramson. She practically salivates over the young handyman, who not only beguiles her but her daughter and housekeeper as well.

The main flaw in this film is that Finney's characterization lacks charm, making it difficult to understand why the three ladies find him so irresistible. John Cutts reviewed

Night Must Fall in *Films and Filming*, saying the picture was "a curious affair (neither good nor bad — just plain curious), that never, for a moment, equals anything like the obvious amount of directorial effort put into it."

Video: None

202. Night of the Big Heat

A Planet Films Ltd. Production (1967); 94 minutes; Eastman Color; U.S. (*Island of the Burning Damned* [a.k.a. *Island of the Burning Doomed*]): United Productions of America (1971)

P: Tom Blakeley; **D:** Terence Fisher; **S:** Ronald Liles; **M:** Malcolm Lockyer; **DP:** Reg Wyer; **E:** Rod Keys; **AD:** Alex Vetchinsky; **Cast:** Christopher Lee, Peter Cushing, Patrick Allen, Jane Merrow, Sarah Lawson, William Lucas, Kenneth Cope, Jack Bligh, Thomas Heathcote, Sydney Bromley, Percy Herbert and Anna Turner.

While the rest of the United Kingdom is in the grip of a cold spell, the inhabitants of a tiny island off the British coast are suffering from rising temperatures. As the heat escalates, irrational behavior abounds. The title *Night of the Big Heat* could also refer to Jane Merrow, who is on the boil for her married ex-lover Patrick Allen and causes him no end of trouble. Christopher Lee is the surly scientist who deduces that an alien life form has come to take over the island. The film is nearly over before we see the aliens, who resemble large, ambulatory fried eggs. A sudden rainstorm kills the creatures and the movie ends abruptly. Good performances from a mostly excellent cast cannot conceal the fact that Terence Fisher's heart simply wasn't in this project.

Video: U.S.

ALBERT FINNEY AS DANNY, THE HOMICIDAL KILLER FROM *NIGHT MUST FALL*.

203. Night of the Demon

A Sabre Production Ltd. (1957); 95 minutes; U.S. (*Curse of the Demon*): Columbia (1958); 82 minutes

P: Hal E. Chester; **D:** Jacques Tourneur; **S:** Charles Bennett and Hal E. Chester; **M:** Clifton Parker; **DP:** Ted Sciafe; **E:** Michael Gordon; **AD:** Ken Adam; **Cast:** Dana Andrews, Peggy Cummins, Niall MacGinnis, Maurice Denham, Athene Seyler, Liam Redmond, Reginald Beckwith, Ewan Roberts, Peter Elliott, Charles Lloyd Pack, Brian Wilde and Percy Herbert.

NORMAN TAYLOR (PETER WYNGARDE) DISCOVERS THAT HIS WIFE TANSY (JANET BLAIR) HAS BEEN PRACTICING WITCHCRAFT IN *NIGHT OF THE EAGLE*.

A true classic of the horror genre. Skeptic John Holden (Dana Andrews) goes to England to disprove the supposed powers of a satanic cult headed by Julian Karswell (Niall MacGinnis). Joanna Harrington (Peggy Cummins) believes that her uncle was destroyed by dark forces conjured up by Karswell and she attempts to save Holden from a similar fate. The screenplay was based on the story "Casting the Ruins" by Montague James. Director Jacques Tourneur, a Val Lewton alumnus, was opposed to the producer's insistance on showing the demon, but the monster is suitably horrific and makes for a memorable climax to a superior motion picture. Niall MacGinnis is very effective as the deceptively benevolent warlock Karswell, whose own black magic eventually gets the better of him.
Video: U.K./U.S.

204. Night of the Eagle

A Julian Wintle–Leslie Parkyn Production (1961); 87 minutes; U.S. *(Burn Witch, Burn)*: American–International (1962); 90 minutes

EXP: Julian Wintle and Leslie Parkyn; **P:** Albert Fennell; **D:** Sidney Hayers; **S:** Richard Matheson, Charles Beaumont and George Baxt; **M:** William Alwyn; **DP:** Reg Wyer; **E:** Ralph Sheldon; **AD:** Jack Shampan; **Cast:** Janet Blair, Peter Wyngarde, Margaret Johnston, Anthony Nicholls, Colin Gordon, Kathleen Byron, Reginald Beckwith, Jessica Dunning, Norman Bird, Judith Stott and Bill Mitchell.

It's hard to believe that this effective exercise in implied horror came from the same team that made the wildly exploitative *Circus of Horrors*. Based on Fritz Leiber's *Conjure Wife*, which had been previously filmed by Universal as *Weird Woman* (1944), *Night of the Eagle* is a story of modern-day witchcraft. Norman Taylor (Peter Wyngarde)

A DISTRAUGHT ELIZABETH TAYLOR BELIEVES SHE HAS WITNESSED A MURDER IN *NIGHT WATCH*.

is an extremely successful university professor who doesn't suspect that much of his success is due to the spells cast by his loving wife Tansy (Janet Blair). Tansy realizes that some of the faculty wives, jealous of Norman's achievements, are doing their best to undermine his position by using some witchcraft of their own. When Norman discovers Tansy's magical implements hidden around the house, he dismisses her beliefs as superstitious nonsense and forces her to burn them. Immediately thereafter, Norman's life goes to hell. A student falsely accuses him of raping her; her boyfriend attacks Norman with a gun; an unknown "thing" screeches outside the Taylor house at night; Tansy becomes possessed and tries to kill Norman with a butcher knife. By the end of the picture, Norman is convinced that witchcraft isn't as irrational a belief as he once thought.

This very good film is somewhat marred by the casting of Janet Blair. Primarily known for her work as a lightweight entertainer on American television, she seems an odd choice for Tansy and tends to overplay the part.

The American release version features a three-minute spoken prologue, added by AIP, which purports to exorcise the theatre of evil spirits before the picture begins.

Video: U.K./U.S. (available in the U.S. on laser disc only)

Night of the Silicates see *Island of Terror*

205. Night Watch

Brut Productions (1973); 100 minutes; Technicolor; U.S.: Avco Embassy

P: Martin Poll, George W. George and Bernard Straus; D: Brian G. Hutton; S: Tony Williamson; M: John Cameron; DP: Billy Williams; E: John Jympson; AD: Peter Murton; Cast: Elizabeth Taylor, Laurence Harvey, Billie Whitelaw, Robert Lang, Tony Britton, Michael Danvers-Walker, Bill Dean, Rosario Serrano, Pauline Jameson, Linda Hayden, Kevin Colson and Laon Maybanke.

Awakened one night during a thunderstorm, neurotic and wealthy Ellen Wheeler (Elizabeth Taylor) witnesses the aftermath of a murder in a derelict house opposite her bedroom window. The police are called and the house is searched but there is no evidence of any killing. Ellen continues to plague the police with what they believe are false alarms. Her husband (Laurence Harvey) and best friend (Billie Whitelaw) begin to think that Ellen is becoming mentally unbalanced. When two gruesome murders are actually committed, the police decline to investigate and dismiss Mrs. Wheeler as a crank. The screenplay for this "Girl Who Cried Wolf" thriller was adapted from the play by Lucille Fletcher, who gained fame with *Sorry, Wrong Number* several years before. Alexander Stuart (reviewing the film in *Films and Filming*) said, "The direction at times has the appearance of a pastiche of the worst of Hammer's Gothic productions." It is often reminiscent of Hammer's psychological thrillers, but one tarted up as a star vehicle to showcase the talents of its renowned leading lady.

Video: U.S.

206. The Nightcomers

An Elliott Kastner–Jay Kanter–Alan Ladd,Jr./ Scimitar Production (1972); 96 minutes; Technicolor; U.S.: A Joseph E. Levine Presentation; Avco Embassy

P/D: Michael Winner; S: Michael Hastings; M: Jerry Fielding; DP: Robert Paynter; E: Frederick Wilson; AD: Herbert Westbrook; Cast: Marlon Brando, Stephanie Beacham, Thora Hird, Harry Andrews, Verna Harvey, Christopher Ellis, and Anna Palk.

This prequel to Henry James' *The Turn of the Screw* might have seemed like an inspired idea at the time, but the uninspired direction of Michael Winner seems to have doomed it from the outset. Marlon Brando plays Peter Quint, the groom whose affair with a governess, Miss Jessell (Stephanie Beacham), ends in their destruction. While James' story is a masterpiece of indirection, this film lays all its cards out on the table; no mystery here! The children are warped little monsters and Quint is not sinister but loutish. During its original release, *The Nightcomers* gained some notoriety because of a rather explicit (for the time) sadomasochistic love scene between Brando and Beacham. The only thing shocking about it now is how overweight Brando looks. Stephanie Beacham, however, is as lovely as ever.

Video: U.S.

207. Nightmare

A Hammer Film Production (1964); 82 minutes; HammerScope; U.S.: Universal–International

P/S: Jimmy Sangster; D: Freddie Francis; M: Don Banks; DP: John Wilcox; E: James Needs; PD: Bernard Robinson; AD: Don Mingaye; Cast: Jennie Linden, David Knight, Moira Redmond, Brenda Bruce, George A. Cooper, Irene Richmond, John Welsh, Timothy Bateson, Clytie Jessop, Hedger Wallace, Julie Samuel and Elizabeth Dear.

Seventeen-year-old Janet (Jennie Linden) is sent home from Hatcher's School for Young Ladies (Oakley Court) because of the terrible nightmares she has been experiencing. Mary (Brenda Bruce), one of Janet's teachers, accompanies her former student back to Hightowers, the family mansion. There, Mary learns from the housekeeper that, on her eleventh birthday, Janet saw her mother stab her father to death. Judged insane, her mother was sent to the local asylum, where she still resides. Janet fears that she may have inherited her mother's insanity. The night of her arrival home, Janet begins to have nightmares about a sinister woman in white who wanders the corridors of the house. This psychological shocker from Hammer has an especially convoluted storyline. It also features a thoroughly demented performance from Moira Redmond as a woman who becomes involved in a murder plot and gets considerably more than she bargained for.

Video: U.S.

Nightmare see *Voices*

208. *1984*

A Holiday Production (1956); 91 minutes; U.S.: Columbia

P: N. Peter Rathvon; **D:** Michael Anderson; **S:** William P. Templeton and Ralph Bettinson; **M:** Malcolm Arnold; **DP:** C. Pennington-Richards; **E:** Bill Lewthwaite; **AD:** Louis Levy; **Cast:** Edmond O'Brien, Jan Sterling, Michael Redgrave, David Kossoff, Mervyn Johns, Donald Pleasence, Carol Wolveridge, Ernest Clark, Patrick Allen, Ronan O'Casey, Michael Ripper and Ewen Solon.

In December 1954, the BBC presented a television version of George Orwell's bleak view of the future, *1984*. The star was Peter Cushing and his performance as Winston Smith was masterful. Why, when the decision was made to bring this story to the big screen, he was passed over in favor of Edmond O'Brien is anybody's guess. O'Brien is the most discordant factor in this disappointing adaptation, which does little justice to Orwell's novel. Following an atomic war, London is the capital city of Oceania, a community where the citizens' lives are continually monitored by television cameras. Free thought is forbidden and sex is carefully controlled by the government, which is represented as the all-knowing "Big Brother." Winston Smith (O'Brien) is a clerk in the Ministry of Truth, where he meets and falls in love with Julia (Jan Sterling). The movie focuses on this love affair to the detriment of Orwell's larger issues. Two different endings were filmed. In the British version, Winston and Julia, unrepentent, are executed for their crime against the state. In the American version, Winston is brainwashed and betrays Julia to the government.

Video: None

209. *No Blade of Grass*

Metro–Goldwyn–Mayer (1970); 96 minutes; MetroColor and Panavision

P/D: Cornel Wilde; **S:** Sean Forestal and Jefferson Pascal; **M:** Burnell Whibley; **DP:** H.A.R. Thomson; **AD:** Elliot Scott; **E:** Frank Clarke and Eric Boyd-Perkins; **Cast:** Nigel Davenport, Jean Wallace, John Hamill, Lynne Frederick, Patrick Holt, Anthony May, Wendy Richard, Nigel Rathbone, George Coulouris, Ruth Kettlewell, Tex Fuller and Christopher Neame.

In the not-too-distant, over-polluted and over-populated future, a new disease is killing all of the grasses throughout the world. With no wheat or other grains available, a world famine is inevitable. Some governments decide to nerve-gas the people in heavily populated areas so that others may survive. David Custance (Nigel Davenport) and his family resolve to leave their home in London and head north to his brother's farm, where a large amount of food supplies have been stored in anticipation of this situation. The trek is difficult; the dangers of a world in the grip of anarchy are many. Director Cornel Wilde has an important message to deliver here but he does it rather heavy-handedly. The story is intercut with continual shots of factories spewing smoke, polluted rivers and dead animals. There is also a pointless and excessive use of flash-forwards which damages the dramatic flow. The material itself was strong enough to carry the film without resorting to these cinematic tricks.

Video: None

No Place Like Homicide see *What a Carve-Up!*

210. Nothing but the Night

A Charlemagne Production (1972); 90 minutes; Color; U.S. *(The Devil's Undead)*: Intercontinental Releasing Corp. (1976)

P: Anthony Nelson-Keys; **D:** Peter Sasdy; **S:** Brian Hayles; **M:** Malcolm Williamson; **DP:** Kenneth Talbot; **E:** Keith Palmer; **AD:** Colin Grimes; **Cast:** Christopher Lee, Peter Cushing, Diana Dors, Georgia Brown, Keith Barron, Gwyneth Strong, Fulton MacKay, John Robinson, Morris Perry, Michael Gambon, Kathleen Byron and Duncan Lamont.

Displeased with the roles he was being offered and the movies he was asked to appear in, Christopher Lee and former Hammer producer Anthony Nelson-Keys formed their own production company, Charlemagne. They secured the screen rights to several of Dennis Wheatley's black magic novels, including *The Satanist* and *To the Devil...A Daughter*. Why the Rank Organization forced Charlemagne to produce this particular project, based on a novel by John Blackburn, for their initial offering instead of one of the Wheatley stories is a mystery. The failure of the film insured that there would be no further productions forthcoming from Charlemagne. In his autobiography, Lee states, "That Charlemagne effort ...failed because it was ahead of its time." Maybe so...but it also really isn't a very good film. The confused storyline has Cushing and Lee investigating the deaths of several trustees of Inver House, an orphanage located on an island off the coast of Scotland. Prime suspect in the killings is Anna Harb (Diana Dors). She is trying to regain custody of her daughter Mary (Gwyneth Strong), who was taken from her when she was sent to prison for murder ten years before. The payoff to the plot is that the trustees are extending their lives by transferring their personalities and memories into the children's bodies. The story is filled with red herrings, including Diana Dors in a red fright wig, hamming it up in another of the "fat mad cow" roles that typified the latter part of her career.

Video: U.S.

211. The Oblong Box

American–International (1969); 91 minutes; Berkey Pathe Color; U.S.: American–International

EXP: Louis M. Heyward; **P/D:** Gordon Hessler; **S:** Lawrence Huntington and Christopher Wicking; **M:** Harry Robinson; **DP:** John Coquillon; **E:** Max Benedict; **AD:** George Provis; **Cast:** Vincent Price, Christopher Lee, Hilary Dwyer, Rupert Davies, Sally Geeson, Alister Williamson, Uta Levka, Peter Arne, Maxwell Shaw, Carl Rigg, Harry Baird, James Mellor and Godfrey James.

The Oblong Box was originally intended as director Michael Reeves' followup film to his *Witchfinder General*, but he bowed out due to illness before filming began in November 1968. Producer Gordon Hessler was recruited to take over the directorial reins. In February 1969, Reeves died at age 25, a possible suicide. The film reunites three of the principal actors from *Witchfinder General*, Vincent Price, Hilary Dwyer and Rupert Davies. Any similarities between the two films ends there. *The Oblong Box* was yet another attempt by AIP to continue their flagging series of Edgar Allan Poe films and, once again, all that remains of Poe is the title. In 1860, Edward (Alister Williamson) and Julian (Price) Markham return to their home in England after spending several years overseeing their plantation in Africa. Edward has come back a raving madman, horribly

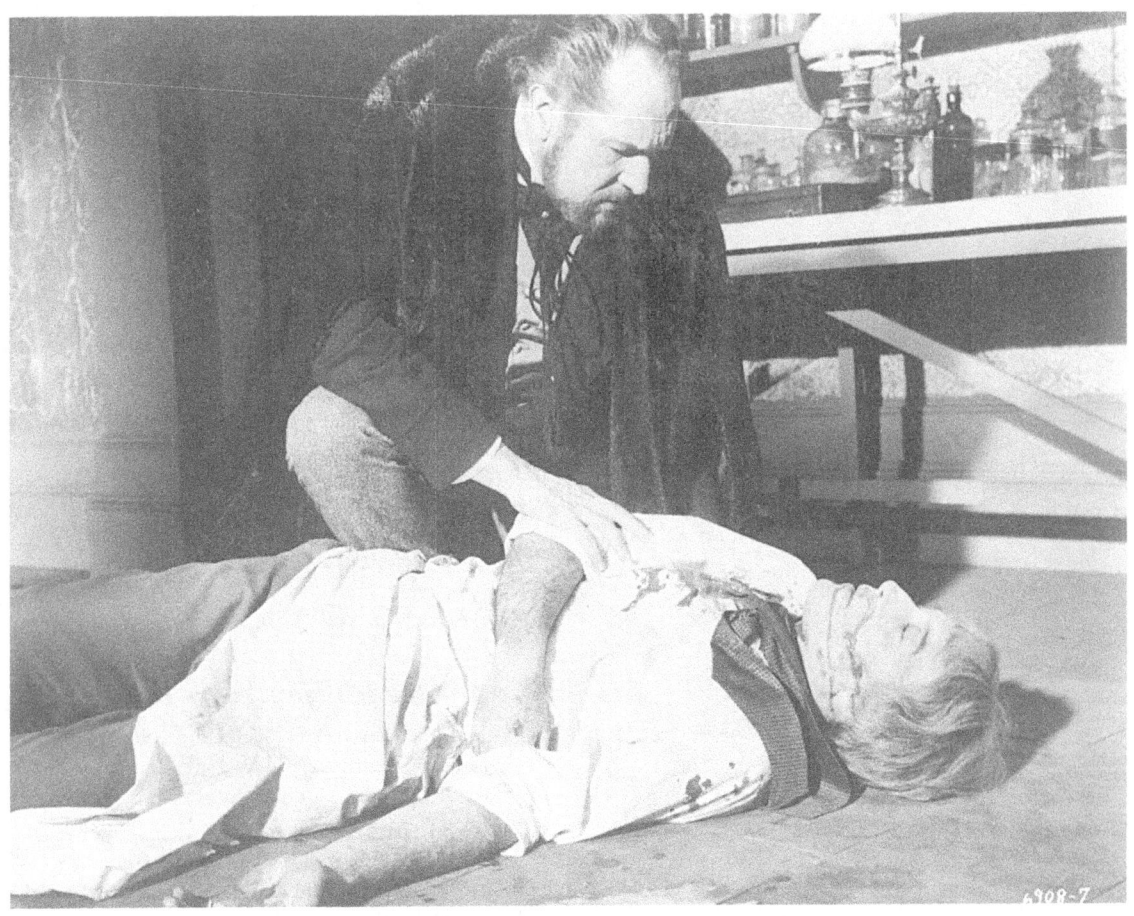

IN *THE OBLONG BOX*, VINCENT PRICE AND CHRISTOPHER LEE SHARE ONE BRIEF SCENE TOGETHER.

disfigured by a voodoo curse, and Julian must keep him hidden away under lock and key. As one might expect in a film of this type, Edward escapes and, with his face hidden behind a scarlet hood, goes on a throat-cutting murder spree. Christopher Lee is on hand in the thankless role of a doctor who reluctantly assists Edward and ends up with his throat slit anyway. The biggest letdown in this film is the revelation of Edward's face, which resembles a pig with acne.

Video: U.K./U.S.

212. The Old Dark House

A William Castle/Hammer Production (1963); 77 minutes; Technicolor; U.S.: Columbia; 86 minutes; Black-and-White

P: William Castle and Anthony Hinds; **D:** William Castle; **S:** Robert Dillon; **M:** Benjamin Frankel; **DP:** Arthur Grant; **E:** James Needs; **PD:** Bernard Robinson; **Cast:** Tom Poston, Robert Morley, Janette Scott, Joyce Grenfell, Mervyn Johns, Fenella Fielding, Peter Bull, Danny Green and John Harvey.

Columbia executives must have thought they would have a sure hit by combining the talents of their resident horror director William Castle with Hammer, the British horror specialists. Instead, it turned out to be a recipe for disaster. J. B. Priestley's novel *Benighted* had been previously filmed in 1932 by Universal, starring Boris Karloff and directed by James Whale. The original version had more than its share of "gallows

GLAMOROUS RAQUEL WELCH IS ONE OF THE REASONS WHY *ONE MILLION YEARS B.C.* WAS HAMMER'S BIGGEST MONEYMAKER.

humor"; Castle turned his version into a total farce played in the broadest of terms. Tom Poston, who had previous starred in Castle's lame comedy *Zotz!*, was unwisely chosen for the lead in *The Old Dark House*. Even a supporting cast of brilliant British character actors couldn't overcome Poston's annoying and unfunny performance. The *San Diego Evening Tribune* said, "Robert Morley, a formidable English actor, and Joyce Grenfell, another Briton of some performing stature, do everything but put on fright wigs to retain attention. And Tom Poston scurries around frantically. It requires suspension of even the smallest degree of sophistication, however, to credit their work as anything more than ridiculous." In America, Columbia chose to release the film in black-and-white. In Britain, it was shelved for three years and then released with a truncated running time. Obviously it was not a high point for William Castle or Hammer. In his autobiography *Step Right Up! I'm Gonna Scare the Pants Off America*, Castle doesn't even mention the film, although it certainly isn't the worst movie he directed.

Video: U.K.

Old Dracula see ***Vampira***

213. One Million Years B.C.

A Hammer/Seven Arts Production (1966); 100 minutes; Technicolor; U.S.: 20th Century–Fox; 91 minutes; DeLuxe Color

P/S: Michael Carreras; **D:** Don Chaffey; **M:** Mario Nascimbene; **DP:** Harry Waxman; **E:** James Needs and Tom Simpson; **AD:** Robert Jones; **SVE:** Ray Harryhausen; **Cast:** Raquel Welch, John Richardson, Percy Herbert, Robert Brown, Martine Beswick, Jean Wladon, Lisa Thomas, Malya Nappi, William Lyon Brown, Yvonne Horner, Richard James and Micky De Rauch.

This flashy color remake of the 1940 film *One Million B.C.* was annnounced as Hammer's one hundredth production. It was the second in their series of "Spectaculars" (or "Glamadventures," as they were sometimes called by the head office) which followed in the prosperous wake of *She*. 20th Century–Fox studio head Richard Zanuck sent Fox starlet Raquel Welch to England to star in the picture, which Fox would distribute. Ray Harryhausen, on a rare hiatus from his association with producer Charles H. Schneer, was engaged to do the special effects sequences.

The cast and crew went to Lanzarote in the Canary Islands for extensive location work which proved hazardous and grueling for everyone involved. The minimal plot details the hardships of life at the dawn of mankind. When the leader of the savage Rock Tribe banishes his son Tumak (John Richardson), the young outcast is befriended by Loana (Raquel Welch), a member of the more advanced Shell People. Together they face the perils of a violent prehistoric world. The highlights of the film are Harryhausen's stupendous stop-motion dinosaurs and a climactic volcanic eruption. Despite some of the worst reviews imaginable (*Time* magazine called it "The Yawn of Mankind"), *One Million Years B.C.* proved to be an even greater box office hit than *She* and went on to become the biggest moneymaker in Hammer's history. The film also made a full-fledged star of Raquel Welch, whose famous pose in her cavegirl outfit became a pin-up icon of the 60s. Welch has spent the subsequent years complaining about this film but, ironically, it is the one she is sure to be remembered for. In August 1969, *One Million Years B.C.* and *She* were reissued on a double bill in England ("Hammer Glamour! Hammer Spectacular!") with considerable success. Each film was cut to approximately 85 minutes for this re-release.

Video: U.K./U.S.

Panic in the Trans-Siberian Train see *Horror Express*

214. Paranoiac

A Hammer Film Production (1963); 80 minutes; U.S.: Universal–International

P: Anthony Hinds; **D:** Freddie Francis; **S:** Jimmy Sangster; **M:** Elisabeth Lutyens; **DP:** Arthur Grant; **E:** James Needs; **AD:** Don Mingaye; **Cast:** Janette Scott, Oliver Reed, Liliane Brousse, Alexander Davion, Sheila Burrell, Maurice Denham, John Bonney, John Stuart, Colin Tapley, Harold Lang, Laurie Leigh and Sydney Bromley.

The already dysfunctional Ashby family has cause for even more anxiety when a young man (Alexander Davion) appears claiming to be Tony, the brother who supposedly committed suicide several years before. His sister Eleanor (Janette Scott) is delighted but brother Simon (Oliver Reed) sees his chances to inherit the family fortune slipping away. As Tony delves deeper into the family affairs, he discovers that madness and murder are close at hand. Jimmy Sangster's script was loosely based on the novel *Brat Farrar*, which had been previously adapted by writer Paul Dehn in 1954 as a proposed Hammer production that was never filmed. This was Freddie Francis' directorial debut for Hammer and it is one of his best efforts. Francis' staging of several sequences is very effective and he draws uniformly good performances from his cast. In 1967, Alexander Davion (billed as Alex Davion) appeared as "Ted Casablanca" in the infamous film version of *Valley of the Dolls*.

Video: U.S.

215. Peeping Tom

A Michael Powell Production (1960); 109 minutes; Eastman Color; U.S.: Astor Pictures Corp.; 86 minutes

P/D: Michael Powell; **S:** Leo Marks; **M:** Brian Easdale; **DP:** Otto Heller; **E:** Noreen Auckland; **AD:** Arthur Lawson; **Cast:** Karl Boehm, Moira Shearer, Anna Massey, Maxine Audley, Esmond Knight, Bartlett Mullins, Shirley Anne Field, Miles Malleson, Brenda Bruce, Pamela Green, Jack Watson and Nigel Davenport.

Reviled in the press and withdrawn from theaters at the time of its original release, *Peeping Tom* has since become a darling of film critics, many of whom consider it to be one of the most important films in the history of British cinema. The film has

OLIVER REED AND LILIAN BROUSSE IN *PARANOIAC*.

often been compared to *Psycho*, which was released the same year. Both films have in common a handsome young anti-hero whose sexuality has been warped by the machinations of an evil parent. Both films also invite the audience to become a voyeur as the main character commits a series of gruesome murders. The major difference lies in the approach each director takes toward his material. Hitchcock's film is an exercise in suspense with an edge of unsettling humor. Powell, on the other hand, makes his statement in a rather cold and academic manner. There is little suspense or humor in *Peeping Tom*. The impact of the film lies the sordid atmosphere of Soho porn shops, sleazy back room photo sessions and Karl Boehm's understated performance, which effectively conveys the depths of his character's twisted psyche.

Video: U.K./U.S.

216. The People That Time Forgot

A Max J. Rosenberg Production (1977); 90 minutes; Color by Movielab; U.S.: American–International;

EXP: Samuel Z. Arkoff; **P:** John Dark; **D:** Kevin Connor; **S:** Patrick Tilley; **M:** John Scott; **DP:** Alan Hume; **E:** John Ireland and Barry Peters; **PD:** Maurice Carter; **AD:** Bert Davey; **Cast:** Patrick Wayne, Doug McClure, Sarah Douglas, Dana Gillespie, Thorley Walters, Shane Rimmer, Tony Britton and Milton Reid.

Two unconvincing dinosaurs threaten *The People That Time Forgot*.

The last gasp of Amicus Productions. Milton Subotsky left Amicus during the production of this film after disputes with John Dark and partner Max Rosenberg. The screenplay is based on the second of three Edgar Rice Burroughs novels about the lost continent of Caprona. *The People That Time Forgot* is not as good as its predecessor *The Land That Time Forgot*, but it is far better than Amicus' other Burroughs adaptation, *At the Earth's Core*. The story picks up where the first film left off: A canister containing Bowen Tyler's tale of his adventures and entrapment in a prehistoric world reaches his friend Ben McBride (Patrick Wayne). McBride organizes an expedition to rescue Tyler but he and his companions also become trapped when their airplane collides with a pterodactyl. Buxom Dana Gillespie is Ajor, a cavegirl who leads them to the City of Skulls where Tyler is imprisoned. The inevitable fiery finale had by now become a convention of the series, as had the poorly designed monsters.

Video: U.S.

217. Persecution

A Tyburn Film Production (1974); 93 minutes; Eastman Color; U.S. *(The Terror of Sheba)*: Fanfare Corp. (1975); 88 minutes

P: Kevin Francis; **D:** Don Chaffey; **S:** Robert B. Hutton, Rosemary Wooten and Frederick Warner; **M:** Paul Ferris; **DP:** Kenneth Talbot; **E:** Mike Campbell; **AD:** Jack Shampan and Peter Williams; **Cast:** Lana Turner, Ralph Bates, Trevor Howard, Suzan Farmer, Olga Georges-Picot, Patrick Allen, Mark Weavers, Catherine

Brandon, Shelagh Fraser, Ronald Howard, Jennifer Guy and John Ryan.

This throughly unpleasant film was an inauspicious debut for Kevin Francis' Tyburn Films. In it, Lana Turner plays a malevolent mother who loves her cat Sheba more than her son David (Ralph Bates). Despite some deep-seated mental problems, David manages to find a wife (Suzan Farmer) and father a son. His mother does everything she can to ruin his marriage and his life. She succeeds all too well and David goes completely mad, finally drowning his mother in a bowl of milk. Turner gives a good performance, far better than the film merits. Her star presence is the sole reason for watching and seems to have been the major motivation for making the film in the first place.

Video: U.K./U.S. (alternate U.S. video title: *The Graveyard*)

218. The Phantom of the Opera

A Hammer Film Production (1962); 84 minutes; Technicolor; U.S.: Universal–International; Eastman Color

P: Anthony Hinds; **D:** Terence Fisher; **S:** John Elder; **M:** Edwin Astley; **DP:** Arthur Grant; **E:** James Needs and Alfred Cox; **PD:** Bernard Robinson; **AD:** Don Mingaye; **Cast:** Herbert Lom, Heather Sears, Edward de Souza, Thorley Walters, Michael Gough, Martin Miller, Renee Houston, Marne Maitland, Michael Ripper, Miles Malleson, Patrick Troughton and Ian Wilson.

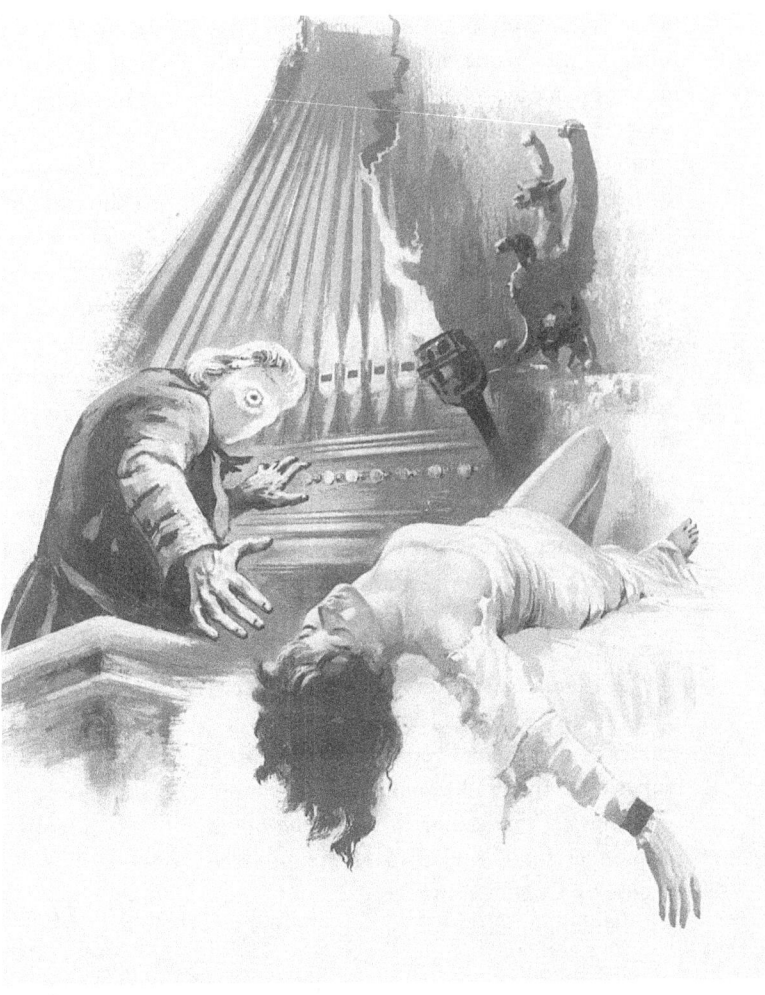

ARTWORK FOR HAMMER'S REMAKE OF *PHANTOM OF THE OPERA*.

As part of their 50th anniversary, Universal entrusted Hammer to remake one of their prize properties. Universal had already filmed two successful versions of Gaston Leroux's novel. The first, in 1925, starred Lon Chaney in the title role. The second was a 1943 Technicolor extravaganza featuring Claude Rains as the Phantom. Cinema legend has it that Hammer's version

OPPOSITE: LANA TURNER OVERSEES THE BURIAL OF HER CAT SHEBA IN THIS SCENE FROM *PERSECUTION*.

was originally intended as a vehicle for Cary Grant. This unique bit of casting obviously did not pan out, but Herbert Lom is a most welcome substitute, giving a performance that is both menacing and touching. As the disfigured composer Prof. Petrie, he wreaks havoc as he attempts to help a gifted singer become the star of his opera and plots to get revenge on the unscrupulous man who stole his music. Terence Fisher's decision to stress the sentimental aspects of the story, rather than the horrific, did not meet with Hammer's approval and the final product was considered a failure. It would be two years before Fisher was asked to direct another film for Hammer. Critical reaction was mixed. *Time* magazine stated, "Herbert Lom looks about as dangerous as dear old granddad" but thought that Michael Gough was "wonderfully sinister." In retrospect, Hammer's *Phantom of the Opera* lacks the sheer shock values of the original version but it is vastly superior to the 1943 remake, which is more of a musical than a horror film. The opera sequences for the Hammer version were staged by Dennis Maunder.

Video: U.K./U.S.

219. *The Plague of the Zombies*

A Hammer/Seven Arts Production (1966); 91 minutes; Technicolor; U.S.: 20th Century–Fox; DeLuxe Color

P: Anthony Nelson-Keys; **D:** John Gilling; **S:** Peter Bryan; **M:** James Bernard; **DP:** Arthur Grant; **E:** James Needs and Chris Barnes; **PD:** Bernard Robinson; **AD:** Don Mingaye; **Cast:** Andre Morell, Diane Clare, Brook Williams, Jacqueline Pearce, John Carson, Alexander Davion, Michael Ripper, Roy Royston, Dennis Chinnery, Louis Mahoney, Marcus Hammond and Ben Aris.

This is the first of two classic Hammer horrors set in Cornwall which were directed back-to-back by John Gilling. Sir James Forbes (Andre Morell) and his daughter Sylvia (Diane Clare) go to a village where several inhabitants have been stricken by a fatal pestilence. It seems that Squire Clive Hamilton (John Carson) has employed voodoo to change the local lads into zombies to be used as free labor in his tin mine. At the time of its release, *The Plague of the Zombies* received more than the usual share of critical attention given to a Hammer film. The story has often been viewed as an analogy to the plight of the Welsh coal miners. In *Boxoffice* magazine, producer Anthony Nelson-Keys simply called it "a morality play." Any way you choose to look at it, the film is an outstanding example of British horror. The often unsung John Carson, so good in all his Hammer roles, is especially fine as the evil Clive Hamilton. Jacqueline Pearce is most affecting as the tragic Alice, who is turned into a zombie. The dream sequence in which the zombies rise from their graves to menace Brook Williams has achieved icon statis among horror film fans — and rightly so.

Video: U.K./U.S.

220. *The Private Life of Sherlock Holmes*

Phalanx/Mirisch Productions (1970); 125 minutes; DeLuxe Color and Panavision; U.S.: United Artists

P/D: Billy Wilder; **S:** Billy Wilder and I.A.L. Diamond; **M:** Miklos Rozsa; **DP:** Christopher Challis; **E:** Ernest Walter; **PD:** Alexander Trauner; **AD:** Tony Inglis; **Cast:** Robert Stephens, Colin Blakely, Genevieve Page, Irene Handl, Stanley Holloway, Christopher Lee, Catherine Lacey, Clive Revill, Peter Madden, Tamara Toumanova, Mollie Maureen and Michael Balfour.

Fifty years after the death of Dr. Watson (Colin Blakely), a locked box is opened; it contains material pertaining to the less successful cases of Sherlock Holmes (Robert Stephens). In the brief opening sequence, a Russian ballerina wants Holmes to father

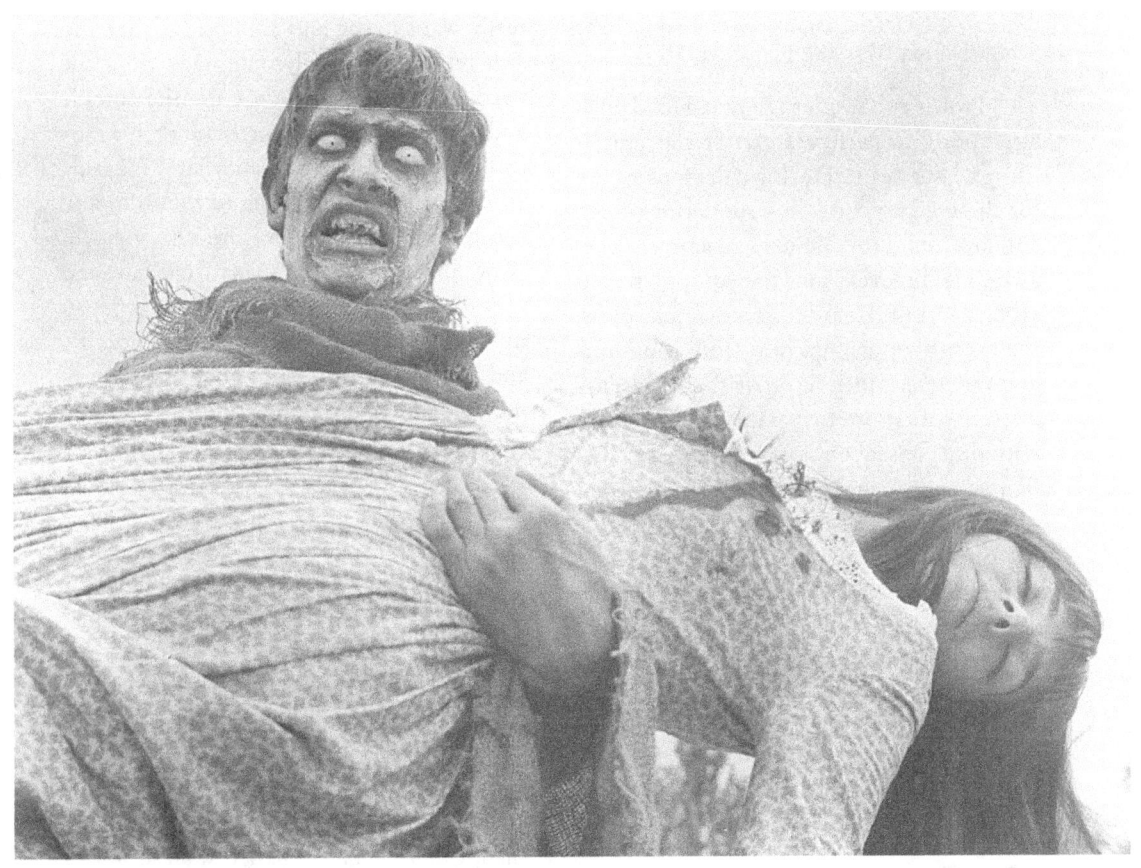

Zombie Ben Aris carries off Jacqueline Pearce in *The Plague of the Zombies*.

her child. Holmes lies his way out of the situation by telling her that he and Watson are a gay couple. The rest of the film involves a beautiful and enigmatic woman, her missing husband, a group of sinister monks and the Loch Ness monster. This main story works on many levels. It is by turns amusing, mysterious and, ultimately, tragic. The action is effectively underscored by Miklos Rozsa's music, adapted from his Violin Concerto at director Wilder's request. Rozsa can be glimpsed briefly, conducting the Swan Lake Ballet in the early part of the film. Unfortunately, the distributors disliked the film and had no faith in its power to attact an audience. Originally running over three hours, it was cut drastically prior to its limited release. Gone are a flashback of a young Holmes at Oxford, "The Curious Case of the Upside Down Room" and "The Dreadful Business of the Naked Honeymooners." Attempts to fully restore this discarded footage have thus far been unsuccessful.

Video: U.S.

221. *The Projected Man*

A Compton/M.L.C. Production (1966); 77 minutes; Technicolor and Techniscope; U.S.: Universal (1967)

EXP: Richard Gordon and Gerald A. Fernback; **P:** John Croydon and Maurice Foster; **D:** Ian Curteis; **S:** John C. Cooper and Peter Bryan; **M:** Kenneth V. Jones; **DP:** Stanley Pavey; **E:** Derek Holding; **AD:** Peter Mullins; **Cast:** Bryant Haliday, Mary Peach, Norman Wooland, Ronald Allen, Derek Farr, Tracey Crisp, Derrick de Marney, Gerald Heinz, Sam Kydd, Terry Scully, Norma West and Frank Gatliff.

Prof. Paul Steiner (Bryant Haliday) is attempting to perfect a matter transmitter using a laser beam. During a demonstration for the executives of the foundation which employs him, Prof. Steiner's experiment goes awry. He discovers that the equipment was sabotaged but, despite his desperate pleas, the executives dismiss him from the foundation. Determined to prove that the transmitter works, Steiner transports himself, with dire consequences. He is horribly disfigured and so charged with electricity that his touch causes electrocution. The remainder of the film has the deranged professor wandering around London zapping people, with the police in hot pursuit. This is a second-rate effort with a slim (and not particularly original) storyline.

Video: U.K.

Psycho-Circus see *Circus of Fear*

222. Psychomania

A Benmar Production (1971); 91 minutes; Technicolor; U.S.: Scotia International (1972)

P: Andrew Donally; **D:** Don Sharp; **S:** Arnaud D'Usseau and Julian Halevy; **M:** John Cameron; **DP:** Ted Moore; **E:** Richard Best; **AD:** Maurice Carter; **Cast:** George Sanders, Beryl Reid, Nicky Henson, Mary Larkin, Roy Holder, Ann Michelle, Robert Hardy, Patrick Holt, Denis Gilmore, Miles Greenwood, Rocky Taylor and Peter Whitting.

This would have been more aptly titled "Cyclemania." Tom Latham (Nicky Henson) is the leader of a motorcycle gang called "The Living Dead." They get their kicks by running motorists off the road and overturning prams and shopping carts at the town square. Tom learns from his spiritualist mother (Beryl Reid) and her mysterious butler Shadwill (George Sanders) that if you really want to die and are positive that you will return, you will come back from the dead. To this end, Tom commits suicide and, sure enough, is resurrected on his motorbike to commit more mayhem. He convinces the rest of the gang to join him and those who truly believe are also reborn. Now, however, their pranks turn deadly and they cannot be killed a second time. A unique concept saves this from mediocrity, and Nicky Henson is quite good as the long-haired, leather-clad anti-hero.

Video: U.S.

223. The Psychopath

An Amicus Production (1965); 83 minutes; Technicolor and Techniscope; U.S.: Paramount (1966)

P: Max J. Rosenberg and Milton Subotsky; **D:** Freddie Francis; **S:** Robert Bloch; **M:** Elisabeth Lutyens; **DP:** John Wilcox; **E:** Oswald Hafenrichter; **AD:** Bill Constable; **Cast:** Patrick Wymark, Margaret Johnston, John Standing, Alexander Knox, Judy Huxtable, Don Borisenko, Colin Gordon, Thorley Walters, Robert Crewdson, Tim Barrett, Frank Forsyth and Olive Gregg.

A London solicitor is intentionally run down by an automobile and a doll, fashioned in his likeness, is found at the scene of the murder. Inspector Holloway (Patrick Wymark) of Scotland Yard traces the doll to Mrs. Von Sturm (Margaret Johnston), the invalid widow of a German aristocrat accused of committing war crimes. Before Holloway can prove any involvement on the part of Mrs. Von Sturm, three more murders are committed and three more dolls are found in the image of the victims. It turns out that the four murdered men served on the Allied High Commission that sentenced Mrs. Von Strum's husband to prison. But the unfortunate lady is confined to a wheelchair...or is she? The screenplay, the first of several written for Amicus by Robert Bloch,

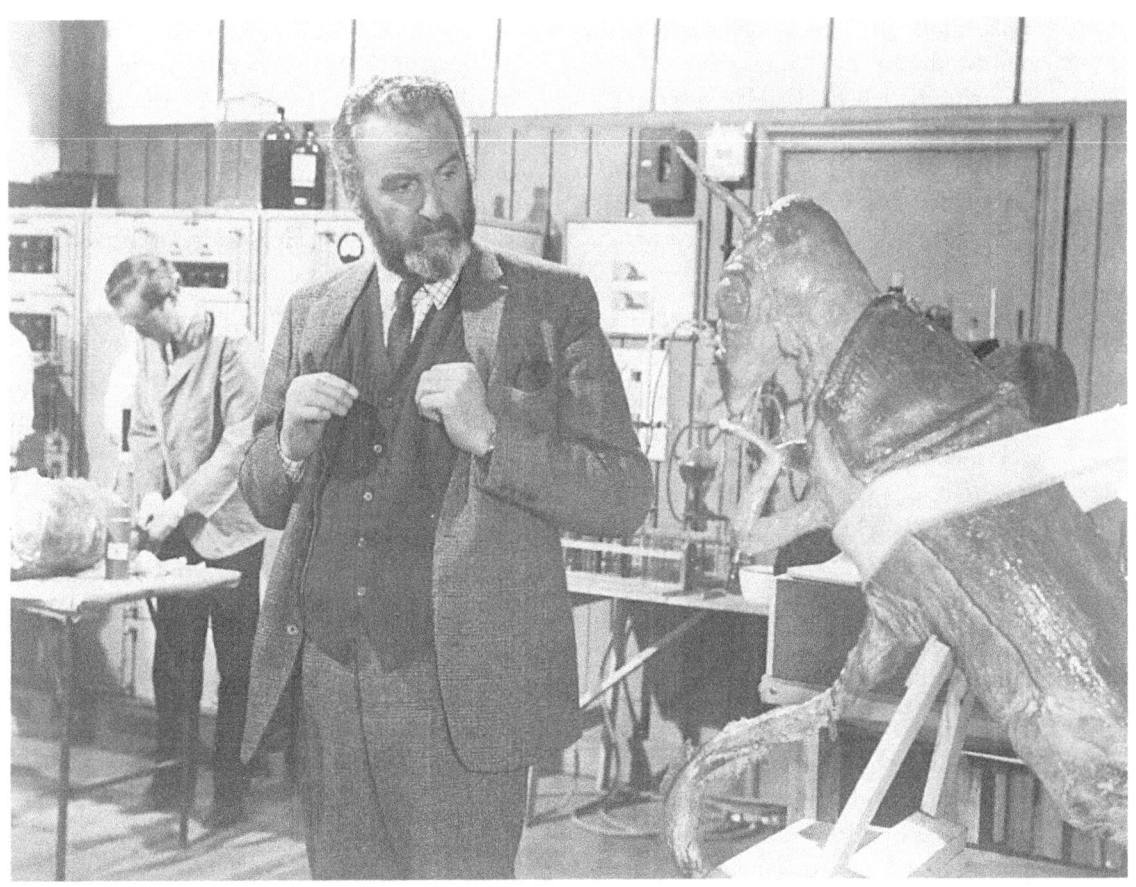

Professor Quatermass (Andrew Keir) contemplates the corpse of an ancient Martian in *Quatermass and the Pit*.

resembles the gimmicky plots he fabricated for William Castle films.

Video: None

224. *Quatermass and the Pit*

A Hammer–Seven Arts Production (1967); 98 minutes; Technicolor; U.S. *(Five Million Years to Earth)*: 20th Century–Fox; DeLuxe Color

P: Anthony Nelson-Keys; **D:** Roy Ward Baker; **S:** Nigel Kneale; **M:** Tristram Cary; **DP:** Arthur Grant; **E:** James Needs and Spencer Reeve; **PD:** Bernard Robinson; **AD:** Ken Ryan; **SVE:** Les Bowie; **Cast:** Andrew Keir, James Donald, Barbara Shelley, Julian Glover, Duncan Lamont, Bryan Marshall, Peter Copley, Edwin Richfield, Robert Morris, Grant Taylor, Maurice Good and Sheila Steafel.

Workers digging a London subway extension unearth a spaceship and the skeletons of primitive men which have been buried together for millions of years. A series of strange occurrences leads Prof. Quatermass (Andrew Keir) to deduce that the ship may be a source of mankind's innermost impulses. This is the third and most elaborate of Hammer's Quatermass trilogy. Nigel Kneale adapted the screenplay from his six-part BBC television serial and, by tightening up the story, actually improves on the original. The complex plot mixes science fiction and the occult to make the fascinating hypothesis that man owes his mental developement to colonizing Martians. Andrew Keir is excellent as Quatermass, replacing Brian Donlevy's bluster with dignified authority. A number of fine actors, including Peter Finch, Jack Hawkins and Peter Cushing, were considered to play Quatermass in this film, but it is hard to imagine any of them bettering Keir's performance.

Video: U.K./U.S.

225. The Quatermass Conclusion (a.k.a. Quatermass)

An Euston Films Production for Thames Television (1979); 105 minutes; Color; U.S.: No theatrical release

EXP: Verity Lambert; P: Ted Childs; D: Piers Haggard; S: Nigel Kneale; M: Marc Wilkinson and Nic Rowley; DP: Ian Wilson; E: Keith Palmer; PD: Arnold Chapkis; Cast: John Mills, Simon MacCorkindale, Barbara Kellerman, Margaret Tyzack, Brewster Mason, Ralph Arliss, Paul Rosebury, Jane Bortish, Toyah Wilbox, Rebecca Saire, David Yip and Bruce Purchase.

In a bleak not-too-distant future, the world is filled with violence and chaos. Cities are the sites of urban warfare and wholesale killing. Groups of young hippie-types called the Planet People wander the countryside in search of ancient stone circles similar to Stonehenge. When they gather in mass at these monolithic locations, a light from space (like a gigantic laser beam) blasts them off the face of the Earth. Prof. Bernard Quatermass is now an old, tired man whose only interest is in finding his missing granddaughter, who may have joined the Planet People. When these large-scale massacres of youths begin to happen with increasing regularity all over the world, Quatermass deduces that the young of the human race are being harvested by an alien force. He devises a way to stop this, but it is at the cost of his own life. Nigel Kneale originally wrote this final Quatermass screenplay in 1972 for the BBC but they rejected it as being too costly to produce. It was eventually produced by Euston Films and Thames Television and aired in the United Kingdom as a four-part TV serial in 1979. An edited-down, feature-length version was prepared for a U.S. theatrical release which never happened. As Prof. Quatermass, John Mills has none of the brashness of Brian Donlevy or authority of Andrew Keir. He is weary of life and, in the words of his creator, "He'd run his course"—which is why Kneale decided to kill him off in the end. Not a patch on the first three films, but still very interesting.

Video: U.K./U.S.

226. Quatermass II

A Hammer Film Production (1957); 85 minutes; U.S. *(Enemy from Space)*: United Artists

EXP: Michael Carreras; P: Anthony Hinds; D: Val Guest; S: Nigel Kneale and Val Guest; M: James Bernard; DP: Gerald Gibbs; E: James Needs; AD: Bernard Robinson; Cast: Brian Donlevy, Sidney James, John Longden, Bryan Forbes, Vera Day, William Franklyn, Charles Lloyd Pack, Tom Chatto, Percy Herbert, John Van Eyssen and Michael Ripper.

This second installment in Hammer's Quatermass trilogy is considered by many to be the best in the series. One person who does not share this opinion is writer Nigel Kneale, who disliked the film in general and star Brian Donlevy in particular. Prof. Bernard Quatermass (Donlevy) discovers that a government plant, supposedly set up for the manufacture of synthetic food, is actually the front for an invasion from outer space. Tiny meteorites, carrying alien life forms, fall to Earth and take over anyone unfortunate enough to come in contact with them. The infected then become the zombie-like slaves of the alien superpower. Quatermass attempts to fight the takeover but discovers that several prominent government positions have already been infiltrated. Donlevy once again gives a no-nonsense performance as Quatermass. He is

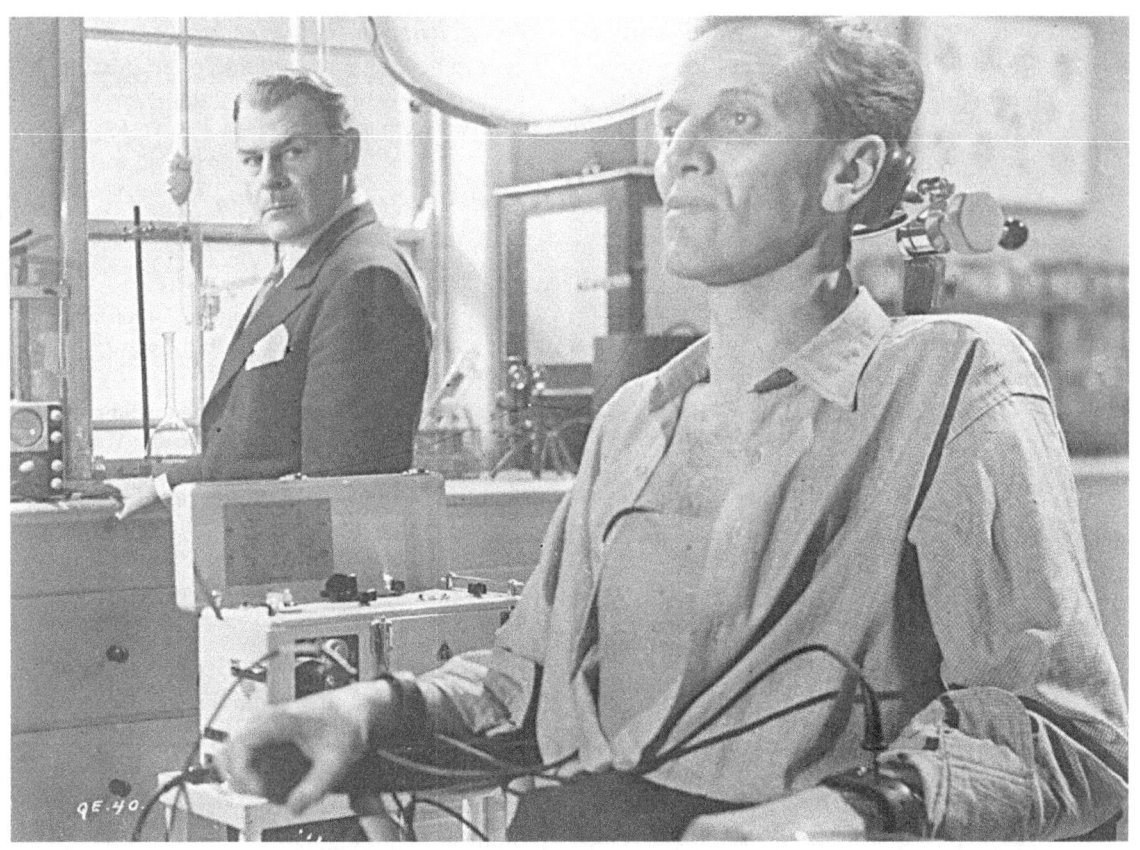

BRIAN DONLEVY AND RICHARD WORDSWORTH IN *THE QUATERMASS XPERIMENT*, HAMMER'S FIRST INTERNATIONAL SUCCESS.

ably assisted by an exceptional supporting cast which does full justice to the excellent script.

Video: U.S.

227. The Quatermass Xperiment

A Hammer Film Production (1955); 82 minutes; U.S. *(The Creeping Unknown)*: United Artists (1956); 78 minutes

P: Anthony Hinds; **D:** Val Guest; **S:** Richard Landau and Val Guest; **M:** James Bernard; **DP:** Walter Harvey; **E:** James Needs; **AD:** J. Elder Wills; **SVE:** Les Bowie; **Cast:** Brian Donlevy, Margia Dean, Jack Warner, Richard Wordsworth, David King Wood, Thora Hird, Gordon Jackson, Harold Lang, Lionel Jeffries, Maurice Kaufmann, Gron Davies and Stanley Van Beers.

Hammer's early penchant for adapting popular British radio and television programs into feature films paid off big when they chose to make a movie version of Nigel Kneale's BBC serial *The Quatermass Experiment*. The film turned out to be Hammer's first big step into the international motion picture market. American star Brian Donlevy was cast as Professor Bernard Quatermass. Although this bit of casting has its champions and detractors, it is impossible to defend the inclusion of the other American performer, Margia Dean. Her poor performance is the only negative factor in an otherwise outstanding film. Quatermass is the head of a space program that has launched an experimental rocket with three men aboard. When the rocket returns to Earth, only one man has survived. Eventually it is discovered that the survivor has been taken over by an alien life force which consumes whatever life forms it comes into contact with. Frightening and sophisticated, *The Quatermass Xperiment* was light years ahead of anything previously produced by Hammer. It also marked the debut of James Bernard as a film composer. When the original composer was taken ill, Hammer's musical director John Hollingsworth suggested his friend Bernard as a replacement. All things considered, this film is a fitting beginning to the "Golden Age of British Horror Films."

Video: U.S.

228. *Rasputin — The Mad Monk*

A Hammer/Seven Arts Production (1966); 91 minutes; Technicolor and CinemaScope; U.S.: 20th Century–Fox; DeLuxe Color and CinemaScope

P: Anthony Nelson-Keys; **D:** Don Sharp; **S:** John Elder; **M:** Don Banks; **DP:** Michael Reed; **E:** James Needs and Roy Hyde; **PD:** Bernard Robinson; **AD:** Don Mingaye; **Cast:** Christopher Lee, Barbara Shelley, Richard Pasco, Francis Matthews, Suzan Farmer, Dinsdale Landen, Renee Asherson, Derek Francis, Alan Tilvern, Joss Ackland, John Welsh and Robert Duncan.

A few facts about the real Rasputin manage to make it into this highly fictionalized account, but since this is a Hammer horror and not a historical epic, facts don't really count all that much. What does count is a truly magnificent performance by Christopher Lee in the title role. His resonant voice and commanding presence dominate the film, helping to create one of the screen's finest interpretations of Rasputin. Holding her own against Lee is Barbara Shelley as Rasputin's doomed mistress Sonia. There has been a great deal of fuss made about Hammer reusing the sets and cast members from *Dracula – Prince of Darkness* for this film. Does anybody recall the Universal horror films where casts and sets were endlessly recycled? Despite Hammer's desire to economize, *Rasputin — The Mad Monk* still manages to have an opulent look, often missing in far more expensive productions.

Video: U.K./U.S.

Raw Meat see ***Death Line***

229. *The Reptile*

A Hammer/Seven Arts Production (1966); 91 minutes; Technicolor; U.S.: 20th Century–Fox; DeLuxe Color

P: Anthony Nelson-Keys; **D:** John Gilling; **S:** John Elder; **M:** Don Banks; **DP:** Arthur Grant; **E:** Roy Hyde; **AD:** Don Mingaye; **Cast:** Noel Willman, Jennifer Daniel, Ray Barrett, Jacqueline Pearce, Michael Ripper, John Laurie, Marne Maitland, David Baron, Charles Lloyd Pack, Harold Goldblatt and George Woodbridge.

Harry Spalding (Ray Barrett) and his wife Valerie (Jennifer Daniel) move into the cottage of his deceased brother, which is located near a small village in Cornwall. They are mostly shunned by the villagers but they do meet their neighbor Dr. Franklyn (Noel Willman) and his pretty daughter Anna (Jacqueline Pearce). Unfortunately, Anna is under the curse of a mysterious Eastern sect which causes her to turn into a deadly cross between a cobra and a woman. As he did with *The Plague of the Zombies*, director John Gilling creates a memorable chiller within the confines of a second-feature status and a limited budget (this was the companion film to *Rasputin — The Mad Monk*). As usual, *Films and Filming* was unimpressed. Their critic Nicholas Gosling wrote, "*The Reptile* lacks grip; nothing much happens for the first half hour and too much time is spent on scene-setting and too little on action."

Video: U.S./U.K.

230. *Repulsion*

A Compton–Tekli Production (1965); 104 minutes; U.S.: Royal Films International

EXP: Tony Tenser and Michael Klinger; **P:** Gene Gutowski; **D:** Roman Polanski; **S:** Roman Polanski and Gerard Brach; **M:** Chico Hamilton; **DP:** Gilbert Taylor; **E:** Alastair McIntyre; **AD:** Seamus Flannery; **Cast:** Catherine Deneuve, Yvonne Furneaux, John Fraser, Ian Hendry, Patrick Wymark, Valerie Taylor, Helen Fraser, Renee Houston, James Villers, Monica Merlin, Imogen Graham and Hugh Futcher.

After the success of his first feature film *Knife in the Water* (1962), Roman Polanski wanted to direct his next film in England. Producer Gene Gutowski approached Anglo–Amalgamated and Hammer but was turned down by both. He and Polanski were finally able to strike a deal with the Compton Group, run by Tony Tenser and Michael Klinger. Polanski said "neither man was a truly professional producer" and he thought the final result was his "shoddiest" effort. Despite his misgivings, Polanski's first English–language film is an immensely powerful depiction of a woman's descent into madness. *Repulsion* is the tragic account of Carol Ledoux (Catherine Deneuve), a beautiful young girl from Brussels, who lives in London with her older sister Helen (Yvonne Furneaux). Although the signs of mental illness in Carol are already pronounced, the self-centered Helen neglects to notice that anything is amiss. Helen goes on holiday to Italy with her married boyfriend (Ian Hendry) and Carol is left alone in the apartment. Her sexual psychosis overwhelms her and she begins to hallucinate; the walls crack and hands reach out to grab her; strange men suddenly appear and violently rape her. When Carol's boyfriend Colin (John Fraser) unexpectedly shows up at the apartment, she bludgeons him to death with a candlestick. She also kills the lecherous landlord (Patrick Wymark) with a razor. Helen returns to find a "house of horrors" and her sister in a catatonic state. Catherine Deneuve gives an eerily understated performance, almost without dialogue. This, combined with Polanski's startling direction, produced a disturbing film which is a genuine masterpiece of the horror genre.

Video: U.S.

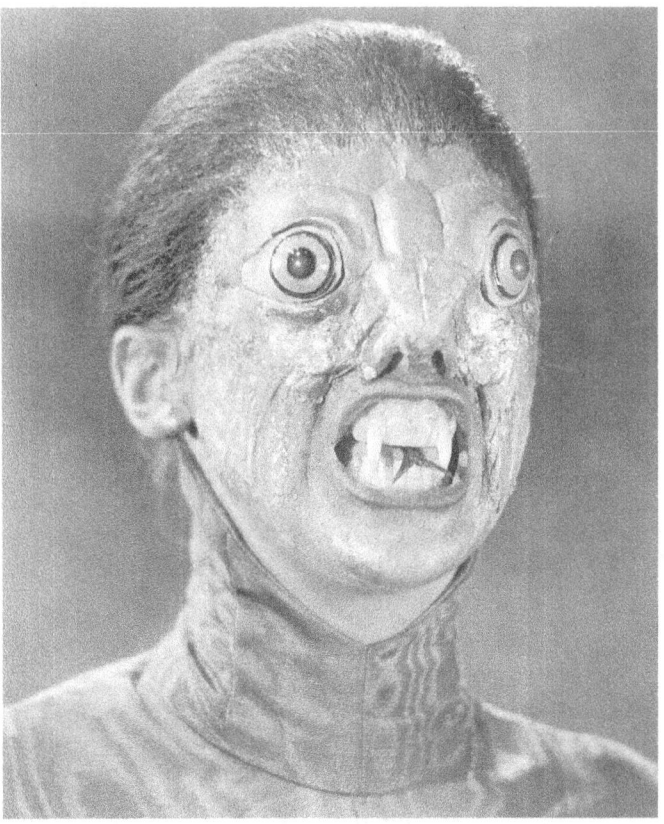

JACQUELINE PEARCE SUFFERS FROM A CURSE WHICH TURNS HER INTO *THE REPTILE*.

231. Revenge (a.k.a. *Inn of the Frightened People*)

A Peter Rogers Production (1971); 89 minutes; U.S. *(Terror from Under the House)*: Hemisphere (1976)

EXP: Peter Rogers; **P:** George H. Brown; **D:** Sidney Hayers; **S:** John Kruse; **M:** Eric Rogers; **DP:** Ken Hodges; **E:** Anthony Palk; **PD:** Tony

Wallis; **AD:** Monte Gough; **Cast:** Joan Collins, James Booth, Ray Barrett, Kenneth Griffith, Tom Marshall, Sinead Cusak, Zuleika Robson, Donald Morley, Barry Andrews, Geoffrey Hughes, Angus Mackay and Ariro Morris.

Two young girls are molested and murdered. When the prime suspect (Kenneth Griffith) is released by the police owing to a lack of evidence, the girls' fathers (James Booth and Ray Barrett) decide to take matters into their own hands. They kidnap Griffith and take him to the basement of Booth's pub, where they attempt to beat a confession out of him, nearly killing the man. Too late they realize the error of their ways and Barrett leaves Booth and his family to suffer the consequences. Eventually the presence of the man in the cellar tears the entire family apart. Joan Collins gives a very convincing performance as Booth's distressed second wife.

Video: U.S.

232. The Revenge of Frankenstein

A Hammer–Cadogan Films Ltd. Production (1958); 89 minutes; Technicolor; U.S.: Columbia

EXP: Michael Carreras; **P:** Anthony Hinds; **D:** Terence Fisher; **S:** Jimmy Sangster; **M:** Leonard Salzedo; **DP:** Jack Asher; **E:** James Needs and Alfred Cox; **PD:** Bernard Robinson; **Cast:** Peter Cushing, Francis Matthews, Eunice Gayson, Michael Gwynn, John Welsh, Lionel Jeffries, Oscar Quitak, Richard Wordsworth, Charles Lloyd Pack, John Stuart, Michael Ripper and George Woodbridge.

This sequel to *The Curse of Frankenstein* was the only time in Hammer's Frankenstein series that any attempt was made to link the new film directly with the previous one. Although not as overtly horrific as its predecessor, *Revenge* has an intelligent script by Jimmy Sangster in which he has combined equitable amounts of wit, pathos and the macabre. Under the guise of Dr. Victor Stein, Baron Frankenstein (Peter Cushing) continues his experiments, this time using the patients of a charity hospital for his "raw material." Although much has been made of the cannibalistic tendencies of Frankenstein's latest creation, it is actually only hinted at in the film. Once again, British critics were not particularly impressed. Tony Beck, writing for *Films and Filming*, found it to be a "lavish and polished production" but curiously stated that "the direction is not sufficiently assured or imaginative to maintain a truly horrific atmosphere. Peter Cushing's performance is too leisurely to remedy these defects." In the United States, Columbia paired it with the splendid *Night of the Demon*, thereby creating one of the great horror double-bills of the 50s.

Video: U.K./U.S.

The Rites of Dracula see ***The Satanic Rites of Dracula***

The Road Builder see ***The Night Digger***

233. The Rocky Horror Picture Show

A Lou Adler–Michael White Production (1975); 100 minutes; Eastman Color; U.S.: 20th Century–Fox; 95 minutes; DeLuxe Color

EXP: Lou Adler; **P:** Michael White; **D:** Jim Sharman; **S:** Jim Sharman and Richard O'Brien; Music and Lyrics by Richard O'Brien; **DP:** Peter Suschitzky; **E:** Graeme Clifford; **PD:** Brian Thomson; **AD:** Terry Ackland-Snow; **Cast:** Tim Curry, Susan Sarandon, Barry Bostwick, Richard O'Brien, Patricia Quinn, Nell Campbell, Jonathan Adams, Peter Hinwood, Meatloaf and Charles Gray.

Richard O'Brien's outrageous and affectionate rock 'n' roll parody of horror and science fiction films had been a big hit on stage in England and at the Roxy Theatre in Los Angeles. A film version must have

Eunice Gayson is threatened by Frankenstein's latest creation (Michael Gwynn) in *The Revenge of Frankenstein*.

DR. FRANK-N-FURTER (TIM CURRY) SHOWS OFF HIS HANDSOME CREATION ROCKY (PETER HINWOOD) TO BRAD (BARRY BOSTWICK) AND JANET (SUSAN SARANDON) IN *THE ROCKY HORROR PICTURE SHOW*.

seemed like a sure bet to the producers. As it turned out, mainstream audiences obviously weren't quite ready for the provocative exploits of Dr. Frank-N-Furter, the "sweet transvestite from Transexual Transylvania." The film bombed badly at the box office in its original release. Shortly thereafter, *The Rocky Horror Picture Show* began to appear as the attraction at midnight movie showings where it built up a loyal following of rabid fans. The film is now the premiere example of a "cult classic" and more than 20 years after its disastrous debut it continues to be shown as a midnight movie in cinemas all over the world. It may not be as shocking as it once was, but the raucous humor and clever songs are as infectious as ever. And who would ever have imagined that dear little Janet Weiss would go on to become a great, Oscar–winning actress? *The Rocky Horror Picture Show* was filmed at Bray Studios, the home of Hammer's early triumphs.

Video: U.K./U.S.

234. The Satanic Rites of Dracula (a.k.a. *Dracula Is Dead and Well and Living in London*)

A Hammer Film Production (1973); 88 minutes; Technicolor; U.S. *(Count Dracula and His Vampire Bride)*: Dynamite Entertainment (1978)

P: Roy Skeggs; **D:** Alan Gibson; **S:** Don Houghton; **M:** John Cacavas; **DP:** Brian Probyn; **E:** Chris Barnes; **AD:** Lionel Couch; **Cast:** Christopher Lee, Peter Cushing, Michael Coles, William Franklyn, Freddie Jones, Joanna Lumley,

VALERIE VAN OST AND CHRISTOPHER LEE IN *THE SATANIC RITES OF DRACULA*.

Richard Vernon, Valerie Van Ost, Patrick Barr, Barbara Yu Ling, Richard Mathews and Lockwood West.

Count Dracula (Christopher Lee) returns to modern London in the guise of a reclusive business tycoon named D.D. Denham. His plan is to release a deadly bacteria that will annihilate the world's population. Once again, Scotland Yard Inspector Murray (Michael Coles) must call on the services of Prof. Van Helsing (Peter Cushing) to help him find and destroy the vampire. *The Satanic Rites of Dracula* is a definite improvement over *Dracula A.D. 1972*, although it often seems more like an espionage thriller than a horror film. Glamourous Joanna Lumley is cast as Jessica Van Helsing, who is a flaming redhead this time around. Joanna's blonde post–Hammer career includes the popular television series *The New Avengers* and *Absolutely Fabulous*. The sequence which finds her trapped in a cellar with a horde of ravenous vampire women is memorably terrifying and the highlight of the film.

Video: U.K./U.S. (alternate U.S. video title: *The Rites of Dracula*)

235. *Satan's Skin* (a.k.a. *The Blood on Satan's Claw*)

A Tigon–British/Chilton Film Production (1970); 93 minutes; Color; U.S.: Cannon (1971); 100 minutes

EXP: Tony Tenser; **P:** Peter L. Andrews and Malcolm B. Heyworth; **D:** Piers Haggard; **S:** Robert Wynne-Simmons and Piers Haggard; **M:**

Marc Wilkinson; **DP:** Dick Bush; **E:** Richard Best; **AD:** Arnold Chapkis; **Cast:** Patrick Wymark, Linda Hayden, Barry Andrews, Michele Dotrice, James Hayter, Wendy Padbury, Tamara Ustinov, Anthony Ainley, Charlotte Mitchell, Simon Williams, Avice Landon and Howard Goorney.

While plowing a field, a young farmer (Barry Andrews) unearths the skull of some inhuman creature. This begins a reign of terror in a small English village which results in rape, dismemberment and death, all committed in the cause of devil worship. Foremost among Satan's servants is the ironically named Angel Blake (Linda Hayden), a beautiful young girl who corrupts the youth of the village to the ways of the devil. Although set in the same time period as *Witchfinder General* (the puritanical rule of Oliver Cromwell), *Satan's Skin* includes supernatural elements that the other film does not. Both movies do share the same disquieting atmosphere and realistic approach to the material, although this film has a far less coherent story line. This may be because the the screenplay was originally conceived as an omnibus film. Plot deficiencies aside, *Satain's Skin* is extremely well-directed and the cast is exceptional.

Video: U.S.

236. *Satan's Slave*

A Monumental Pictures Ltd. Production (1976); 86 minutes; Technicolor and Techniscope; U.S.: Crown International (1979)

P: Les Young and Richard Crafter; **D:** Norman J. Warren; **S:** David McGillivray; **M:** John Scott; **DP:** Les Young; **AD:** Hayden Pearce; **Cast:** Michael Gough, Martin Potter, Candace Glendenning, Barbara Kellerman, Michael Craze, Gloria Walker, James Bree, David McGillivray and Celia Hewitt.

Catherine York (Candace Glendenning) and her parents are driving to the secluded estate of her uncle. As they pass through the gates leading to the house, her father loses control of the car and crashes into a tree. Catherine escapes injury but the car explodes, killing her parents. Kindly Uncle Alexander (Michael Gough) and his son Stephen (Martin Potter) do their best to help Catherine cope with her loss. Wandering around the grounds of the estate, Catherine sees a blackened tree stump which causes her to have a vision of a young woman tied to a tree and tortured by Puritans. Later, at her parents' funeral, she notices a neglected gravestone with the name Camilla Yorke on it. Catherine discovers that Uncle Alexander and Stephen are part of a coven. They plan to sacrifice her in order to reincarnate their ancestor, who was burnt as a witch in 1753. There are some interesting plot twists and, as with several other films of the period, the director's answer to the present trend in horror movies seemed to be the addition of more sadism and gore. There is also an excessive amount of full frontal female nudity that seems, at times, to be from another film altogether.

Video: U.K./U.S.

237. *Satellite in the Sky*

A Tridelta/Danzinger Production (1956); 85 minutes; WarnerColor and CinemaScope; U.S.: Warner Bros.

P: Harry and Edward Danzinger; **D:** Paul Dickson; **S:** John Mather, J.T. McIntosh and Edith Dell; **M:** Albert Elms; **DP:** Georges Perinal and James Wilson; **E:** Sydney Stone; **AD:** Eric Blakemore; **SVE:** Wally Veevers; **Cast:** Kieron Moore, Lois Maxwell, Donald Wolfit, Bryan Forbes, Jimmy Hanley, Tea Gregory, Barry Keegan, Alan Gifford, Shirley Lawrence, Walter Hudd, Donald Gray and Peter Neil.

The first British manned satellite takes off with a tritonium bomb aboard. The plan is to explode it above the Earth's atmosphere. Unfortunately, the bomb cannot be detached from the rocket, putting the lives of the crew in grave jeopardy. With its impressive special effects, this is a surprisingly elaborate endeavor, quite unlike any other film produced in England at the time. Sadly, the quality of the script is not up to that of the production, and the considerable amount of technical effort that obviously went into this movie is mostly wasted.

Video: None

238. Scars of Dracula

A Hammer Film Production (1970); 96 minutes; Technicolor; U.S.: American Continental (1971)

P: Aida Young; **D:** Roy Ward Baker; **S:** John Elder; **M:** James Bernard; **DP:** Moray Grant; **E:** James Needs; **AD:** Scott MacGregor; **Cast:** Christopher Lee, Dennis Waterman, Jenny Hanley, Christopher Matthews, Patrick Troughton, Michael Gwynn, Wendy Hamilton, Anoushka Hempel, Delia Lindsay, Bob Todd, Michael Ripper and Toke Townley.

When Randy Wastrel Paul (Christopher Matthews) vanishes, his brother Simon (Dennis Waterman) and their friend Sarah (Jenny Hanley) go to find him. Their search leads to Castle Dracula, where the vampire Count attempts to put Sarah under his spell. This is the last of the Gothic Hammer Draculas starring Christopher Lee. The next film in the series (*Dracula A.D. 1972*) updates the story to "mod" London. This time around the connection with the previous film (*Taste the Blood of Dracula*) is cursory and the production values are not up to Hammer's typical high standards. On the positive side, Dennis Waterman and Jenny Hanley make an attractive pair of young lovers and Lee is given more to do than usual. James Bernard's background score includes a love theme which is one of his loveliest compositions.

Video: U.K./U.S.

239. Schizo

A Peter Walker/Heritage Ltd. Production (1976); 109 minutes; Technicolor; U.S.: Niles International

P/D: Peter Walker; **S:** David McGillvray; **M:** Stanley Myers; **DP:** Peter Jessop; **E:** Alan Brett; **AD:** Chris Burke; **Cast:** Lynne Frederick, John Leyton, Stephanie Beacham, John Fraser, Jack Watson, Queenie Watts, Raymond Bowers, Paul Alexander, Victor Winding, Colin Jeavons, Terry Duggan and Victoria Allum.

In this tedious and bloody thriller, Lynne Frederick stars as Samantha Falconer, a newlywed who believes that she is being stalked by the man who was convicted of murdering her mother. The illogical and poorly constructed plot is filled with false leads and uninteresting characters. There is even a half-hearted attempt to bring in a supernatural element when Samantha attends a séance held during a meeting of the Psychic Brotherhood. Lynne Frederick plays her part like a somnambulist, pausing every now and then to run her fingers through her hair for the thousandth time. Only Stephanie Beacham gives anything resembling a performance, despite the fact that she is saddled with a thankless "best friend" role. This is a surprisingly uninteresting effort from Peter Walker, who can usually be counted on for holding your attention at the very least.

Video: U.S.

240. Scream and Die

A Blackwater Film Production (1973); 99 minutes; Eastman Color; U.S. *(The House That Vanished)*: American–International (1974); 84 minutes

P: Diana Daubeney; **D:** Joseph (Jose) Larraz; **S/E:** Derek Ford; **DP:** Trevor Wrenn; **AD:** John Hoesli; **Cast:** Andrea Allan, Karl Lanchbury, Maggie Walker, Peter Forbes-Robertson, Judy Matheson, Anabella Wood, Alex Leppard, Daphne Lea, Lawrence Keane, Edmund Pegge and Richard Aylen.

An example of British horror at its most exploitative. A more accurate title would have been "Strip and Die." In this "breasts and blood" thriller, gorgeous model Valerie

> "Composite Beings, half synthetic, half human transplant. They live, they love, they kill, but they cannot die. Only boiling acid will dissolve them, halt their unearthly lust."

Scream and Scream Again

(Andrea Allan) and her photographer boyfriend witness a murder in an old country house. Valerie escapes alone but, for some reason, doesn't inform the police. She then becomes convinced that she is being stalked by the same black-gloved killer. When her roommate is brutally raped and killed, Valerie runs off with her new boyfriend to his old house in the country. The identity of the killer is a surprise only to dimwitted Valerie. This is one of those illogical thrillers where you want to throttle the characters because of their stupidity. There is so much gratuitous nudity that eventually you may find yourself saying, "Oh, no, here come those boring boobs again." Then again, you might not.

Video: U.S.

241. Scream and Scream Again

An Amicus Production (1970); 95 minutes; Color by Movielab; U.S.: American–International

EXP: Louis M. Heyward; **P:** Max J. Rosenberg and Milton Subotsky; **D:** Gordon Hessler; **S:** Christopher Wicking; **M:** David Whitaker; **DP:** John Coquillon; **E:** Peter Elliot; **AD:** Bill Constable; **Cast:** Vincent Price, Christopher Lee, Peter Cushing, Marshall Jones, Michael Gothard, Judy Huxtable, Alfred Marks, Anthony Newlands, Peter Sallis, David Lodge, Uta Levka, Christopher Matthews and Yutte Stensgaard.

Peter Saxton's novel *The Disorientated Man* becomes a disorientated film. The three seemingly disparate story lines include a runner who collapses while jogging and awakes in hospital to find his limbs amputated; a power struggle in a Nazi–like military state; and a series of vampire murders in London. That they are all connected in the end with some sort of coherence is a minor miracle. Dr. Browning (Vincent Price) is attempting to create a "super race" by transplanting limbs and organs from different bodies to create composite beings. The first of these experiments (Michael Gothard) goes a bit wrong and develops a craving for human blood. In one of the most gruesome sequences, the police manage to capture the vampire-killer and handcuff him to the bumper of a car. In his mania to escape, the composite severs his own hand, leaving it dangling from the handcuff. Although they are star-billed, Price, Lee and Cushing have little actual screen (Cushing is in only one scene while Price and Lee are in about four each). Hammer starlet Yutte Stensgaard appears briefly, in one of her earliest screen roles, as a political prisoner undergoing torture.

Video: U.K./U.S.

Scream of Fear see *Taste of Fear*

242. Séance on a Wet Afternoon

A Beaver Films Ltd./Allied Film Makers Presentation; A Richard Attenborough and Bryan Forbes Production (1964); 115 minutes; U.S.: An Artixo Productions Release

P: Richard Attenborough; **D/S:** Bryan Forbes; **M:** John Barry; **DP:** Gerry Turpin; **E:** Derek York; **AD:** Ray Simm; **Cast:** Kim Stanley, Richard Attenborough, Mark Eden, Nanette Newman, Judith Donner, Patrick Magee, Gerald Sim, Margaret Lacey, Maria Kazan, Lionel Gamlin, Marian Spencer and Ronald Hines.

Myra Savage (Kim Stanley) is a spiritual medium who conceives a plan to kidnap the daughter of a wealthy man and then use her powers to help locate the missing child. Myra reasons that the notoriety she gains from this will make the public aware of her psychic gifts. Myra is mentally unbalanced and her meek husband Billy (Richard Attenborough) is completely powerless to stop her. Instead he allows himself to be dominated by his wife and participates in her mad scheme. Based on the novel by Mark McShane, this remarkable film is a masterpiece of tension and restraint. Stanley gives a stunning performance as a woman whose mind was unhinged by the death of her own child and slips deeper into insanity. Attenborough is tormented by his devotion to her and by the realization that she is losing her already tenuous hold on reality. An outstanding motion picture in every respect.

Video: U.S.

The Secret of Dorian Gray see *Dorian Gray*

See No Evil see *Blind Terror*

The Seven Brothers Meet Dracula see *The Legend of the 7 Golden Vampires*

243. The Shadow of the Cat

A B.H.P./Jon Pennington Production (1961); 79 minutes; U.S.: Universal International

P: Jon Pennington; **D:** John Gilling; **S:** George Baxt; **M:** Mikis Theodorakis; **DP:** Arthur Grant; **E:** James Needs and John Pomeroy; **PD:** Bernard Robinson; **AD:** Don Mingaye; **Cast:** Andre Morell, Barbara Shelley, William Lucas, Freda Jackson, Conrad Phillips, Alan Wheatley, Andrew Crawford, Catherine Lacey, Vanda Godsell, Richard Warner, Henry Kendall and Vera Cook.

There has always been some controversy as to whether or not this is actually a Hammer film. Although it was filmed at Bray Studios using Hammer technicians, *The House of Horror: The Complete Story of Hammer Films*, a book authorized by the company itself, states in the filmography, "*Shadow of the Cat* and *Light Up the Sky*, two films that have been characterised as

The Shadow of the Cat ... is it a Hammer Film or isn't it?

Hammer pictures, are in fact not productions of the company." Despite this statement, recent books devoted to Hammer insist that it is a Hammer production.

In a pre-credits sequence, wealthy Ella Venable (Catherine Lacey) is bludgeoned to death by her butler Andrew (Andrew Crawford). Ella's husband Walter (Andre Morell) is behind the killing, and he and the housekeeper Clara (Freda Jackson) help Andrew bury the body in the forest. The sole witness to the dastardly deed is the dead woman's cat, Tabitha. During the remainder of the film, Tabitha enacts her revenge on the guilty persons by causing them each to suffer a fatal "accident." Some inventive "cat's-eye-view" sequences enliven this otherwise routine endeavor. For once the cat in question is a tabby rather than the usual black variety seen in many horror films. She gives a commendable performance.

Video: None

244. She

A Hammer/Seven Arts Production (1965); 105 minutes; Technicolor and HammerScope; U.S.: Metro–Goldwyn–Mayer; MetroColor and CinemaScope

P: Michael Carreras; **D:** Robert Day; **S:** David T. Chantler; **M:** James Bernard; **DP:** Harry Waxman; **E:** James Needs and Eric Boyd-Perkins; **AD:** Robert Jones and Don Mingaye; **Cast:** Ursula Andress, John Richardson, Peter Cushing, Bernard Cribbins, Rosenda Monteros, Christopher Lee, Andre Morell, John Maxim, Cherry Larman, Bula Coleman, Soraya, Julie Mendez and Lisa Peake.

Holly (Peter Cushing) voices his disapproval of her tyrannical rule to Ayesha (Ursula Andress) and Leo (John Richardson) in *She*.

Though the setting is updated to 1918 and the location is changed from Africa to Palestine, the essential elements of H. Rider Haggard's famous novel were retained for this ornate Hammer remake. Three English adventurers set out across the desert to find the lost city of Kuma. Despite many hardships, they finally arrive at their destination to discover an ancient city ruled by a fantastically beautiful queen. This is Ayesha (Ursula Andress), also know as She-Who-Must-Be-Obeyed. Ayesha believes that one of the English men, Leo Vincey (John Richardson), is the reincarnation of the lover she murdered in a jealous rage 2000 years before. In an effort to make Leo her eternal consort, Ayesha takes him to the sacred flame which has given her everlasting life. She does not know that to enter the flame a second time revokes the gift of immortality. As Ayesha bathes in the fire, the full span of her 2000 years catches up with her and, before Leo's horrified gaze, She turns into a hideous old woman and then crumbles into dust.

In 1962, Kenneth Hyman had brought the novel to the attention of Anthony Hinds as a venture to be undertaken in association with Seven Arts. This was to be Hammer's most expensive production to date; the project was temporarily put on hold while Hammer endeavored to attain additional financing from Universal. They eventually ended up making a deal with MGM instead and *She* began filming in August 1964. Hammer temporarily abandoned their tiny Bray Studios for the greater space provided by Elstree. Here the elaborate sets for the lost city of Kuma were constructed while the cast and crew went on location to the Negev desert in Southern Israel to shoot scenes for the early part of the film. Despite mixed critical reaction, *She* became Hammer's biggest world wide grosser up to that time. This financial success encouraged Hammer to embark on a series of fantasy "spectaculars" which provided a money-making alternative to their Gothic horror films. Andress' exotic and imaginative costumes were designed by Carl Toms, who would design the costumes for most of Hammer's subsequent "spectaculars." Toms went on to become an outstanding production designer for the theater, opera and ballet and has received an OBE (Officer in the Order of the British Empire) for his achievements.

Video: U.K./U.S.

245. The Shuttered Room

A Troy Schenck Production (1966); 99 minutes; Technicolor; U.S.: Warner Bros.–Seven Arts (1967)

EXP: Bernard Schwartz; **P:** Phillip Hazelton; **D:** David Greene; **S:** D.B. Ledrov and Nathaniel Tanchuck; **M:** Basil Kirchin; **DP:** Ken Hodges; **E:** Brian Smedley-Aston; **AD:** Brian Eatwell; **Cast:** Gig Young, Carol Lynley, Flora Robson, Oliver Reed, William Devlin, Judith Arthy, Bernard Kay, Robert Cawdron, Celia Hewitt, Ingrid Bower and Charles Lloyd Pack.

Adapted from a book by H.P. Lovecraft and August Derleth, *The Shuttered Room* is set in New England but was shot entirely Britain. Mike Kelton (Gig Young) and his wife Susannah (Carol Lynley) return to her family home on Dunwich Island. They are greeted with foreboding by her aunt Agatha Whateley (Flora Robson), who warns them to stay out of the old mill house which they are planning to turn into a summer home. This, of course, only fires their curiosity. Susannah eventually enters the mystery room at the top of the stairs and discovers that she has a sister who is a homicidal maniac. Aunt Agatha has kept her locked away there for years and faithfully watches over her. Although there are a number of tense scenes, the denouement is a slim payoff after all the buildup. Oliver Reed is Susannah's hateful and disgusting cousin Ethan, who causes her no end of trouble until his death at the hands of the mad sister.

Video: U.S. (video title: *Blood Island*)

246. The Skull

An Amicus Production (1965); 83 minutes; Technicolor and Techniscope; U.S.: Paramount

P: Milton Subotsky and Max J. Rosenberg; **D:** Freddie Francis; **S:** Milton Subotsky; **M:** Elisabeth Lutyens; **DP:** John Wilcox; **E:** Oswald Hafenrichter; **AD:** Bill Constable; **Cast:** Peter Cushing, Christopher Lee, Patrick Wymark, Jill Bennett, Michael Gough, George Coulouris, Nigel Green, Peter Woodthorpe, April Olrich, Patrick Magee, Maurice Good and Anna Palk.

Amicus' second horror entry is one of their best. Based on a short story by Robert Bloch, *The Skull* tells the tragic tale of occult collector Christopher Maitland (Peter Cushing), who acquires the skull of the Marquis De Sade from an unscrupulous dealer (Patrick Wymark). The skull is possessed by an evil spirit and eventually Maitland is driven to madness and murder. The film is populated by an excellent cast of familiar faces but, and as usual, it is Cushing who shines brightest. He is very convincing in a particularly harrowing nightmare sequence. This is one of those all-too-infrequent occasions when Freddie Francis directs with imagination. He disliked being pigeonholed in the horror genre and it is sometimes all too obvious in his lackluster approach.

PETER CUSHING IN THE TRULY HORRIFIC DREAM SEQUENCE FROM *THE SKULL*.

The Skull is an exception. The final third of the film is played almost completely without dialogue and Francis keeps it moving with some interesting visuals. The point-of-view shots from inside the skull are especially effective (he would use this technique again in *The Creeping Flesh*).

Video: U.S.

247. *Slave Girls*

A Hammer/Seven Arts Production (1966); 74 minutes; Technicolor and CinemaScope; U.S.: 20th Century–Fox (1967); 91 minutes; DeLuxe Color and CinemaScope

P/D: Michael Carreras; **S:** Henry Younger; **M:** Carlo Martelli; **DP:** Michael Reed; **E:** James Needs and Roy Hyde; **AD:** Robert Jones; **Cast:** Martine Beswick, Michael Latimer, Edina Ronay, Stephanie Randall, Carol White, Alexandra Stevenson, Yvonne Horner, Sydney Bromley, Frank Hayden, Robert Raglan, Mary Hignett and Louis Mahoney.

Intending to make good use of the extensive sets for *One Million Years B.C.* which were still standing at Elstree Studios, Michael Carreras (under the pseudonym Henry Younger) concocted a script called *Slave Girls of the White Rhino*. For the lead in his new production, he choose Martine Beswick, who had given an impressive performance in the previous stone age epic. *Slave Girls* is a fascinatingly puerile piece of entertainment, sure to quicken the pulse of red-blooded schoolboys everywhere. Big

Martine Beswick is Kari, the ruler of a tribe of prehistoric women and Michael Latimer is her captive in *Slave Girls*.

game hunter David Marchant (Michael Latimer) is thrown back in time to a mysterious land where dark-haired Amazons hold blonde slave girls in cruel bondage. Kari (Martine Beswick) is the barbarous queen who rules over them all with an iron hand. Marchant rejects Kari's amorous advances and leads a revolt which liberates the slaves. Beswick realized the film was an intellectual wash out but nevertheless gave an amazing performance as the evil Kari. *Slave Girls* languished on the shelf in England until 1968 when it was finally released, shorn of 17 minutes running time. *Films and Filming*, which usually found little good to say about Hammer, printed a curious review of the film by Michael Armstrong. He closed this review by writing, "Yes — the film may be boring as a mere piece of entertainment, but it is certainly a very sincere work of art, with a lot to say."

Video: U.S.

248. *The Snake Woman*

A Caralan Production (1960); 68 minutes; U.S.: United Artists (1961)

P: George Fowler; **D:** Sidney J. Furie; **S:** Orville H. Hampton; **M:** Buxton Orr; **DP:** Stephen Dade; **E:** Anthony Gibbs; **AD:** John G. Earl; **Cast:** John McCarthy, Susan Travers, Geoffrey Denton, Elsie Wagstaff, Arnold Marle, John Cazabon, Frances Bennett, Jack Cunningham,

Hugh Moxey, Michael Logan and Stevenson Lang.

In the tiny English village of Bellingham, a scientist cures his wife's insanity by repeatedly injecting her with snake venom. When she gives birth to a daughter, the infant is cold-blooded and has the lidless eyes of a serpent. The mother takes one look at her progeny and promptly dies. During the next 20 years, the village is continually plagued by mysterious deaths in which the victim bears the mark of a cobra bite. Scotland Yard sends a man to investigate and the villagers tell him that they are suffering from the curse of a snake woman. He is skeptical until he meets a beautiful young girl on the moors who loves flute music and is prone to shedding her skin. Slow-moving and endlessly talky, *The Snake Woman* was conceived and released as the companion feature to *Dr. Blood's Coffin*. Hammer would use a similar idea to far greater effect in *The Reptile*.

Video: None

249. The Snorkel

A Hammer/Clarion Films Ltd. Production (1958); 90 minutes; U.S.: Columbia; 74 minutes

P: Michael Carreras; **D:** Guy Green; **S:** Peter Myers and Jimmy Sangster; **M:** Francis Chagrin; **DP:** Jack Asher; **E:** James Needs; **AD:** John Stoll; **Cast:** Peter Van Eyck, Betta St. John, Mandy Miller, Gregoire Aslan, William Franklyn, Marie Burke, Henry Vidon, Irene Prador and Robert Rietty.

Based on an original story by actor Anthony Dawson, *The Snorkel* is a precursor to Hammer's series of psychological thrillers which began with *Taste of Fear* in 1961. Candy Brown's (Mandy Miller) mother is found dead and the verdict is suicide. Although her mother was in a sealed room with the gas on, Candy is convinced that she was murdered by her second husband Jacques Duval (Peter Van Eyck). Candy persists in her accusations until her stepfather is forced to target her as his next victim. Filmed in the town of Alassio on the Italian Riviera, *The Snorkel* is a taut thriller with some clever plot twists. Mandy Miller had a very successful career as a child star in England, making her debut at age six in *The Man in the White Suit* (1951). During the filming of *The Snorkel* she celebrated her thirteenth birthday. This was her last film. Like many other child stars, she had outgrown the traits responsible for her success.

Video: None

250. Son of Dracula

Apple Films Ltd. (1973); 90 minutes; Color; U.S. *(Young Dracula)*: Cinemation (1974)

P: Ringo Starr; **D:** Freddie Francis; **S:** Jay Fairbank; **M:** Paul Buckmaster; Songs by Harry Nilsson; **DP:** Norman Warwick; **E:** Derek York; **AD:** Andrew Sanders; **Cast:** Harry Nilsson, Ringo Starr, Dennis Price, Freddie Jones, Suzanna Leigh, Peter Frampton, Keith Moon, John Bonham, Shakira Baksh, Skip Martin, Jenny Runacre and Rosanna Lee.

Singer Harry Nilsson plays Count Down, the son of Dracula. (Ringo Starr had wanted David Bowie for the lead but the rock star wisely turned it down.) The film was originally intended as a mere comedy but, a week prior to shooting, Starr decided to also make it a musical. Harry Nilsson quickly wrote seven songs which director Freddie Francis then had to incorporate into the script. Starr plays Merlin the Magician and the whole sorry affair smacks greatly of extreme self-indulgence. The soundtrack album of *Son of Dracula* received a far wider release than the film itself. The film is, at best, curious footnote in the history of vampire cinema and pop music.

Video: None

251. The Sorcerers

A Tony Tenser–Curtwel–Global Production (1967); 86 minutes; Eastman Color; U.S.: Allied Artists

EXP: Arnold L. Miller; **P:** Patrick Curtis and Tony Tenser; **D:** Michael Reeves; **S:** Michael Reeves and Tom Baker; **M:** Paul Ferris; **DP:** Stanley A. Long; **AD:** Tony Curtis; **E:** David Woodward and Susan Michie; **Cast:** Boris Karloff, Ian Ogilvy, Elizabeth Ercy, Victor Henry, Catherine Lacey, Susan George, Dani Sheridan, Alf Joint, Ivor Dean, Peter Fraser, Meier Tzelniker, Gerald Campion and Martin Terry.

Dr. Marcus Monserrat (Boris Karloff) is a "Practitioner of Medical Hypnosis." He has invented a device which will allow him and his wife Estelle (Catherine Lacey) to tap into the sensations and experiences of another person. The doctor lures a bored young swinger named Mike (Ian Ogilvy) to his flat with the promise of new "kicks" and hooks him up to the machine. Afterwards, Mike remembers nothing of the incident but Marcus and Estelle are able to "tune in" at will. Estelle becomes addicted to the new sensations and uses her will to drive Mike to commit increasingly more extreme acts, eventually causing him to murder two young women. The script was based on an idea by British horror writer John Burke, who wrote the novelizations of several Hammer and Amicus films. With this movie, Michael Reeves secured his position as the "boy wonder" of horror film directors. He would direct only one more motion picture, but it would be a masterpiece.

Video: U.S.

252. Spaceflight IC-1

A Lippert Films Production (1965); 65 minutes; U.S.: 20th Century–Fox

P: Robert L. Lippert and Jack Parsons; **D:** Bernard Knowles; **S:** Harry Spalding; **M:** Elisabeth Lutyens; **DP:** Geoffrey Faithfull; **E:** Robert Winter; **AD:** Harry White; **Cast:** Bill Williams, John Cairney, Linda Marlowe, Kathleen Breck, Donald Churchill, Margo Mayne, Jeremy Longhurst, Norma West, Tony Doonan, Andrew Downie, John Lee and Chuck Julian.

In the computer-controlled government of the future, a group of carefully selected people are sent into space with the purpose of colonizing another planet. Under the harsh, tyrannical command of Capt. Ralston (Bill Williams), the conditions aboard Spaceflight IC-1 become intolerable. A mutiny lead by Dr. Thomas (John Cairney) eventually reinstitutes a benevolent society which will be carried on to their new world. This is probably the most obscure of the films produced in England by Lippert for 20th Century–Fox. Like many of the others, it has an interesting premise that is let down by indifferent direction and meager production values.

Video: None

253. Spaceways

A Hammer Film Production (1953); 76 minutes; U.S.: Lippert

P: Michael Carreras; **D:** Terence Fisher; **S:** Paul Tabori and Richard Landau; **M:** Ivor Slaney; **DP:** Reg Wyer; **E:** Maurice Rootes; **AD:** J. Elder Wills; **Cast:** Howard Duff, Eva Bartok, Andrew Osborn, Anthony Ireland, Alan Wheatley, David Horne, Michael Medwin, Cecile Chevreau and Hugh Moxey.

Britain's first space movie is an adaptation of a radio play by Charles Eric Maine. Stephen Mitchell (Howard Duff) is a space research scientist working in England. His wife (Cecile Chevreau) is having an affair with one of her husband's colleagues (Andrew Osborn). When the illicit lovers disappear, Mitchell is suspected of having killed them and sent their bodies into outer space on a test rocket. Mitchell decides that in order to prove his innocence he must go on another rocket to retrieve the first one. Sound interesting? It isn't! With endless dialogue

John Cairney rebels against Bill Williams' harsh command of *Spaceflight IC-1*.

(after all, it was a radio play) and no budget, this Hammer production certainly didn't anticipate the studio's later efforts.

Video: None

254. *The Spaniard's Curse*

A Wentworth Film (1958); 80 minutes; U.S.: Independent Film Distributors

EXP: A.M.G. Gelardi; **P:** Roger Proudlock; **D:** Ralph Kemplen; **S:** Kenneth Hyde; **M:** Lambert Williamson; **DP:** Arthur Grant; **E:** Stanley Hawks; **PD:** Tony Masters; **Cast:** Tony Wright, Lee Patterson, Susan Beaumont, Michael Hordern, Ralph Truman, Olga Dickie, Henry Oscar, Brian Oulton, Evelyn Roberts, Roddy Hughes, Jessica Cairns and Constance Fraser.

A man accused of murder is condemned to death by the court. Professing his innocence, he puts a fifteenth century Spanish curse, "The Assize of Dying," on the men who judged him. The condemned man dies of a heart attack and, shortly thereafter, the jury foreman is hit by a bus and killed. The ward (Susan Beaumont) of the judge (Michael Hordern) who tried the case is convinced that the man was innocent. She meets the murder victim's half-brother (Lee Patterson) and together they set out to discover the true identity of the killer. At this point, "the curse" is all but forgotten and the film becomes a lethargic murder mystery with a very peculiar ending. An unfortunate case of wasted potential.

Video: None

Spider's Venom see ***Venom***

255. The Spiral Staircase

A Raven Film Production (1975); 89 minutes; Technicolor; U.S.: Warner Bros.

EXP: Josef Shaftel; **P:** Peter Shaw; **D:** Peter Collinson; **S:** Andrew Meredith; **M:** David Lindup; **DP:** Ken Hodges; **E:** Raymond Poulton; **AD:** Disley Jones; **Cast:** Jacqueline Bisset, Christopher Plummer, Mildred Dunnock, Sam Wanamaker, Gayle Hunnicutt, John Phillip Law, Elaine Stritch, John Ronane, Sheila Brennan, Ronald Radd, Heather Lowe and Christopher Malcolm.

Helen Mallory (Jacqueline Bisset) is mute because of the trauma she suffered seeing her husband and daughter die in a fire. She comes to visit her ailing grandmother (Mildred Dunnock), who lives in a rambling mansion with her sons (Christopher Plummer and John Phillip Law). Five people, all with physical disabilities, have been recently murdered in the area and the police suspect that Helen is a potential target because of her affliction. This is a tepid remake of the classic 1946 thriller which starred Dorothy McGuire. Director Peter Collinson, who seemed to make a career of "women in peril" films, shows no particular flair for the material and directs without style. The identity of the killer is fairly obvious early on, negating what little suspense the story might have otherwise generated. The staircase of the title barely figures into the plot at all.

Video: U.S.

Spirit of the Dead see *The Asphyx*

Stop Me Before I Kill! see *The Full Treatment*

256. Straight on Till Morning

A Hammer Film Production (1972); 96 minutes; Technicolor; U.S.: International Co-Productions (1974)

P: Howard Brandy; **D:** Peter Collinson; **S:** John Peacock; **M:** Roland Shaw; **DP:** Brian Probyn; **E:** Alan Pattillo; **AD:** Scott MacGregor; **Cast:** Rita Tushingham, Shane Briant, Tom Bell, Annie Ross, Katya Wyeth, James Bolam, Clare Kelly, Harold Berens, John Clive, Tommy Godfrey and Mavis Villiers.

Homely Brenda Thompson (Rita Tushingham) leaves her mother in Liverpool and goes to London to search for a "handsome prince" to father her baby. Instead she meets Peter (Shane Briant), a psychotic killer who hates beauty and whose murder weapon of choice seems to be a box cutter. Filled with endless "jump cuts" and pointless references to Peter Pan, this was a particularly unappetizing stew cooked up by Hammer. Tushingham is tiresome in yet another one of her perpetual "ugly duckling" roles, and Briant is at his most petulant. Briant and screenwriter John Peacock had a previous association: In 1969, Briant was cast the West End production of Peacock's play *Children of the Wolf*. It's nice to see Katya Weyth in a fairly substantial role after her brief but striking appearance as Mircalla Karnstein in *Twins of Evil*.

Video: U.S. (video title: *Till Dawn Do We Part*)

257. The Strange World of Planet X

A John Bash/Artistes Alliance Production (1957); 75 minutes; U.S. *(Cosmic Monsters)*: DCA Pictures (1958)

P: George Maynard; **D:** Gilbert Gunn; **S:** Paul Ryder; **M:** Robert Sharples; **DP:** Joe Ambor; **E:** Francis Bieber; **AD:** Bernard Sarron; **Cast:** Forrest Tucker, Gaby Andre, Wyndham Goldie, Martin Benson, Hugh Latimer, Alec Mango, Dandy Nicholls, Richard Warner, Patricia Sinclair, and Geoffrey Chater.

A scientist's experiments tear a hole in the Earth's ionosphere, causing various upheavals of nature, including a horde of giant insects. An alien using the clever name "Mr. Smith" arrives in time to save the day and prevent further disasters from occurring. A fairly thoughtful story is given a dull execution with lots of talk and little action until the final scenes. Even then the townspeople seem far more concerned about television reception and last call at the local pub than the threat of rampaging monster insects. As with several other British science fiction movies of the period, *The Strange World of Planet X* was adapted from a television serial. In the U.S. it was the companion film to the far superior *The Trollenberg Terror*.

Video: U.S.

258. Stranger from Venus (a.k.a. *Immediate Disaster*)

A Rich and Rich–Princess Pictures Production (1954); 75 minutes; U.S.: *No theatrical release*

P: Burt Balaban and Gene Martel; **D:** Burt Balaban; **S:** Hans Jacoby; **M:** Eric Spear; **DP:** Kenneth Talbot; **E:** Peter Hunt; **AD:** John Elphick; **Cast:** Helmut Dantine, Patricia Neal, Derek Bond, Cyril Luckham, Arthur Young, Marigold Russell, Willoughby Gray, Kenneth Edwards, David Garth, Stanley Van Beers, Nigel Green and Graham Stuart.

A nameless stranger (Helmut Dantine) arrives at a country inn and discloses that he is an emissary from the planet Venus. There is considerable skepticism until it is revealed that he has healed Patricia Neal of some serious car crash injuries. He also cures the innkeeper's limp. The stranger has come to Earth to meet with world authorities to warn them against the uncontrolled use of nuclear weapons on our planet. A hasty meeting is arranged with British government officals but they respond by stealing his communication device and trying to intercept the spaceship that is scheduled to take him back to Venus. He is able to warn the mother ship before it lands, at great expense to his own well-being. The presence of Patricia Neal and the anti-nuclear message recall *The Day the Earth Stood Still*, but the minimal special effects, talky script and low-key exposition put to rest any further comparisons with that film.

Video: U.S.

259. The Stranglers of Bombay

A Hammer Film Production (1960); 81 minutes; MegaScope; U.S.: Columbia

EXP: Michael Carreras; **P:** Anthony Hinds; **D:** Terence Fisher; **S:** David Z. Goodman; **M:** James Bernard; **DP:** Arthur Grant; **E:** James Needs and Alfred Cox; **PD:** Bernard Robinson; **AD:** Don Mingaye; **Cast:** Guy Rolfe, Allan Cuthbertson, Andrew Cruickshank, George Pastell, Marne Maitland, Jan Holden, Paul Stassino, Tutte Lemkow, David Spenser, John Harvey, Roger Delgado and Marie Devereux.

This story of British colonialism in nineteenth century India is based on the true events surrounding the religious fanatics called Thuggees, who were said to have been responsible for the deaths of more than a million people. Capt. Harry Lewis (Guy Rolfe) discovers the cult of stranglers who worship Kali, the Goddess of Destruction. Unable to convince his superior officers of the cult's existence, he vows to bring the killers to justice despite the terrible danger he will be facing. Shot in a black-and-white semi-documentary style, it is different from anything Terence Fisher directed before or after for Hammer. It also contains some of the most gruesome sequences in the entire Hammer lexicon. Bernard Robinson's production design replicates the Indian atmosphere so convincingly that it is often hard to believe the film was not shot on location.

Video: U.K.

260. A Study in Terror

A Compton–Sir Nigel Film Production (1965); 94 minutes; Eastman Color; U.S.: Columbia

EXP: Herman Cohen and Tony Tenser (uncredited); **P:** Henry E. Lester; **D:** James Hill; **S:** Donald and Derek Ford; **M:** John Scott; **DP:**

Desmond Dickinson; **E:** Henry Richardson; **PD:** Alex Vetchinsky; **Cast:** John Neville, Donald Houston, John Fraser, Anthony Quayle, Adrienne Corri, Robert Morley, Judi Dench, Peter Carsten, Frank Finlay, Barry Jones, John Cairney, Edina Ronay and Georgia Brown.

Sherlock Holmes meets Jack the Ripper in this interesting, if not entirely notable, movie. Holmes (John Neville) and Dr. Watson (Donald Houston) become involved in deducing the identity of the infamous killer who is slaughtering the prostitutes of Whitechapel. Obviously heavily influenced by the Hammer films but lacking their atmosphere and flair, *A Study in Terror* does have its moments. Barbara Windsor does a saucy turn as a doomed prostitute and Edina Ronay, as another of the victims, features in a stylish sequence where the camera takes the point of view of the Ripper as she attempts to seduce him. With a Holmes the caliber of Peter Cushing's and direction by Terence Fisher, this could have been a memorable film indeed. Georgia Brown, who played Nancy in the original stage production of the musical *Oliver*, belts out two songs. Holmes and the Ripper were to meet again in the 1979 film *Murder by Decree*, which starred Christopher Plummer as the famous detective.

Video: U.K./U.S.

Sudden Terror see *Eyewitness*

261. *Sumuru*

Sumuru Films Ltd. (1967); 84 minutes; Technicolor and Techniscope; U.S. *(The Million Eyes of Su-Muru)*: American–International; 95 minutes

P: Harry Alan Towers; **D:** Lindsay Shonteff; **S:** Kevin Kavanagh; **M:** John Scott; **DP:** John Kotze; **E:** Allan Morrison; **AD:** Scott MacGregor; **Cast:** Frankie Avalon, George Nader, Shirley Eaton, Wilfrid Hyde-White, Klaus Kinski, Patti Chandler, Salli Sachse, Ursula Rank, Christa Nell, Maria Rohm, Paul Chang and Denise Davreux.

Once again producer Harry Alan Towers turned to the works of author Sax Rohmer for inspiration. Trouble shooters Nick West (George Nader) and Tommy Carter (Frankie Avalon) are persuaded by British Intelligence to investigate the murder of a government official from the tiny Asian country of Sinonesia. They uncover an organization of women who are plotting to take over the world. Their leader is the evil mastermind Su-Muru (Shirley Eaton). Operating from an island stronghold, they attempt to realize their ambition by using torture, murder and a gun which can turn people into stone. Nick is taken prisoner and Tommy must fight to save his friend and the world. This works better than some because of the tongue-in-cheek approach to the material and interesting Hong Kong location photography.

Video: None

262. *Svengali* (a.k.a. *Trilby and Svengali*)

A George Minter–Renown Production (1955); 82 minutes; Eastman Color; U.S.: Metro–Goldwyn–Mayer

P: George Minter; **D/S:** Noel Langley; **M:** William Alwyn; **DP:** Wilkie Cooper; **E:** John Pomeroy; **AD:** Fred Pusey; **Cast:** Hildegarde Neff (Knef), Donald Wolfit, Terence Morgan, Derek Bond, Paul Rogers, Harry Secombe, Noel Purcell, Alfie Bass, David Kossoff, Hubert Gregg, David Oxley and Hugh Cross.

Although the 1931 version of *Svengali* starring John Barrymore is often mentioned in surveys of horror films, this color remake is not. Based on the novel *Trilby* by George du Maurier, the story begins in turn-of-the-century Paris where Trilby (Hildegarde Neff) is an artist's model. She falls in love with Billy (Terence Morgan), a British art student, but when his family disapproves of their relationship, she goes into hiding. Svengali (Donald Wolfit) is a mad musical

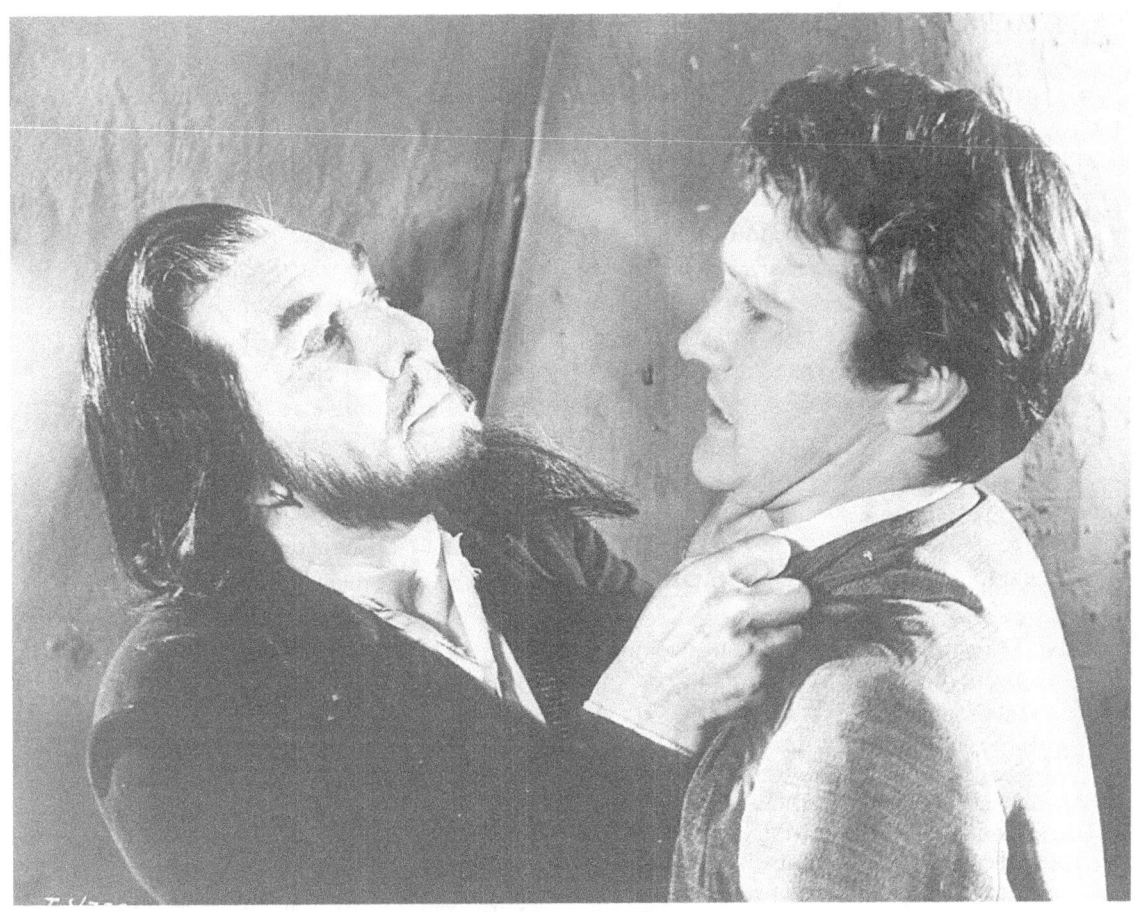

DONALD WOLFIT AND TERENCE MORGAN ARE RIVALS FOR THE LOVELY TRILBY IN *SVENGALI*.

genius who is smitten with Trilby. Under the pretext of curing her headaches, he gains a powerful hypnotic control over her. He summons her to him and, using his powers of hypnosis, transforms her into a brilliant opera singer. His control over her is complete and he vows that when he dies, she will follow him shortly thereafter. (Originally the title role was to have gone to Robert Newton.) The macabre aspects of the story don't really take over until the final third of the film, but the fine performances and good production values make it of more than passing interest. The look of this movie anticipates the color Gothic Hammer films which were still two years in the future.

Video: U.S.

263. Symptoms

Finition Productions (1974); 91 minutes; Eastman Color; U.S.: Bryanston (1976); 81 minutes

P: Jean Dupuis; **D:** Joseph (Jose) Larraz; **S:** Joseph Larraz and Stanley Miller; **M:** John Scott; **DP:** Trevor Wrenn; **E:** Brian Smedley-Aston; **Cast:** Angela Pleasence, Lorna Heilbron, Peter Vaughan, Ronald O'Neil, Raymond Huntley, Michael Grady, Nancy Levinson and Marie-Paul Mailleux.

Helen Ramsey (Angela Pleasence) invites her friend Ann (Lorna Heilbron) to visit her at yet another decaying country home (the English countryside is apparently littered with them). This one appears to be haunted by the spirit of Cora (Marie Paul

Mailleux), one of Helen's former house guests. Helen is a lesbian who becomes pathologically jealous of her friends. When Ann's boyfriend shows up, Helen cannot repress her anger. She goes berserk and kills them both in a particularly gruesome sequence. This is the second of three horror films directed by Jose Larraz in a two-year period. He later continued to make horror films in his native country, Spain. In 1981 he returned to England to film *Los Ritos Sexuales Del Diablo* (a.k.a. *Black Candles*). Although this story of devil worship is set in England, it was a Spanish production.

Video: U.S.

264. Tales from the Crypt

An Amicus Production (1972); 92 minutes; Eastman Color; U.S.: Cinerama Releasing

EXP: Charles Fries; P: Max J. Rosenberg and Milton Subotsky; D: Freddie Francis; S: Milton Subotsky; M: Douglas Gamley; DP: Norman Warwick; E: Teddy Darvas; AD: Tony Curtis; Cast: Joan Collins, Peter Cushing, Roy Dotrice, Richard Greene, Ian Hendry, Patrick Magee, Barbara Murray, Nigel Patrick, Robin Phillips, Ralph Richardson, Geoffrey Bayldon and Chloe Franks.

This Amicus anthology film is based on publisher Bill Gaines' notorious *EC Comics*, which were banned because of their adult themes and violent content. Max Rosenberg said that Gaines was very pleased that Amicus wanted to film his stories, but apparently he was not that happy with the end result. True to their source material, the five stories herein all deal with those favorite *EC* themes: greed, infidelity and murder. Five people are gathered and each is told a story by the Crypt Keeper (Ralph Richardson). The first is "All Through the House," a Christmas Eve tale with Joan Collins pursued by a homicidal Santa Claus. The second and weakest entry is titled "Reflection of Death" and features Ian Hendry as an unfaithful husband. "Poetic Justice" is the best of the lot. Peter Cushing is the lovable rubbish collector Arthur Grimsdyke, who is hounded to death by his greedy neighbor Robin Phillips. Grimsdyke returns from the grave as a rotting corpse bent on revenge. Robert Hutton can be spotted briefly as one of Grimsdyke's disgruntled neighbors. "Wish You Were Here" stars Richard Greene in a variation on the classic story "The Monkey's Paw." The last tale is "Blind Alleys," in which Nigel Patrick is the heartless administrator of a home for the blind, whose suffering charges get even with him in a particularly unpleasant manner. Despite the varying quality of the stories, this is one of Amicus' best productions and it is also a bit bloodier than their usual fare.

Video: U.S.

265. Tales That Witness Madness

A World Film Services Ltd. Production (1973); 90 minutes; Color; U.S.: Paramount

P: Norman Priggen; D: Freddie Francis; S: Jay Fairbank; M: Bernard Ebbinghouse; DP: Norman Warwick; E: Bernard Gribble; AD: Roy Walker; Cast: Kim Novak, Joan Collins, Jack Hawkins, Donald Houston, Michael Jayston, Suzy Kendall Peter McEnery, Michael Petrovitch, Donald Pleasence, Russell Lewis, Georgia Brown and Leslie Nunnerley.

The box office success of *Tales from the Crypt* prompted Paramount to cofinance this anthology film from the same director. The screenplay by Jay Fairbank (actually actress Jennifer Jayne and her husband Art Fairbank) consists of four stories about the patients in a mental institution. The format is very much like the Amicus film *Asylum*, produced the previous year. The first story is about a young boy and his "imaginary" tiger. The second tells of an antique bicycle that transports its rider into the past. In the third, a jealous tree stump competes with a wife for her husband's affections. The final tale has Kim Novak planning a luau where

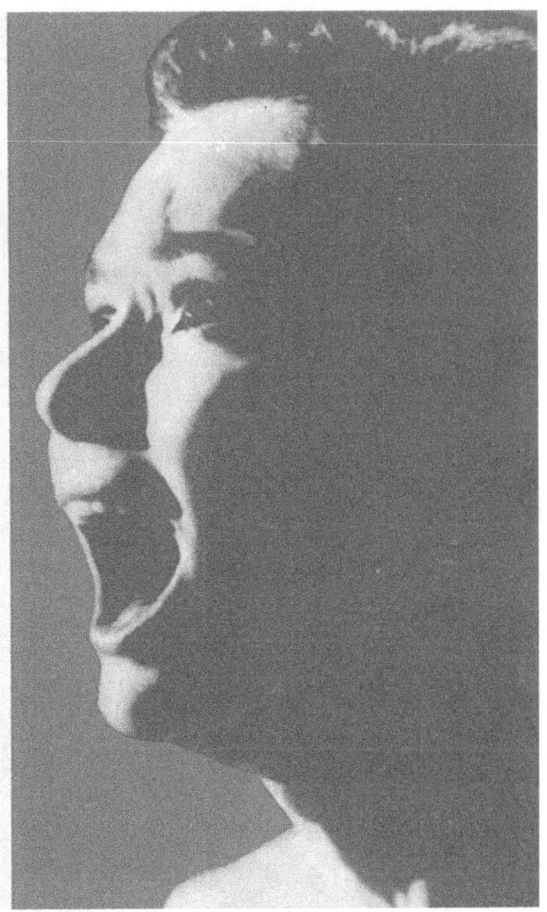

TASTE OF FEAR

her daughter ends up as the main course. (Originally Rita Hayworth was to have played the lead in the final segment but her frequent absences, due to illness, caused the producers to replace her with Novak.) The solid cast and wry tone of the stories work in the film's favor.
   Video: U.S.

Tam-Lin see *The Devil's Widow*

266. *Taste of Fear*

A Hammer Film Production (1961); 82 minutes; U.S. *(Scream of Fear)*: Columbia

EXP: Michael Carreras; **P/S:** Jimmy Sangster; **D:** Seth Holt; **M:** Clifton Parker; **DP:** Douglas Slocombe; **E:** James Needs and Eric Boyd-Perkins; **PD:** Bernard Robinson; **AD:** Tom Goswell; **Cast:** Susan Strasberg, Ronald Lewis, Ann Todd, Christopher Lee, Leonard Sachs, John Serret, Anne Blake, Fred Johnson and Bernard Brown.

Jimmy Sangster originally wrote this screenplay for producer Sidney Box. When Box decamped due to ill health, the rights went to his brother-in-law, producer Peter Rogers. Fearing the script might never be filmed, Sangster began shopping it around to other producers, including the producing team of Baker and Berman and Hammer's Michael Carreras. Carreras optioned the rights from Rogers and it became the first, and best, in Hammer's series of psychological thrillers.

RALPH BATES MADE HIS MOTION PICTURE DEBUT AS THE DEBAUCHED LORD COURTLEY IN *TASTE THE BLOOD OF DRACULA*.

Susan Strasberg stars as Penny Appleby, an invalid confined to a wheelchair. She receives a letter from the father she has not seen for ten years, asking her to join him at his house on the Riviera. When she arrives, her stepmother Jane (Ann Todd) explains that Penny's father is away on a business trip but will return shortly. When the corpse of her father turns up, Penny suspects that he was the victim of foul play. The story is tightly plotted and includes a number of enjoyable shocks. The climax is sure to keep most viewers guessing until the final minutes. Seth Holt's direction and the camerawork by Douglas Slocombe are first-rate.

Video: U.S.

267. Taste the Blood of Dracula

A Hammer Film Production (1970); 95 minutes; Technicolor; U.S.: Warner Bros.; 91 minutes

P: Aida Young; **D:** Peter Sasdy; **S:** John Elder; **M:** James Bernard; **DP:** Arthur Grant; **E:** Chris Barnes; **AD:** Scott MacGregor; **Cast:** Christopher Lee, Linda Hayden, Geoffrey Keen, Anthony Corlan, John Carson, Ralph Bates, Gwen Watford, Isla Blair, Martin Jarvis, Roy Kinnear, Peter Sallis, Michael Ripper, Russell Hunter and Maddy Smith.

This is the fourth in Hammer's series of films starring Christopher Lee as the arch vampire, Count Dracula. Although Lee has little actual screen time in this outing, the compensations are many. Peter Sasdy's direction is highly imaginative and the juvenile leads (Anthony Corlan and Linda Hayden) are both talented and appealing. Ralph Bates (as the dissolute Lord Courtley) gives a wonderfully over-the-top performance in his first of many roles for Hammer. Technical credits are exemplary, with Arthur Grant's color photography and James Bernard's background score standouts. Anthony Corlan also appears in Hammer's *Vampire Circus* (1972). He later changed his name to Anthony Higgins and has appeared in many films, including *The Draughtsman's Contract* (1982), *Young Sherlock Holmes* (1985) and, more recently, *Alive and Kicking* (1997). Future Hammer leading lady Madeleine Smith (billed here as Maddy Smith) can be seen in a small supporting role during the brothel sequence.

Video: U.K./U.S.

268. The Tell-Tale Heart

A Danziger Production (1960); 78 minutes; U.S.: Brigadier Films (1961)

P: Harry and Edward Danziger; **D:** Ernest Morris; **S:** Brian Clemens and Elden Howard; **M:** Tony Crombie and Bill Le Sage; **DP:** James Wilson; **E:** Derek Parsons; **AD:** Peter Russell; **Cast:** Laurence Payne, Adrienne Corri, Dermot Walsh, Selma Vaz Diaz, John Scott, John Martin, Annette Carell, Rosemary Rotheray, Suzanne Fuller, David Lander, Yvonne Buckingham and Richard Bennett.

This Edgar Allan Poe adaptation was filmed in England the same year that Roger Corman directed his first Poe film for AIP. Like the Corman adaptations, this has little to do with the original Poe story. Edgar (Lawrence Payne) is a socially inept man who spends much of his time looking at photographs of naked women and peeping through the window at his pretty new neighbor, Betty (Adrienne Corri). He finally gets up the nerve to ask her out but bungles the evening by making inappropriate advances towards her. She reluctantly agrees to go out with him again and, at a nightclub, Edgar introduces her to his best friend, Carl (Dermot Walsh). Big mistake! Carl is a handsome knave and before very long he and Betty are in bed together with Edgar peering through the window at them. Edgar invites Carl to his house, murders him and buries the body under the floorboards in his lounge. Although Carl is dead, Edgar continues to hear the beating of his heart. This is quite an effective little film until the stupid "it was all a nightmare" ending.

Video: None

269. Ten Rillington Place

Genesis Productions Ltd. (1970); 111 minutes; Eastman Color; U.S.: Columbia (1971)

P: Martin Ransohoff and Leslie Linder; **D:** Richard Fleischer; **S:** Clive Exton; **M:** John Dankworth; **DP:** Denys Coop; **E:** Ernest Walter; **AD:** Maurice Carter; **Cast:** Richard Attenborough, Judy Geeson, John Hurt, Pat Heywood, Isobel Black, Robert Hardy, Geoffrey Chater, Andre Morell, Sam Kydd, and Gabrielle Daye.

This is the true story of London's most infamous mass murderer since Jack the Ripper. The film begins in 1944 with the murder of a young woman by John Christie (Richard Attenborough). The story then resumes in 1949 when a young couple, the Evans, rent a flat in Christie's building in the Notting Hill area of London. Timothy Evans (John Hurt) is an illiterate bloke who constantly berates his wife Beryl (Judy Geeson). The Evans already have an infant daughter; when Beryl discovers that she is pregnant again, a terrible fight ensues. When Beryl confides her problem to Christie, he convinces her that he has medical training and can perform an abortion. Instead, Christie murders Beryl and her daughter. He then gives testimony which incriminates Timothy, who ends up being hanged for the crimes. Christie continues to compulsively commit murders and is eventually caught and hanged. Timothy Evans was pardoned posthumously. The public outcry was so great at this miscarriage of justice that the death penalty was abolished in Great Britain. These disturbing events are told without any sensationalism, which greatly inhances the impact — as does Richard Attenborough's chillingly understated performance as John Christie.

Video: U.S.

Terror from Under the House see *Revenge*

The Terror of Sheba see *Persecution*

270. *The Terror of the Tongs*

A Hammer Film Production (1961); 79 minutes; Technicolor; U.S.: Columbia; Black-and-White

EXP: Michael Carreras; **P:** Kenneth Hyman; **D:** Anthony Bushell; **S:** Jimmy Sangster; **M:** James Bernard; **DP:** Arthur Grant; **E:** James Needs and Eric Boyd-Perkins; **PD:** Bernard Robinson; **Cast:** Geoffrey Toone, Christopher Lee, Yvonne Monlaur, Burt Kwouk, Brian Worth, Barbara Brown, Marie Burke, Marne Maitland, Charles Lloyd Pack, Richard Leech, Ewen Solon and Milton Reid.

In 1910, Hong Kong is held in a grip of fear by the ruthless Chung King (Christopher Lee), leader of the deadly crime syndicate called the Red Dragon Tong. When his daughter is murdered by the Tong, Jackson (Geoffrey Toone), a British sea captain, vows to get revenge on the secret society. This could be considered a companion piece to *The Stranglers of Bombay*, with British colonialism once again in opposition to an evil Eastern sect. *The Terror of the Tongs* has always been one of Hammer's under-appreciated gems. Bernard Robinson's production design is especially noteworthy as he manages to create what seem to be extensive sets within the tiny confines of Bray Studios. The dock scenes, originally built for Hammer's *Visa to Canton*, are particularly impressive. Yvonne Monlaur returns to Hammer as the ill-fated Lee, a Eurasian concubine who loves Capt. Jackson to the bitter end. Lee seems to be doing an extensive screen test for the Fu Manchu series a few years in his future. This may be the reason why the Fu Manchu movies have mistakenly been classified as Hammer productions over the years. Until just before its U.S. theatrical showings, Columbia planned to release this film in color. Pressbook inserts state, "Please note: *The Terror of the Tongs* is in black-and-white. All references to Eastman Color must be removed!"

Video: None

271. *The Terrornauts*

An Amicus Production (1967); 75 minutes; Eastman Color by Pathe; U.S.: Embassy

P: Max J. Rosenberg and Milton Subotsky; **D:** Montgomery Tully; **S:** John Brunner; **M:** Elisabeth Lutyens; **DP:** Geoffrey Faithfull; **E:** Peter Musgrave; **PD:** Bill Constable; **AD:** Scott Slimon; **Cast:** Simon Oates, Zena Marshall, Charles Hawtrey, Stanley Meadows, Max Adrian, Patricia Hayes, Frank Berry, Richard Carpenter, Leonard Cracknell, Robert Jewell and Frank Forsyth.

English scientists at Project Startalk receive mysterious radio signals from a distant asteroid. Believing them to be distress signals, the scientists attempt to respond. This results in the entire Earth lab being scooped up by an enormous spaceship and taken off into outer space. The nonsensical story involves a doomed civilization which is trying to save the Earth from destruction by marauding invaders. Based on a Murray Leinster novel entitled *The Wailing Asteroid*, *The Terrornauts* is proof positive that science fiction was not Amicus' forte. Every aspect of the film is astoundingly silly, from the cheapjack special effects to an alien

ROBERT MORLEY IS ABOUT TO EAT HIS PET POODLES BAKED IN A PIE COURTESY OF VINCENT PRICE IN *THEATRE OF BLOOD*.

monster whose ridiculous appearance defies description. Strictly "kiddie matinee" stuff.

Video: U.S.

272. Theatre of Blood

A Sam Jaffe and Harbor Productions Inc. Presentation; A Cineman Films Ltd Production (1973); 104 minutes; DeLuxe Color; U.S.: United Artists

EXP: Gustave Berne and Sam Jaffe; **P:** John Kohn and Stanley Mann; **D:** Douglas Hickox; **S:** Anthony Greville-Bell; **M:** Michael J. Lewis; **DP:** Wolfgang Suschitsky; **E:** Malcolm Cooke; **PD:** Michael Seymour; **Cast:** Vincent Price, Diana Rigg, Ian Hendry, Harry Andrews, Coral Browne, Robert Morley, Jack Hawkins, Michael Hordern, Dennis Price, Diana Dors, Milo O'Shea and Madeline Smith.

Savaged by theater critics and denied the prestigious Critics Circle Award, Shakespearean actor Edward Lionheart (Vincent Price) apparently commits suicide by jumping into the Thames. Not long thereafter, the critics who denounced his performances begin to die one by one, their deaths reminiscent of murders from the plays of Shakespeare. It isn't too difficult to understand why Price often cited *Theatre of Blood* as his favorite film. It is an extremely deft combination of horror and the blackest of black comedy, offering Price the opportunity to essay a wide variety of Shakespearean roles. Of Price's performance, the *Los Angeles Times* review said: "If horror pictures were taken seriously, he would surely be an Oscar contender next year." The marvelous Diana Rigg, who has not been served well by the big screen, for once has a part that enabled her to show her considerable talents. As Lionheart's daughter Edwina, Rigg also enacts a variety of roles. On the set of this film, Price met co-star Coral Browne, who became his third wife and the great love of his golden years.

Video: U.K./U.S.

273. Theatre of Death

A Pennea Production (1966); 91 minutes; Technicolor and Techniscope; U.S.: Hemisphere (1967); 86 minutes

EXP: William Gell; **P:** Michael Smedley-Aston; **D:** Samuel Gallu; **S:** Ellis Kadison and Roger Marshall; **M:** Elisabeth Lutyens; **DP:** Gilbert Taylor; **E:** Barrie Vince; **AD:** Peter Proud; **Cast:** Christopher Lee, Lelia Goldoni, Julian Glover, Evelyn Laye, Jenny Till, Ivor Dean, Joseph Furst, Steve Plytas, Miki Iveria, Betty Woolfe, Leslie Handford and Fraser Kerr.

Dani (Lelia Goldoni) and Nicole (Jenny Till) are actresses who perform at the Grand Guignol–style Theatre du Morte in Paris. The director of the theater is Philippe Darvas (Christopher Lee), an arrogant and overbearing egotist who is obsessed by his art. Darvas has a strange hypnotic influence over Nicole and plans to make her the star of his next production. When Paris is beset by a series of vampire-like murders, Darvas becomes a primary suspect. Lee gives one of his best-ever performances in this often overlooked film. He has also never appeared more handsome. Unfortunately, his character disappears about halfway through the story, causing the film to lose much of its momentum. The production values are of a high caliber and the widescreen color photography is outstanding.

Video: U.S.

These Are the Damned see **The Damned**

274. They Came from Beyond Space

An Amicus Production (1967); 85 minutes; Eastman Color by Pathe; U.S.: Embassy

P: Max J. Rosenberg and Milton Subotsky; **D:** Freddie Francis; **S:** Milton Subotsky; **M:** James Stevens; **DP:** Norman Warwick; **E:** Peter Musgrave; **PD:** Bill Constable; **AD:** Don Mingaye and Scott Slimon; **Cast:** Robert Hutton, Jennifer Jayne, Bernard Kay, Zia Mohyeddin, Michael Gough, Geoffrey Wallace, Maurice Good, John Harvey, Luanshya Greer, Diane King, Paul Bacon and Dermot Cathie.

Yet another terrible science fiction movie from Amicus! The perpetually dull Robert Hutton plays a scientist who is attempting to stave off an invasion by aliens. The aliens, who are made up of pure energy, arrive via small meteorites and take over any Earthlings who are exposed to them. They are unable to take over Hutton because he has a silver plate in his head. The aliens also create a plague which seemingly kills many people but is really a ploy to provide more bodies for subjugation. The finale finds Hutton and two companions stowing away on a rocket to the Moon. There they meet the "Master of the Moon" (Michael Gough), who convinces the Earth people that he and his fellow extraterrestrials really aren't so bad. This atrocious movie seems to be trying to emulate *The Avengers* (Robert Hutton's character even drives a vintage auto *à la* John Steed) but any comparisons would be an insult to that wonderful television series. *They Came from Beyond Space* was released on a double-bill with *The Terrornauts*, a combination almost too awful to contemplate, let alone sit through.

Video: U.S.

Thin Air see **The Body Stealers**

Those Fantastic Flying Fools see **Jules Verne's Rocket to the Moon**

275. The 3 Worlds of Gulliver

A Morningside Production (1960); 100 minutes; Eastman Color and SuperDynamation; U.S.: Columbia

P: Charles H. Schneer; **D:** Jack Sher; **S:** Arthur Ross and Jack Sher; **M:** Bernard Herrmann; **DP:** Wilkie Cooper; **E:** Raymond Poulton; **AD:** Gil Parrendo and Derek Barrington; **SVE:** Ray Harryhausen; **Cast:** Kerwin Mathews, June Thorburn, Jo Morrow, Lee Patterson, Basil Sydney, Sherri Alberoni, Martin Benson, Peter Bull, Mary Ellis, Gregoire Aslan and Charles Lloyd Pack.

Jonathan Swift's classic *Gulliver's Travels* loses most of its satiric bite in this delightful fantasy geared toward children. There is, however, a good lesson to be learned about man's reaction to anyone who is "different." While sailing on a ship headed for the East Indies, Dr. Lemuel Gulliver (Kerwin Mathews) falls overboard in a storm. He is washed ashore on the island of Lilliput, whose inhabitants are only a few inches high, making Gulliver a giant. Gulliver attempts to make the Lilliputians' land a paradise, but their mistrust and petty squabbles eventually force him to flee. He next arrives in the kingdom of Brobdingnag, a land populated by giants. Once again Gulliver's size causes all manner of troubles as the giants refuse to believe that such a diminutive person could possess greater intelligence than themselves. This time around, Ray Harryhausen's stop-motion magic is subordinate to other forms of trick photography, but Gulliver's fight with a giant alligator is an exciting animation highlight.

Video: U.K./U.S.

Till Dawn Do We Part see *Straight on Till Morning*

276. Timeslip

A Merton Park Studios Ltd Production (1956); 93 minutes; U.S. *(The Atomic Man)*: Allied Artists; 78 minutes

P: Alec C. Snowden; **D:** Ken Hughes; **S:** Charles Eric Maine; **M:** Richard Taylor; **DP:** A.T. Dinsdale; **E:** Geoffrey Muller; **AD:** George Haslam; **Cast:** Gene Nelson, Faith Domergue, Joseph Tomelty, Peter Arne, Vic Perry, Donald Gray, Carl Jaffe, Launce Maraschal, Charles Hawtrey, Martin Wyldeck, Paul Hardtmuth and Barry Mackay.

Exposure to a radioactive isotope during an atomic research experiment hurls a man's mind seven seconds into the future. He is kidnapped by criminals who plan to use his powers to commit a robbery. Despite the unique premise, the plot never really rises above the level of a standard spy melodrama. Charles Eric Maine based the screenplay on his own novel *The Isotope Man* but the end result is more espionage thriller than science fiction. Gene Nelson, who gained fame as a dancer, plays the reporter who attempts to unravel the mystery, with perennial "scream queen" Faith Domergue at his side.

Video: U.S.

To Love a Vampire see *Lust for a Vampire*

277. To the Devil...A Daughter

A Hammer–Terra/Anglo–German Co-Production (1976); 92 minutes; Technicolor; U.S.: Cine Artists Pictures

P: Roy Skeggs; **D:** Peter Sykes; **S:** Christopher Wicking and John Peacock; **M:** Paul Glass; **DP:** David Watkin; **E:** John Trumper; **AD:** Don Picton; **Cast:** Christopher Lee, Richard Widmark, Nastassja Kinski, Honor Blackman, Denholm Elliott, Michael Goodliffe, Eva Marie Meineke, Anthony Valentine, Derek Francis, Isabella Telezynska, Anna Bentinck and Constantin De Goguel.

Hammer's last theatrical horror film was a major disappointment on many levels. Fans of the Dennis Wheatley novel on which the film was based were disheartened when they discovered that very little of it was retained for the screenplay. In the book,

IN *TO THE DEVIL...A DAUGHTER*, CHRISTOPHER LEE PLAYS THE EXCOMMUNICATED PRIEST FATHER MICHAEL.

the satanist Canon Copely-Syle creates a homunculus into which he hopes to transfer the soul of a virgin. The film deals with the typical horror movie theme of good versus evil. Good is represented by occult writer John Verney (Richard Widmark) and evil by the defrocked priest Father Michael Rayner (Christopher Lee); they battle for the soul of the virginal Catherine Beddows (Nastassja Kinski). Except for a hasty and unsatisfying climax, the movie isn't really all that bad. It simply isn't what fans had come to expect of Hammer. Reviews were mixed. *Variety* was unenthusiastic, rightly saying that "the finale registers well below socko climax standards." *Boxoffice*, however, called it a "spine-chilling occult thriller" and said, "Australian Peter Sykes has directed with a minimum of violence and an emphasis on brooding atmosphere." The box office failure of *To the Devil...A Daughter* seriously hampered Hammer's plans to produced any more horror films. Projects such as *Nessie* and *Vampirella*, which were already well into development, would never come to light as a result.

Video: U.K./U.S. (alternate U.S. video title: *Child of Satan*)

278. *Tom Thumb*

A George Pal Production/A Galaxy Picture; Metro-Goldwyn-Mayer (1958); 92 minutes; Eastman Color

P/D: George Pal; **S:** Ladislas Fodor; **M:** Douglas Gamley and Ken Jones; **DP:** Georges Perinal; **E:** Frank Clarke; **AD:** Elliot Scott; **SVE:** Tom Howard, Gene Warren, Wah Chang, Don Sahlin and Herb Johnson; **Cast:** Russ Tamblyn, Alan Young, Terry-Thomas, Peter Sellers, Jessie Matthews, June Thorburn, Bernard Miles, Ian Wallace, Peter Butterworth, Peter Bull and Barbara Ferris.

George Pal approached MGM executives with a proposal to make a Donald O'Connor-starring film based on the fairy tale *Tom Thumb*. The production department estimated that such a film, which would require extensive special effects, could not be filmed domestically for less than two million dollars. It was suggested that the project be shot at MGM's British studio where costs were lower and advantage could be taken of the Eady Plan, which was then in effect to encourage film production in England. MGM also insisted that Russ Tamblyn star in the title role. Pal himself directed as he thought a British director might give the film "too British an attitude." As it is, the best thing about *Tom Thumb* is the wonderful cast of British supporting players, including Terry-Thomas and Peter Sellers as a couple of bumbling villians. The special effects, which featured Pal's Puppetoons, were executed in Hollywood. The finished film cost less than one million dollars and went on to become one of MGM's top moneymakers in 1958. Viewed today, *Tom Thumb* is very juvenile and Russ Tamblyn's excessive exuberance is a bit cloying.

Video: U.S.

279. *The Tomb of Ligeia*

Alta Vista Film Productions (1964); 81 minutes; ColorScope; U.S.: American-International (1965)

P/D: Roger Corman; **S:** Robert Towne; **M:** Kenneth V. Jones; **DP:** Arthur Grant; **E:** Alfred Cox; **AD:** Colin Southcott; **Cast:** Vincent Price, Elizabeth Shepherd, John Westbrook, Oliver Johnston, Derek Francis, Richard Vernon, Ronald Adam, Frank Thornton and Denis Gilmore.

This was the final film in the series of Edgar Allan Poe adaptations that Roger Corman directed for American-International. It is also one of his very best efforts. In many ways, this is the antithesis of the seven films which preceded it. The others are very claustrophobic and sound stage bound, but *The Tomb of Ligeia* has extensive exterior location photography. Vincent Price also plays what amounts to a romantic lead, albeit a rather strange one. Verden Fell (Price) marries Lady Rowena Trevanion (Elizabeth Shepherd) and takes her to live at the decrepit abbey which is his home. Rowena discovers that Verden's deceased first wife Ligeia (also played by Shepherd) still has a powerful hold on her husband and may be reaching out from the grave to possess her. There really isn't much more to the story than this, but plot is not of the essence here. The film consists mainly of a series of surreal sequences which are greatly enhanced by Arthur Grant's sumptuous color photography. This was a fitting finale to the Corman-Price collaboration; they have seldom been better.

Video: U.S.

280. *Torture Garden*

An Amicus Production (1967); 92 minutes; Technicolor; U.S.: Columbia

P: Max J. Rosenberg and Milton Subotsky; **D:** Freddie Francis; **S:** Robert Bloch; **M:** James Bernard and Don Banks; **DP:** Norman Warwick; **E:** Peter Elliott; **DP:** Bill Constable; **AD:** Don Mingaye and Scott Slimon; **Cast:** Peter Cushing, Burgess Meredith, Jack Palance, Beverly Adams, Maurice Denham, Barbara Ewing, Michael Bryant, John Standing, Robert Hutton, Michael Ripper, John Phillips and Niall MacGinnis.

Dr. Diablo (Burgess Meredith) runs a carnival sideshow called "Torture Garden,"

VERDEN FELL (VINCENT PRICE) HOLDS THE BODY OF HIS WIFE ROWENA (ELIZABETH SHEPHERD) DURING THE FIERY FINALE OF *THE TOMB OF LIGEIA*.

a chamber of horrors where some of the patrons see more than they bargained for. In the first story, Michael Bryant lets his sick uncle (Maurice Denham) die so that he can inherit the old man's fortune. Instead, he inherits a cat named Balthazar, an evil creature with an insatiable appetite for human heads. The next story is about an ambitious starlet (Beverly Adams) who is determined to gain success at any price. The third features Barbara Ewing as a young woman in love with a concert pianist (John Standing). Unfortunately, his piano has a very jealous temperament. The final, and best, narrative has Peter Cushing and Jack Palance as rival collectors of Edgar Allan Poe memorabilia. Cushing, it turns out, has the ultimate prize ... Poe himself! Vincent Canby's *New York Times* review found *Torture Garden* to be "a simple-minded forthright horror movie, made without condescension." It is actually one of Amicus' middling efforts, distinguished by some very imaginative production design and art direction, particularly the third segment.

Video: U.K./U.S.

281. Tower of Evil

A Grenadier Films Ltd. Production (1971); 86 minutes; Eastman Color; U.S. *(Horror on Snape Island)*: Fanfare Corporation (1972); MetroColor

EXP: Joe Solomon; **P:** Richard Gordon; **D/S:** Jim O'Connolly; **M:** Kenneth V. Jones; **DP:**

PETER CUSHING AND JACK PALANCE IN "THE MAN WHO COLLECTED POE" SEQUENCE OF *TORTURE GARDEN*.

Desmond Dickinson; **E:** Henry Richardson; **AD:** Disley Jones; **Cast:** Bryant Haliday, Jill Haworth, Anna Palk, Jack Watson, Mark Edwards, Derek Fowlds, John Hamill, Gary Hamilton, Anthony Valentine, George Coulouris, Robin Askwith and Dennis Price.

Four young American tourists go to Snape Island to stay at a deserted lighthouse. Three of them are brutally murdered and the fourth is found in a state of catatonic shock. Later, a group of archaeologists go to Snape Island to search for the treasure from an ancient Phoenician shipwreck. One by one the mystery killer strikes again. In an interview, producer Richard Gordon said that this film "was intended as a straight horror picture with enough blood and guts to compete with a Hammer–type picture."

The film is far more gory than any Hammer film and also has an excess of nudity, sexual innuendo and bell-bottom trousers. There is also a fairly strong sex scene between Gary Hamilton and Anna Palk. The screenplay was based on an original story by genre regular George Baxt. In 1981, Independent International rereleased *Tower of Evil* under the title *Beyond the Fog* to capitalize on John Carpenter's film *The Fog*.

Video: U.K./U.S.

Tower of Terror see *Assault*

282. *Trog*

A Herman Cohen Production (1970); 91 minutes; Technicolor; U.S.: Warner Bros.

Trog (Joe Cornelius) on a rampage.

P: Herman Cohen; **D:** Freddie Francis; **S:** Aben Kandel; **M:** John Scott; **DP:** Desmond Dickinson; **E:** Oswald Hafenrichter; **AD:** Geoffrey Tozer; **Cast:** Joan Crawford, Michael Gough, Bernard Kay, Kim Braden, David Griffin, Thorley Walters, David Warbeck, Joe Cornelius, Robert Hutton, Rona Newton-John, Maurice Good and Chloe Franks.

This may well be the silliest film to come out of Britain's "Golden Age." Once again Herman Cohen exploits Joan Crawford in one of his ridiculous shockers. Crawford, in her last screen appearance, plays her part with utmost sincerity, which couldn't have been easy. Working with Cohen always seemed to bring out the worst in Michael Gough and this film is no exception. His performance is wildly unhinged.

Three enthusiastic young spelunkers discover a previously unexplored cave in a not-too-remote area of England. To their dismay, they also discover a living troglodyte (Joe Cornelius) who promptly kills one of them. Crawford plays an anthropologist who believes she can tame the beast. She succeeds in teaching Trog to play with dolls, enjoy classical music and even wear her pretty pink scarf. A further scientific experiment taps into Trog's memory to reveal stock footage from the prehistoric sequence of *The Animal World* (1956). Trog eventually goes on the inevitable murderous rampage before being dispatched by army bullets and a conveniently placed stalagmite. Aben Kandel's lamentable script was based

on an original story by Peter Bryan and John Gilling, who should have known better!
Video: U.S.

283. The Trollenberg Terror

Eros/Tempean Films (1958); 85 minutes; U.S. *(The Crawling Eye)*: DCA Pictures

P: Robert S. Baker and Monty Berman; **D:** Quentin Lawrence; **S:** Jimmy Sangster; **M:** Stanley Black; **DP:** Monty Berman; **E:** Henry Richardson; **AD:** Duncan Sutherland; **SVE:** Les Bowie; **Cast:** Forrest Tucker, Laurence Payne, Jennifer Jayne, Janet Munro, Warren Mitchell, Andrew Faulds, Stuart Sanders, Frederick Schiller, Colin Douglas, Derek Sydney, Richard Golding and Anne Sharpe.

Another in the wave of British sci-fi films which followed in the wake of *The Quatermass Xperiment*. Like its predecessor, this was also adapted from a British television serial. A radioactive cloud has settled on Trollenberg mountain in the Alps. Shortly thereafter, a number of mountain climbers vanish or, in some cases, are found with their heads torn off. Anne (Janet Munro), a young girl with highly developed ESP powers, is drawn to the Trollenberg by visions of impending doom. Scientists Forrest Tucker and Warren Mitchell have studied similar occurrences in the Andes mountains and come to the conclusion that alien creatures are paving the way for an invasion of Earth. When these aliens are finally revealed, they resemble gigantic tentacled eyeballs. An interesting and highly suspenseful storyline is somewhat impaired by some mediocre special effects but, as a whole, and considering the small budget, the film has a strong impact.
Video: U.S.

Twins of Dracula see *Twins of Evil*

284. Twins of Evil (a.k.a. Twins of Dracula)

A Hammer Film Production (1971); 87 minutes; Technicolor; U.S.: Universal (1972); 85 minutes

P: Harry Fine and Michael Style; **D:** John Hough; **S:** Tudor Gates; **M:** Harry Robinson; **DP:** Dick Bush; **E:** Spencer Reeve; **AD:** Roy Stannard; **Cast:** Peter Cushing, Madeleine and Mary Collinson, Dennis Price, Damien Thomas, Kathleen Byron, David Warbeck, Isobel Black, Alex Scott, Luan Peters, Katya Wyeth and Harvey Hall.

Original entitled *The Gemini Twins*, this is the final installment in Hammer's Karnstein Trilogy. It is also one of the best films from Hammer's later period. In one of the most unsympathetic roles of his career, Peter Cushing portrays Gustav Weil, the leader of a Puritanical religious sect called "The Brotherhood." His identical twin nieces, Frieda and Maria (Madeleine and Mary Collinson), are orphaned and come to live with him and his kindly wife in the village of Karnstein. The overlord of the village is Count Karnstein (Damien Thomas), a corrupt nobleman who worships the devil. During a black mass at his castle, the Count conjures up the spirit of his dead ancestor, Mircalla Karnstein (Katya Wyeth), who promptly turns him into a vampire. Shortly thereafter, Frieda, who is drawn to the evil ways of the Count, is turned into a vampire by him. She then goes on a killing spree which eventually implicates her innocent sister. Fast-paced and creatively directed, *Twins of Evil* is a prime example of Hammer horror at its best. Screenwriter Tudor Gates also penned an extensive story outline for a fourth entry in the Karnstein series. It was called *The Vampire Virgins* and, in a curious bit of casting, was to have featured Peter Cushing as Count Karnstein. Unfortunately, it was never produced.
Video: U.K./U.S.

285. Twisted Nerve

A Boulting Brothers Production (1968); 116 minutes; Technicolor; U.S.: National General Pictures (1969)

Damien Thomas seems delighted with his two lovely co-stars Mary and madeleine Collinson on the set of *Twins of Evil*.

P: George W. George and Frank Granat; **D:** Roy Boulting; **S:** Leo Marks and Roy Boulting; **M:** Bernard Herrmann; **DP:** Harry Waxman; **E:** Martin Charles; **Cast:** Hayley Mills, Hwyel Bennett, Billie Whitelaw, Phyllis Calvert, Barry Foster, Thorley Walters, Salmaan Peer, Christian Roberts, Timothy West, Gretchen Franklin, Clifford Cox and Frank Finlay.

This film caused some indignation and acquired a bad reputation at the time of its release because the script hinted that there might be a link between Mongolism and insanity. The producers eventually tacked a disclaimer to the front of the film in an attempt to exonerate themselves of this allegation. Martin Durnley (Hywel Bennett) is a seriously disturbed young man who wheedles his way into the rooming house of Susan Harper (Hayley Mills) and her mother Joan (Billie Whitelaw). Martin pretends to be "Georgie," a childlike character he has created to cope with times of emotional distress. He is attracted to Susan but she becomes suspicious of his helpless act when he makes sexual advances toward her at a picnic. Martin's impulses eventually overcome him and he kills Joan with an axe. When his crime is discovered and the police are called in, he takes Susan hostage. This was the second teaming for Hayley Mills and Hywel Bennett, who had previously appeared together in *The Family Way* (1966). Both films were directed by her future husband, Roy Boulting, who was attempting to dispel Hayley's pristine Disney image. Today, the

HAYLEY MILLS AND HYWEL BENNETT, SHOWN HERE IN *TWISTED NERVE*, WERE TEAMED IN THREE FILMS.

main reason *Twisted Nerve* is remembered is because of an excellent Bernard Herrmann score.

Video: U.K.

286. *The Two Faces of Dr. Jekyll*

A Hammer Film Production (1960); 88 minutes; Technicolor & MegaScope; U.S. (*House of Fright* [1961]; 80 minutes): American–International; PatheColor and MegaScope

P: Michael Carreras; **D:** Terence Fisher; **S:** Wolf Mankowitz; **M:** Monty Norman and David Heneker; **DP:** Jack Asher; **E:** James Needs and Eric Boyd-Perkins; **PD:** Bernard Robinson; **AD:** Don Mingaye; **Cast:** Paul Massie, Dawn Addams, Christopher Lee, David Kossoff, Francis De Wolff, Norma Marla, William Kendal, Helen Goss, Pauline Shepherd, Magda Miller, Oliver Reed and Janina Faye.

Hammer's underrated version of *Dr. Jekyll and Mr. Hyde* offers an interesting variation on the original story. Henry Jekyll is an unattractive and socially inept research scientist married to the beautiful, but faithless Kitty (Dawn Addams). Kitty is having an affair with her husband's best friend, Paul Allen (Christopher Lee), and together they frequent some of the more sordid nightspots of Victorian London. Jekyll injects himself with an experimental drug and becomes Edward Hyde. Hyde turns out to be a handsome and thoroughly immoral rogue who sets out to sample London's baser entertainments. During his quest, he meets Paul and Kitty in a debauched nightclub called the Sphinx. Hyde befriends Paul and offers to pay off his considerable gambling debts if Paul will show him the dissolute side of London's night life. Hyde eventually murders Paul and rapes Kitty, thereby driving her to suicide. Paul Massie is quite effective in the Jekyll-Hyde roles and most of the other performances are first-rate. The problem with the film lies in the fact that all the characters are unpleasant, leaving the audience no one to really care about. Columbia was originally to have released the film in the United States but they sold it to American–International, who changed the title to *Jekyll's Inferno*. Just prior to release, it was retitled *House of Fright* to capitalize on AIP's very successful *House of Usher*.

Video: U.S.

287. *2001: A Space Odyssey*

A Stanley Kubrick Production (1968); 141 minutes; MetroColor and Super Panavision; U.S.: Metro–Goldwyn–Mayer

P/D: Stanley Kubrick; **S:** Arthur C. Clarke and Stanley Kubrick; **DP:** Geoffrey Unsworth; **E:** Ray Lovejoy; **AD:** John Hoesli; **PD:** Tony Masters, Harry Lange and Ernie Archer; **SVE:** Wally Veevers, Douglas Trumbull, Con Pederson and Tom Howard; **Cast:** Keir Dullea, Gary Lockwood, William Sylvester, Daniel Richter, Leonard Rossiter, Robert Beatty, Sean Sullivan, Frank Miller, Penny Brahms, Alan Gifford and Margaret Tyzack.

During its original release, *2001: A Space Odyssey* took audiences by surprise. The powerful visuals and enigmatic storyline created word-of-mouth that filled cinemas with fascinated viewers who left speculating on and debating the meaning of Kubrick's intriguing opus. Controversy over the message being delivered in *2001* has persisted ever since. Is the film filled with deep meaning or is it merely Stanley Kubrick at his most pretentious?

Based on Arthur C. Clarke's *The Sentinel*, the screenplay manages to avoid most of the pitfalls and clichés present in multitudes of previous space operas. The plot, stated as simply as possible, traces the forward progression of mankind each time a black stone monolithic slab appears. The prologue shows the effect of this monolith on a group of prehistoric ape men. Next it is discovered near the American colony located on the surface of the Moon. This leads to the central portion of the film in which astronaut David Bowman (Keir Dullea) engages in a battle of wills with his ship's computer HAL 9000 (voiced by Douglas Rain). In the final symbolism-heavy sequence, Bowman travels through a space warp where he encounters the monolith and is reborn on a higher level. The unprecedented state-of-the-art special effects set a new standard for science fiction movies and have influenced virtually every space movie made since. Originally Alex North was hired to write the score for *2001: A Space Odyssey* and he composed and recorded over 40 minutes of music before Kubrick decided to use classical pieces for the background score instead.

Video: U.K./U.S.

288. *The Ugly Duckling*

A Hammer Film Production (1959); 84 minutes; U.S.: No theatrical release

P: Michael Carreras; **D:** Lance Comfort; **S:** Sid Colin and Jack Davies; **M:** Douglas Gamley; **DP:** Michael Reed; **E:** James Needs and John Dunsford; **AD:** Bernard Robinson; **Cast:** Bernard Bresslaw, Reginald Beckwith, Jon Pertwee, Maudie Edwards, Jean Muir, Richard Wattis, David Lodge, Michael Ripper, Norma Marla, Elwyn Brook-Jones, Harold Goodwin and Keith Smith.

Hammer's first version of Robert Louis Stevenson's *Dr. Jekyll and Mr. Hyde* was this comedy, the premise of which recalls the 1963 Jerry Lewis' film *The Nutty Professor*.

Bernard Bresslaw plays poor, put-upon Henry Jekyll, an untalented dancer who is a constant object of derision by local teenage gang members. While looking after his family's chemist shop, Henry happens upon a formula which turns him into Teddy Hide, a suave ladies' man. Unfortunately this new persona soon becomes involved with gangland connections. Hammer would produce two more unorthodox variations on the Stevenson story, *The Two Faces of Dr. Jekyll* (1960) and *Dr. Jekyll and Sister Hyde* (1971).

Video: None

289. Unearthly Stranger

A Julian Wintle–Leslie Parkyn Production (1963); 75 minutes; U.S.: American–International (1964); 68 minutes

EXP: Julian Wintle and Leslie Parkyn; **P:** Albert Fennell; **D:** John Krish; **S:** Rex Carlton; **M:** Edward Williams; **DP:** Reg Wyer; **E:** Tom Priestly; **AD:** Harry Pottle; **Cast:** John Neville, Gabriella Licudi, Philip Stone, Patrick Newell, Jean Marsh and Warren Mitchell.

Four scientists, working on similiar space projects, are killed mysteriously. Dr. Mark Davidson (John Neville) is chosen to carry on in their place. Recently married, he begins to notice some unusual things about his wife Julie (Gabriella Licudi). She sleeps with her eyes open, registers no pulse and removes dishes from a hot oven with her bare hands. When another of his colleagues dies, Mark begins to suspect that his wife may somehow be involved. Eventually she confesses to him that she is an alien who has been sent to Earth to sabotage the space project. This low-key and highly effective film has been seldom seen since the time of its original release and deserves to be revived.

Video: None

The Unseen see *House of Mystery*

290. Vampira

A World Film Services Production (1974); 88 minutes; Color by Movielab; U.S. (*Old Dracula* [1975]): American–International

P: Jack H. Wiener; **D:** Clive Donner; **S:** Jeremy Lloyd; **M:** David Whitaker; **DP:** Anthony Richmond; **E:** Bill Butler; **AD:** Philip Harrison; **Cast:** David Niven, Teresa Graves, Jennie Linden, Nicky Henson, Peter Bayliss, Bernard Bresslaw, Linda Hayden, Veronica Carlson, Freddie Jones, Frank Thornton, Luan Peters and Minah Bird.

This spoof of vampire films manages to run its interminable course without a single laugh. A horror writer (Nicky Henson) and several *Playboy* Playmates go to Transylvania for a photo shoot at Castle Dracula. Count Dracula (David Niven) takes this opportunity to use the Playmates' blood to revive his beloved Countess Vampira. Something goes wrong with the transfusion and Vampira turns into a beautiful black woman (Teresa Graves). Annoyed by this change of color, Dracula follows the Playmates back to London to try and discover what went wrong.

The lowbrow humor includes such hilarious *bons mots* as Graves calling Niven a "jive turkey." No wonder he looks so utterly trapped and unhappy. The cast has many familiar names, including two former heroines from Hammer's Dracula films, Veronica Carlson and Linda Hayden. Hayden is memorable in her very brief stint as a vampire but Carlson is totally wasted as one of the Playmates.

AIP retitled the film to capitalize on Mel Brooks' *Young Frankenstein* using the catchline, "If you liked *Young Frankenstein*, you'll love *Old Dracula*." Not bloody likely!

Video: U.K.

The Vampire-Beast Craves Blood see *The Blood Beast Terror*

LINDA HAYDEN AND DAVID NIVEN BARE THEIR FANGS IN *VAMPIRA*.

291. Vampire Circus

A Hammer Film Production (1972); 87 minutes; Eastman Color; U.S.: 20th Century–Fox; 82 minutes; DeLuxe Color

P: Wilbur Stark; **D:** Robert Young; **S:** Judson Kinberg; **M:** David Whitaker; **DP:** Moray Grant; **E:** Peter Musgrave; **AD:** Scott MacGregor; **Cast:** Adrienne Corri, Laurence Payne, Thorley Walters, John Moulder-Brown, Lynne Frederick, Anthony Corlan, Elizabeth Seal, Richard Owens, Domini Blythe, Robert Tayman, David Prowse and Skip Martin.

Count Mitterhouse (Robert Tayman) is the nobleman who rules over the village of Schtettel. He is also a vampire who, with the help of his human mistress, lures innocent children to their deaths at his castle. The villagers finally have enough and kill the count and burn his castle, but not before he puts a curse on the village. Fifteen years later, the mysterious "Circus of Nights" arrives in plague-torn Schtettel to exact the slain vampire's revenge. Judson Kinberg's script, based on an original story by Wilbur Stark and George Baxt, is densely populated with characters and offers some original twists on the usual vampire themes. Anthony Corlan, who played the hero in *Taste the Blood of Dracula*, herein is the sexy gypsy Emil, a circus performer who is actually the cousin of Count Mitterhouse. Hissing with fangs bared, he is certainly a vampire to reckon with! *Vampire Circus* suffered greatly at the hands of the American distributor, who eliminated all of the blood and nudity in order to get a PG rating. (The ending, when the body count really escalates, is almost unintelligible due to the excessive cutting.) Despite this, the film received some enthusiastic reviews. Fredric Milstein said

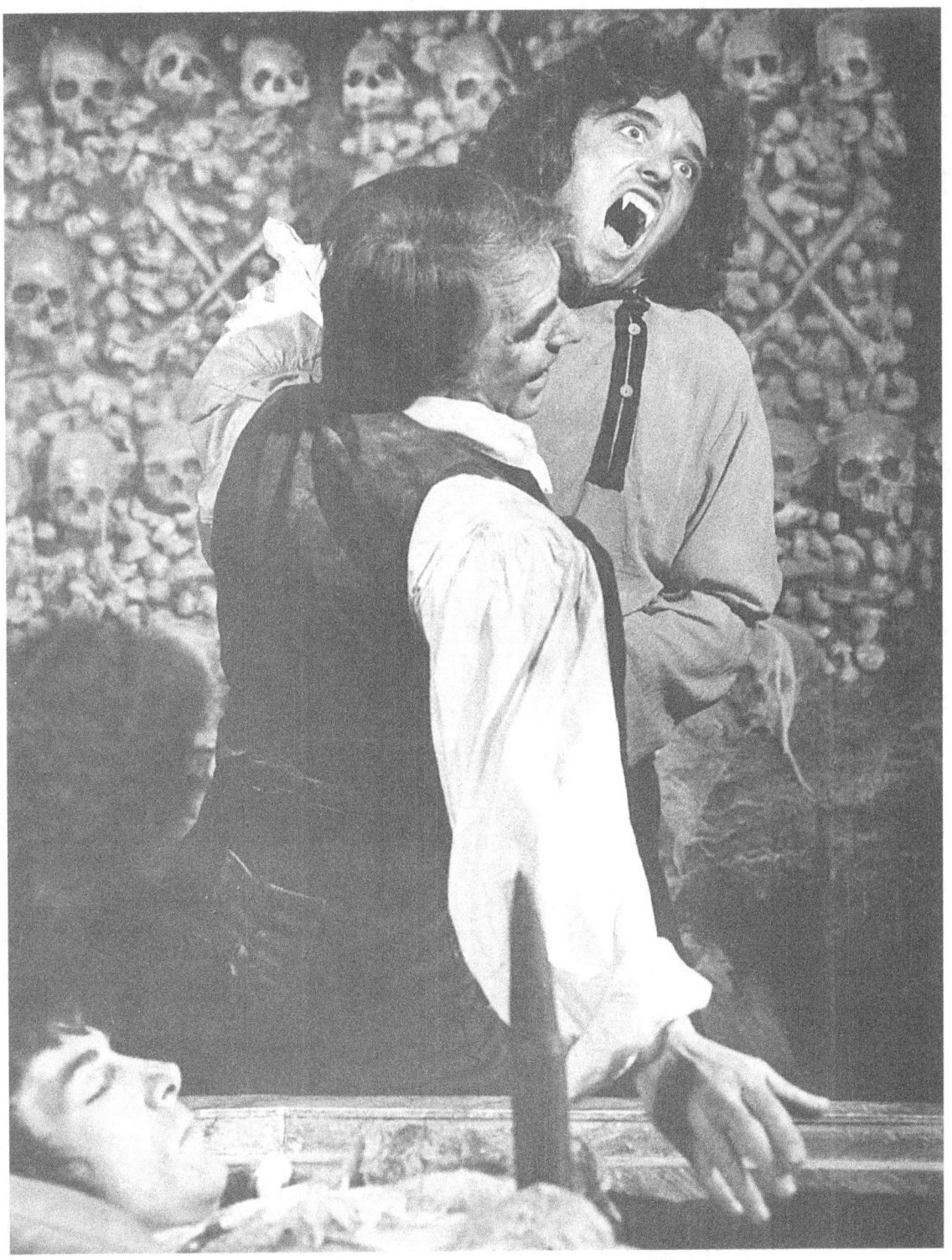

Laurence Payne fights with Anthony Corlan while Robert Tayman lies in his coffin in *Vampire Circus*.

Producer Harry Fine on the set of *The Vampire Lovers*.

in the *Los Angeles Times,* "Robert Young's true chiller, *Vampire Circus,* offers lots of real-looking teeth, believable gore, and — save for a very lurid ending — a lot of pace, a certain sense of subtlety and a definite, consistent style."

Video: U.K.

292. The Vampire Lovers

A Hammer/American–International Production (1970); 91 min; Technicolor; U.S.: American–International; 89 min; Color by Movielab

EXP: Louis M. Heyward; **P:** Harry Fine and Michael Style; **D:** Roy Ward Baker; **S:** Tudor Gates; **M:** Harry Robinson; **DP:** Moray Grant; **E:** James Needs; **AD:** Scott MacGregor; **Cast:** Ingrid Pitt, Pippa Steele, Madeleine Smith, Peter Cushing, Dawn Addams, George Cole, Kate O'Mara, Jon Finch, Douglas Wilmer, Harvey Hall, Janet Key, Ferdy Mayne, Kirsten Betts and John Forbes-Robertson.

Those two purveyors of cinematic horror, AIP and Hammer, joined forces for this, their only coproduction. *The Vampire Lovers* is the first entry in Hammer's lesbian vampire trilogy, based on characters from J. Sheridan Le Fanu's *Carmilla.* This was also the first Hammer film to take full advantage of the new permissive trend in movies by including lots of female nudity and more overt sexuality. Carmilla (Ingrid Pitt) is a voracious female vampire who preys on the young women of Styria, first taking them as her lovers and then draining them of their blood. Roy Ward Baker directs the film with tremendous style and some macabre touches

This definitive example of Hammer Glamour from *The Vampire Lovers* shows Ingrid Pitt surrounded by Kate O'Mara, Pippa Steele, Madeline Smith and Kirsten Betts.

of humor, and Ingrid Pitt is certainly one of the screen's most alluring vampires. Once again, Hammer's stalwart vampire hunter Peter Cushing is on hand to bring an end to the evil. John Forbes-Robertson, who would later portray Dracula for Hammer, is the sinister "Man in Black." The other films in the trilogy are *Lust for a Vampire* and *Twins of Evil*.

Video: U.K./U.S.

293. Vampyres

Essay Films Ltd. (1974); 87 minutes; Color; U.S.: *Vampyres, Daughters of Dracula* (1975); 84 minutes; Cambist Films

P: Brian Smedley-Aston; **D:** Joseph (Jose) Larraz; **S:** Diana Daubeney; **M:** James Clarke; **DP:** Harry Waxman; **E:** Geoff R. Brown; **AD:** Ken Bridgeman; **Cast:** Marianne Morris, Anulka, Murray Brown, Brian Deacon, Sally Faulkner, Michael Byrne, Margaret Heald, Douglas Jones, Gerald Case, Karl Lanchbury, Bessie Love and Elliott Sullivan.

Spanish director Jose Larraz manages to rise above his usual sexploitation fare with this atmospheric vampire tale. This is not to say that there are not the usual excessive amounts of nudity that are a trademark of his films. There is nudity galore, but herein it is part of the overall dreamlike mood which makes the movie seem like an

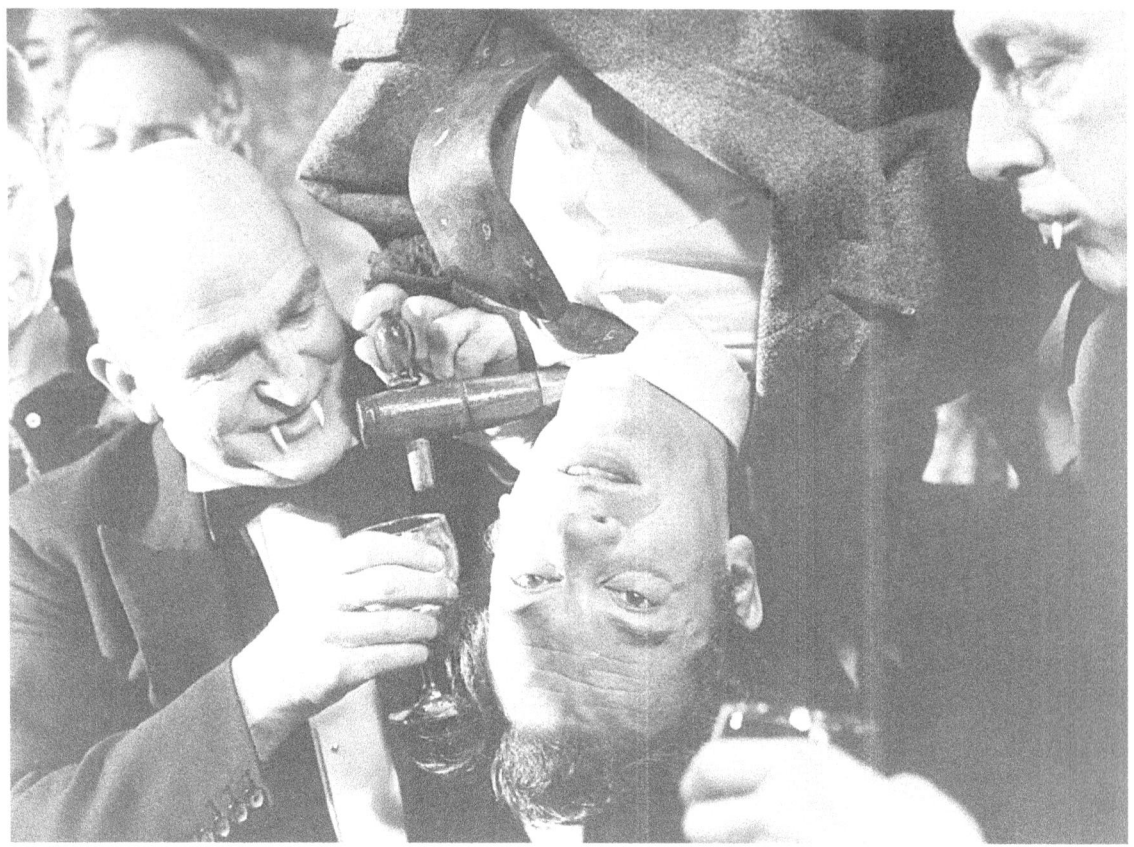

DANIEL MASSEY BECOMES THE MAIN COURSE IN A RESTAURANT FULL OF VAMPIRES IN *VAULT OF HORROR*.

erotic nightmare. The story is a slight one. In a brief prologue, two young women are in bed together making love. A man, seen only in silhouette, comes into the room and kills them with a gun. For the remainder of the film these same two women, Fran (Marianne Morris) and Miriam (Anulka), pose as hitchhikers to lure men to their home (once again Oakley Court) where they drain them of blood. One of their victims (Murray Brown) is kept by Fran for a sex slave and an occasional repast. Many of the scenes were obviously inspired by earlier films such as *The Vampire Lovers*, *Count Yorga, Vampire* and *Daughters of Darkness*, but *Vampyres* has its own distinctively disturbing quality which sets it apart from the rest.

Video: U.S.

Vampyres, Daughters of Dracula see *Vampyres*

294. Vault of Horror

A Metromedia Producers Corporation Presentation; An Amicus Production (1973); 86 minutes; Eastman Color

EXP: Charles Fries; **P:** Max J. Rosenberg and Milton Subotsky; **D:** Roy Ward Baker; **S:** Milton Subotsky; **M:** Douglas Gamley; **DP:** Denys Coop; **E:** Oswald Hafenrichter; **AD:** Tony Curtis; **Cast:** Dawn Addams, Tom Baker, Michael Craig, Denholm Elliott, Glynis Johns, Edward Judd, Curt Jurgens, Anna Massey, Daniel Massey, Terry-Thomas, John Forbes-Robertson and Eric Chitty.

In this follow-up to their *Tales from the Crypt*, Amicus once again turned to Bill

Gaines' horror comics for inspiration. The results, however, are only mildly inspiring. Five men take an unexpected elevator ride to the sub-basement of an office building and find themselves trapped in a room they mistake for a club. To amuse themselves while they await rescue, they begin to relate unusual dreams they have had. In "Midnight Mess," Daniel Massey kills his sister (Anna Massey) for the fortune she inherited from their father. He ends up as the main course in a restaurant which caters to vampires. "The Neat Job" has a tormented wife (Glynis Johns) driven to murder by the unrelenting fastidiousness of her husband (Terry-Thomas). In "This Trick'll Kill You," a magician (Curt Jurgens) and his wife (Dawn Addams) commit murder in order to steal an Indian rope trick for their magic act. The fourth story features Michael Craig and Edward Judd as two men who make a "Bargain in Death" with fatal results for both. In the last episode, "Drawn and Quartered," Tom Baker plays a painter who is out to get revenge on the trio of men who cheated him. The first story is the most memorable and Glynis Johns does a wonderful comic turn in the second. The rest of the film has little to offer in the way of thrills. American prints employed freeze frames to tone down some of the more gruesome scenes and thereby obtain a more lenient rating.

Video: U.K./U.S.

Velvet House see *The Corpse*

295. Vengeance

A CCC–Stross/Garrick–British Lion Film (1962); 83 minutes; U.S. (*The Brain* [1964]): Governor Films

P: Raymond Stross; **D:** Freddie Francis; **S:** Phil Mackie and Robert Stewart; **M:** Kenneth V. Jones; **DP:** Bob Hulke; **E:** Oswald Hafenrichter; **AD:** Arthur Lawson; **Cast:** Anne Heywood, Peter Van Eyck, Cecil Parker, Bernard Lee, Jack MacGowran, Ellen Schwiers, Miles Malleson, Frank Forsyth, Allan Cuthbertson, Maxine Audley, Ann Sears and Jeremy Spenser.

Ruthless business tycoon Max Holt is killed in an airplane crash which may not have been an accident. Dr. Peter Corrie (Peter Van Eyck) and his colleagues "rescue" Holt's brain and keep it alive in their laboratory. Holt's brain exerts a powerful influence over Dr. Corrie, who begins to act like Holt as he searches for the dead man's assassin. This British–West German coproduction was the third film version of Curt Siodmak's novel *Donovan's Brain*. It was also one of Freddie Francis' earliest directorial efforts. This time around, the horror–sci-fi elements take a back seat and the story comes across as a slow-moving whodunit. The performances are of a generally high caliber with Maxine Audley a standout as Holt's double-crossing former mistress.

Video: U.K./U.S.

296. The Vengeance of Fu Manchu

Babasdave Films (1967); 91 minutes; Color; U.S.: Warner Bros–Seven Arts (1968)

P: Harry Alan Towers; **D:** Jeremy Summers; **S:** Peter Welbeck; **M:** Malcolm Lockyer; **DP:** John Von Kotze; **E:** Allan Morrison; **AD:** Scott MacGregor; **Cast:** Christopher Lee, Douglas Wilmer, Tsai Chin, Horst Frank, Noel Trevarthen, Maria Rohm, Tony Ferrer and Howard Marion Crawford.

In the third entry to this increasingly declining series, Fu Manchu (Christopher Lee) attempts once again to take control of the world. This time he replaces the police chiefs of various countries with duplicates under his evil command. He also creates a duplicate of his enemy Nayland Smith (Douglas Wilmer) and uses him to implicate the real Smith in a murder. Featuring extensive Hong Kong location filming, this was the last of the British productions. Lee

CHRISTOPHER LEE AS FU MANCHU. LEE PORTRAYED SAX ROHMER'S INFAMOUS VILLAIN IN FIVE FILMS FOR PRODUCER HARRY ALAN TOWERS.

had by now become as disenchanted playing this Oriental villain as he had with Dracula. In 1968, Towers rushed two more Fu Manchu movies through production. These Spanish–German coproductions were both directed by Jess Franco and featured Richard Greene as Nayland Smith. The first was shot in Turkey and was titled *The Castle of Fu Manchu* (a.k.a. *Assignment Istabul*). The last, and arguably the worst, was *The Blood of Fu Manchu* (a.k.a. *Kiss and Kill*), shot in Spain and Brazil.

Video: U.K./U.S.

297. *The Vengeance of She*

A Hammer–Seven Arts Production (1968); 101 minutes; Technicolor; U.S.: 20th Century–Fox; 90 min; DeLuxe Color

P: Aida Young; **D:** Cliff Owen; **S:** Peter O'Donnell; **M:** Mario Nascimbene; **DP:** Wolfgang Suschitzky; **E:** James Needs and Raymond Poulton; **PD:** Lionel Couch; **Cast:** Olinka Berova, John Richardson, Edward Judd, Colin Blakely, Jill Melford, George Sewell, Andre Morell, Noel Willman, Derek Godfrey, Daniele Noel, Gerald Lawson and Zohra Segal.

Considering the success of *She*, a sequel was inevitable. In 1967, Hammer announced plans to film *Ayesha, The Daughter of She* starring Susan Denberg. (Ursula Andress had already moved on to bigger films and higher salaries.) Nothing more was heard of a *She* sequel until Aida Young, who

PERFECT PROFILES: JOHN RICHARDSON AND OLINKA BEROVA IN *THE VENGEANCE OF SHE*.

had been associate producer on the original film, announced that she had discovered a Czechoslovakian actress who was perfect for the part of *She*. Time magazine was quick to report that Olinka Berova "will be the first actress from Eastern Europe to toil in a capitalist movie." Berova had already made several films in her own country and appeared in *Playboy* under her real name Olga Schoberova. *The Vengeance of She* begins in Monte Carlo where a young girl named Carol (Berova) is being tormented by visions of Ayesha. With the help of a sympathetic psychiatrist (Edward Judd), she finds the lost city of Kuma where Kallikrates (once again played by John Richardson) awaits her as the reincarnation of his beloved queen. With the exception of Richardson, there are few direct connections to the previous movie. Extensive location work in Spain and the South of France is a major attribute to the overall effectiveness of the film, but it opened to considerably less favorable reviews than its predecessor. *The New York Times* said it was "a scriptwriter's mindless sequel" and *Variety* called it "lack luster hokum." The box office returns were also far less than expected, so no further *She* sequels were forthcoming from Hammer. Watch for singer-actress Dana Gillespie in a very minor role during the party aboard the yacht.

Video: U.K./U.S.

298. Venom (a.k.a. *The Legend of Spider Forest*)

A Cupid Production Ltd. (1971); 84 minutes; Association with Action Plus Productions; Techcnicolor

P: Michael Pearson and Kenneth F. Rowles; D: Peter Sykes; S: Donald and Derek Ford; M:

John Simco Harrison; **DP:** Peter Jessop; **E:** Stephen Collins; **AD:** Hayden Pearce; **Cast:** Simon Brent, Neda Arneric, Derek Newark, Sheila Allen, Gerald Heinz, Gertan Klauber, Bette Vivian, Terence Soall, Sean Gerrard, Ray Barron and George Fisher.

On holiday in a remote Bavarian town, painter Paul Greville (Simon Brent) meets a mysterious girl named Anna (Neda Arneric). The villagers believe Anna is the forest Spider Goddess and may be responsible for the deaths of several men. Paul does not heed their warnings and becomes enmeshed in a web of murder and intrigue. This independent British production (shot in Germany) was Peter Sykes' first horror movie. Like many other directors in Britain at this time, Sykes had cut his cinematic teeth directing episodes of *The Avengers*. The stylish and atmospheric direction of this film led to his being hired by Hammer to helm *Demons of the Mind*. Indeed, it is Sykes' direction that makes *Venom* worth watching as the plot quickly degenerates into a confused hodgepodge of scientific experiments involving spider venom and valuable art pieces being sold on the black market. Christopher Wicking had a hand in the *Venom* script and he would later team with Sykes on both of the director's Hammer features.

Video: U.S. (video title: *Spider's Venom*)

299. Village of the Damned

Metro–Goldwyn–Mayer (1960); 78 minutes

P: Ronald Kinnoch; **D:** Wolf Rilla; **S:** Stirling Silliphant, Wolf Rilla and George Barclay; **M:** Ron Goodwin; **DP:** Geoffrey Faithfull; **E:** Gordon Hales; **AD:** Ivan King; **Cast:** George Sanders, Barbara Shelley, Martin Stephens, Michael Gwynn, Laurence Naismith, Richard Vernon, John Phillips, Jenny Laird, Richard Warner, Thomas Heathcote, Peter Vaughan and Keith Pyott.

The entire population of the small English village of Midwich is rendered unconscious by some mysterious force. Afterwards, all the women of child-bearing age discover that they are pregnant. Following an accelerated pregnancy, they all give birth to blonde-haired babies with unusual eyes. The children mature rapidly, possessed of exceptional intelligence as well as the ability to control people by the power of their will. The leader of the children is David (Martin Stephens), whose mother's husband (George Sanders) suspects they may have been sired by beings from outer space. This outstanding adaptation of John Wyndham's novel *The Midwich Cuckoos* is a thoroughly compelling motion picture. Filmed in a straightforward manner with an excellent cast, the story is never anything less than riveting. John Carpenter's 1995 remake was unable to duplicate the impact of the original despite a big budget, sophisticated special effects and slick production values.

Video: U.K./U.S.

300. Virgin Witch

Univista Productions Ltd. (1970); 87 minutes; Eastman Color; U.S.: Joseph Brenner (1971)

P: Ralph Solomons; **D:** Ray Austin; **S:** Klaus Vogel; **M:** Ted Dicks; **DP:** Gerald Moss; **E:** Philip Barnikel; **AD:** Paul Bernard; **Cast:** Ann Michelle, Vicki Michelle, Patricia Haines, Keith Buckley, James Chase, Neil Hallett, Helen Downing, Paula Wright, Christopher Strain, Esme Smythe, Garth Watkins and Peter Halliday.

This truly lousy sexploitation film is more for the "raincoat crowd" than horror fans. It pulls no punches as even the opening credits are over a succession of bare breasts. Christine and Betty (Ann and Vicki Michelle) go to London to seek their fortune. Christine goes to a modelling agency run by Sybil Waite (Patrica Haines) and is promptly sent to Wychwold on a photographic shoot. Betty accompanies her sister. At Wychwold, Christine discovers that Sybil is not only the high priestess of a coven of witches but also a lesbian who has designs on her new protege. Many bare boobs later, Christine uses her new found powers to kill Sybil and takes over as the leader of the coven.

Video: U.K./U.S.

301. Voices

A Robert Enders–Warden Production Ltd. (1973); 91 minutes; Technicolor; U.S.: No theatrical release

P: Robert Enders; **D:** Kevin Billington; **S:** George Kirgo and Robert Enders; **M:** Richard Rodney Bennett; **DP:** Geoffrey Unsworth; **E:** Peter Thornton; **AD:** Len Townsend; **Cast:** David Hemmings, Gayle Hunnicutt, Lynn Farleigh, Russell Lewis, Peggy Ann Clifford, Eva Griffith, and Adam Bridge.

Claire (Gayle Hunnicutt) and Robert (David Hemmings) lose their young son in a drowning accident. After two suicide attempts, Claire is committed to a mental institution. When she recovers, the couple go to an isolated country home which was left to Claire by a deceased relative. Once they arrive at the house, most of the remainder of the movie is confined to one room where Claire and Robert continually bicker and verbally abuse each other. Claire hears voices and sees what she believes are ghosts, but Robert is too insensitive and horny to take her seriously. Adapted from a play by Richard Lortz, the film seems to exist mainly as a vanity piece to showcase the talents of Hemmings and Hunnicutt. Unfortunately, they are no Lunt and Fontanne and the endless stretches of dialogue are not involving enough to carry this seemingly interminable film. There is also a pointless "twist" ending in which the couple discover that they died in an automobile accident on the way to the house.

Video: U.S. (video title: *Nightmare*)

302. The Vulture

A Homeric–Iliad–Film Financial Co. Production (1966); 91 minutes; Color; U.S.: Paramount (1967); Black-and-White **EXP:** Jack O. Lamont; **P/D/S:** Lawrence Huntington; **M:** Eric Spear; **DP:** Stephen Dade; **E:** John S. Smith; **AD:** Duncan Sutherland; **Cast:** Robert Hutton, Akim Tamiroff, Broderick Crawford, Diane Clare, Philip Friend, Patrick Holt, Annette Carell, Edward Caddick, Gordon Sterne, Keith McConnell and Margaret Robertson.

In a village in Cornwall, a woman is found in a complete state of shock; her hair has turned white with fright. She claims to have seen "a big black bird, like a vulture" with a human face and human hands. Everyone thinks she's gone off her nut until the local squire, Brian Stroud (Broderick Crawford), is carried off in the night and found dead the next morning, his body horribly mutilated. Local legend has it that in the 1700s, a Spaniard who had settled in the village was accused of witchcraft and buried alive. Before he died, he placed a curse on the descendants of his accusers, the Stroud family. Know-it-all scientist Eric Lutyens (Robert Hutton) is convinced that any supernatural explanation is preposterous and that it is most certainly a case of "nuclear transmutation." How he arrived at this conclusion is explained at great length and makes no sense whatsoever. The terrifying vulture, when glimpsed (very briefly) at the end of the film, turns out to be a large bird with the head of Akim Tamiroff.

Video: U.S.

War-Gods of the Deep see *City Under the Sea*

303. Warlords of Atlantis

A John Dark–Kevin Connor–Individual Pictures Ltd. Production (1978); 96 minutes; Technicolor; U.S.: Columbia

P: John Dark; **D:** Kevin Connor; **S:** Brian Hayles; **M:** Mike Vickers; **DP:** Alan Hume; **E:** Bill Blunden; **PD:** Elliot Scott; **AD:** Jack Maxsted; **Cast:** Doug McClure, Peter Gilmore, Cyd Charisse, Daniel Massey, Shane Rimmer, Lea

Brodie, Michael Gothard, Robert Brown, Hal Galili, John Ratzenberger, Derry Power and Donald Bisset.

This was the first John Dark–Kevin Connor offering away from the auspices of Amicus, but it greatly resembles their previous productions for that company. Originally entitled *Seven Cities to Atlantis*, this Victorian adventure combines elements from Burroughs, Wells and Verne. Once again, all–American hero type Doug McClure is on hand, this time as part of an underwater expedition that discovers the lost city of Atlantis. The hierarchy of Atlantis are the descendants of Martians who landed on Earth millions of years before and were trapped beneath the sea. They are readying their forces to dominate the world by using their superior intellect. The slaves of the Atlanteans are people who have been shipwrecked by an enormous octopus which prowls the seas above the sunken city.

This film is no better or worse than the other Dark–Connor collaborations and, as usual, the emphasis is on action. Chief among its liabilities are the lamentable costuming and wigs of the Atlanteans. How an actor could deliver a line with any conviction while dressed like that is beyond me! The monsters, designed by Roger Dicken, are also ill-concieved save for the giant octopus which is actually very impressive.

Video: U.K.

304. Welcome to Blood City

A Canada–United Kingdom Co.–Production Film; A Stanley Chase Presentation; An EMI–Len Herberman Production (1977); 96 minutes; Technicolor and Panavision; U.S.: No theatrical release

P: Marilyn Stonehouse; **D:** Peter Sasdy; **S:** Stephen Schneck and Michael Winder; **M:** Roy Budd; **DP:** Reginald H. Morris; **E:** Keith Palmer; **PD:** Jack McAdam; **AD:** Tony Hall; **Cast:** Jack Palance, Keir Dullea, Samantha Eggar, Barry Morse, Hollis McLaren, Chris Wiggins, Harry Ramer, Ken James, Allan Royale, John Evans, Larry Reynolds and Jack Greley.

A man caught in a traffic jam suddenly awakens to find himself in a desert with four strangers. None of them can remember how they got there. A cowboy in black on a white horse finds them and leads them to Blood City, a nightmare of a wild west town where extreme violence and death are commonplace. Blood City is actually a "psuedo reality" that has been created at a governmental computer center where scientists can program the events which will befall their plugged-in human subjects. This often fascinating British–Canadian coproduction anticipates the idea of virtual reality. Vaguely suggestive of *Westworld*, but with far less linear plot developement, *Welcome to Blood City* is another example of just how good a director Peter Sasdy can be when he puts his mind to it. Jack Palance plays Frendlander, the Marshall of Blood City and, of course, plays it at full tilt. Keir Dullea gives him stiff competition as Lewis, the understandably confused, but ever resourceful, hero. Amicus executive Max J. Rosenberg was an uncredited producer on this film.

Video: U.K./U.S. (U.S. video title: *Blood City*)

305. What a Carve-Up!

New World Films Ltd (1961); 88 minutes; U.S. *(No Place Like Homicide)*: Embassy Pictures (1962)

P: Robert S. Baker and Monty Berman; **D:** Pat Jackson; **S:** Ray Cooney and Tony Hilton; **M:** Muir Mathieson; **DP:** Monty Berman; **E:** Gordon Pilkington; **AD:** Ivan King; **Cast:** Sidney James, Kenneth Connor, Shirley Eaton, Dennis Price, Donald Pleasence, Michael Gough, Esma Cannon, Michael Gwynn, Valerie Taylor, Philip O'Flynn, George Woodbridge and Frederick Piper.

A creaky old house, a family of crazies and an inheritance from a dead relative.

Sound familiar? These are the plot elements in just about every horror parody to come out of England. This one is supposed to be a remake of the 1933 Boris Karloff thriller *The Ghoul*, but precious little of that film is in evidence here. Sidney James and Kenneth Connor both appeared in several of the "Carry On" movies and that particular style of comedy permeates *What a Carve-Up!*. The sequence with James and Connor in bed together (quite innocently) is very funny and makes one realize how much times have changed. A supporting cast of familiar faces, including a pre–*Goldfinger* Shirley Eaton, also make this worth a look. British pop singer Adam Faith makes a cameo appearance as Eaton's boyfriend.

Video: None

306. What Became of Jack and Jill?

An Amicus Production (1971); 93 minutes; A Palomar Pictures International Presentation; DeLuxe Color; U.S.: 20th Century–Fox (1972)

EXP: Edgar J. Scherick; **P:** Max J. Rosenberg and Milton Subotsky; **D:** Bill Bain; **S:** Roger Marshall; **M:** Carl Davis; **DP:** Gerry Turpin; **E:** Peter Tanner; **AD:** Tony Curtis; **Cast:** Vanessa Howard, Paul Nicholas, Mona Washbourne, Peter Copley, Peter Jeffrey, Patricia Fuller, George A. Cooper, Renee Roberts, Lillias Walker, Angela Down and George Benson.

In this seldom-seen production from Amicus, Jack (Paul Nicholas) and Jill (Vanessa Howard) attempt to scare his grandmother (Mona Washbourne) to death in order to inherit her estate. They tell her that the elderly are being put to death because the young don't want to look after them any more. Granny does die of fright when she mistakenly thinks a protest march is a gang of youths come to execute her. Although the film can boast Amicus' usual fine production values, it is a rather tasteless and forgettable endeavor.

Video: None

What the Peeper Saw see ***Night Hair Child***

307. When Dinosaurs Ruled the Earth

A Hammer Film Production (1970); 100 minutes; Technicolor; U.S.: Warner Bros. (1971); 96 minutes

P: Aida Young; **D/S:** Val Guest; **M:** Mario Nascimbene; **DP:** Dick Bush; **E:** Peter Curran; **AD:** John Blezard; **SVE:** Jim Danforth; **Cast:** Victoria Vetri, Robin Hawdon, Patrick Allen, Drewe Henley, Sean Caffrey, Magda Konopka, Imogen Hassall, Patrick Holt, Jan Rossini, Carol-Anne Hawkins, Maria O'Brien and Connie Tilton.

This was the follow-up film to Hammer's box office blockbuster *One Million Years B.C.* A cosmic cataclysm interrupts the virgin sacrifice of three blonde cavegirls by their dark haired tribe. One of them, Sanna (Victoria Vetri), escapes by jumping into the ocean. She is rescued by a handsome fisherman named Tara (Robin Hawdon) and is taken to his people. Sanna's tribe pursues her and she must flee. During her flight, she encounters carnivorous plants, prehistoric beasts and a tidal wave. As a brunette, and using the name Angela Dorian, Victoria Vetri had already been a *Playboy* Playmate of the Year and appeared briefly in a few films (including *Rosemary's Baby*). Hammer, hoping to duplicate the audience response received by Ursula Andress and Raquel Welch, gave Vetri the full star buildup. Despite her beauty and superstructure, she failed to click with the public and plans to star her in the sequel *The Dinosaur Gril*, were cancelled. When Ray Harryhausen was not available to do the special effects, Hammer hired Jim Danforth. He was unable to finish his work in the time allocated and several proposed effects sequences had to be scrapped. To save time and money, Hammer included stock shots of optically enlarged lizards lifted

WHEN DINOSAURS RULED THE EARTH ROBIN HAWDON SPENT MUCH OF HIS TIME PROTECTING VICTORIA VETRI FROM THE PERILS OF NATURE.

from the 1960 version of *The Lost World*. Danforth's stop-motion special effects are nothing short of spectacular and they garnered him an Academy Award nomination.

Video: U.K./U.S.

308. Where has Poor Mickey Gone?

A Ledeck–Indigo Production (1964); 59 minutes; U.S.: No theatrical release

P/D: Gerry Levy; **S:** Peter Marcus; **M:** Graham Whettam; **DP:** Alan Pudney; **E:** Howard Lanning; **Cast:** Warren Mitchell, John Malcom, Raymond Armstrong, John Challis, Christopher Robbie, Karol Hagar, Philip Newman and Joseph Cook.

An unexpectedly fine effort from Gerry Levy, the man responsible for helping to ruin Michael Armstrong's *The Dark* (see *The Haunted House of Horror*) and the even worse *The Body Stealers*. This feature was shot in 11 days with a cast of mainly unknowns, the exception being Warren Mitchell. A gang of teenage thugs terrorize Emilio Dinelli (Mitchell), an Italian immigrant who is a stage magician. They force him to put on a magic show for them, and during the course of which he causes three of them to disappear. An inconclusive ending fails to reveal the true nature of Emilio's "magic" powers. This is a modest production which manages to generate a considerable impact.

Video: None

Who Slew Auntie Roo? see *Whoever Slew Auntie Roo?*

309. *Whoever Slew Auntie Roo?*

An American–International–Hemdale Production (1971); 90 minutes; Color by Movielab; U.S. *(Who Slew Auntie Roo?)*: American–International

EXP: Louis M. Heyward; **P:** Samuel Z. Arkoff and James H. Nicholson; **D:** Curtis Harrington; **S:** Robert Blees and Jimmy Sangster; **M:** Kenneth V. Jones; **DP:** Desmond Dickinson; **E:** Tristam Cones; **AD:** George Provis; **Cast:** Shelley Winters, Mark Lester, Ralph Richardson, Michael Gothard, Lionel Jeffries, Hugh Griffith, Judy Cornwell, Chloe Franks, Rosalie Crutchley, Pat Heywood, Jacqueline Cowper and Richard Beaumont.

DIRECTOR CURTIS HARRINGTON AND SHELLEY WINTERS ON THE SET OF *WHOEVER SLEW AUNTIE ROO?*

Each year the wealthy widow Mrs. Forrest (Shelley Winters) invites children from the local orphanage to attend a Christmas Eve party at her home. Outwardly, she seems the very picture of kindness, but she has actually become mentally unbalanced since the death of her daughter several years before. Christopher (Mark Lester) and Katy (Chloe Franks) are a brother and sister who come to the party. Katy resembles Mrs. Forrest's daughter Katherine and the looney lady decides to "adopt" her. Christopher, who does not want to be separated from his sister, has other ideas. This "Hansel and Gretel" takeoff is an entertaining but ultimately sick affair, with Winters giving yet another of the shrill and overwrought performances that have plagued her later career.

Video: U.S.

310. *The Wicker Man*

A Peter Snell–British Lion Production Ltd. (1973); 102 minutes; Color; U.S.: Warner Bros. (1974); 87 minutes

P: Peter Snell; **D:** Robin Hardy; **S:** Anthony

Shaffer; **M:** Paul Giovanni; **DP:** Harry Waxman; **E:** Eric Boyd-Perkins; **AD:** Seamus Flannery; **Cast:** Edward Woodward, Britt Ekland, Diane Cilento, Christopher Lee, Ingrid Pitt, Lindsay Kemp, Russell Waters, Aubrey Morris, Irene Sunters, Walter Carr, Roy Boyd and Leslie Mackie.

The Wicker Man has been called the "*Citizen Kane* of Horror Movies," which is a gross exaggeration of its virtues. It is a very good film but not quite the masterpiece it has been proclaimed in some circles. Much of the acclaim seems to have been in response to Warner Bros. cutting the film by 15 minutes and then giving it a very minor distribution. The resulting furor by fans of the film did much to enhance its reputation.

Police Sgt. Neil Howie (Edward Woodward) receives an anonymous letter from Summerisle, an island off the west coast of Scotland, claiming that a young girl has disappeared. Sgt. Howie, a self-righteous prig, goes to the island, where his inquiries are met mostly with indifference. He is disgusted by the sexual mores he encounters there and soon becomes convinced that the girl has met with foul play. As his search escalates, the mystery only seems to deepen. He eventually comes to the conclusion that the islanders plan to conduct a human sacrifice to their pagan gods to insure a good harvest. One element that has not been exaggerated is the excellent performance by Christopher Lee as Lord Summerisle.

Video: U.K./U.S.

311. Witchcraft

A Lippert Films Ltd. Production (1964); 79 minutes; U.S.: 20th Century–Fox

P: Robert L. Lippert and Jack Parsons; **D:** Don Sharp; **P:** Harry Spalding; **M:** Carlo Martelli; **DP:** Arthur Lavis; **E:** Robert Winter; **AD:** George Provis; **Cast:** Lon Chaney, Jr., Jack Hedley, Jill Dixon, Marie Ney, David Weston, Diane Clare, Viola Keats, Yvette Rees, Barry Linehan, Victor Brooks, Marianne Stone and John Dunbar.

The generations-old feud between the Laniers and the Whitlocks began in the seventeenth century when Vanessa Whitlock (Yvette Rees) was buried alive by the Laniers because they believed she was a witch. Now, centuries later, the Lanier family is bulldozing the Whitlock family cemetery to make room for a housing project they are developing. The bulldozer unearths the tomb of Vanessa and she returns to life to get revenge for herself and her descendants. To complicate matters, Todd Lanier (David Weston) is in love with Amy Whitlock (Diane Clare) to the extreme displeasure of her warlock uncle (Lon Chaney Jr.). This very low-budget film is helped greatly by Don Sharp's canny direction but is hindered by the miscasting of Lon Chaney, Jr., who blusters his way through his part.

Video: None

312. The Witches

A Hammer–Seven Arts Production (1966); 90 minutes; Technicolor; U.S. (*The Devil's Own*): 20th Century–Fox (1967); DeLuxe Color

P: Anthony Nelson-Keys; **D:** Cyril Frankel; **S:** Nigel Kneale; **M:** Richard Rodney Bennett; **DP:** Arthur Grant; **E:** James Needs and Chris Barnes; **PD:** Bernard Robinson; **AD:** Don Mingaye; **Cast:** Joan Fontaine, Kay Walsh, Alec McCowen, Ann Bell, Ingrid Brett, John Collin, Michele Dotrice, Gwen Ffrangcon-Davies, Duncan Lamont, Martin Stephens, Viola Keats and Leonard Rossiter.

Gwen Mayfield (Joan Fontaine) is a teacher in an African mission school. A tribal rebellion, led by the local witch doctor, results in her suffering a nervous breakdown. Later, back in England, Miss Mayfield recovers and takes a job as a schoolteacher in the rural village of Heddaby. Following a series of peculiar incidents, she suspects that the some of the villagers may be practicing witchcraft. The strange goings-on cause her to have a relapse and she is sent to

VINCENT PRICE AS MATTHEW HOPKINS *WITCHFINDER GENERAL.*

a nursing home to recover. She returns to Heddaby just as the local coven of witches is about to perform a virgin sacrifice. The novel *The Devil's Own* by Peter Curtis (pseudonym of Norah Lofts) was brought to Hammer by Joan Fontaine as a starring vehicle for herself. The first three quarters of the film are very engrossing as Fontaine's character attempts to uncover the town's secrets. The final quarter deteriorates somewhat when the sacrificial ritual begins to resemble a jazz dance class filled with particularly untalented students. And is it my imagination, or does the rather butch Stephanie Bax (Kay Walsh), leader of the witches' coven, seem to have designs on Miss Mayfield?

Video: U.S.

313. *Witchfinder General*

A Tigon–British–American–International Production (1968); 87 minutes; Eastman Color; U.S. *(Conqueror Worm)*: American-International; Color by Perfect

EXP: Tony Tenser; **P:** Louis M. Heyward, Philip Waddilove and Arnold L. Miller; **D:** Michael Reeves; **S:** Michael Reeves and Tom Baker; **M:** Paul Ferris; **DP:** John Coquillon; **E:** Howard Lanning; **AD:** Jim Morahan; **Cast:** Vincent Price, Ian Ogilvy, Hilary Dwyer, Rupert Davies, Robert Russell, Patrick Wymark, Wilfred Brambell, Nicky Henson, Anthony Selby, Maggie Kimberley, Hira Talfrey and Bernard Kay.

In 1645, while England is the scene of a civil war between the Royalists and Cromwell, Matthew Hopkins (Vincent Price) engages in a highly profitable crusade to rid the country of witchcraft. With his henchman John Stearne (Robert Russell), he journeys from town to town extracting "confessions" from people accused of being in league with the devil.

A disturbing exercise in sadism, the movie is more a piece of historical fiction than a horror film. This expertly directed and handsomely mounted production features a cast of memorable players, not the least of which is Price in one of the best performances of his lengthy career. Although Price was rather ill-treated by his young director Michael Reeves (who wanted Donald Pleasence for the lead), he did not let this interfere with his work as an actor. The film also introduces the lovely and talented Hilary Dwyer. She and Ian Ogilvy make a very handsome pair of lovers. Composer Paul Ferris appears in the film as Paul, the understandably distressed husband of condemned witch Maggie Kimberley. In the credits he is billed as "Morris Jar" (Maurice Jarre ... get it?). For the U.S. release, AIP retitled the film and added some quotes from Edgar Allan Poe (read by Price) to pass it off as part of their Poe series.

Because of the brutal content, it was condemned by many critics at the time of its release. *Witchfinder General* is now considered to be a classic and was chosen to be shown as a part of the BBC's Centenary of the Cinema. A note of warning regarding the U.S. video tape release: Due to contractual conflicts, Paul Ferris' unforgettable music has been replaced by a synthesized score by Kendall Schmidt. For fans of the original, this renders the tape nearly unwatchable. The U.K. video release has the original score intact.

Video: U.K./U.S.

The Woman Eater see *Womaneater*

The Woman Who Wouldn't Die see *Catacombs*

314. Womaneater

A Fortress Film Production (1957); 70 minutes; U.S. *(The Woman Eater)*: Columbia (1959)

P: Guido Coen; **D:** Charles Sanders; **S:** Brandon Fleming; **M:** Edwin Astley; **DP:** Ernest Palmer; **E:** Seymour Logie; **AD:** Herbert Smith; **Cast:** George Coulouris, Vera Day, Joy Webster, Peter Wayn, Jimmy Vaughn, Sara Leighton, Joyce Gregg, Maxwell Foster, Edward Higgins, Robert MacKenzie, Marpessa Dawn and Roger Avon.

Dr. James Moran (George Coulouris) comes back from an expedition to the Amazon with an unusual specimen of the local flora. It is a tree, sacred to the natives, which exudes sap that can raise the dead. The major drawback is that, to produce the sap, the tree must feed on beautiful young women. Dr. Moran has his eye on sexy showgirl Sally (Vera Day), who seems just perfect for the truculent tree's next repast. Once again producer Guido Coen and director Charles Sanders trap poor George Coulouris in a miasma of awful material. As with their film *The Man Without a Body*, if this had been just a little more over-the-top, it might have been a lot more fun. Some of the same plot elements were later used in *Konga* (scientist returns from jungle with carnivorous plant; scientist throws over faithful housekeeper-mistress for buxom blonde) with more deliriously deranged results.

Video: None

315. Wuthering Heights

American–International (1971); 105 minutes; Color by Movielab; U.S.: American–International

EXP: Louis M. Heyward; **P:** Samuel Z. Arkoff and James H. Nicholson; **D:** Robert Fuest; **S:** Patrick Tilley; **M:** Michel Legrand; **DP:** John Coquillon; **E:** Reginald Mills; **PD:** Philip Harrison; **Cast:** Anna Calder-Marshall, Timothy Dalton, Ian Ogilvy, Harry Andrews, Judy Cornwell, Hugh Griffith, Hilary Dwyer, Pamela

Brown, James Cossins, Rosalie Crutchley, Julian Glover and Peter Sallis.

Emily Brontë's classic novel of an obsessive and destructive love is given a first-class treatment in this sadly underrated American–International production. The tragic story of Heathcliff (Timothy Dalton) and Cathy (Anna Calder-Marshall) is afforded a far more realistic interpretation than the famous 1939 version. It also includes more of the novel, which accounts for the somewhat break-neck pacing of the film. Cathy and Heathcliff have been in love since childhood but her selfishness and his wild nature continally cause rifts in their relationship. When Cathy marries another man, Heathcliff vows to make her endure the same torment that he is suffering. Together they manage to ruin the lives of just about everybody in close proximity. In the climax, the ghost of Cathy lures Heathcliff to his death and then claims his spirit to be with her for eternity. Planned as a prestige release by AIP, it somehow still comes across as one of their British–produced horror films. You keep expecting Vincent Price to pop up at any minute. Even the advertising hints at the darker aspects of the tale: "The power, the passion, the terror of Emily Bronte's unforgettable love story."

WUTHERING HEIGHTS

Not a true horror film, but the presence of many familiar genre players in the cast and director Robert Fuest make this of more than passing interest to fans of AIP's British output. Heyward, Fuest and Tilly hoped to follow this film with a version of Nathaniel Hawthorne's the *Seven Gables* but this project never saw fruition.

Video: U.S.

316. X — The Unknown

A Hammer Film Production (1956); 78 minutes; U.S.: Warner Bros. (1957)

EXP: Michael Carreras; **P:** Anthony Hinds; **D:** Leslie Norman; **S:** Jimmy Sangster; **M:** James Bernard; **DP:** Gerald Gibbs; **E:** James Needs and Alfred Cox; **PD:** Bernard Robinson; **Cast:** Dean Jagger, Edward Chapman, Leo McKern, William Lucas, John Harvey, Peter Hammond, Anthony Newley, Michael Ripper, Edwin Richfield, Ian MacNaughton, Kenneth Cope and Marianne Brauns.

After the success of *The Quatermass Xperiment*, Hammer began to search for a follow-up science fiction project. Longtime Hammer employee Jimmy Sangster was given his first opportunity to write a feature-length script; the result is very close tone to the *Quatermass* film but offers its own highly original theorem. Radioactive mud from the Earth's core makes its way to the surface on the Scottish moors in search of new sources to replenish its energy, killing a number of people along the way. Dr. Royston (Dean Jagger) is the dedicated research scientist who must find a way to destroy this seemingly unstoppable menace. Once again Hammer was able to incorporate the "X" adult rating into the title of a film. Joseph Losey (under the pseudonym of Joe Walton) was originally set to direct, but he was replaced by Leslie Norman shortly before filming began.

The completed film was picked up by RKO to be released in America on a double-bill with the Bert I. Gordon potboiler *The Cyclops*. When the failing RKO was forced to liquidate some of its assets, Warner Bros. acquired the rights and released *X — The Unknown* as the cofeature to Hammer's seminal gothic horror *The Curse of Frankenstein*.

Video: U.K./U.S.

Young Dracula see **Son of Dracula**

317. Zardoz

20th Century–Fox (1974); 105 minutes; DeLuxe Color and Panavision

P/D/S: John Boorman; **M:** David Munrow; **DP:** Geoffrey Unsworth; **E:** John Merritt; **PD:** Anthony Pratt; **Cast:** Sean Connery, Charlotte Rampling, Sara Kestelman, Sally Anne Newton, John Alderton, Niall Buggy, Bosco Hogan, Jessica Swift, Christopher Casson, Reginald Jarman and Bairbre Dowling.

In the year 2293, the Outlands are inhabited by the Brutals. Only the chosen can breed and, to this end, the Brutals are policed by the violent Exterminators. All are ruled over by the god Zardoz, a gigantic stone head that floats through the sky intoning, "The gun is good. The penis is evil." One of the Exterminators, Zed (Sean Connery), hitches a ride aboard Zardoz and is whisked away to the Vortex, a peaceful valley inhabited by the Eternals. There he is reviled by the people and treated like a beast because he is capable of attaining an erection. A faction of women agree to give Zed the total of their knowledge if he will inseminate them. And this is only the coherent part of the story! There is no denying that John Boorman has a magnificent visual sense, but unfortunately the content of his films is often not equal to the stylish execution (remember *Exorcist II: The Heretic?*). *Zardoz* tries hard to be erotic but only succeeds in being idiotic, pretentious claptrap. The costumes (designed by Christel Kruse Boorman) and hairstyles of the Eternals are especially silly. Sean Connery fans get to see a lot of their hirsute hero as he spends most of the film clad in what looks like a red diaper. Every cloud has a silver lining.

Video: U.S.

318. Zero Population Growth (a.k.a. Z.P.G.)

A Sagittarius Production (1971); 96 minutes; Color; U.S.: Paramount

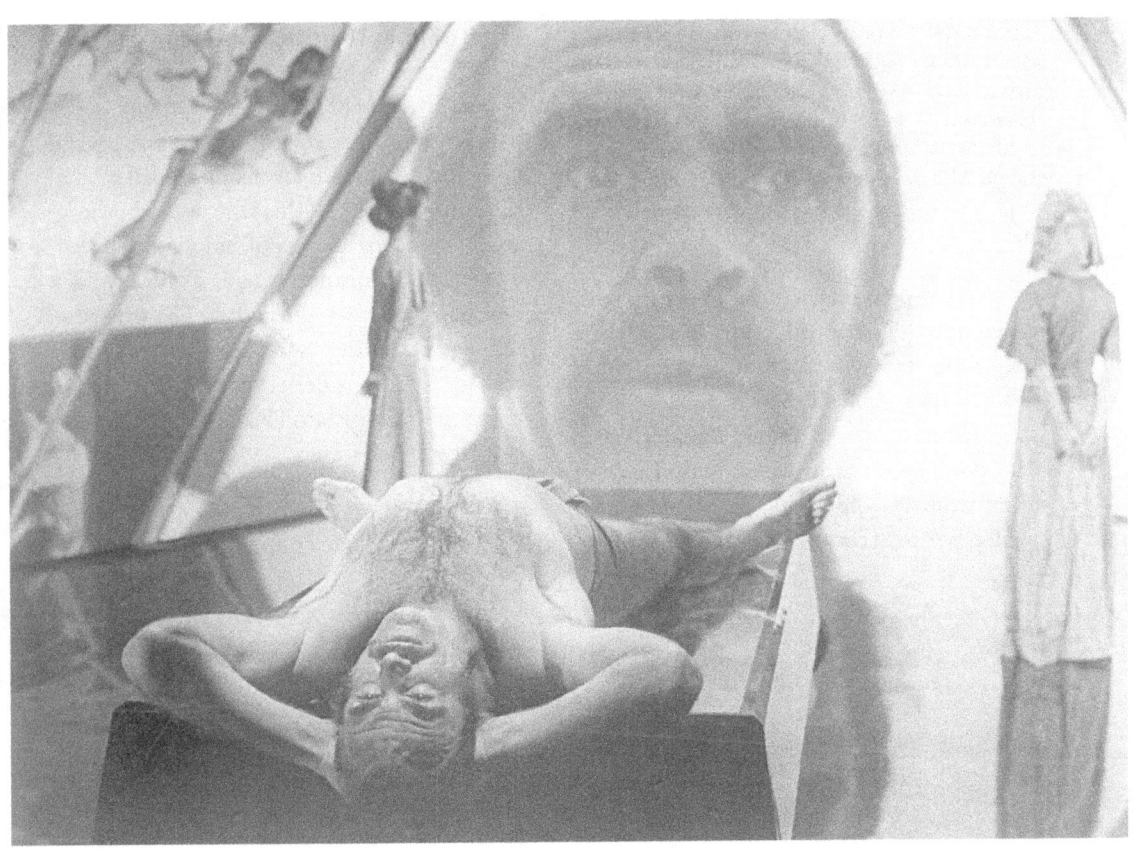

ZED (SEAN CONNERY) IS PUT THROUGH A SERIES OF EXAMINATIONS BY THE ETERNALS IN *ZARDOZ*.

EXP: Frank De Felitta; **P:** Thomas F. Madigan; **D:** Michael Campus; **S:** Max Ehrlich and Frank De Felitta; **M:** Jonathan Hodge; **DP:** Michael Reed; **E:** Richard C. Meyer and Dennis Lanning; **PD:** Tony Masters; **AD:** Harry Lange and Peter Hojmark; **Cast:** Oliver Reed, Geraldine Chaplin, Diane Cilento, Don Gordon, Bill Nagy, Aubrey Woods, David Markham, Sheila Reid, Wayne John Rhodda, Ditte Maria, Belinda Donkin, Jeff Slocombe and Dale Robinson.

In the horribly polluted, over-populated twenty-first century, world leaders issue orders that no infants are to be born for 30 years. To have a baby is a crime punishable by death. Carol (Geraldine Chaplin) is desperate to conceive a child. When she discovers that she is pregnant, she hides this information from her husband Russ (Oliver Reed). Four months into the pregnancy, she tells him about the forthcoming blessed event. With his help, Carol eventually gives birth in the cellar of their home, where she will have to keep the child in hiding ... apparently for the rest of its life. Combine *1984* with *Fahrenheit 451* (substituting babies for books) and you've got the idea. This British–American coproduction is deadly dull and Geraldine Chaplin's sullen performance does nothing to enliven the proceedings. Although set in the future, the look of the film is hopelessly entrenched in the 70s.

Video: U.S.

319. Zeta One

A Tigon–British Film Production (1969); 82 minutes; Color; U.S. *(The Love Factor)*: Edward Montoro Enterprises (1973)

EXP: Tony Tenser; **P:** George Maynard; **D:** Michael Cort; **S:** Alastair McKenzie and Michael

Cort; **M:** Johnny Hawksworth; **DP:** Jack Atchelor; **E:** Jack T. Knight and Dennis Lanning; **AD:** Martin Gasciogne; **Cast:** Robin Hawdon, James Robertson Justice, Dawn Addams, Charles Hawtrey, Yutte Stensgaard, Lionel Murton, Anna Gael, Brigitte Skay, Wendy Ingham, Valerie Leon, Rita Webb and Paul Baker.

Based on a magazine comic strip, this deplorable Tigon production is a softcore sex spoof of the James Bond films, with a dash of *Barbarella* thrown in for bad measure. Secret Agent James Word (Robin Hawdon) becomes involved with a race of alien women, known as Angvians, whose leader is Zeta (Dawn Addams). The Angvians seem to come in two types. The first dress in orange mini-skirts and white go-go boots. The second have Louise Brooks–style pageboy hairdos and wear black pasties with G-strings to match. Actually, most of the time the women in this film wear nothing at all. It is a virtual sea of bouncing boobs. The story makes no sense and the psychedelic special effects are awful. The sole reason for watching is to see starlets Yutte Stensgaard and Valerie Leon in pre–Hammer roles. Stensgaard shows a nice flair for comedy in her scenes.

Video: U.S. (video title: *Alien Women*)

Z.P.G. see ***Zero Population Growth***

BIBLIOGRAPHY

Adkinson, Robert, Allen Eyles and Nicholas Fry. *The House of Horror: The Story of Hammer Films.* London: Lorrimer, 1973.
Baer, D. Richard. *The Film Buff's Bible.* Hollywood, California: Hollywood Film Archive, 1972.
Beck, Calvin Thomas. *Heroes of the Horrors.* New York: Collier Books, 1975.
Bilbow, Marjorie. *The Facts About a Feature Film.* London: G. Whizzard Publications, 1978.
Brosnan, John. *The Horror People.* New York: St. Martin's Press, 1976.
Butler, Ivan. *Horror in the Cinema.* London: A. Zwemmer, 1970.
Castle, William. *Step Right Up! I'm Gonna Scare the Pants Off America.* New York: Putnam, 1976.
Clarens, Carlos. *Horror Movies: An Illustrated Survey.* London: Secker and Warburg, 1968.
Crocker, Keith, and George Reis. "The Richard Gordon Interview." *The Exploitation Journal.* 1995, vol. 2, no. 2-3, pp. 6-12.
Cushing, Peter. *An Autobiography.* London: Weidenfeld and Nicolson, 1986.
Dixon, Wheeler Winston. *The Charm of Evil: The Life and Films of Terence Fisher.* Metuchen, N.J.: Scarecrow Press, 1991.
Gifford, Denis. *Karloff: The Man, the Monster, the Movies.* New York: Curtis Books, 1973.
Harryhausen, Ray. *Film Fantasy Scrapbook.* Cranbury, N.J.: A.S. Barnes, 1972.
Heard, Colin. "Hammering the Box Office." *Films and Filming.* June 1969, vol. 15, no. 9, pp. 17-19.
Hearn, Marcus, and Alan Barnes. *The Hammer Story.* London: Titan Books, 1997.
Hickman, Gail Morgan. *The Films of George Pal.* Cranbury, N.J.: A.S. Barnes, 1977.
Humphries, Reynold. "Tyburn." *Cinefantastique.* 1976, vol. 4, no. 4, pp. 40-44.
Hutchings, Peter. *Hammer and Beyond: The British Horror Film.* Manchester, England: Manchester University Press, 1993.
Lamparski, Richard. *What Ever Became of...?* Vol. 10. New York: Crown, 1986.
Lee, Christopher. *Tall, Dark and Gruesome: An Autobiography.* London: Granada, 1978.
Mangravite, Andrew. "The House of Hammer." *Film Comment.* May-June 1992, vol. 28, no. 3, pp. 46-50.
Maxford, Howard. *Hammer, House of Horror.* London: Batsford Film Books, 1996.
McGee, Mark Thomas. *Fast and Furious: The Story of American International Pictures.* Jefferson, N.C.: McFarland, 1984.
Mulay, James J. *The Horror Film: A Guide to More Than 700 Films on Videocassette.* Evanston, Ill.: CineBooks, 1989.
Newman, Kim. *Nightmare Movies.* New York: Harmony Books, 1988.
Pirie, David. *Hammer: A Cinema Case Study.* London: BFI Education, 1980.
_____. *A Heritage of Horror.* London: Gordon Fraser, 1973.
Polanski, Roman. *Roman by Polanski.* New York: Ballantine, 1985.
Price, Vincent. *Vincent Price.* New York: Doubleday, 1978.
Ringel, Harry. "The Horrible Hammer Films of Terence Fisher." *Take One.* Jan.-Feb. 1972, vol. 3, no. 9, pp. 8-12.

Rose, Tony. "Horror Movies: Methods and Mystique." *Movie Maker*. Dec 1971, vol. 5, no. 12, pp. 797–800.
Sangster, Jimmy. *Do You Want It Good or Tuesday?* Baltimore: Midnight Marquee Press, 1997.
Silver, Alain, and James Ursini. *The Vampire Film*. Cranbury, N.J.: A.S. Barnes, 1975.
Speed, F. Maurice. *Film Review 1955-1956*. London: MacDonald, 1956.
Spoto, Donald. *The Dark Side of Genius: The Life of Alfred Hitchcock*. New York: Ballantine, 1983.
Strick, Philip. *Science Fiction Movies*. London: Octopus, 1976.
Svehla, Gary J. "A Tribute to Hammer Films." *Midnight Marquee*. Summer 1994, no. 47.
Swires, Steve. "When the Movies Got Tenser." *Fangoria*. Nov. 1993, no. 128, pp. 12–17; Dec. 1993, no. 129, pp. 68–73.
Williams, Lucy Chase. *The Complete Films of Vincent Price*. New York: Citadel, 1995.
Willis, John. *Screen World 1975*. New York: Crown, 1975.

Series Periodicals

Filmfax. Evanston, Illinois. Publisher, Michael Stein; editors, Michael Stein and Ted Okuda.
Films and Filming. London, England. Publisher, Hansom Books; editor, Robin Bean.
Hammer Horror. London, England. Publisher, Marvel Comics U.K.; editor, Marcus Hearn.
House of Hammer. London, England. Publisher, General Book Distribution; editor, Dez Skinn.
Little Shoppe of Horrors. Des Moines, Iowa. Publisher/editor, Richard Klemensen.
Monster Mania. New York. Publisher, Rennaissance Productions; editor, Russ Jones.

INDEX

Abney, William 169
The Abominable Dr. Phibes 1
The Abominable Snowman 2
Abraham, Edward 85
Abraham, Valerie 85
Ackland, Joss 48, 129, 154, 228
Ackland-Snow, Terry 233
Adam, Ken 203
Adam, Ronald 141, 279
Adams, Beverly 280
Adams, Jonathan 233
Adams, Nick 184
Adams, Tom 154
Addams, Dawn 286, 292, 294, 319
Adler, Lou 233
Adrian, Max 72, 83, 271
Agutter, Jenny 85
Ainley, Anthony 8, 168, 193, 235
Alberge, Betty 49, 77
Alberoni, Sherri 275
Alcott, John 39
Alderton, John 317
Alexander, Paris 64
Alexander, Paul 239
Alexiou, Nicos 64
Alison, Dorothy 3, 18, 81
Allen, Andrea 240
Allen, Elizabeth 136
Allen, Irving 102
Allen, Jack 142
Allen, Lewis M. 104
Allen, Michael 66
Allen, Patrick 23, 27, 202, 208, 217, 307
Allen, Ronald 107, 221
Allen, Sheila 34, 298
Allison, John 102
Allnutt, Wendy 124
Allum, Victoria 239
Alston, Andy 78
Alwyn, William 204
The Amazing Mr. Blunden 3
Ambler, Dial 197
Ambler, Joss 129
Ambor, Joe 258
Ambrosino, Mario 89
Amer, Nick 77

An, Feng Ko 171
And Now the Screaming Starts 4
And Soon the Darkness 5
Anderson, Daphne 27
Anderson, Gene 63
Anderson, Gerald 147
Anderson, Gerry 88
Anderson, Jean 199
Anderson, Michael 85
Anderson, Rona 74
Anderson, Sylvia 88
Andress, Ursula 244
Andrews, Barry 29, 93, 231, 235
Andrews, Bill 192
Andrews, Dana 125, 203
Andrews, Harry 26, 109, 200, 206, 272, 315
Andrews, Peter L. 235
Angers, Avril 74
Annett, Paul 13
Annis, Francesca 101
The Anniversary 6
Anthony, Olga 191
Antony, Scott 191
Antrobus, Yvonne 84
Anulka 293
Arbeid, Ben 34
Archard, Bernard 116, 145
Archdale, Alexander 142
Archer, Ernie 287
Archibald, William 159
Arent, Eddi 35
Argyle, John 60
Aris, Ben 219
Arkoff, Samuel Z. 1, 10, 82, 175, 184, 190, 216, 309, 315
Arliss, Ralph 7, 226
Armstrong, Hugh 67, 189
Armstrong, Michael 140
Armstrong, Raymond 308
Armstrong, Todd 164
Armstrong, Vic 99
Arnall, Julia 179
Arnatt, John 49, 79, 155
Arne, Peter 11, 17, 190, 211, 276
Arneric, Neda 298
Arnold, Grace 167
Arnold, Malcolm 208

Arnold, Norman 70
Arnold, Wilfred 23, 97, 142, 147, 167, 197
Arnould, Norma 110
Arpino, Tony 98
Arrighi, Nike 44, 71
Arthy, Judith 245
Asher, Jack 24, 51, 90, 176, 187, 232, 249, 286
Asher, Jane 181
Asherson, Renee 63, 228
Ashton, Don 75
Askwith, Robin 113, 144, 281
Aslan, Gregorie 133, 249, 275
The Asphyx 7
Assault 8
Astley, Edwin 15, 70, 218, 314
Asylum 9
At the Earth's Core 10
Atchelor, Jack 140, 319
Atkins, Eileen 156
The Atomic Man see *Timeslip*
Attenborough, Richard 242, 269
Aubrey, Diane 136
Auckland, Noreen 215
Audley, Maxine 22, 119, 215, 295
Auric, Georges 159, 182
Austin, Ray 300
Avalon, Frankie 140, 261
Avon, Roger 57, 314
Ayers, Robert 11, 32, 111
Aylen, Richard 240
Aylmer, Felix 138, 187, 196
Aylward, Derek 149

Bachardy, Don 120
Bachmann, Lawrence P. 34, 201
Bacon, Norman 93
Bacon, Paul 7, 274
Badel, Alan 34
Baide, Doon 46
Bailey, Robin 18
Bain, Bill 306
Baines, John 66, 138
Baird, Antony 69
Baird, Harry 211
Baird, Roy 109
Baker, George 54

Index

Baker, Jane 29
Baker, Paul 319
Baker, Pip 29
Baker, Robert S. 21, 114, 163, 283, 305
Baker, Roy Ward 4, 6, 9, 81, 171, 185, 224, 238, 292, 294
Baker, Tom 133, 191, 251, 294, 313
Baksh, Shakira 250
Balaban, Burt 257
Balch, Antony 144
Balcon, Michael 66, 133
Balfour, Michael 108, 220
Ball, Vincent 21
Banes, Lionel 108, 136
Bankhead, Tallulah 105
Banks, Don 27, 98, 125, 155, 184, 188, 207, 228, 229, 280
Bannen, Ian 87, 122, 124
Barber, Antonia 3
Barclay, George 69, 299
Baring, Aubrey 2
Barnes, Chris 46, 48, 68, 139, 145, 171, 173, 219, 234, 267, 312
Barnes, Julian 140
Barnikel, Philip 198, 201, 300
Baron, David 229
Baron, Lynda 139
Barr, Patrick 113, 153, 234
Barrett, Ray 229, 231
Barrett, Sean 115
Barrett, Tim 65, 188, 223
Barrie, Maxine 107
Barrington, Derek 53, 275
Barron, Keith 10, 168, 210
Barron, Ray 298
Barry, Hilda 147, 151
Barry, John (composer) 242
Barry, John (production designer) 39
Bartok, Eva 128, 253
Bass, Alfie 59, 262
Bastedo, Alexandra 132
Bastow, Michael 195
Bate, Anthony 130
Bates, Michael 14, 39, 121
Bates, Ralph 81, 106, 145, 156, 174, 217, 267
Bateson, Timothy 6, 207
Batt, Bert 119
Battle Beneath the Earth 11
Bauer, David 96
Bayliss, Peter 290
Baxt, George 36, 37, 204, 243
Baxter, Les 50
Bayldon, Geoffrey 9, 119, 154, 264
Beach, Ann 37
Beacham, Stephanie 4, 75, 92, 151, 206, 239
The Beast in the Cellar 12
The Beast Must Die 13
The Beast of Morocco see *The Hand of Night*
Beatty, Robert 287
Beaumont, Charles 181, 204

Beaumont, Gabrielle 41
Beaumont, Richard 309
Beaumont, Susan 254
Beaver, Paul 109
Beckley, Tony 8, 107, 173
Beckwith, Reginald 63, 203, 204, 288
Bedazzled 14
Beesley, David 191
Beeson, Paul 48, 173, 184, 185, 191
Behemoth the Sea Monster 15
Behling, Bob 73
Belbin, George 77, 119
Bell, Arnold 54
Bell, Keith 139, 161
Bell, Michael 111
Bell, Tom 256
Benda, Kenneth 144
Benedict, Max 190, 211
Benfield, Derek 156
Benjamin, Adrian 80
Bennett, Charles 38, 203
Bennett, Frances 248
Bennett, Hywel 96, 285
Bennett, Jill 126, 194, 246
Bennett, John 150, 154
Bennett, Richard 268
Bennett, Richard Rodney 176, 194, 301, 312
Benson, George 306
Benson, Martin 11, 27, 47, 134, 258, 275
Bentinck, Anna 277
Benzencent, Peter 163
Bergen, Candice 64
Berger, Helmut 89
Berger, William 64
Bergner, Elisabeth 50
Berkeley, Ballard 198
Berman, Monty 21, 114, 163, 283, 305
Bernard, Carl 142
Bernard, James 51, 58, 71, 90, 93, 94, 117, 118, 119, 135, 148, 166, 171, 219, 226, 227, 238, 244, 259, 267, 270, 280, 316
Bernard, Paul 300
Berne, Gustave 4, 45, 272
Bernstein, Elmer 3, 18
Berova, Olinka 191, 297
Berry, Frank 271
Berry, Owen 110
Berserk 16
Bertrand, Claude 5
Best, Richard 85, 222, 235
Beswick, Martine 81, 213, 247
Bettison, Ralph 208
Betts, Kirsten 48, 292
Bevan, Stewart 132, 151
Beware the Brethren see *The Fiend*
Beyond the Fog see *Tower of Evil*
Bidmead, Stephanie 160
Bieber, Francis 129, 258
Bill, David 144
Billington, Kevin 301

Birch, Derek 136
Bird, Minah 290
Bird, Norman 17, 139, 180, 182, 204, 296
Birkin, Jane 61
Birks, David 148
Bishop, Edward 11, 88
Bislani, Fernando 73
Bisset, Donald 142, 303
Bisset, Jacqueline 255
Black Isobel 166, 269, 284
Black, Stanley 21, 38, 63, 114, 127, 152, 163, 180, 283
Black, Stewart 89
The Black Torment 17
Blackman, Honor 31, 122, 164, 277
Blair, Isla 267
Blair, Janet 204
Blair, John 137
Blake, Ann 266
Blake, Beverly 50
Blake, Josephine 142
Blakely, Colin 64, 220, 297
Blakely, Tom 74, 161, 202
Blakemore, Eric 237
Blanshard, Joby 87, 185
Blast Off! see *Jules Verne's Rocket to the Moon*
Blees, Robert 82, 309
Blezard, John 37, 112, 138, 307
Bligh, Jack 202
Blind Terror 18
Bloch, Robert 9, 154, 223, 246, 280
Block, Irving 15
Blood Beast from Outer Space see *The Night Caller*
The Blood Beast Terror 19
Blood City see *Welcome to Blood City*
Blood from the Mummy's Tomb 20
Blood Island see *The Shuttered Room*
Blood of the Vampire 21
Blood on Satan's Claw see *Satan's Skin*
Blood Will Have Blood see *Demons of the Mind*
Bloodsuckers see *Incense for the Damned*
Bloom, Claire 141
Bluebeard's Ten Honeymoons 22
Blum, Harry N. 10
Blunden, Bill 150, 183
Blythe, Domini 291
Blythe, Peter 118
Boddey, Martin 32, 61
The Body Stealers 23
Boehm, Karl 215
Bogarde, Dirk 182
Bohun, Carl 13
Boize, Sandra 155
Bolam, James 49, 256
Bolling, Claude 138

Index

Bolster, Anita Sharp 149
Bond, Derek 257, 262
Bonham, John 250
Bonner, Tony 46, 102
Bonney, John 214
Boone, Pat 146
Boorman, John 317
Booth, Anthony 43, 195
Booth, James 231
Borelli, Carlo 97
Borisenko, Don 223
Borodin, Alexander 110
Bortish, Jane 225
Boscoe Holder Dancers 137
Bostwick, Barry 233
Boulting, Roy 285
Boulton, David 34, 125, 141, 162
Bower, Ingrid 245
Bowers, Lally 92
Bowers, Raymond 239
Bowie, David 177, 250, 140
Bowie, Les 63, 185, 224, 227, 283
Bowles, Peter 96, 102, 170
Bown, John 84, 106
Box, John 128
Boyd, Roy 210
Boyd-Perkins, Eric 27, 55, 134, 135, 209, 244, 266, 270, 286, 310
Brach, Gerard 59, 230
Braden, Bernard 63, 127
Bradford, Ernie 26
Bradley, Elizabeth 113
Bradley, Stephen 77
Bradley-Smith, Douglas 79
Bradsell, Michael 72
Braga, Tony Sarza 164
Brahms, Penny 287
The Brain see *Vengeance*
Brambell, Wilfred 313
Brando, Marlon 206
Brandon, Catherine 217
Brandy, Howard 20
Brauns, Marianne 316
Brayne, William 77
Breaks, Sebastian 199
Breck, Kathleen 125, 252
Bree, James 236
Brennan, Ed 61
Brennan, Michael 122
Brennan, Sheila 255
Brent, Simon 298
Bresslaw, Bernard 21, 30, 185, 288, 290
Brett, Alan 40
Brett, Ingrid 312
Briant, Shane 28, 68, 117
The Bride of Fengriffen see *And Now the Screaming Starts*
The Brides of Dracula 24
The Brides of Fu Manchu 25
Bridge, Adam 301
Bridgeman, Ken 293
Bridges, Alan 160
Bridges, Ronald 193

Briley, Jack 34
Brill, Michael 2
Brittany, John 7
Britton, Tony 205, 216
Brock, Patrick 40
Brodie, Lea 303
Brodrick, Susan 44, 81
Brogan, Harry 103
Bromley, Sydney 27, 59, 184, 202, 214, 247
Bron, Eleanor 14
Brook, Lyndon 160
Brook-Jones, Elwyn 288
Brooke, Steven 38
Brooks, Ray 57, 113, 153
Brooks, Victor 74, 101
Broome, Marianne 169
Brousse, Liliane 180, 214
Brown, Barbara 270
Brown, Bernard 266
Brown, Gay 181
Brown, Geoff R. 293
Brown, George H. 8, 231
Brown, Georgia 210, 260, 265
Brown, Murray 91, 293
Brown, Pamela 91, 199, 315
Brown, Robert 2, 68, 213, 303
Brown, Walter 94
Brown, William Lyon 213
Browne, Coral 79, 272
Browne, Laidman 129
Bruce, Brenda 207, 215
Brunner, John 271
Bryan, Dora 139, 186
Bryan, Peter 19, 24, 148, 219, 221
Bryant, Michael 182, 189, 280
Buck, David 188
Buckingham, Yvonne 268
Buckley, Keith 300
Budd, Roy 304
Buggy, Niall 317
Bull, Peter 212, 275, 278
Burden, Hugh 20, 129, 150
Burke, Alfred 34, 194, 198
Burke, Barbara 163
Burke, Chris 123, 151, 239
Burke, Marie 249, 270
Burke, Patricia 64
Burke and Hare 26
Burn, Jonathan 102
Burn Witch Burn see *Night of the Eagle*
Burnham, Jeremy 145
Burnley, Fred 195
Burrell, Sheila 214
Burroughs, Edgar Rice 10, 168, 216
Burton, Julian 181
Burton, Richard 22, 80
Bush, Dick 92, 169, 235, 284, 307
Bush, Maurice 47
Bushell, Anthony 131, 270
Butcher, Kim 123, 151
Butler, Bill 290
Butler, David 41

Butterworth, Peter 63, 278
Buxton, Judy 156
Byrne, Eddie 74, 161, 163, 187
Byrne, Michael 293
Byron, Kathleen 45, 204, 210, 284

Cacavas, John 143, 234
Cacoyannis, Michael 64
Caddick, Edward 302
Caffrey, Sean 307
Caffrey, Liam 161
Cagan, Steven 31
Cain, Sydney 104
Caine, Henry 51
Cairney, John 114, 164, 252, 260
Cairns, Jessica 254
Calder-Marshall, Anna 315
Callan, Michael 31, 192
Callard, Kay 32, 97
Calley, John 100
Calvert, Phyllis 285
Calvet, Corrine 22
Calvin, Tony 81
Calvo, Jose 190
Cameron, Earl 11
Cameron, Isa 159
Cameron, John 205, 222
Cameron, Rod 97
Campbell, Mike 217
Campbell, Nell 233
Campbell, R. Wright 29, 181
Campion, Gerald 251
Campus, Michael 318
Cannon, Esma 305
Capote, Truman 159
Captain Clegg 27
Captain Kronos Vampire Hunter 28
Captain Nemo and the Underwater City 29
Carayiannis, Costa 73
Cardiff, Jack 191
Carell, Annette 268, 302
Carey, Joyce 101
Carey, Macdonald 58
Caridia, Michael 128
Carlos, Walter 39
Carlson, Veronica 93, 119, 132, 145, 290
Carlton, Rex 289
Carlton, Vivienne 53
Carmet, Jean 5
Carmichael, Ian 124, 129
Carol, Joan 129
Carpenter, Paul 79, 110
Carpenter, Richard 271
Carr, Walter 310
Carrel, Dany 138
Carreras, Michael 2, 20, 24, 46, 48, 51, 55, 56, 58, 90, 92, 105, 106, 115, 173, 176, 180, 185, 187, 196, 213, 226, 232, 244, 247, 249, 253, 259, 266, 270, 286, 288, 316
Carrick, Edward 180, 194, 155
Carruthers, Benito 173

Carry on Screaming 30
Carson, Charles 54
Carson, John 28, 178, 198, 219, 267
Carsten, Peter 260
Carte, Eric 13
Carter, Fred 59, 96, 120
Carter, Maurice 10, 124, 150, 168, 216, 222, 269
Cartwright, Robert 72
Carwardine, Richard 80
Cary, Tristram 20, 224
Case, Gerald 293
Casey, Bernie 177
Cass, Henry 21
Casson, Christopher 317
Castle, Roy 83, 84, 172
Castle, William 212
The Cat and the Canary 31
Cat Girl 32
Catacombs 33
Cater, John 1, 28, 82
Cathie, Dermot 274
Caunter, Tony 7
Cavalcanti, Alberto 66
Cawdron, Robert 245
Cawthorne, James 168
Cazabon, John 248
Celi, Adolfo 116, 190
Chadbon, Tom 13
Chadwick, June 40
Chaffey, Don 46, 164, 213, 217
Chagrin, Francis 249
Challis, Christopher 220
Challis, John 308
Chan, Wong Han 171
Chandler, Patti 261
Chaney, Lon, Jr. 311
Chang, Paul 261
Chang, Wah 278
Chantler, David T. 244
Chapkis, Arnold 49, 225, 235
Chaplin, Geraldine 318
Chapman, Edward 178, 316
Chappell, Diane 107
Charisse, Cyd 303
Charles, Martin 285
Chase, James 300
Chase, Stephen 50
Chater, Geoffrey 258, 269
Chatto, Tom 125, 162, 226
Chegwidden, Ann 5, 57, 165, 181
Cheshire, Geoffrey 57
Chester, Hal E. 203
Chevreau, Cecile 253
Chiang, David 171
Chilcott, Barbara 127
Child of Satan see *To the Devil...A Daughter*
Children of the Damned 34
Childs, Ted 225
Chin, Anthony 2
Chin, Tsai 25, 103, 160, 296
Chinnery, Dennis 219
Chitty, Eric 112, 146, 174, 294

Choice, Elisabeth 12
Chopra, Ram 80
Christian, Kurt 133, 144
Christiansen, Arthur 63
Christie, Helen 174
Christie, Julie 86, 104
Christodoulou, Raymond 124
Churchill, Donald 252
Cilento, Diane 127, 310, 318
Cipriani, Stelvio 200
Circus of Fear 35
Circus of Horrors 36
City of the Dead 37
City Under the Sea 38
Clair, A.C.T. 110
Clare, Diane 137, 141, 219, 302, 311
Clark, Candy 177
Clark, Ernest 162, 208
Clark, Fred 55
Clark, James 159
Clark, Jim 175
Clark, Marlene 13
Clarke, Arthur C. 287
Clarke, Frank 209, 278
Clarke, James 293
Clarke, James Kenelm 99
Clarke, Robin 124
Clarke, Warren 39
Clarke-Smith, D.A. 131
Clay, Nicholas 199
Claydon, George 16, 156
Clayton, Jack 159
Clein, John 79
Clegg, Tom 30
Clemens, Brian 18, 55, 28, 81, 133, 268
Clements, John 182
Clerk, Jacqueline 197
Clifford, Graeme 86, 177, 233
Clifford, Peggy Ann 136, 301
Clitheroe, Jimmy 165
Clive, John 39, 256
A Clockwork Orange 39
Coates, Anne V. 169
Cobert, Dan 91
Coen, Guido 26, 179, 314
Coghill, Neville 80
Cohen, Herman 16, 45, 129, 142, 147, 167, 260, 282
Cole, George 122, 292
Coleman, Bryan 21
Coleman, Bula 244
Coleman, Richard 193
Coles, Michael 84, 92, 234
Colin, Sid 288
Collier, Patience 44, 96
Collin, John 312
Collings, Lisa 191
Collins, Joan 61, 106, 156, 231, 264, 265
Collins, John D. 93
Collins, Stephen 298
Collinson, Madeleine and Mary 284

Collinson, Peter 122, 255, 256
Collinson, Tara 122
Colson, Kevin 205
Colville, John 26
The Comeback 40
Comfort, Lance 74, 288
Comport, Brian 7, 107, 189
Compton, Fay 141
Computer Killers see *Horror Hospital*
Cones, Tristam 1, 76, 82, 189, 309
The Confessional see *House of Mortal Sin*
Connell, Maureen 2
Connell, Thelma 18, 83, 161
Connery, Neil 23
Connery, Sean 317
Connock, Jim 99
Connor, Kenneth 29
Connor, Kevin 10, 124, 168, 216, 303
Connors, Chuck 29
The Conqueror Worm see *Witchfinder General*
Conrad, Jess 167
Constable, Bill 65, 83, 84, 183, 233, 241, 246, 271, 274, 280
Constantine, Frixos 73
Conte, Richard 101
Conti, Tom 126
Cook, Joseph 308
Cook, Peter 14
Cook, Vera 24, 166, 196, 243
Cooke, Alan 183
Cooke, Malcolm 116, 272
Cookson, Georgina 33
Cooney, Ray 305
Coop, Denys 4, 9, 182, 269, 294
Cooper, George A. 93, 207, 396
Cooper, John C. 111, 136, 221
Cooper, Wilkie 164, 180, 192, 262, 275
Cope, Kenneth 58, 202, 306
Copley, Peter 179, 224, 306
Coquillon, John 23, 50, 53, 211, 241, 313, 315
Corbett, Harry H. 30
Cordell, Shane 108
Corlan, Anthony 267, 291
Corman, Roger 181, 279
Cornelius, Billy 30, 183
Cornelius, Joe 282
Corney, Norma 156
Cornford, Robert 77
Cornwell, Judy 309, 315
The Corpse 41
Corri, Adrienne 39, 42, 70, 175, 185, 260, 268, 291
Corridors of Blood 42
Corruption 43
Cort, Michael 319
Coscia, Marcello 89
Cosmic Monsters see *The Strange World of Planet X*
Cosmo, James 8

Index

Cossins, James 6, 20, 65, 67, 106, 145, 173, 315
Costello, Deidre 68
Costelloe, John 130
Cotten, Joseph 1
Couch, Lionel 8, 201, 234, 297
Coulouris, George 20, 22, 34, 109, 179, 209, 246, 281, 314
Count Dracula and His Vampire Bride see *The Satanic Rites of Dracula*
Countess Dracula 44
Court, Hazel 51, 70, 78, 129, 176, 181
Courtney, Alan D. 199
Courtney, Tom 64
Cowper, Jacqueline 309
Cox, Alfred 24, 56, 148, 184, 187, 196, 218, 232, 259, 279, 316
Cox, Clifford 285
Cox, Jack 70
Cox, Vincent 46
Crabtree, Arthur 108, 147
Cracknell, Leonard 271
Crafter, Richard 236
Craig, Michael 192, 294
Craig, Wendy 182, 194
Crawford, Andrew 243
Crawford, Broderick 302
Crawford, Howard Marion 25, 103, 296
Crawford, Joan 6, 16, 282
Crawford, Lillybelle 177
The Crawling Eye see *The Trollenberg Terror*
Craze 45
Craze, Michael 195, 236
Craze, Peter 12
Creatures the World Forgot 46
The Creepers see *Assault*
The Creeping Flesh 47
The Creeping Unknown see *The Quatermass Xperiment*
Crescendo 48
Crewdson, Robert 223
Cribbins, Bernard 57, 121, 244
Crichton, Charles 66
The Crimson Cult see *Curse of the Crimson Alter*
Crisp, Tracey 221
Croft, Jon 183
Crombie, Tony 268
Cross, Beverly 164
Cross, Henry 95
Cross, Hugh 262
Cross, Larry 97
Crosthwait, Julie 175
Crowden, Graham 3, 109, 199
Croydon, John 42, 108, 111, 136, 221
Crucible of Horror see *The Corpse*
Crucible of Terror 49
Cruickshank, Andrew 259
Crutchley, Rosalie 4, 20, 46, 128, 141, 150, 309, 315

Cry of the Banshee 50
Cuadrado, Luis 200
Culver, Michael 23
Culver, Roland 116, 170
Cummins, Peggy 203
Cunningham, Beryl 89
Cunningham, Christopher 93, 117, 174
Cunningham, Jack 248
Cunningham, June 147
Curnow, Graham 147
Curran, Peter 307
Currie, Finlay 42
Curry, Tim 233
The Curse of Frankenstein 51
Curse of Simba 52
Curse of the Crimson Alter 53
Curse of the Demon see *Night of the Demon*
The Curse of the Fly 54
The Curse of the Mummy's Tomb 55
Curse of the Voodoo see *Curse of Simba*
The Curse of the Werewolf 56
Curteis, Ian 221
Curtis, Alan 76
Curtis, Dan 91
Curtis, Jacqueline 110
Curtis, Patrick 251
Curtis, Tony (art director) 4, 9, 154, 157, 175, 251, 264, 294, 306
Curzon, Fiona 173
Curzon, Jill 57
Cusak, Cyril 75, 104
Cusak, Sinead 75, 231
Cushing, Peter 2, 4, 7, 9, 10, 13, 19, 24, 27, 43, 47, 51, 57, 73, 82, 83, 84, 90, 92, 98, 106, 114, 117, 118, 119, 124, 132, 135, 143, 148, 154, 157, 158, 161, 171, 172, 175, 187, 202, 208, 210, 232, 234, 241, 244, 246, 264, 280, 292
Cuthbertson, Allan 8, 23, 29, 259, 295

Dade, Stephen 22, 38, 78, 198, 248, 302
Dahl, Roald 199
Daine, Lois 28
Daisika 77
Dalby, Lynn 172
Dale, Jim 175
Daleks' Invasion Earth: 2150 A.D. 57
Dallamano, Massimo 89
Dalrymple, Ian 131
Dalton, Timothy 315
Daltry, Roger 169
The Damned 58
Dance of the Vampires 59
Dane, Alexandra 43
Danforth, Jim 307
Danielly, Lisa 52
Daniel, Jennifer 166, 229

Daniels, Danny 52
Dankworth, John 269
Dann, Larry 130
Dantine, Helmut 257
Danvers-Walker, Michael 205
Danzinger, Harry and Edward 70, 237, 268
Dark, John 10, 168, 216, 303
Dark, Rodney 110
The Dark see *The Haunted House of Horror*
Dark Eyes of London 60
Dark Places 61
Darvas, Teddy 3, 61, 178, 264
Daubeney, Diana 240, 293
Dauphin, Claude 127
Davenport, Nigel 91, 209, 215
Davey, Bert 10, 30, 168, 216
David, Karen 153
Davidson, L.W. 139
Davies, Deddie 3
Davies, Gron 227
Davies, Jack 91
Davies, Peter Maxwell 72
Davies, Rupert 25, 53, 93, 123, 211, 313
Davion, Alexander 158, 214, 219
Davis, Bette 6, 194
Davis, Carl 157, 306
Davreux, Denise 261
Dawe, Cedric 62
Dawn, Doreen 181
Dawn, Marpessa 314
Dawson, Anthony 56, 136, 249
Day, Robert 42, 111, 136, 244
Day, Vera 136, 226, 314
The Day of the Triffids 62
The Day the Earth Caught Fire 63
The Day the Fish Came Out 64
The Day the Screaming Stopped see *The Comeback*
Daye, Gabrielle 269
Deacon, Brian 293
Deacon, Don 43
Dead of Night 66
The Deadly Bees 65
Dean, Bill 205
Dean, Ivor 81
Dean, Margia 227
DeAngeles, Nato 156
Dear, Elizabeth 207
Dearberg, Robert 123, 143, 144
Dearden, Basil 66, 178, 182
Dearman, Glyn 115
Dearman, Jennifer 115
Death Line 67
Decker, Diane 74
De Cuir, John 80
Deeley, Michael 177
De Felitta, Frank 318
De Goguel, Constantin 277
Dehn, Paul 116, 159, 214
Delamain, Aimee 150, 157
Delgado, Roger 111, 182, 188, 259
de los Rios, Waldo 190

Index

De Luca, Peppino 89
de Marney, Derrick 221
de Marney, Terence 137, 184
de Mendoza, Alberto 143
The Demon Master see *Craze*
Demons of the Mind 68
Dempster, Austin 14
Denberg, Susan 118
Dench, Judi 260
Deneuve, Catherine 230
Denham, Maurice 44, 194, 155, 198, 203, 280
Dennen, Barry 175
Dennis, Winifred 105
Denton, Geoffrey 149
de Pozo, Angel 143
De Rauch, Mickey 213
Derbyshire, Delia 170
Derosa, Franco 88
de Souza, Edward 165, 166, 218
Des Rarres, Michael 157
Devereux, Marie 24, 259
Devil Doll 69
Devil Girl from Mars 70
The Devil Rides Out 71
The Devils 72
The Devil's Bride see *The Devil Rides Out*
The Devil's Men 73
Devils of Darkness 74
The Devil's Own see *The Witches*
The Devil's Undead see *Nothing But the Night*
The Devil's Widow 75
The Devil Within Her see *I Don't Want to Be Born*
Devlin, William 21, 245
Dewey, Christopher 41
De Witt, Louis 15
De Wolfe 144
De Wolff, Francis 17, 42, 69, 148, 176, 286
Dexter, Anthony 110
Dexter, William 137
Diamond, Arnold 6, 180
Diamond, I.A.L. 220
Dickie, Olga 90, 166, 254
Dickinson, Desmond 12, 16, 26, 107, 138, 147, 158, 167, 260, 281, 282, 309
Dicks, Ted 300
Dickson, Hugh 67
Dickson, Paul 237
Die, Die My Darling see *Fanatic*
Die Monster Die see *Monster of Terror*
Die Screaming Marianne 76
Diffring, Anton 13, 36, 104, 176, 168
Dignam, Basil 42, 134, 193
Dillon, Robert 212
Dilworth, Carol 140
Dinsdale, A.T. 276
Disciple of Death 77
Dix, William 194

Dixon, Jill 311
Dobtcheff, Vernon 12
Doctor Blood's Coffin 78
Dr. Crippen 79
Doctor Faustus 80
The Doctor from Seven Dials see *Corridors of Blood*
Dr. Jekyll and Sister Hyde 81
Dr. Phibes Rises Again 82
Dr. Terror's House of Horrors 83
Dr. Who and the Daleks 84
Dodge, David 27
Dodimead, David 12
Doig, Lee 5, 79
Doleman, Guy 65
Domergue, Faith 276
Dominique 85
Dominique Is Dead see *Dominique*
Donaggio, Pino 86
Donahue, Troy 165
Donald, James 224
Donally, Andrew 85, 222
Donen, Stanley 14
Donkin, Belinda 318
Donlevy, Brian 54, 226, 227
Donnelly, Donal 183
Donner, Clive 290
Donner, Judith 242
Don't Look Now 86
Doomwatch 87
Doonan, Tony 252
Doppleganger 88
Dor, Karen 103
Doran, Veronica 140
Dorian Gray 89
Dorne, Sandra 69, 149
Dors, Diana 3, 16, 45, 124, 210, 272
Dotrice, Michele 5, 235, 312
Dotrice, Roy 264
Douglas, Angela 30
Douglas, Colin 283
Douglas, Johnny 35
Douglas, Josephine 92
Douglas, Karin 103
Douglas, Paul 128
Douglas, Sarah 91, 216, 109
Dowling, Bairbre 317
Down, Leslie-Anne 8, 44, 124
Down, Terry 59
Downie, Andrew 252
Doyle, David 40
Drache, Heinz 25, 35
Dracula (1958) 90
Dracula (1973) 91
Dracula A.D. 1972 92
Dracula and the 7 Golden Vampires see *The Legend of the 7 Golden Vampires*
Dracula Has Risen from the Grave 93
Dracula Is Dead and Well and Living in London see *The Satanic Rites of Dracula*
Dracula—Prince of Darkness 94

Dracula Today see *Dracula A.D. 1972*
Drago, Eleonora Rossi 89
Drake, Fabia 75
Drake, Geoffrey 164
Dress, Michael 154, 183
Drewett, Pauline 128
Duering, Carl 39, 97
Duff, Howard 253
Duffell, Bee 104
Duffell, Peter 154
Duggan, Terry 239
Dullea, Keir 126, 287, 304
Dunas, Ronald S. 1
Dunbar, John 311
Duncan, Archie 146
Duncan, Betty 195
Duncan, Trevor 110
Dunlop, Joe 77
Dunn, Michael 191
Dunning, Jessica 204
Dunning, Ruth 150
Dunnock, Mildred 255
Dunsford, John 105, 176, 288
Dupuis, Jean 263
D'Usseau, Arnaud 143, 222
Dwyer, Hilary 23, 50, 211, 313, 315
Dwyer, Leslie 85, 184
Dyall, Valentine 37, 141, 146
Dyneley, Peter 152
Dyrenforth, James 37, 108

Earl, John G. 149, 248
Earl, John St. John 74
The Earth Dies Screaming 95
Easdale, Brian 215
East, Susanna 107
Eastwood, James 70
Eaton, Shirley 261, 305
Eatwell, Brian 1, 82, 177, 245
Ebert, Gunter 89
Ebbinghouse, Bernard 160, 189, 193, 265
Eccles, Jeremy 80
Eddington, Paul 71
Eden, Mark 53, 242
Edwards, Bill 111
Edwards, Glynn 19, 26, 116
Edwards, Mark 20, 281
Edwards, Maudie 288
Edwards, Meredith 97
Ege, Julie 45, 46, 109, 171, 191
Eggar, Samantha 79, 304
Ehrlich, Max 318
Ekland, Britt 9, 96, 200, 310
Elder, John 27, 56, 98, 117, 118, 132, 166, 172, 218, 228, 229, 267
The Electronic Monster see *Escapement*
Eles, Sandor 5, 44, 98
Elliott, Denham 154, 277, 294
Elliott, Peter 11, 203, 280
Elliott, Sam 169

Ellis, Christopher 206
Ellis, Don 185
Ellis, Mary 275
Ellis, William 92
Ellsworth, Paul 154
Elms, Albert 22, 179
Elphick, John 21, 108, 114, 136, 257
Emmott, Basil 54
Encore see *The Comeback*
Enders, Robert 301
Endfield, Cy 192
Endless Night 96
Enemy from Space see *Quatermass II*
Eno, Brian 73
Ercy, Elizabeth 251
Erich, Heidi 69
Escapement 97
Eshley, Norman 18, 151
Essex, David 8
Estate of Insanity see *The Black Torment*
Estridge, Robin 100
Evans, Barry 76
Evans, Clifford 56, 166
Evans, Edith 45
Evans, Gene 15
Evans, Jessie 44
Evans, John 304
Evans, Maurice 23
Evans, Roy 61
The Evil of Frankenstein 98
Ewing, Barbara 93, 280
Exorcism at Midnight see *Naked Evil*
Expose 99
Exton, Clive 87, 150, 201, 269
Eye of the Devil 100
The Eyes of Annie Jones 101
Eyewitness 102

The Face of Fu Manchu 103
Fahey, Brian 52
Fahrenheit 451 104
Fairbank, Jay 250, 265
Fairhurst, Lyn 74
Fairman, Churton 77
Faithfull, Geoffrey 42, 111, 193, 252, 271, 299
Faithfull, Marianne 130
Fanatic 105
Farbrother, Pamela 50, 123
Farleigh, Lynn 301
Farmer, Suzan 94, 184, 217, 228
Farrell, Charles 44
Farrell, Colin 168
Farrow, Mia 18, 126
Faulds, Andrew 72, 283
Faulkner, Max 18
Faulkner, Sally 23, 293
Faye, Janina 62, 90, 138, 142, 196, 286
Fear in the Night 106
The Fearless Vampire Killers see *Dance of the Vampires*

Feller, Catherine 56
Felton, Felix 97
Fennell, Albert 5, 28, 170, 81, 170, 204, 159, 289
Fenton, Bernie 74
Fernback, Gerald A. 221
Ferrer, Mel 138
Ferrer, Tony 296
Ferris, Barbara 34, 278
Ferris, Paul 19, 47, 217, 251, 313
Fetterman, Peter 126, 195
Ffrangcon-Davies, Gwen 71, 312
Fiander, Lewis 81, 82
Field, Alexander 60
Field, Shirley Anne 58, 147, 215
Field, Virginia 95
Fielding, Fenella 30, 212
Fielding, Jerry 206
The Fiend 107
The Fiendish Ghouls see *The Flesh and the Fiends*
Fiend Without a Face 108
The Final Programme 109
Finch, Jon 109, 121, 145, 292
Fine, Harry 122, 174, 284, 292
Finlay, Frank 8, 65, 195, 285
Finn, Catherine 47, 65
Finney, Albert 201
Fire Maidens of Outer Space 110
First Man Into Space 111
First Men in the Moon 112
Fisher, Gerry 3, 18
Fisher, George 298
Fisher, Terence 24, 51, 56, 71, 90, 94, 95, 115, 117, 118, 119, 135, 146, 148, 176, 187, 202, 161, 218, 232, 253, 259, 286
Five Million Years to Earth see *Quatermass and the Pit*
Flannery, Seamus 230
Fleischer, Richard 18, 269
Fleming, Brandon 314
Flemyng, Gordon 57, 84
Flemyng, Robert 19, 23
The Flesh and Blood Show 113
The Flesh and the Fiends 114
Flood, Gerald 123
Fodor, Ladislas 278
Fontaine, Joan 312
Foot, Geoffrey 67, 170
Forbes, Bryan 225, 237, 242
Forbes, Scott 183
Forbes-Robertson, John 171, 292, 294
Forbes-Robertson, Peter 197, 161, 240
Ford, Brylo 193
Ford, Carole Ann 62
Ford, Derek 17, 240, 298
Ford, Donald 17, 298
Fores, Helen 111
Force, Lewis J. 197
Forsyth, Brigit 199
Forsyth, Frank 4, 65, 98, 223, 271, 295

Fortescue, Kenneth 25
Foster, Barry 121, 285
Foster, David 169
Foster, Maurice 221
Four Sided Triangle 115
Fowlds, Derek 118, 281
Fowler, George 110
Fowler, Harry 110
Fox, Edward 31, 125, 182
Fox, Marcia 46
Fragment of Fear 116
Frampton, Peter 250
Francis, Derek 27, 228, 277, 279
Francis, Freddie 45, 47, 62, 65, 83, 93, 98, 132, 155, 159, 172, 189, 196, 202, 207, 214, 223, 246, 250, 264, 265, 274, 280, 282, 295
Francis, Kevin 132, 172, 217
Francis, Scott 18
Frank, Horst 296
Frankel, Benjamin 212
Frankel, Cyril 196, 312
Frankenstein and the Monster from Hell 117
Frankenstein Created Woman 118
Frankenstein Must Be Destroyed 119
Frankenstein: The True Story 120
Franklin, Gretchen 184, 285
Franklin, Pamela 5, 159, 170, 194
Franklyn, John 5
Franklyn, William 226, 234, 249
Franks, Chloe 154, 264, 282, 309
Fraser, Bill 29
Fraser, Constance 254
Fraser, Helen 230
Fraser, John 230, 239
Fraser, Peter 251
Fraser, Shelagh 23, 87, 217
The Freak Maker see *The Mutations*
Frederick, Lynn 3, 209, 239, 291
French, Barbara 198
Frenzy 121
Friedland, Dennis 41
Friend, Philip 302
Fright 122
Frightmare 123
Frobe, Gert 165
From Beyond the Grave 124
The Frozen Dead 125
Fuchsberger, Joachim 103
Fuest, Robert 1, 5, 82, 109, 315
Full Circle 126
Fuller, Suzanne 268
Fuller, Tex 209
The Full Treatment 127
Furie, Sidney J. 78, 248
Furneaux, Yvonne 187, 230
Furse, Judith 186
Furst, Joseph 25, 102, 273

Gabriel, John 56
Gael, Anna 319
Gale, John 82

Galicia, Jose Luis 190
Galili, Hal 303
Gallu, Samuel 273
Gambon, Michael 13, 210
Gamley, Douglas 4, 9, 13, 37, 124, 146, 168, 175, 197, 264, 278, 288, 294
Gamlin, Lionel 242
The Gamma People 128
Gammell, Robin 126
Garady, Ken 84
Gardner, Ava 75
Gardner, Caron 98
Garfield, John D. 133
Garrie, John 175
Garth, David 195, 257
Gasciogne, Martin 319
Gates, Tudor 122, 174, 284, 292
Gatliff, Frank 221
Gaunt, Valerie 51, 90
Gayson, Eunice 232
Gearon, Valerie 160
Geesin, Ron 130
Geeson, Judy 16, 85, 87, 106, 269
Geeson, Sally 50, 211
Gelardi, A.M.G. 254
Gell, William 273
Genn, Leo 35, 76, 96, 123
George, George W. 205, 285
George, Susan 76, 102, 122, 251
Georges-Picot, Olga 178, 217
Gershwin, Jerry 75
Gerrard, Sean 298
Getty, J. Ronald 191
Ghost Ship 129
Ghost Story 130
The Ghoul (1933) 131
The Ghoul (1975) 132
The Giant Behemoth see *Behemoth the Sea Monster*
Gibbs, Anthony 78, 248
Gibbs, Gerald 52, 69, 226, 316
Gibson, Alan 48, 92, 234
Gidding, Nelson 141
Gielgud, John 120
Gifford, Alan 69, 237, 287
Gilbert, Philip 105, 125
Gill, John 201
Gillespie, Dana 173, 216, 297
Gilliat, Sidney 96
Gilling, John 114, 128, 135, 186, 188, 198, 219, 243
Gilmore, Denis 222, 279
Gilmore, Peter 303
Gilpin, Toni 135
Gingold, Hermoine 165
Giovanni, Paul 310
The Girl and the Monster see *Four Sided Triangle*
Girly see *Mumsy, Nanny, Sonny and Girly*
Gladwin, Joe 201
Glass, Paul 277
Glendenning, Candace 113, 236
Glover, Julian 224, 273, 315

Godfrey, Derek 1, 139, 297
Godfrey, Tommy 256
Godsell, Vanda 95, 167, 243
Godwin, Frank 68
Goffe, Rusty 77
Goldblatt, Harold 34, 182, 229
Golden, Michael 179
The Golden Voyage of Sinbad 133
Goldie, Wyndham 258
Golding, Richard 283
Goldoni, Lelia 155, 273
Goldstein, William 1
Goldstone, John 109
Gomez, Ramiro 143
Gonzalez, Fernando 133
Good, Maurice 65, 224, 246, 274, 282
Goode, Frederick 137
Goodliffe, Michael 63, 135, 277
Goodman, David Z. 259
Goodwin, Harold 119, 187, 288
Goodwin, Ron 34, 62, 121, 299
Goolden, Richard 162
Goorney, Howard 14, 41, 98, 235
Gordon, Bernard 62, 143
Gordon, Claire 167
Gordon, Colin 152, 204, 223
Gordon, Don 318
Gordon, Dorothy 136, 153
Gordon, Michael 203
Gordon, Nora 147, 194
Gordon, Richard 31, 42, 52, 108, 111, 136, 144, 161, 193, 221, 281
Gordon-Orr, Denis 67
Gorgo 134
The Gorgon 135
Gorman, Shay 101, 161
Goss, Helen 148, 286
Gossage, John 128
Goswell, Tom 266
Gotell, Walter 58
Gothard, Michael 72, 241, 303, 309
Gough, Michael 16, 41, 83, 90, 144, 147, 167, 170, 218, 236, 246, 274, 282, 305
Gough, Monte 231
Gough, Simon 41
Goulder, Stanley 193
Grace, Martin 144
Grace, Sally 130
Grady, Michael 263
Graham, Imogen 230
Graham, Michael 54
Graham Scott, Peter 27, 142
Grainer, Ron 156, 201
Granat, Frank 285
Granger, Marc 3
Grant, Arthur 2, 20, 27, 56, 58, 68, 71, 93, 106, 118, 119, 188, 212, 214, 218, 219, 224, 229, 243, 254, 259, 267, 270, 279, 312
Grant, Cy 10
Grant, Moray 145, 157, 238, 291, 292

Grant, Stanley 129
Graves, Bryan 3
Graves, Theresa 290
The Graveyard see *Persecution*
Gray, Barry 88
Gray, Carole 25, 54, 74, 161
Gray, Charles 13, 71, 169, 233
Gray, Donald 237, 276
Gray, Nadia 180
Gray, Steve 99
Gray, Willoughby 257
Graysmark, Jon 75
Grayson, Diane 18
Gregg, Hubert 262
Gregg, Joyce 314
Green, Danny 212
Green, Frances 196
Green, Guy 249
Green, Nigel 42, 44, 103, 164, 181, 246, 257
Green, Pamela 215
Green, Pat 184
Greenberg, Robert 13
Greene, David 245
Greene, Leon 71
Greene, Richard 264, 296
Greenlaw, Verina 181
Greenwood, Jack 142, 147, 160
Greenwood, Joan 192
Greenwood, Miles 222
Greenwood, Paul 123
Greer, Luanshya 274
Gregory, Johnny 198
Gregory, Tea 237
Gregson, John 122
Greley, Jack 304
Grellis, Brian 106
Grenfell, Joyce 212
Greville, Edmond T. 138
Greville-Bell, Anthony 272
Grey, David 7
Gribble, Bernard 142, 265
Griffin, David 19, 282
Griffith, Eva 301
Griffith, Hugh 1, 45, 50, 109, 172, 309, 315
Griffith, Kenneth 36, 50, 231
Griffiths, Leon 114
Grimes, Bruce 43
Grimes, Colin 87, 210
Grip of the Strangler 136
Grote, William 179
Guest, Val 2, 63, 127, 226, 227, 307
Gunn, Gilbert 258
Gunning, Christopher 139
Gur, Alizia 137
Gurney, Sharon 41, 67
Gutowski, Gene 59, 230
Guy, Jennifer 217
Gwillim, Jack 36, 55, 164
Gwynn, Michael 164, 196, 232, 238, 299, 305
Gynt, Greta 22, 60

Index

Haddon, Carol 197
Hafenrichter, Oswald 47, 50, 65, 84, 138, 223, 246, 282, 294, 295
Hafner, Ingrid 22
Hagar, Karol 308
Hagg, Robert 39
Haggard, Piers 225, 235
Haines, Alan 101
Haines, Patricia 198, 300
Haisman, Mervyn 53
Hale, Georgina 72
Hale, John 183
Hales, Gordon 38, 299
Halevy, Julian 143, 222
Haliday, Bryant 52, 69, 221, 281
Hall, Brian 168
Hall, Cameron 21
Hall, Harvey 174, 181, 284, 292
Haller, Daniel 38, 181, 184
Hallett, May 60
Hallett, Neil 300
Halliday, Peter 300
Hallowi, Maria 137
Hamer, Robert 66
Hamill, John 12, 209, 281
Hamilton, Chico 230
Hamilton, Gary 281
Hamilton, Wendy 238
Hamlett, Dilys 8
Hammond, Marcus 219
Hammond, Peter 316
Hampshire, Susan 195, 201
Hampton, Orville H. 248
Hancock, Sheila 6, 201
Handford, Leslie 273
The Hand of Night 137
Handl, Irene 220
The Hands of Orlac 138
Hands of the Ripper 139
The Hands of the Strangler see *The Hands of Orlac*
Hanley, Jenny 75, 113, 238
Hanley, Jimmy 173, 237
Hanna, Robert 171
Hannah, James Jr. 61
Hannon, Peter 126
Harback, William O. 199
Hardiman, Marguerite 77
Hardin, Ty 16
Harding, Reg 18
Harding, Vincent 29
Hardtmuth, Paul 51, 78, 276
Hardwicke, Cedric 131
Hardy, Robert 16, 61, 222, 269
Hare, Ken 46
Hargreaves, Lance Z. 11, 111
Harlow, April 197
Harrington, Curtis 309
Harris, Alan 17
Harris, Brad 191
Harris, Graham 12, 158, 200
Harris, Johnny 116
Harris, Julie 141
Harris, Richard A. 91

Harrison, John 176
Harrison, John Simco 298
Harrison, Kathleen 131
Harrison, Philip 5, 44, 109, 290, 315
Harrison, Richard 80
Harrison, Roger 31
Harrison, Sally 4
Harryhausen, Ray 112, 133, 164, 192, 213, 275
Hart, Susan 38
Hartford-Davis, Robert 17, 43, 107, 158
Hartstone, Christopher 29
Harvard, Dafydd 12
Harvey, Edward 32, 58
Harvey, James 149
Harvey, John 65, 212, 259, 274
Harvey, Laurence 205
Harvey, Verna 206
Harvey, Walter 227
Harwood, Ronald 102
Hassall, Imogen 158, 189, 307
Hasse, Charles 66
Hastings, Michael 206
The Haunted House of Horror 140
The Haunted Strangler see *Grip of the Strangler*
The Haunting 141
The Haunting of Julia see *Full Circle*
Hauser, Gilgi 62
Havers, Nigel 126
Hawdon, Robin 14, 26, 63, 182, 307, 319
Hawkins, Carol-Anne 307
Hawkins, Jack 265, 272
Hawkins, Michael 148
Hawks, Stanley 254
Hawksworth, John 319
Haworth, Jill 140, 162, 191, 281
Hawtrey, Charles 30, 271, 276, 319
Hayden, Frank 247
Hayden, Linda 99, 175, 205, 235, 267, 290
Hayden, Sterling 109
Hayers, Sidney 8, 36, 204, 231
Hayes, Brian 85, 303
Hayes, Melvin 51, 114
Hayes, Patricia 271
Hayles, Brian 210
Hayter, James 26, 115, 145
Hazelton, Phillip 245
Head, Nicholas 53
The Headless Ghost en>142
Heald, Margaret 293
Healy, David 174
Heathcote, Thomas 202, 299
Heathcott, Roger 161
Hedley, Jack 6, 311
Heffer, Richard 80
Heilbron, Lorna 47, 263
Heiman, Nachum 195
Heinz, Gerald 74, 221, 298

Heller, Otto 55, 215
Hemmings, David 100, 116, 301
Hempel, Anouska 238
Hendel, Kenneth 76
Henderson, Don 132
Hendry, Ian 28, 34, 88, 230, 264, 272
Heneker, David 286
Henley, Drewe 307
Hennessy, Peter 32, 101
Henry, Buck 177
Henry, Victor 251
Hensen, Basil 109, 125
Henson, Gladys 112
Henson, Nicky 22, 290, 313
Herbert, Bryan 60
Herbert, George 144
Herbert, Percy 45, 87, 107, 192, 202, 203, 213, 226
Herder, Lawrence 112
Herrmann, Bernard 96, 104, 164, 192, 199, 275, 285
Hessler, Gordon 33, 50, 133, 190, 211, 241
Hewitt, Celia 236, 245
Heyland, Michael 38
Heyward, Louis M. 1, 38, 50, 53, 82, 190, 211, 241, 292, 309, 313, 315
Heywood, Anne 295
Heywood, Pat 189, 269, 309
Heyworth, Malcolm B. 235
Hickox, Douglas 272
Higgins, Edward 314
Hignett, Mary 41, 247
Hildyard, Jack 13
Hill, Douglas 197
Hill, James 29
Hiller, Wendy 31
Hillier, Erwin 100
Hilton, Tony 305
Hinde, Madeline 107, 158
Hinds, Anthony 24, 51, 56, 58, 90, 98, 105, 166, 196, 212, 214, 218, 226, 227, 232, 259, 316
Hines, Ronald 152, 242
Hinwood, Peter 233
Hird, Thora 206, 227
Hitchcock, Alfred 121
Hobbs, Carlton 61
Hobbs, William 28
Hodge, Jonathan 318
Hodges, Ken 8, 15, 231, 245, 255
Hodgson, Brian 170
Hoesli, John 18, 240, 287
Hogan, Bosco 317
Hogg, Ian 169
Hojmark, Peter 318
Holden, Jan 110, 140, 259
Holden, Maxine 37
Holder, Roy 168, 222
Holding, Derek 160, 221
Holland, Hilary 177
Holloway, Stanley 220
Holmes, David 102

Holt, Patrick 172, 209, 222, 302
Holt, Seth 20, 194
Honeymoon of Fear see *Fear in the Night*
Hood, Noel 51
Hooker, Ted 49
Hooper, Ewan 93
Hope, Gary 197
Hordern, Michael 68, 254, 272
Horne, David 253
Horner, Penelope 91
Horner, Yvonne 213, 247
Horror Express 143
Horror Hospital 144
Horror Hotel see *City of the Dead*
Horror House see *The Haunted House of Horror*
Horror of Dracula see *Dracula*
The Horror of Frankenstein 145
The Horror of It All 146
Horror on Snape Island see *Tower of Evil*
The Horrors of Burke and Hare see *Burke and Hare*
Horrors of the Black Museum 147
Hotchkis, John 41
Hough, John 102, 170, 284
Houghton, Don 92, 171, 234
The Hound of the Baskervilles 148
House in Marsh Road 149
The House in Nightmare Park 150
House of Crazies see *Asylum*
House of Fright see *The Two Faces of Dr. Jekyll*
House of Mortal Sin 151
House of Mystery 152
House of Whipcord 153
The House on Straw Hill see *Expose*
The House That Dripped Blood 154
The House That Vanished see *Scream and Die*
Houston, Donald 180, 260, 265
Houston, Glyn 160
Houston, Renee 114, 172, 218, 230
Howard, Ben 168
Howard, Elden 268
Howard, Ronald 55, 217
Howard, Tom 134, 141, 278, 287
Howard, Trevor 45, 217
Howard, Vanessa 19, 43, 189, 306
Howells, Ursula 83, 189
Howerd, Frankie 150
Howes, Sally Ann 66
Howey, David 113
Howlett, Noel 166
Howman, Karl 99
Huby, Robert 97
Hudd, Roy 19
Hudd, Walter 237
Hudson, Vanda 36
Hughes, Geoffrey 231
Hughes, Ken 276
Hughes, Raymond 44
Hughes, Roddy 254

Hulke, Bob 295
The Human Monster see *Dark Eyes of London*
Hume, Alan 10, 30, 83, 124, 166, 168, 169, 170, 216
Hume, Marjorie 51
Humphries, Barry 14
Humphries, Dave 126
Hunnicut, Gayle 116, 170, 255, 301
Hunt, Martita 24
Hunt, Peter 257
Hunter, Ian 78
Hunter, John 196
Hunter, Russell 267
Hunter, T. Hayes 131
Hunter, Tab 38
Huntington, Lawrence 211, 302
Huntley, Raymond 17, 187, 263
Hurndall, Richard 157
Hurndell, William 38
Hurst, David 186
Hurst, Peter 130
Hurt, John 132, 269
Hurt, Marsha 92
Hussey, Olivia 31
Hutcheson, David 98
Hutchinson, Harry 149
Huth, Harold 131
Hutton, Brian G. 205
Hutton, Linda 177
Hutton, Robert 50, 179, 264, 274, 280, 282, 302
Hutton, Robert B. 217
Huxtable, Judy 76, 223, 241
Hyde, Kenneth 254
Hyde, Roy 228, 229
Hyde-White, Wilfrid 31, 261
Hyer, Martha 112
Hylton, Jane 36, 152
Hyman, Kenneth 270
Hyman, Prudence 135
Hysteria 155

I Don't Want to Be Born 156
I, Monster 157
Ibbetson, Arthur 105, 120
Illing, Peter 22, 74, 97
Immediate Disaster see *Stranger from Venus*
In the Devil's Garden see *Assault*
Incense for the Damned 158
Ingham, Barrie 84, 160
Ingham, Wendy 319
Inglis, Tony 52, 220
Inn of the Frightened People see *Revenge*
The Innocents 159
Invasion 160
Invisible Creature see *House in Marsh Road*
Ireland, Anthony 253
Ireland, John 10, 124, 216
Irving, Penny 40, 153
Isherwood, Christopher 120

Island of Terror 161
Island of the Burning Damned see *Night of the Big Heat*
It! 162
Iveria, Miki 273
Ives, Burl 165
Ives, Frederick 137

Jack, Colette 200
Jack the Ripper 163
Jackson, Dan 183, 192, 193
Jackson, David 20
Jackson, Freda 24, 184, 243
Jackson, Jocelyn 32
Jacoby, Hans 257
Jaffe, Carl 97, 111, 276
Jaffe, Sam 272
Jagger, Dean 316
James, Donald 88
James, Godfrey 10, 168, 211
James, Graham 145
James, Ken 304
James, Richard 213
James, Robert 28
James, Sidney 225
Jameson, Louise 77
Jameson, Pauline 126, 205
Jameson, Susan 157
Janson, Horst 28
Jarman, Reginald 317
Jarvis, Martin 267
Jason and the Argonauts 164
Jaspe, Jose 143
Jayne, Jennifer 83, 155, 274, 283
Jayston, Michael 45, 85, 265
Jeavons, Colin 239
Jeffrey, Peter 1, 44, 82, 396
Jeffries, Lionel 3, 102, 112, 165, 232, 309
Jessel, Patricia 37
Jessop, Clytie 159, 207
Jessop, Peter 40, 113, 123, 151, 153, 239, 298
Jewell, Robert 271
John, Robert 46
Johns, Glynis 294
Johns, Margo 167
Johns, Mervyn 66, 151, 208, 212
Johnson, Bari 193
Johnson, Fred 37, 51, 78, 266
Johnson, Herb 278
Johnson, Laurie 5, 28, 112
Johnson, Michael 174, 193
Johnson, Richard 40, 141
Johnston, Margaret 204, 223
Johnston, Oliver 79, 162, 279
Jones, Barry 260
Jones, Ceri 67
Jones, Disley 122, 169, 255, 281
Jones, Douglas 293
Jones, Freddie 8, 119, 178, 234, 250, 290
Jones, Gemma 72
Jones, Jack 40

Jones, Kenneth V. (aka Ken Jones) 11, 37, 79, 221, 278, 279, 281, 295, 309
Jones, Marshall 50, 190, 241
Jones, Nicholas 41
Jones, Norman 1, 183
Jones, Paul 68
Jones, Robert 28, 79, 81, 170, 181, 244, 247
Jones, Roger Glyn 61
Jordon, Patrick 8
Jordon, William 137
Josephs, Wilfred 50, 61, 65, 105
Journey to the Far Side of the Sun see *Doppleganger*
Joyce, Yootha 26, 105, 116, 199
Judd, Edward 63, 112, 160, 161, 294, 297
Jules Verne's Rocket to the Moon 165
Julian, Chuck 252
Julius, Maxine 7, 49
Junge, Alfred 131
Juraga, Boris 80
Juran, Jerry 78
Juran, Nathan 112
Jurgens, Curt 294
Justice, James Robertson 79, 103, 319
Jympson, John 121, 205

Kahn, Ronald J. 189
Kalinski, Edward 123
Kandel, Aben 16, 45, 147, 167, 282
Kane, Jackson D. 177
Kann, Lilly 32
Kanter, Jay 67, 206
Karlin, Miriam 39
Karloff, Boris 42, 53, 131, 136, 184, 251
Kastner, Elliott 75, 206
Kaufmann, Christine 190
Kaufmann, Maurice 1, 15, 35, 105, 122, 152, 179, 227
Kavanagh, Kevin 261
Kay, Bernard 245, 274, 282, 313
Kaye, Clarissa 120
Kaye, Lila 18
Kazan, Maria 242
Keane, Lawrence 240
Keats, Viola 311, 312
Keel, Howard 62
Keeling, Kenneth 49
Keen, Geoffrey 16, 147, 182, 267
Keigan, Berry 237
Keir, Andrew 57, 94, 224
Keith, Sheila 40, 123, 151, 153
Kelland, John 12
Kellerman, Barbara 226
Kellner, William 163
Kelly, Claire 5
Kelly, James 12, 200
Kelly, Sean 112
Kemp, Jeremy 102
Kemp, Lindsay 310
Kemp, Valli 82

Kempinski, Thomas 58
Kemplen, Ralph 254
Kendal, William 286
Kendall, Henry 243
Kendall, Suzy 8, 35
Kennaway, James 182
Kent, Jean 22, 136
Keogh, Barbara 1
Kerr, Deborah 100, 159
Kerr, Fraser 273
Kerr, Richard 107
Kerridge, Mary 52
Kettlewell, Ruth 209
Key, Janet 4, 92, 156, 292
Keys, Rod 30, 202
Kier, Udo 99
Kilburn, Terence 108
Kimberley, Maggie 188, 313
Kinberg, Judson 291
King, Diane 105, 274
King, Frank 134
King, Ivan 305
King, Maurice 134
King, Roger 12
Kingston, Kiwi 98, 155
Kinnear, Roy 267
Kinski, Klaus 35, 261
Kinski, Nastassja 277
Kirchin, Basil 1, 191, 245
Kirgo, George 301
Kirwan, Patrick 60
Kiss of Evil see *The Kiss of the Vampire*
The Kiss of the Vampire 166
Klauber, Gertan 298
Klinger, Michael 17, 230
Knapp, Bud 196
Kneale, Nigel 2, 112, 224, 225, 226, 227, 312
Knef (aka Neff, Hildegard) 173, 262
Knight, David 207
Knight, Esmond 215
Knight, Jack T. 319
Knight, Peter 53
Knight, Terence 14
Knowles, Bernard 252
Knox, Alexander 58, 223
Kohn, John 272
Komeda, Christopher 59
Konga 167
Konopka, Magda 307
Kopelson, Arnold 169
Kossoff, David 208, 262, 286
Kotze, John 261
Koumani, Maya 110
Kovack, Nancy 164
Krampf, Gunther 131
Krause, Bernard 109
Krish, John 289
Kronos see *Captain Kronos Vampire Hunter*
Kruger, Hardy 200
Kruse, John 8, 231
Kubrick, Stanley 39, 287

Kwouk, Burt 54, 270
Kydd, Sam 148, 149, 221, 269

Lacey, Catherine 188, 220, 243, 251
Lacey, Margaret 242
Lacey, Ronald 49, 59
Ladd, Alan, Jr. 67, 75, 206
Ladd, David 67
Laffan, Patricia 70
Laing, Robert 121
Laird, Jenny 299
Lambert, Jack 94, 195
Lambert, Verity 225
Lamont, Duncan 26, 47, 98, 118, 210, 224, 312
Lamont, Jack O. 302
Lanchbury, Karl 292
Landau, Richard 227, 253
Landen, Dinsdale 228
Lander, David 268
Landi, Marla 111, 148
Land of the Minotaur see *The Devil's Men*
The Land That Time Forgot 168
Landon, Avice 235
Landor, Ray 69
Landor, Rosalyn 3, 171
Lane, Jackie 128
Lang, Harold 214, 227
Lang, Howard 141
Lang, Robert 205
Lang, Stevenson 248
Lange, Harry 287, 318
Langley, Bryan 60
Langley, Noel 262
Lanning, Dennis 318, 319
Lanning, Howard 19, 23, 53, 308, 313
Lantry, Kenneth 142
Lapotaire, Jane 7, 48
Larkin, Mary 222
Larman, Cherry 244
Larraz, Joseph (Jose) 240, 263, 293
Larussa, Adrienne 177
Lassally, Walter 64
The Last Days of Man on Earth see *The Final Programme*
Latham, Philip 94
Latimer, Hugh 129, 258
Latimer, Michael 247
Laurenson, James 8
Laurie, John 1, 70, 229
Laurimore, John 76
Lavagnino, Angelo Francisco 134
Laverick, June 114
Lavi, Daliah 165
Lavis, Arthur 33, 95
Law, John Phillip 133, 255
Law, Pamela 69
Lawrence, Andrea 44, 117
Lawrence, Delphi 176
Lawrence, John 7
Lawrence, Marjie 139, 157

Lawrence, Oswald 146
Lawrence, Quentin 283
Lawrence, Sheldon 22, 179
Lawrence, Shirley 237
Lawson, Arthur 173, 215, 295
Lawson, Gerald 78, 297
Lawson, Leigh 130
Lawson, Sarah 71, 202
Lea, Daphne 240
Leader, Anton M. 34
Leaver, Philip 163, 186
Lebor, Stanley 156
Le Borg, Reginald 101
Leder, Herbert J. 108, 125, 162
Ledrov, D.B. 245
Lee, Bernard 83, 117, 295
Lee, Christopher 25, 35, 37, 42, 51, 53, 61, 67, 71, 83, 90, 93, 94, 103, 138, 135, 143, 148, 154, 157, 176, 187, 202, 210, 211, 220, 228, 234, 238, 241, 244, 246, 266, 267, 270, 273, 277, 286, 296, 310
Lee, David 181
Lee, John 32, 79, 252
Lee, Margaret 35, 89
Lee, Rosanna 250
Leech, Richard 270
The Legacy 169
The Legend of Hell House 170
The Legend of Spider Forest see *Venom*
The Legend of the Seven Golden Vampires 171
Legend of the Werewolf 172
Leggatt, Alison 62, 196
Legrand, Michel 315
Lehmann, Beatrix 31
Leigh, Laurie 214
Leigh, Suzanna 65, 107, 173, 174, 250
Leigh-Hunt, Barbara 121
Leigh-Hunt, Ronald 52
Leighton, Margaret 120, 124
Leighton, Sara 314
Le Mesurier, John 21, 38, 100, 148
Lemkow, Tutte 259
Lemont, John 167
Lennon, Toby 191
Lennox, Michael 84
Lenny, Bill 2, 63, 90, 127
Leon, Valerie 20, 319
Leonard, Don 46
Leppard, Alex 240
Le Sage, Bill 268
Lester, Henry E. 260
Lester, Mark 102, 104, 200, 309
Levine, Joseph E. 163, 206
Levinson, Barry 3
Levinson, Nancy 263
Levison, Ken 175
Levka, Uta 211, 241
Levy, Gerry 23, 140, 308
Levy, Louis 131, 208
Levy, Ori 185

Lewis, Fiona 59, 82, 91
Lewis, Michael J. 169, 178, 272
Lewis, Ronald 127, 266
Lewis, Russell 265, 301
Lewiston, Denis 99
Lewthwaite, Bill 29, 208
Leyton, John 239
Licudi, Gabriella 289
Lidstone, Gail 12
Lightfoot, John 107
Liles, Ronald 198, 202
Liljedahl, Marie 89
Lincoln, Henry 53
Lind, Gillian 4, 106
Linden, Jennie 84, 207, 290
Linder, Leslie 18, 269
Lindfors, Viveca 58
Lindley, Barbara 91
Lindsay, Delia 238
Lindup, David 255
Line, Helga 143
Linehan, Barry 311
Ling, Barbara Yu 234
Lippert, Robert L. 54, 95, 252, 311, 146
Liter, Monia 110
Littledale, Anabel 8
Litvinoff, Si 39, 177
Lloyd, Jeremy 290
Lloyd, Lala 108
Lloyd, Sue 43
Lloyd, Ted 15
Lockhart, Calvin 13
Lockyer, Malcolm 161, 202
Lodge, Andrew 13
Lodge, David 3, 158, 288
Lodge, Jean 52, 101, 160
Logan, Michael 248
Logie, Seymour 314
Logue, Christopher 72
Lom, Herbert 4, 9, 61, 88, 89, 190, 192, 218
Loncraine, Richard 126
Long, Stanley A. 19, 251
Longden, John 226
Longhurst, Jeremy 135, 252
Loong, Chen Tien 171
Lord, Justine 180, 197
Loring, Lynn 88
Losey, Joseph 58
The Lost Continent 173
Lotis, Dennis 37
Lourie, Eugene 15, 134
Love, Bessie 293
The Love Factor see *Zeta One*
Lovejoy, Ray 287
Lovell, Angela 137
Lovell, Roderick 186
Lowe, Heather 255
Lucan, Arthur 186
Lucas, William 202, 243, 316
Luckham, Cyril 257
Lugosi, Bela 60, 186
Lumley, Joanna 75, 234
Lust for a Vampire 174

Lutyens, Elisabeth 83, 95, 196, 214, 223, 246, 252, 271, 273
Lyle, Jane 73
Lynch, Sean 10
Lynley, Carol 31, 245
Lynn, Ann 17
Lynn, Robert 79
Lyon, Richard 142

Ma, James 171
Macaulay, Tom 12
MacAvin, Josie 46
MacCorkindale, Simon 225
Macdonald, David 70
MacGinnis, Niall 161, 164, 196, 203, 280
MacGowran, Jack 15, 27, 59
MacGregor, Scott 20, 26, 48, 78, 110, 117, 125, 145, 162, 185, 238, 256, 261, 267, 291, 292, 296
MacIlwraith, Bill 6
Mackay, Angus 231
Mackay, Barry 276
MacKay, Fulton 210
MacKenzie, Robert 314
Mackerell, Vivian 130
Mackey, John 41
Mackie, Leslie 310
Mackie, Phil 295
MacLennon, Elizabeth 150
MacNaughton, Alan 118, 316
Macnee, Patrick 158
MacOwan, Norman 37
MacPhail, Angus 66
Madden, Ciaran 13
Madden, Peter 108, 117, 166, 220
Maddern, Victor 21, 35, 173
Madhouse 175
Madhouse Mansion see *Ghost Story*
Madigan, Thomas F. 318
Madison, Leigh 15
Madoc, Philip 16, 57, 81, 88
Magee, Patrick 4, 9, 39, 68, 107, 109, 181, 184, 242, 246, 264
Mahoney, Louis 219, 247
Mailleux, Marie-Paul 263
Maine, Charles Eric 97, 253, 276
Mainwaring, Daniel 33
Maitland, Marne 112, 218, 229, 259, 270
Malcolm, Christopher 255
Malcolm, John 308
Malleson, Miles 24, 66, 90, 112, 148, 215, 218, 295
Mallone, Wil 67
The Man Who Could Cheat Death 176
The Man Who Fell to Earth 177
The Man Who Haunted Himself 178
The Man Without a Body 179
Mango, Alec 258
Mania see *The Flesh and the Fiends*
Maniac 180

Mankowitz, Wolf 63
Mann, Edward Andrew 161, 191
Mann, Stanley 75, 272
Mansaray, Sam 13
Manson, Mary 54
Maraschal, Launce 276
Marcus, Peter 23, 308
Marder, Richard 14, 120
Marie, Ditte 318
Markham, Barbara 153
Markham, David 20, 318
Marks, Alfred 241
Marla, Norma 286, 288
Marle, Arnold 2, 176, 248
Marlowe, Linda 197, 252
Marmont, Percy 115
Marquand, Richard 169
Marriott, Anthony 65
Marriott, Sylvia 137
Marsden, Betty 102
Marsh, Carol 90
Marsh, Jean 61, 121, 289
Marsh, Keith 57
Marshall, Bryan 224
Marshall, Roger 4, 160, 273, 306
Marshall, Ted 2
Marshall, Zena 271
Martell, Philip 6
Martelli, Carlo 33, 55, 162, 247, 311
Marter, Ian 80
Martin, Gene (Eugenio) 143
Martin, John 268
Martin, Skip 35, 144, 181, 250, 291
Mascia, Tony 177
Maslansky, Paul 67, 102
Mason, Bert 97
Mason, Hilary 86, 156
Mason, James 120
The Masque of the Red Death 181
Massey, Anna 121, 215, 294
Massey, Daniel 31, 116, 294, 303
Massie, Paul 286
Masters, Tony 42, 63, 127, 254, 287, 318
Matania, Clelia 86
Mather, John 70, 237
Matheson, Judy 49, 113, 240
Matheson, Richard 71, 91, 105, 170, 204
Mathews, Kerwin 11, 180, 275
Mathews, Richard 234
Mathie, Marion 93
Mathieson, Muir 36, 305
Matthews, Christopher 18, 238, 241
Matthews, Francis 42, 94, 228, 232
Matthews, Geoffrey 62
Matthews, Jessie 278
Maude, Mary 49
Maureen, Molly 220
Maurey, Nicole 62
Maxim, John 94, 118, 244

Maxsted, Jack 164, 303
Maxted, Stanley 108
Maxwell, James 58, 78
Maxwell, Lois 96, 141, 237
Maxwell, Paul 141, 162
May, Anthony 209
May, Jack 32, 197
Maybanke, Laon 205
Mayersberg, Paul 177
Mayhew, Peter 111, 136
Maynard, George 258, 319
Mayne, Ferdy 59, 292
Mayne, Margo 252
Mayne, Tony 191
McAdam, Jack 304
McCabe, John 106
McCallum, David 120
McCallum, Neil 33, 83, 173, 185
McCarthy, John 97
McCarthy, Julia 151
McCarthy, Matt 151, 153
McClure, Doug 10, 168, 216, 303
McConnell, Keith 302
McCowen, Alec 121, 312
McCracken, Jenny 199
McCulloch, Ian 132, 162
McCullogh, Andrew 168
McDermott, Hugh 70, 112
McDonald, David 144
McDowall, Betty 112, 163
McDowall, Roddy 75, 162, 170
McDowell, Malcolm 39
McEnery, John 168
McEnery, Peter 31, 265
McFarland, Gary 100
McGillvray, David 123, 151, 153, 236, 239
McGreevy, Oliver 125
McGuffie, Bill 7, 57
McHugh, Jimmy 163
McIntosh, David 80
McIntosh, J.T. 237
McIntyre, Alastair 17, 59, 230
McKenna, T.P. 12
McKenzie, Alastair 319
McKern, Leo 63, 316
McLaren, Hollis 304
McLaren, John 111
McNaughton, R.Q. 108
McShane, Ian 75
McStay, Michael 55
McWhorter, Richard 80
Meaden, Dan 81
Meadows, Stanley 271
Meatloaf 233
Meddings, Derek 88
Medwin, Michael 201, 253
Meincke, Eva Marie 277
Melachrino, George 128
Melford, Jill 297
Melle, Gil 120
Mellor, James 197, 211
Melly, Andree 24, 146
Melvin, Murray 72, 130
Melzack, Julian 126

Mendez, Julie 244
Mercedes, Maria 186
Merchant, Vivien 121
Meredith, Andrew 255
Meredith, Burgess 280
Meredith, Penny 113
Merivale, John 36, 152
Merlin, Monica 230
Merrill, Gary 33, 192
Merritt, George 127, 157
Merrow, Jane 33, 139, 202
Metzger, Radley 31
Michael, Ralph 66
Michelle, Ann 153, 222, 300
Michelle, Vicki 300
Michie, Susan 251
Middlemass, Frank 119
Mikell, George 88
Mikhelson, Andre 34
Miles, Bernard 278
Milland, Ray 150
Miller, Arnold L. 19, 313
Miller, Frank 287
Miller, Garry 3
Miller, Magda 286
Miller, Mandy 249
Miller, Martin 34, 128, 218
Miller, Philip 92
Miller, Stanley 263
The Million Eyes of Su-Muru see *Sumuru*
Mills, Hayley 96, 285
Mills, Reginald 36, 315
Milton, Billy 184
Milton, Ernest 32
The Mind Benders 182
The Mind of Mr. Soames 183
Mingaye, Don 27, 56, 92, 94, 98, 118, 135, 166, 174, 183, 187, 188, 207, 214, 218, 219, 228, 229, 243, 244, 259, 274, 280, 286, 312
Minter, George 262
Minty, David 85
Miranda, Isa 89
Mitchell, Arthur 64
Mitchell, Bill 204
Mitchell, Charlotte 235
Mitchell, Norman 172
Mitchell, Warren 56, 185, 198, 283, 289, 308
Mitchell, Yvonne 41, 68
Mohyeddin, Zia 274
Moll, Peter 137
Mollison, Clifford 117
Monlaur, Yvonne 24, 36, 270
Monster of Terror 184
Montague, Lee 169
Monteros, Rosenda 244
Montez, Conchita 200
Montgomery, Bruce 25
Moody, Ron 172
Moon, George 184
Moon, Keith 250
Moon Zero Two 185

Moorcock, Michael 109, 168
Moore, Dudley 14
Moore, Evelyn 14
Moore, John 125
Moore, Kieron 62, 78, 237
Moore, Roger 178
Moore, Ted 62, 85, 128, 133, 222
Moorhead, Agnes 120
Morahan, Jim 11, 182, 313
More, Julian 158
Morell, Andre 15, 148, 188, 219, 243, 244, 269, 297
Morgan, Stanley 167
Morgan, Terence 55, 262
Morley, Donald 231
Morley, Robert 212, 260, 272
Morris, Ariro 231
Morris, Aubrey 20, 39, 198, 310
Morris, Beth 49
Morris, Brian 126
Morris, Ernest 268
Morris, Marianne 293
Morris, Mary 126
Morris, Oswald 91, 116
Morris, Reginald H. 304
Morris, Robert 118, 224
Morris, Wolfe 2
Morrison, Allan 25, 261, 296
Morrison, Greg 175
Morrow, Jo 275
Morse, Barry 9, 304
Mortimer, Tricia 123
Moss, Gerald 300
Mother Riley Meets the Vampire 186
Moulder-Brown, John 291
Mower, Patrick 50, 71, 158
Moxey, Hugh 248, 253
Moxey, John 35, 37
Moyens, Judi 148
Mueller, Andre 163
Muir, David 174, 189
Muir, Jean 288
Mulhare, Edward 100
Mulholland, Declan 168
Muller, Geoffrey 97, 147, 276
Mullins, Peter 221
Mulock, Al 11
The Mummy 187
The Mummy's Shroud 188
Mumsy, Nanny, Sonny and Girly 189
Munro, Caroline 1, 10, 28, 92, 133, 156
Munro, Janet 63, 283
Munroe, Carmen 193
Munt, Peter 97
Murcell, George 21
Murders in the Rue Morgue 190
Murphy, Dennis 100
Murphy, Mary 97
Murray, Barbara 264
Murray, Bill 43
Murray, Stephen 115
Murton, Lionel 319
Murton, Peter 205

Musgrave, Peter 42, 193, 271, 274, 291
The Mutations 191
My Son the Vampire see *Mother Riley Meets the Vampire*
Myers, Andy 52
Myers, Douglas 21
Myers, Stanley 75, 123, 151, 153, 239
Myles, Bruce 199
Mysterious Island 192

Nader, George 261
Nagy, Bill 11, 318
Naismith, Laurence 3, 299
Naked Evil 193
The Nanny 194
Napier, Russell 19, 162
Napier-Bell, Nicholas 12
Nappi, Malya 213
Nascimbene, Mario 46, 80, 213, 297, 307
Nash, Michael 173
Nasseck, Ralph 29
Nation, Terry 5, 84
Naylor, Tom 37
Neal, Patricia 199, 257
Neame, Christopher 92, 174, 209
Needs, James 6, 24, 27, 28, 51, 56, 55, 58, 71, 81, 90, 92, 93, 94, 98, 105, 117, 118, 135, 148, 155, 166, 173, 177, 180, 187, 188, 194, 196, 207, 212, 213, 214, 218, 219, 224, 226, 227, 228, 232, 238, 243, 244, 247, 249, 259, 266, 270, 286, 288, 292, 297, 312, 316
Neff, Hildegard see Knef, Hildegard
Neil, Hildegard 169, 178
Neil, Peter 237
Neither the Sea Nor the Sand 195
Nell, Christa 261
Nelson, Gene 276
Nelson-Keys, Anthony 71, 94, 118, 119, 135, 188, 210, 219, 224, 228, 229
Nesbitt, Cathleen 126
Nesbitt, Derren 26
Nettleton, John 5
Never Take Sweets from a Stranger 196
Neville, John 260, 289
Newark, Derek 38, 298
Newbrook, Peter 7, 17, 43, 49
Newlands, Anthony 35, 241
Newley, Anthony 316
Newman, Nanette 29, 242
Newman, Philip 308
Newton, Sally Anne 317
Newton-John, Rona 282
Ney, Marie 311
Nicholas, Paul 18
Nicholls, Anthony 204
Nicholls, Dandy 258

Nicholson, James H. 1, 82, 170, 190, 309, 315
Nicholson, Nora 69
Nick, Bill 111
Nicolaidis, Dimitris 64
Nielson, Peter 108
Night After Night, After Night 197
The Night Caller 198
Night Caller from Outer Space see *The Night Caller*
Night Creatures see *Captain Clegg*
The Night Digger 199
Night Hair Child 200
Night Must Fall 201
Night of the Big Heat 202
Night of the Demon 203
Night of the Eagle 204
Night of the Silicates see *Island of Terror*
Night Watch 205
The Nightcomers 206
Nightengale, Michael 52, 197
Nightmare 207
Nightmare see *Voices*
Nilsson, Harry 250
1984 208
Niven, David 100, 290
No Blade of Grass 209
No Place Like Homicide see *What a Carve-Up!*
Noel, Daniele 297
Noel, Hubert 74
Nordoff, Puppel 108
Norman, Monty 286
Norman, Philip 130
North, Virginia 1
Nothing but the Night 210
Novak, Kim 100, 265
Nunnerley, Leslie 265

Oates, Simon 271
The Oblong Box 211
O'Brien, Edmond 208
O'Brien, Maria 307
O'Brien, Richard 233
O'Brien, Willis 15
O'Casey, Ronan 208
O'Connolly, Jim 16, 198, 281
O'Connor, Derrick 109
O'Connor, Joseph 87, 134
O'Doherty, Mignon 129
O'Donnell, Peter 297
O'Donovan, Elizabeth 80
O'Flynn, Philip 305
Ogilvy, Ian 4, 64, 124, 251, 313, 315
O'Grady, Tony 52
The Old Dark House 212
Old Dracula see *Vampira*
Olrich, April 246
Olson, James 48, 185
O'Mara, Kate 43, 145, 292
One Million Years B.C. 213
O'Neil, Colette 119
O'Neil, Ronald 263

Ornadel, Cyril 76, 113
Orr, Buxton 42, 78, 101, 108, 111, 136, 248
Osbiston, Alan 128
Osborne, Tony 107
Oscar, Henry 24, 38, 254
Oscarsson, Per 96
O'Shaughnessy, Brian 46
O'Shea, Milo 272
Ostrer, Bertram 29
O'Sullivan, Richard 140
Oulton, Brian 74, 166, 254
Owen, Arthur E. 60
Owen, Bill 40
Owen, Dickie 55, 188
Owens, Patricia 129
Oxley, David 148, 262

Paal, Alexander 44, 115
Pack, Charles Lloyd 14, 42, 90, 117, 176, 178, 186, 203, 225, 229, 232, 245, 270, 275
Pack, Roger Lloyd 122
Padbury, Wendy 235
Page, Genevieve 220
Pagett, Nicola 120
Pal, George 278
Palance, Holly 40
Palance, Jack 45, 91, 280, 304
Palk, Anna 95, 104, 125, 206, 246, 281
Palk, Anthony 8, 91, 231
Palmer, Ernest 314
Palmer, Keith 87, 156, 210, 226, 304
Palmer, Lilli 190, 200
Palmer, Terry 182
Pallos, Steven 29, 138, 193
Paluzzi, Luciana 29
Panic in the Trans-Siberian Train see *Horror Express*
Pantera, Malou 147
Paranoiac 214
Parfitt, Judy 183
Paris, Edith 72
Pariser, Alfred 126
Parke, Macdonald 196
Parker, Cecil 35, 295
Parker, Clifton 203, 266
Parker, Kim 108, 179
Parker, Willard 95
Parkins, Barbara 9
Parkinson, Roy 22
Parkinson, Tom 49, 77
Parkyn, Leslie 36, 152, 204, 289
Parrendo, Gil 275
Parrish, Robert 88
Parslow, Ray 154
Parsons, Derek 268
Parsons, Jack 33, 54, 95, 101, 252, 311
Pascal, Francoise 26
Pascal, Jefferson 209
Paseo, Richard 135, 228

Pastell, George 55, 167, 180, 187, 259
Patrice, Ann 29
Patrick, Dian 199
Patrick, Nigel 38
Patrick, Roy 38
Patterson, Lee 163, 254, 275
Pattillo, Alan 107, 256
Paul, Jeremy 44
Paul, John 19, 55, 87
Pavey, Stanley 66, 221
Pavitt, Denys 77
Payne, Laurence 268, 283, 291
Paynter, Robert 206
Payton, Barbara 115
Peach, Mary 221
Peacock, John 256, 277
Peake, Lisa 244
Peake, Michael 135
Pearce, Hayden 140, 236, 298
Pearce, Jacqueline 219, 229
Pearson, Michael 298
Pederson, Con 287
Peel, David 24, 138
Peeping Tom 215
Peer, Salmaan 285
Peers, Leon 180
Pegge, Edmund 240
Pelling, Maurice 16
Pemberton, Reece 6
Pena, Julio 143
Penhaligon, Susan 151, 168
Pennington, Jon 243
Pennington-Richards, C. 208
Penrose, Charles 60
The People That Time Forgot 216
Percy, Edward 24
Perinal, Georges 237, 278
Perrins, Leslie 136
Perry, Morris 210
Persecution 217
Perschy, Maria 190
Persson, Essy 50
Pertwee, Jon 30, 154, 288
Pertwee, Roland 131
Pes, Carlo 89
Peters, Barry 216
Peters, Dennis Alaba 52
Peters, Luan 73, 113, 174, 284, 290
Petersen, Mark 84
Peterson, Barry 10
Peterson, Pete 15
Petrovitch, Michael 195, 265
Pettingell, Frank 42
The Phantom of the Opera 218
Phillips, Conrad 35, 243
Phillips, John (actor) 188, 280, 299
Phillips, John (musical director) 177
Phillips, John (producer) 198
Phillips, Leslie 128
Phillips, Redmond 135
Phillips, Robin 264
Pickwood, Mike 40

Picton, Don 48, 106, 173, 277
Pilkington, Gordon 305
Pinhorn, Maggie 189
Piper, Frederick 33, 305
Pitcher, George 62
Pitt, Ingrid 44, 154, 292, 310
Pitt, Peter 140
The Plague of the Zombies 219
Pleasence, Angela 124, 263
Pleasence, Donald 36, 67, 73, 79, 100, 114, 124, 138, 156, 191, 208, 265, 305
Plummer, Christopher 255, 260
Poerio, Adelina 86
Pogany, Gabor 80
Poggi, Fernando 133
Pokras, Barbara 109
Polanski, Roman 59, 230
Poll, Martin 205
Pollock, Ellen 144
Pollock, Nicholas 41
Pomeroy, John 37, 243, 262
Pooley, Olaf 41, 128, 193
Pope, Ron 113
Porter, Eric 139, 173
Porter, Nyree Dawn 124, 154
Poston, Tom 212
Potter, Martin 45, 236
Pottle, Harry 289
Poulton, Raymond 16, 122, 255, 275, 297
Powell, Clive 34
Powell, Eddie 188
Powell, June 114
Powell, Michael 215
Powell, Norman S. 199
Powell, Robert 7, 9
Power, Derry 303
Power, Hartley 66
Power, Sandra 194
Powers, Stefanie 48, 105
Prador, Irene 249
Pratt, Anthony 31, 199, 317
Pravda, George 91, 119
Pravda, Hana-Marie 5
Prebble, John 192
Prehistoric Women see *Slave Girls*
Prescod, Pearl 193
Prescott, Kerrigan 108
Preston, Trevor 200
Price, Dennis 52, 95, 140, 144, 145, 146, 165, 250, 272, 281, 284, 305
Price, Penny 28
Price, Stanley 156
Price, Vincent 1, 38, 50, 175, 181, 211, 241, 272, 279, 313
Priestly, Tom 289
Priggen, Norman 47, 265
Pring, Gerald 60
The Private Life of Sherlock Holmes 220
Probyn, Brian 117, 234, 256
The Projected Man 221
Proud, Peter 105, 273

Index

Proudlock, Roger 254
Provis, George 33, 45, 47, 50, 57, 95, 101, 107, 158, 193, 211, 309, 311
Prowse, David 39, 117, 145, 291
Psycho Circus see *Circus of Fear*
Psychomania 222
The Psychopath 223
Pudney, Alan 308
Purcell, Mara 101
Purcell, Noel 262
Purchase, Bruce 226
Pusey, Fred 262
Puttnam, David 109
Pyne, Natasha 175
Pyott, Keith 299

Quarrier, Ian 59
Quarry, Robert 82, 175
Quatermass and the Pit 224
The Quatermass Conclusion 225
Quatermass II 226
The Quatermass Xperiment 227
Quayle, Anthony 260
Quinn, Tony 179
Quitak, Oscar 232

Raab, Max L. 39
Rabin, Jack 15
Radd, Ronald 255
Radford, Basil 66
Raglan, Robert 247
Raine, Jack 131
Rakoff, Alvin 6
Rampling, Charlotte 9, 317
Ramsen, Alan 161
Randall, Stephanie 247
Rank, Ursula 261
Ransohoff, Martin 18, 100, 269
Rasputin — The Mad Monk 228
Rathbone, Nigel 209
Rathvon, N. Peter 208
Raven, Mike 49, 77, 157, 174
Rawlings, Margaret 139
Rawlinson, Brian 18
Raw Meat see *Death Line*
Ray, Philip 118
Raymond, Gary 164
Read, Jan 112, 136, 164
Read, John 88
Rebel, Bernard 55
Redbourn, Michael 47
Redgrave, Michael 66, 159, 208
Redgrave, Vanessa 72
Redmond, Liam 203
Redmond, Moira 207
Reed, Michael 94, 228, 247, 318
Reed, Myrtle 101
Reed, Oliver 27, 56, 58, 72, 214, 245, 286, 318
Reed, Tracy 74
Reede, Rosemarie 53
Rees, Angharad 139
Rees, Llewellyn 149
Rees, Yvette 54, 311

Reeve, Spencer 71, 93, 174, 185, 284
Reeves, Bernard 1
Reeves, Kynaston 108, 115
Reeves, Michael 251, 211, 313
Regin, Nadja 179
Reid, Alastair 199
Reid, Beryl 12, 82, 222
Reid, Milton 16, 21, 27, 82, 270
Reid, Sheila 318
Reisz, Karel 201
Reizenstein, Franz 36, 187
Relph, Michael 66, 178, 182
Remberg, Erika 36
The Reptile 229
Repulsion 230
Revenge 231
The Revenge of Frankenstein 232
Revill, Clive 170, 220
Reynolds, Barry 73
Reynolds, Charles 11
Reynolds, Larry 304
Reynolds, Peter 57, 70, 138
Rhodda, Wayne John 318
Rhodes, Christopher 134
Rhodes, Marjorie 139
Riccardo, Rick 177
Rice, Joan 145
Richard, Jean-Louis 104
Richard, Wendy 209
Richards, Aubrey 96, 162
Richards, E.G. 60
Richards, Robert (Bobby) 17, 158
Richardson, Henry 44, 45, 132, 172, 260, 283
Richardson, John 213, 244, 297
Richardson, Larry 171
Richardson, Ralph 120, 131, 264, 309
Richfield, Edwin 224, 316
Richmond, Anthony 86, 177, 290
Richmond, Irene 207
Richter, Daniel 287
Rietty, Robert 249
Rigg, Carl 23, 50, 211
Rigg, Diana 272
Riguad, Jorge 143
Rilla, Walter 103, 128
Rilla, Wolf 299
Rimmer, Shane 216, 303
Rintoul, David 172
Ripper, Michael 24, 27, 47, 55, 56, 65, 93, 172, 173, 185, 187, 188, 189, 208, 218, 219, 226, 232, 238, 267, 280, 288, 316
Ritelis, Viktors 41
Rive, Kenneth 52, 69
Rivera, Luis 190
The Road Builder see *The Night Digger*
Robards, Jason 190
Robbie, Christopher 308
Robbins, Jessie 59
Roberts, Christian 6, 183, 285
Roberts, Evelyn 254

Roberts, Ewan 62, 203
Roberts, Renee 306
Robertson, Cliff 85
Robinson, Bernard 2, 24, 27, 51, 55, 56, 58, 71, 90, 93, 94, 118, 119, 135, 148, 166, 176, 186, 187, 188, 196, 207, 212, 218, 219, 224, 226, 228, 232, 243, 259, 266, 270, 286, 288, 312, 316
Robinson, Bruce 75
Robinson, Gordon 112
Robinson, Harry 44, 68, 122, 132, 150, 172, 174, 284, 292
Robinson, John 129, 210
Robson, Flora 12, 85, 100, 116, 245
Roc, Patricia 22
The Rocky Horror Picture Show 233
Roeg, Nicolas 79, 86, 104, 177, 181
Rogan, Beth 192
Rogers, Anton 178
Rogers, Eric 8, 30, 231
Rogers, Erica 146
Rogers, Jean Scott 42
Rogers, Paul 262
Rogers, Peter 8, 30, 231
Rogers, Tristan 113
Rohm, Marie 261, 296
Roland, Jeanne 55
Rolfe, Guy 4, 259
Romain, Yvonne 27, 36, 42, 56, 69
Romano, Renato 89
Ronane, John 255
Ronay, Edina 17, 247, 260
Rootes, Maurice 112, 115, 164, 253
Rosay, Francoise 127
Rose, David 142
Rose, George 114, 163
Rosebury, Paul 225
Rosenberg, Max J. 4, 9, 10, 13, 65, 57, 83, 84, 124, 154, 157, 175, 183, 216, 223, 246, 264, 271, 274, 280, 294, 304, 306
Ross, Arthur 275
Ross, Katherine 169
Rossini, Jan 307
Rossiter, Leonard 287, 312
Roth, Cy 110
Rotheray, Rosemary 268
Rothwell, Talbot 30
Rowe, Arthur 73
Rowles, Kenneth F. 298
Rowley, Nic 225
Royale, Allan 304
Royston, Roy 219
Rozsa, Miklos 133, 220
Rugolo, Pete 163
Rumbold, Jonathan 47
Runacre, Jenny 47, 109, 250
Rusoff, Lou 32
Russell, Ken 72
Russell, Marigold 257
Russell, Peter 268
Russell, Robert 313

Russell, Ray 146
Russell, Roy 136
Rutherford, Paris 49
Ryan, Edmond 60
Ryan, Ken 224
Ryan, Madge 39, 96
Ryan, Robert 29
Ryder, Paul 258

Sachs, Leonard 15, 128, 167, 266
Sachse, Sally 261
Sadler, Avril 137
Sahlin, Don 278
St. Clair, Mike 23
St. John, Betta 37, 42, 249
Saint Simon, Lucille 138
Saire, Rebecca 225
Sallis, Peter 126, 199, 241, 267, 304, 315
Salter, Ivor 153
Salter, Nicholas 86
Salzedo, Leonard 232
Sambrel, Aldo 133
Samuel, Julie 207
Sanders, Andrew 250
Sanders, Charles 179, 314
Sanders, George 22, 23, 87, 96, 222, 299
Sanders, Stuart 283
Sandford, Christopher 76
Sangster, Jimmy 6, 21, 24, 48, 51, 90, 94, 106, 145, 155, 163, 169, 174, 177, 180, 187, 194, 207, 232, 249, 266, 270, 283, 309, 316
Sansom, John 94
Sarafian, Richard C. 116
Sarandon, Susan 233
Sarrazin, Michael 120
Sarron, Bernard 258
Sasdy, Peter 44, 87, 139, 156, 210, 267
The Satanic Rites of Dracula 234
Satan's Skin 235
Satan's Slave 236
Satellite in the Sky 237
Savalas, Telly 143
Saville, Edith 115
Saw, Eric 32
Saxon, John 198
Scarpa, Renato 86
Scars of Dracula 238
Scherick, Edgar J. 306
Schiller, Frederick 283
Schizo 239
Schneck, Stephen 304
Schneer, Charles H. 112, 133, 164, 192, 275
Schurmann, Gerard 142, 147, 167, 173
Schwartz, Bernard 245
Schwiers, Ellen 295
Sciafe, Ted 203
Scott, Alex 7, 104, 284
Scott, Allan 86

Scott, Elliot 34, 100, 134, 141, 209, 278, 303
Scott, Janette 62, 212, 214
Scott, John (actor) 268
Scott, John (aka Patrick John Scott) 16, 45, 87, 165, 216, 236, 261, 263, 282
Scott, Margaretta 48
Scott, Peter Graham *see* Graham Scott, Peter
Scream and Die 240
Scream and Scream Again 241
Scream of Fear see *Taste of Fear*
Scully, Terry 7, 197, 221
Seal, Elizabeth 291
Seance on a Wet Afternoon 242
Searle, Humphrey 2, 141
Sears, Ann 295
Sears, Heather 17, 218
Secombe, Harry 262
The Secret of Dorian Gray see *Dorian Gray*
See No Evil see *Blind Terror*
Segal, Zohra 297
Sekely, Steve 62
Sekka, Johnny 158
Selby, Anthony 38, 313
Sellers, Alan 162
Sellers, Elizabeth 188
Sellers, Peter 278
Serato, Massimo 86
Serrano, Rosario 205
Serret, John 266
Seton, Bruce 134
Seven Brothers Meet Dracula see *The Legend of the Seven Golden Vampires*
Sewell, George 88, 140
Sewell, Vernon 19, 26, 53, 129, 152
Seyler, Athene 203
Seymour, Jane 120
Seymour, Michael 272
The Shadow of the Cat 243
Shaffer, Anthony 121, 310
Shaftel, Josef 255
Shakespeare, Joan 137
Shampan, Jack 36, 132, 152, 172, 204, 217
Sharman, Jim 233
Sharp, Anthony 76, 160
Sharp, Don 25, 54, 61, 103, 165, 166, 222, 228, 311
Sharpe, Anne 163, 283
Sharples, Robert 258
Shaughnessy, Alfred 32, 48, 113
Shaw, Dennis 176, 187
Shaw, Martin 133
Shaw, Maxwell 211
Shaw, Peter 255
Shaw, Richard 111
Shaw, Roland 256
Shaw, Susan 110
Shaw, Vanessa 144
Shaw, Vee King 171

She 244
Shearer, Moira 215
Shefter, Bert 54
Sheldon, Ralph 204
Shelley, Barbara 21, 32, 94, 130, 135, 224, 228, 243, 299
Shelley, Norman 179
Shen, Chan 171
Shenderey, Dee 26
Shepherd, Albert 6
Shepherd, Elizabeth 279
Shepherd, Pauline 286
Sher, Jack 275
Sheridan, Dani 251
Sheriff, Paul 22
Sherman, Gary 67
Sherwood, William 179
Sheybal, Vladek 88
Shields, Peter 39
Shields, Stan 69
Shine, Bill 163
Shingleton, Wilfred 3, 59, 96, 120, 159
Shipman, Kenneth 26
Shirley, John 80
Shiu, Paula Li 11
Shonteff, Lindsay 52, 69, 197, 261
Shrimpton, Chrissie 185
The Shuttered Room 245
Silk, Jeff 40
Silliphant, Stirling 299
Sim, Gerald 81, 82, 121, 178, 242
Simm, Ray 116
Simmons, Jean 85
Simmons, Stan 54
Simon, Melvin 85
Simpson, Edward 183
Simpson, Tom 22, 125, 162, 179, 180, 194, 213
Sims, Joan 30
Sims, Sylvia 9
Sinclair, Patricia 258
Singer, Campbell 138
Skay, Brigitte 319
Skeaping, Colin 144
Skeggs, Roy 28, 117, 234, 277
Skouras, Costas 73
The Skull 246
Slade, Jack 114, 128, 167
Slaney, Ivor 253
Slave Girls 247
Slesar, Henry 190
Slimon, Scott 271, 274, 280
Sloan, John R. 116
Sloane, Oliver 149
Slocombe, Douglas 36, 59, 66, 266
Slocombe, Jeff 318
Smart, Patsy 99, 169
Smedley-Aston, Brian 99, 263, 293
Smedley-Aston, Michael 273
Smethurst, Jack 197
Smight, Jack 120
Smith, Clive 175

Smith, Herbert 32, 164, 191, 314
Smith, Jack 195
Smith, John S. 302
Smith, John Victor 75
Smith, Keith 288
Smith, Madeleine (aka Maddy) 3, 75, 117, 267, 272, 292
Smith, Murray 40, 76
Smythe, Esme 300
Smythe, Vernon 55
The Snake Woman 248
Snell, Peter 310
The Snorkel 249
Snowden, Alec C. 97, 276
Soall, Terence 298
Soblosky, Perry 28
Soccol, Giovanni 86
Solo, Robert H. 72
Solomon, Joe 281
Solomons, Ralph 300
Solon, Ewen 56, 129, 148, 163, 208, 270
Son of Dracula 250
Soraya 244
The Sorcerers 251
Sottane, Liliane 142
Soundrama 97
Southcott, Colin 184, 279
Southworth, Lindo 186
Spaceflight IC-1 252
Spaceways 253
Spalding, Harry 54, 252, 311
The Spaniard's Curse 254
Spear, Bernard 14
Spear, Eric 57, 129, 257, 302
Spenceley, Peter 47
Spencer, Marian 42, 242
Spencer, Sally-Jane 6
Spenser, David 11, 95, 259
Spenser, Jeremy 104, 295
Spider's Venom see *Venom*
Spier, William 75
Spikings, Barry 177
Spila, Otello 89
The Spiral Staircase 255
Spirit of the Dead see *The Asphyx*
Spratling, Tony 178
Stacy, John 142
Stafford, Brendan 179
Stambouileh, Anthony 102
Stamp, Terence 183
Standing, John 169, 223, 280
Stanley, Kim 242
Stannard, Roy 139, 156, 284
Stanton, Barry 68
Stark, Graham 165
Stark, Wilbur 291
Starr, Ringo 250
Stassino, Paul 76, 259
Stavrou, Ari 73
Steafel, Sheila 224
Steele, Barbara 53
Steele, Pippa 174, 292
Steiner, John 156
Stensgaard, Yutte 26, 174, 241, 319

Stepanek, Karl 69, 125
Stephens, Martin 159, 299, 312
Stephens, Robert 7, 220
Stephenson, Pamela 40
Sterling, Jan 208
Sterne, Gordon 302
Stevens, Jack 32
Stevens, James 274
Stevenson, Alexandra 247
Stevenson, Venetia 37
Steward, Ernest 25, 35, 61, 103, 152
Stewart, Bruce 137
Stewart, Robert 295
Stewart, Robin 140
Stewart, Sophie 70
Stock, Nigel 173
Stockman, Paul 78
Stoll, John 7, 13, 46, 133, 249
Stone, Marianne 16, 155, 198, 311
Stone, Philip 289
Stone, Sydney 11, 237
Stonehouse, Marilyn 304
Stoney, Heather 67
Stoney, Kevin 19
Stop Me Before I Kill! see *The Full Treatment*
Stott, Judith 204
Stott, Wally 29
Straight on Till Morning 256
Strain, Christopher 300
The Strange World of Planet X 258
Stranger from Venus 257
The Stranglers of Bombay 259
Strasberg, Susan 266
Stratton, John 117
Straus, Bernard 205
Stribling, Melissa 49, 90, 129
Stringer, Michael 68
Stritch, Elaine 255
Stromberg, Hunt, Jr. 120
Strong, Gwyneth 210
Stross, Raymond 295
Struthers, Ian 110
Stuart, Graham 257
Stuart, John 115, 187, 214, 232
A Study in Terror 260
Style, Michael 122, 174, 284, 292
Styles, Edwin 127
Subotsky, Milton 4, 9, 10, 13, 37, 57, 65, 83, 84, 85, 124, 154, 157, 168, 175, 183, 216, 223, 241, 246, 264, 271, 274, 280, 284, 306
Sudden Terror see *Eyewitness*
Suedo, Julie 60
Sullivan, Elliott 293
Sullivan, Sean 287
Summers, Jeremy 296
Summers, Walter 60
Sumpter, Donald 197
Sumuru 261
Sunters, Irene 310
Suschitzky, Peter 233
Suschitsky, Wolfgang 272, 297

Sutcliff, Rosemary 130
Sutherland, Donald 83, 86, 105
Sutherland, Duncan 283, 302
Sutton, Dudley 72
Svengali 262
Swann, Robert 47, 189
Swift, Clive 67, 121
Swift, Jessica 317
Sydney, Basil 138, 275
Sydney, Derek 283
Sykes, Peter 68, 150, 277, 298
Sylvester, William 69, 74, 134, 137, 287
Symptoms 263
Syropoulos, Vassilis 64
Syson, Michael 106
Szu, Shih 171

Tabori, Paul 115, 253
Tafler, Sydney 16, 110
Tait, Kenneth McCallam 28
Talbot, Kenneth 11, 44, 87, 139, 156, 210, 217, 257
Tales from the Crypt 264
Tales That Witness Madness 265
Talfrey, Hira 56, 313
Tamblyn, Russ 141, 278
Tamiroff, Akim 302
Tam Lin see *The Devil's Widow*
Tanchuck, Nathaniel 245
Tani, Yoko 160
Tanner, Peter 4, 9, 13, 154, 157, 306
Tansley, Derek 53
Tapley, Colin 214
Taste of Fear 266
Taste the Blood of Dracula 267
Tate, Sharon 59, 100
Taylor, Brough 70
Taylor, Donald 37, 138
Taylor, Elaine 6
Taylor, Elizabeth 80, 205
Taylor, Gilbert 121, 127, 230, 273
Taylor, Grant 224
Taylor, Richard 276
Taylor, Rocky 222
Taylor, Roy 46
Taylor, Valerie 230, 305
Tayman, Robert 153, 185, 291
Telezynska, Isabella 277
The Tell-Tale Heart 268
Temple-Smith, John 27
Templeton, William P. 208
Ten Rillington Place 269
Tenser, Tony 12, 17, 19, 23, 47, 53, 87, 123, 140, 195, 230, 235, 251, 260, 313, 319
Terror from Under the House see *Revenge*
The Terror of the Tongs 270
The Terrornauts 271
Terry, Martin 251
Terry-Thomas 1, 82, 165, 278, 294
Teuber, Andreas 80

Thanisch, Jennifer 61
Thawnton, Tony 52
Theatre of Blood 272
Theatre of Death 273
Theodorakis, Mikis 64, 243
These Are the Damned see *The Damned*
Thesiger, Ernest 131
They Came from Beyond Space 274
Thin Air see *The Body Stealers*
Thinnes, Roy 88
13 see *Eye of the Devil*
Thomas, Damien 284
Thomas, Gerald 30
Thomas, Lisa 213
Thomas, Rachel 33
Thompson, Ian 175
Thompson, J. Lee 100
Thompson, Marshall 108.111
Thompson, Peter J. 195
Thomson, Alex 31, 67, 82, 199
Thomson, Brian 233
Thomson, H.A.R. 209
Thorn, Ronald Scott 127
Thornburn, June 275, 278
Thornton, Frank 279, 290
Thornton, Peter 301
Thornton, Philip 129
Those Fantastic Flying Fools see *Jules Verne's Rocket to the Moon*
The Three Worlds of Gulliver 275
Tierney, Lawrence 193
Til Dawn Do We Part see *Straight on Till Morning*
Till, Jenny 273
Tilley, Patrick 169, 216, 315
Tilsely, Reg 23, 140
Tilton, Connie 307
Tilvern, Alan 125, 228
Timeslip 276
Tingwell, Charles 94
Tirard, Ann 127
To Love a Vampire see *Lust for a Vampire*
To the Devil...A Daughter 277
Todd, Ann 107, 266
Todd, Bob 238
Todd, Richard 9, 89
Tohl, Jerry 184
Tom Thumb 278
The Tomb of Ligeia 279
Tomelty, Joseph 17, 70, 276
Tomlinson, David 38, 85
Toms, Carl 244
Toone, Geoffrey 79, 84, 270
Torn, Rip 177
Tortosa, Silvia 143
Torture Garden 280
Toumanova, Tamara 220
Tourneur, Jacques 38, 203
Tovey, Roberta 57, 84
Tower of Evil 281
Tower of Terror see *Assault*
Towers, Harry Alan 25, 35, 89, 103, 165, 261, 296

Towne, Robert 279
Townley, Toke 238
Towns, Colin 126
Townsend, Len 301
Tozer, Geoffrey 282
Tracy, Kim 167
Train, Jack 33
Trauner, Alexander 220
Travers, Bill 134
Travers, Susan 248
Tree, David 86
Trend, Jean 87
Trestini, Giorgio 86
Trevarthan, Noel 43, 162, 296
Trevor, Austin 63, 147, 167
Trevor, Howard 189
Trieste, Leopoldo 86
Trog 282
The Trollenberg Terror 283
Troughton, Patrick 17, 117, 135, 164, 218, 238
Trouncer, Ruth 178
Trubshawe, Michael 14
Truffaut, Francois 104
Truman, Ralph 254
Trumbull, Douglas 287
Trumm, Len 186
Trumper, John 35, 74, 103, 152, 277
Tsau, Johnson 171
Tu, Poulet 103
Tucker, Alan 26
Tucker, Forrest 2, 258, 283
Tully, Brian 28
Tully, Montgomery 11, 97, 149, 271
Turner, Anna 202
Turner, John 15, 29
Turner, John Hastings 131
Turner, June 67
Turner, Lana 217
Turner, Peter 40
Turner, Stephen 145
Turner, Tim 136
Turner, Vickery 183
Turpin, Gerry 242, 306
Tushingham, Rita 256
Twins of Dracula see *Twins of Evil*
Twins of Evil 284
The Twisted Nerve 285
The Two Faces of Dr. Jekyll 286
2001: A Space Odyssey 287
Tyzack, Margaret 39, 169, 225, 287
Tzelniker, Meier 251

The Ugly Duckling 288
Ullman, Daniel 192
Ulloa, Alejandro 143
Umberg, Warner 190
Underdown, Edward 79, 137
Unearthly Stranger 289
Unger, Anthony B. 75
Unger, Oliver A. 103, 200
The Unseen see *House of Mystery*
Unsworth, Geoffrey 287, 301, 317

Ure, Mary 182
Urquhart, Molly 152
Urquhart, Robert 51
Ustinov, Tamara 20, 235

Valentine, Anthony 277, 281
Valentine, Val 186
Valk, Frederick 66
Vampira 290
The Vampire Beast Craves Blood see *The Blood Beast Terror*
Vampire Circus 291
The Vampire Lovers 292
Vampire Over London see *Mother Riley Meets the Vampire*
Vampyres 293
Van Beers, Stanley 227, 257
Van Eyck, Peter 249, 295
Van Eyssen, John 90, 115, 226
Van Ost, Valerie 43, 158, 234
Van Winkle, Joseph 61
Vance, Leigh 79
Varley, Beatrice 147
Varnals, Wendy 43
Vassiliou, Spyros 64
Vaughn, Jimmy 314
Vaughn, Peter 102, 105, 263, 299
Vaughn, Robert 183
Vault of Horror 294
Vaz Diaz, Selma 22, 268
Veale, John 149
Veevers, Wally 62, 237
Vegoda, Joe 57, 84
Velvet House see *The Corpse*
Vengeance 295
The Vengeance of Fu Manchu 296
The Vengeance of She 297
Venom 298
Ventham, Wanda 19, 28
Ventura, Vivianne 11
Verlekis, Nikos 73
Vernon, Richard 234, 279, 299
Versini, Marie 25
Vetchinsky, Alex 202, 260
Vetri, Victoria 307
Vetter, Charles F. Jr. 11, 111
Vickers, Mike 10, 92, 303
Vidon, Henry 15, 249
Village of the Damned 299
Villiers, James 3, 9, 20, 58, 194, 230
Villiers, Mavis 256
Vince, Barrie 52, 273
Virgin Witch 300
Vittes, Louis 101
Vivian, Bette 298
Vogel, Klaus 300
Voices 301
Von Friedl, Loni 88
Von Kotz, John 296
Von Schell, Catherina 185
The Vulture 302

Waddilove, Philip 313
Wagner, Anthony 198

Wagstaff, Elsie 248
Walker, Fiona 7
Walker, Gloria 236
Walker, Lillias 306
Walker, Maggie 240
Walker, Peter 76, 113, 123, 151, 153, 239
Walker, Roy 265
Wallace, Geoffrey 274
Wallace, Hedger 47, 207
Wallace, Ian 278
Wallace, Jean 209
Wallis, Jacquie 166
Wallis, Tony 231
Walsh, Dermot 114, 129, 268
Walsh, Kay 312
Walsh, Sally 51
Walter, Ernest 34, 100, 141, 220, 269
Walter, Len 88
Walter, Richard 110
Walter, Wilfrid 60
Walters, Thorley 94, 95, 118, 178, 216, 218, 223, 282, 285, 291
Walton, Tony 104
Wanamaker, Sam 64, 255
Wanstall, Norman 195
War-Gods of the Deep see *City Under the Sea*
Warbeck, David 45, 282, 284
Ward, Derek 46
Ward, Dervis 134
Ward, Michael 30
Ward, Simon 85, 91, 119, 126
Warlords of Atlantis 303
Warner, David 124
Warner, Frederick 217
Warner, Jack 85, 227
Warner, Richard 188, 243, 258, 299
Warren, Barry 118, 166
Warren, Gene 278
Warren, Kenneth J. 47, 68, 78, 157
Warren, Michele 53
Warren, Yvonne *see* Romain, Yvonne
Warwick, Gina 140
Warwick, John 147
Warwick, Norman 1, 47, 81, 109, 250, 264, 265, 274, 280
Washbourne, Mona 24, 116, 201, 306
Waterman, Dennis 122, 238
Waters, Jan 43
Waters, Russell 71, 310
Watford, Gwen 196
Watkins, David 72, 277
Watkins, Garth 300
Watling, Jack 194
Watson, Alan 144
Watson, Jack 32, 135, 167, 198, 215, 239, 281
Watson, Ralph 6
Wattis, Richard 2, 75, 186, 288

Watts, Gwendolyn 105
Watts, Queenie 239
Watts, Roy 133
Waxman, Harry 6, 12, 63, 96, 194, 200, 213, 244, 285, 293, 310
Wayn, Peter 314
Wayne, Naughton 66
Wayne, Patrick 216
Weatherly, Peter 6, 20, 106
Weavers, Mark 172, 217
Webb, Rita 319
Webb, Roger 26
Webber, Robert 155
Webster, Joy 314
Webster, Patricia 32
Weeks, Stephen 130, 157
Weelnough, Russell 191
Weinbach, Robert D. 191
Weinstein, Henry T. 75
Welbeck, Peter 25, 35, 103, 296
Welch, Raquel 14
Welcome to Blood City 304
Wells, Jerold 180
Welsh, John 178, 207, 228, 232
Wendy, Barbara 144
Wentworth, Nicholas 89, 200
Werner, Oscar 104
West, Lockwood 234
West, Norma 252
West, Timothy 285
Westbrook, Herbert 102, 206
Westbrook, John 181, 279
Weston, David 181, 311
Wetherell, Virginia 53, 68, 77, 81, 91
What a Carve-Up! 305
What Became of Jack and Jill? 306
What the Peeper Saw see *Night Hair Child*
Wheatley, Alan 243, 253
Wheatley, Dennis 71, 173, 280
Wheeler, Paul 169
Whelan, Christopher 103
When Dinosaurs Ruled the Earth 307
Where Has Poor Mickey Gone? 308
Whettam, Graham 308
Whibley, Burnell 209
Whitaker, David 81, 85, 102, 241, 290, 291
White, Carol 247
White, Frank 25, 35, 38, 103, 165
White, Harry 15, 54, 146, 179, 198, 252
White, Michael 233
White, Patrick 34
Whitehead, Geoffrey 4
Whitelaw, Billie 114, 121, 205, 285
Whitely, Annette 17
Whiting, Leonard 120
Whitman, David 75
Whiton, James 1
Whitsun-Jones, Paul 81
Whitting, Peter 222
Whoever Slew Auntie Roo? 309

The Wicker Man 310
Wicking, Christopher 19, 50, 68, 190, 211, 241, 277, 298
Widmark, Richard 277
Wiener, Jack H. 290
Wiggins, Chris 304
Wilbox, Toyah 255
Wilbur, Crane 192
Wilcox, John 45, 57, 65, 84, 98, 132, 155, 171, 172, 207, 223, 246
Wild, Janette 107
Wild, Katy 65, 83, 98
Wild, William 19
Wilde, Brian 203
Wilde, Colette 36, 62, 152
Wilde, Cornel 209
Wilde, Lorna 23
Wilder, Billy 220
Wilder, Myles 22
Wilder, W. Lee 22, 179
Wilding, Michael 120
Wiles, John 142
Wilkins, Jeremy 54
Wilkinson, Marc 225, 235
Williams, Bill 252
Williams, Billy 75, 183, 205
Williams, Brook 219
Williams, Edward 289
Williams, Emlyn 100
Williams, Kenneth 30
Williams, Peter 217
Williams, Trevor 91
Williamson, Alister 211
Williamson, Lambert 254
Williamson, Malcolm 24, 48, 145, 210
Williamson, Tony 205
Willman, Noel 166, 229, 297
Willmer, Catherine 72, 175
Willoughby, George 38
Wills, J. Elder 115, 227, 263
Wilmer, Douglas 25, 133, 164, 292, 296
Wilson, Frederick 192, 206
Wilson, Ian 5, 28, 122, 186, 218, 225
Wilson, James 160, 237, 268
Wilson, Maurice J. 149
Wilson, Sue 46
Wimbush, Mary 116
Winder, Michael 13, 304
Winding, Victor 151, 239
Winfield, Gil 108
Wing, Anna 126
Winner, Michael 206
Winter, Robert 33, 54, 95, 101, 146, 311
Winter, Vincent 134
Winters, Shelley 309
Wintle, Julian 36, 152, 204, 289
Wise, Robert 141
Wiseman, Ron 126
Witchcraft 311
The Witches 213
Witchfinder General 313

Witherick, Albert 178
Withers, Googie 66
Witty, John 52
Wladon, Jean 213
Wolfit, Donald 21, 79, 138, 237, 262
Wolveridge, Carol 208
The Woman Who Wouldn't Die see *Catacombs*
Womaneater 314
Wood, Anabella 240
Woodbridge, George 56, 87, 90, 94, 114, 163, 187, 229, 232, 305
Woodburn, Eric 159
Woods, Aubrey 318
Woods, Wilfred 19
Woodthorpe, Peter 98, 155, 246
Woodward, Edward 158, 310
Wooland, Norman 221
Woolfe, Betty 273
Woolgar, Jack 67

Wooten, Rosemary 217
Wordsworth, Richard 56, 227, 232
Worth, Brian 270
Wrenn, Trevor 240, 263
Wright, Paula 300
Wright, Tony 149, 254
Wuthering Heights 315
Wyatt, Tess 12
Wyer, Reg 74, 115, 161, 165, 202, 204, 253, 289
Wyeth, Katya 26, 139, 256, 284
Wyldeck, Martin 76, 201, 276
Wymark, Patrick 34, 88, 223, 230, 235, 246, 313
Wyngarde, Peter 159, 204
Wynne-Simmons, Robert 235

X the Unknown 316

Yates, Marjorie 172

Yip, David 225
Yordan, Philip 62
York, Derek 242, 250
Young, Aida 93, 139, 238, 267, 297, 307
Young, Alan 278
Young, Arthur 257
Young, Eric 25, 160
Young, Freddie 7
Young, Gig 245
Young, Les 236
Young, Robert 291
Young Dracula see *Son of Dracula*
Younger, Henry 55, 247
Yule, John 123, 151
Yung, Liu Chia 171

Zardoz 317
Zero Population Growth 318
Zeta One 319

www.ingramcontent.com/pod-product-compliance
Lightning Source LLC
Chambersburg PA
CBHW081546300426
44116CB00015B/2774